D1104347

A World Beneath the Sands

A
WORLD
BENEATH
THE SANDS

The Golden Age of Egyptology

Toby Wilkinson

W. W. NORTON & COMPANY
Independent Publishers Since 1923

Manufacturing by LSC Communications, Harrisonburg
Production manager: Beth Steidle

Library of Congress Cataloging-in-Publication Data

Names: Wilkinson, Toby A. H., author.
Title: A world beneath the sands : the golden age of Egyptology / Toby Wilkinson.
Description: First American edition. | New York : W. W. Norton & Company,
2020. | Includes bibliographical references and index.
Identifiers: LCCN 2020010916 | ISBN 9781324006893 (hardcover) |
ISBN 9781324006909 (epub)
Subjects: LCSH: Egyptology—History. | Excavations (Archaeology)—Egypt. |
Egypt—Antiquities.
Classification: LCC DT60 .W63 2020 | DDC 932.009/09—dc23
LC record available at https://lccn.loc.gov/2020010916

W. W. Norton & Company, Inc., 500 Fifth Avenue, New York, N.Y. 10110
www.wwnorton.com

W. W. Norton & Company Ltd., 15 Carlisle Street, London W1D 3BS

1 2 3 4 5 6 7 8 9 0

I dedicate this book, with deepest gratitude,
to the memory of Sir Ernest Alfred Thompson Wallis Budge,
Egyptologist and author, for his generosity in endowing a
fund for Egyptology at Christ's College, Cambridge;
and to successive Masters, Fellows and Scholars of Christ's
for maintaining and nurturing the Lady Wallis Budge Fund
over the past eighty-five years. Its beneficiaries (of which
I am proud to be one) have played, and will continue to play,
their part in shaping Egyptology.

CONTENTS

List of Illustrations

Mono

PROLOGUE Frontispiece of the English edition of Norden's *Travels in Egypt and Nubia*, 1757 (Gg. 1. 12-13 reproduced by kind permission of the Syndics of Cambridge University Library)

1. The Rosetta Stone (Granger Historical Picture Archive / Alamy Stock Photo)

2. Frontispiece of the Napoleonic *Description de l'Egypte* (By Impr. impériale – https://digitalcollections.nypl.org/items/510d47e0-0f27-a3d9-e040-e00a18064a99, Public Domain, https://commons.wikimedia.org/w/index.php?curid=49898981)

3. John Gardner Wilkinson (The Harpur Crewe Collection / National Trust Photographic Library / Mike Williams / Bridgeman Images)

4. Richard Lepsius and members of his Prussian expedition (bpk Bildagentur / Aegyptisches Museum und Papyrussammlung / Mardarete Buesing / Art Resource, NY)

5. A seated statue of King Khafra (akg-images / Fototeca Gilardi)

6. Lucie Duff Gordon (National Portrait Gallery, London, UK / Photo © Stefano Baldini / Bridgeman Images)

7. Flinders Petrie outside a rock-cut tomb (which served as his home) on the first of his many archaeological expeditions to Egypt (Courtesy of The Egypt Exploration Society)

8. Ernest Alfred Thompson Wallis Budge (© Trustees of the British Museum)

9. Theodore Davis, Arthur Weigall, Mrs Weigall and Edward Ayrton in the Valley of the Kings (MS 3196/360/25 reproduced with the permission of the Library of Birmingham)

10. Ludwig Borchardt (bpk Bildagentur / Vorderasiatisches Museum, Staatliche Museen, Berlin, Germany / Art Resource, NY)

11. Howard Carter meeting his patron Lord Carnarvon and Lady Evelyn Herbert at Luxor (Bentley Archive / Popperfoto / Contributor)

12. Carter with King Fuad I and Egyptian officials in the Valley of the Kings (© Tallandier / Bridgeman Images)

Colour

1. Napoleon Bonaparte (GL Archive / Alamy Stock Photo)

2. Giovanni Battista Belzoni (Fitzwilliam Museum, University of Cambridge, UK / Bridgeman Images)

3. The 'Young Memnon': a stone bust of pharaoh Ramesses II (© Trustees of the British Museum)

4. Jean-François Champollion (Louvre, Paris, France / Photo © Luisa Ricciarini / Bridgeman Images)

5. The temple of the goddess Hathor at Dendera (Juergen Ritterbach / Alamy Stock Photo)

6. A watercolour by David Roberts of the great temple at Abu Simbel (akg-images / Erich Lessing)

7. A wall decoration from one of the Tombs of the Nobles at Thebes (Francis Dzikowski / akg-images)

8. Muhammad Ali, the Albanian mercenary (Lebrecht Music & Arts / Alamy Stock Photo)

Decade	Rulers of Egypt	Events
1790s		
1800s	Muhammad Ali, 1805–48	
1810s		'Young Memnon' brought to London, 1818
1820s		Dendera zodiac brought to Paris, 1821
1830s		First antiquities laws and *Antiqakhana*, 1835 Luxor obelisk erected in Paris, 1836
1840s	Ibrahim, 1848 Abbas I, 1848–54	
1850s	Said, 1854–63	Mariette appointed Director of Antiquities Service and Museum, 1858
1860s	Ismail, 1863–79	Opening of Suez Canal, 1869
1870s	Tewfiq, 1879–92	Cleopatra's Needle erected in London, 1878

Expeditions and Excavations	Discoveries	Publications
Napoleonic expedition, 1798–1801	Rosetta Stone, 1799	
		Voyage dans la Basse et la Haute Egypte (Denon), 1802
Belzoni's expedition, 1815–19		*Description de l'Egypte*, 1810–28
Wilkinson's first visit, 1821–33	**Decipherment of hieroglyphics, 1822**	*Lettre à M. Dacier* (Champollion), 1822
Lane's first visit, 1825–8		*Précis du système hiéroglyphique* (Champollion), 1824
Franco-Tuscan expedition, 1828–9		
Vyse's 'operations' at Giza, 1836–8		*Manners & Customs* (Lane), 1836
		Manners & Customs, (Wilkinson), 1837
Prussian expedition, 1842–5		*Handbook for Travellers in Egypt* (Wilkinson), 1847
		Denkmäler aus Ägypten und Äthiopien (Lepsius), 1849–59
Mariette's first visit, 1850–54	Serapeum, 1851	
Duff Gordon's sojourn, 1862–9		
Edwards's visit, 1873–4		*A Thousand Miles Up the Nile* (Edwards), 1877

Decade	Rulers of Egypt	Events
1880s		Ecole française founded, 1880
		Mariette dies, Maspero succeeds, 1881
		Cleopatra's Needle erected in New York, 1881
		British invasion, 1882
		EEF founded, 1882
		Grébaut succeeds Maspero, 1886
		Egyptian Museum moves to Giza, 1889
1890s	Abbas II, 1892–1914	de Morgan succeeds Grébaut, 1892
		Loret succeeds de Morgan, 1897
		Maspero returns as Director, 1899
		Wörterbuch project initiated, 1899
1900s		Egyptian Museum opens in central Cairo, 1902
		Kaiserlich Deutsche Institut founded, 1907
1910s	Hussein Kamal, 1914–17	Maspero retires, Lacau succeeds, 1914
	Fuad, 1917–36	Oriental Institute founded, 1919
1920s		Egyptian independence declared, 1922

Expeditions and Excavations	Discoveries	Publications
Petrie's first visit, 1880 Budge's first visit, 1886–7	Hawara mummy portraits, 1888	*Ägypten und Ägyptisches Leben in Altertum* (Erman), 1885
Breasted's first visit, 1895 Borchardt appointed scientific attaché, 1899	Tombs of Thutmose III and Amenhotep II, 1898	
Davis's excavations in Valley of Kings, 1902–14 Epigraphic Survey of Nubia, 1905– Carter and Carnavon begin excavations, 1907	Karnak cachette, 1903 Tomb of Thutmose IV, 1903 Tomb of Nefertari, 1904 Tomb of Yuya and Tjuyu, 1905 Tomb of Kha, 1906 Gold Tomb, 1908	*Ancient Records of Egypt* (Breasted), 1906–7
Carter and Carnarvon start work in Valley of the Kings, 1914	Bust of Nefertiti, 1912	
	Tomb of Tutankhamun, 1922	

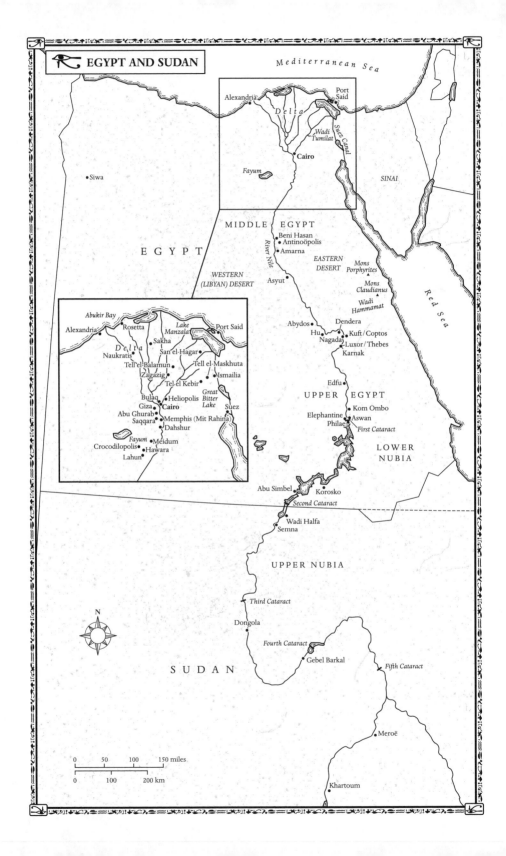

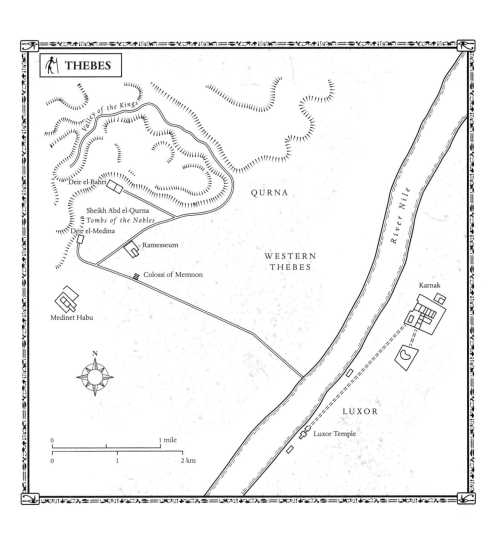

THEBES

Valley of the Kings

Deir el-Bahri

QURNA

Sheikh Abd el-Qurna
Tombs of the Nobles
Deir el-Medina

Ramesseum

Colossi of Memnon

WESTERN
THEBES

River Nile

Karnak

Medinet Habu

N

LUXOR

Luxor Temple

0   1 mile

0   1   2 km

Introduction

On my approaching the temple, the hope I had formed
of opening its entrance vanished at once; for the
amazing accumulation of sand was such, that it
appeared an impossibility ever to reach the door.[1]

GIOVANNI BATTISTA BELZONI, 1821

Rudyard Kipling wrote of archaeology that it 'furnishes a
scholarly pursuit with all the excitement of a gold pros-
pector's life'.[2] If that is true of archaeology, it is all the more
true of Egyptology. For what could be more exciting, more
exotic or more intrepid than digging in the sands of Egypt in
the hope of discovering golden treasures from the age of the
pharaohs? The antiquities of the Nile Valley have a special
allure, a particular romance, that have spoken to the Western
imagination for centuries. Our fascination with ancient Egypt
goes back to the ancient Greeks, while the practice of collecting
Egyptian antiquities was already well known in ancient Rome.
But the heyday of Egyptology – the period when it emerged
from its antiquarian origins to develop as a proper scientific
discipline, and the period that witnessed all the great discoveries,
prompting recurrent bouts of 'Egyptomania' in the West – was
undoubtedly the nineteenth and early twentieth centuries. This
golden age of scholarship and adventure is neatly bookended
by two epoch-making events: the decipherment of hieroglyphics
in 1822, and the discovery of Tutankhamun's tomb exactly a

hundred years later. The first provided the key to unlocking the secrets of pharaonic civilization, and initiated a headlong rush to find out more, sparking intensive Western engagement with Egypt. The second revealed the full glory and sophistication of pharaonic civilization, and gave legitimacy to the Egyptians' desire for self-determination, sounding the death knell for Western dominance in the country's affairs.

As we approach the bicentenary of decipherment and the centenary of Tutankhamun's rediscovery, there has never been a better time to retell – and, in retelling, to reassess – the story of Egyptology. New discoveries, new research and new insights since 1922 have transformed both our understanding of ancient Egypt and the discipline of Egyptology itself. Recent years have seen an upsurge of interest in the early history of archaeology and travel in the Middle East; many of Egyptology's nineteenth-century protagonists – its lesser-known figures, as well as its more famous names – have been the focus of detailed biographical study; and the opening up of private and institutional archives has shed new light on the motives and methods of archaeologists and their imperialist colleagues.

Indeed, the close relationship between scientific excavation and colonial expansion has emerged as a major theme in recent studies of Egyptology. As one scholar has observed: 'For rising empires, both ancient and modern, Egypt has always been a symbol of ancient sovereignty.'[3] This has long been understood and appreciated. When Julius Caesar sailed up the Nile with Cleopatra, the trip was a double celebration: on a personal level, it marked his amorous conquest of the most famous woman in the world; on a political level, it announced Rome's vice-like embrace of the fabled land of the pharaohs. Shortly afterwards the Romans began the practice of appropriating archaeological monuments in order to demonstrate their hegemony, and their successors – the colonial powers of Western Europe and, latterly,

America – followed suit. Roman emperors may have been content to ship the odd Egyptian obelisk, sphinx or statue back to the imperial capital, to adorn public spaces and private retreats, and to signal both their sophisticated taste and their all-encompassing authority, all the while squeezing every drop of profit out of their Egyptian possessions. European and American interest in Egypt was more complex, if no less naked. The exploration and description of the Nile Valley and its antiquities – carried out, with an accelerating pace, throughout the nineteenth century – was motivated by religious, philosophical or antiquarian interests, and helped to create and shape the new disciplines of archaeology and Egyptology; but these ostensibly scholarly activities also served, wittingly or unwittingly, to open up Egypt to Western involvement and interference, economic, social and political. From its very inception, Egyptology was thus the handmaid of imperialism, in a manner that Caesar would have recognized and applauded.

At the same time, Egypt's exposure to Western influences – some willingly encouraged, many impossible to resist – served to change Egyptian society from the inside. During the course of the nineteenth century, notions of modernity, progress, and national identity – concepts that had barely stirred in Egypt during the preceding 1,800 years of foreign occupation and control – slowly began to take root. By the beginning of the twentieth century, after a hundred years of engagement with foreigners, Egyptians themselves had begun to think about, and plan for, their own independent future. The story of Egyptology is thus also the story of Egyptian self-determination. The detailed understanding and appreciation of the country's ancient past paved the way for its modern rebirth. As the West rediscovered Egypt, so Egypt discovered itself.

This book seeks to tell both stories, for they are deeply interwoven. It also seeks to take a balanced approach; for

Western interest in Egypt, despite the arguments of some commentators, was neither wholly malign nor wholly benign. In the world of antiquarianism and archaeology there were good and bad individuals, scholars and scoundrels, those motivated by a desire for knowledge and those motivated by personal greed. So too, in the world of economics and politics, some (albeit rather few) had genuine aspirations for Egypt's development, while others (all too frequently) saw a chance for making a fast buck. Western engagement with Egypt featured more than its fair share of charlatans and condescending imperialists, but also a handful of more enlightened souls who sought to understand the Egyptians on their own terms, sympathized with their predicament, and sought to ameliorate their condition. They, too, are part of the tapestry that is the history of the golden age of Egyptology.

In the pages that follow, well-known giants, from Champollion to Carter and Carnarvon, will each get their moment in the sun. But so too will their lesser-known contemporaries, men and women whose painstaking but less headline-grabbing work helped to enrich and transform our understanding of the Nile Valley and its people, and left a lasting impression on Egypt, too. Travellers and treasure-hunters, ethnographers and epigraphers, antiquarians and archaeologists: whatever their motives, whatever their methods, all understood that in pursuing Egyptology they were part of a greater endeavour – to reveal a lost world, buried for centuries beneath the sands.

PROLOGUE

Travellers in an antique land

Frontispiece of the English edition of Norden's *Travels in Egypt and Nubia* (1757). Enlightenment Europe is depicted revealing the secrets of an exotic, degenerate and subjugated civilization.

When you are got to the entrance of the first pyramid, you discharge some pistols, to fright away the bats: after which you make two Arabs enter, and remove the sand, which almost entirely stops up the passage.[1]

FREDERIK NORDEN, 1757

In the summer of 47 BC, with Egypt's last queen at his side, Julius Caesar became Egypt's first tourist. Sailing up the Nile, he set a trend that would be followed by adventurous travellers over the succeeding two millennia. During the years of Roman occupation, legionaries and dignitaries visited some of Egypt's most spectacular monuments, as attested by their surviving graffiti. One of the most notable excursions was that undertaken by the emperor Hadrian, an extended trip through Egypt in AD 130 with his lover Antinous. The youth's subsequent death by drowning in the Nile spurred the establishment of a whole new cult and a new imperial city, Antinoöpolis, to perpetuate his memory.

Following the collapse of the Roman empire, records of foreigners visiting Egypt during the years of Byzantine rule (in the fifth and sixth centuries AD) are few and far between. By contrast, the Arab conquest of 641 made Egypt an integral part of a new, multicultural and multifaith empire – moreover one founded on trade, exploration and intellectual inquiry. It was in this context that Rabbi Benjamin of Tudela visited Egypt during his journey of 1165–71, entering from Abyssinia to the south. A few decades later, a scholar from present-day Iraq, Abdel Latif el-Baghdadi, arrived in Cairo and took up residence as a teacher. Around 1238, Jamal al-Din al-Idrisi wrote a book on the pyramids, the earliest known work on Egypt's most iconic ancient monuments.

While Egypt, and especially Cairo, featured on the mental map of Arabic scholars, and was relatively accessible from other Arab lands, the Nile Valley was altogether more remote, both psychologically and practically, for medieval Europeans. The earliest continental travellers were drawn to Egypt because of its biblical associations; such pilgrims mostly confined themselves to Alexandria and Cairo, and never ventured south of the pyramids. For example, Felix Fabri, a Dominican monk born in Zurich in 1441, reached the port city of Alexandria and penned an early description of Cleopatra's Needle: 'a very remarkable column, all of one stone, yet of wonderful height and width. On the four sides were carved men and animals and birds from top to bottom; and no one knows what these friezes signify.'[2]

From the beginning of the sixteenth century, Europe's trading empires increasingly came into contact with Arab vessels on the high seas. The resulting clashes were often bloody. In 1501, the Portuguese navy sank an Egyptian fleet moored at Calicut (modern Kozhikode), on the west coast of India; seven years later, it attacked and destroyed the entire Egyptian Red Sea fleet, dealing a fatal blow to the importance of Suez as a trading and trans-shipment centre, and forcing merchant ships to sail around the Cape of Good Hope, which the Portuguese controlled. It was an early indication both of Egypt's strategic potential and of the European desire to dominate trade routes. These two factors, one way or another, would determine the relationship between Europe and Egypt for the next four and a half centuries. With its fleet destroyed and its economy weakened, Egypt was in a vulnerable position, and in 1517 the Turks invaded and added the Nile Valley to their expanding territory, beginning four hundred years of suzerainty.

Egypt's incorporation into the Ottoman empire had the unintended consequence of making it more, not less, accessible to adventurous Europeans. Western nations maintained active diplomatic relations with the Sublime Porte, and this helped to facilitate travel to Ottoman lands. As a result, towards the end of the sixteenth century, a flurry of visitors reached the Nile Valley. In 1583, a Polish nobleman, Prince Nicholas Christopher Radziwill, spent about two months in Egypt during his two-year pilgrimage to the Holy Land. He visited Alexandria and Memphis, purchased two mummies, described the Sphinx and climbed the Great Pyramid at Giza, and – significantly – wrote up his travels in a book published on his return. A Latin translation appeared in 1601 followed by German editions in 1603 and 1605, and a Polish edition in 1607. *Hierosolymitana peregrinatio* was one of the earliest European works on Egypt to mention its ancient monuments. Three years after Radziwill's sojourn, two Englishmen reached Egypt. John Evesham arrived in Alexandria aboard the merchant vessel *Tyger*, while a London merchant, Laurence Aldersey, ventured further afield, visiting all the sites of interest around Cairo. Finally, in what seems to have been the busiest decade for European travel to Egypt since the days of the Romans, an anonymous Venetian travelled as far south as Upper Egypt in 1589. He explained to his incredulous readers: 'For some years I had a lively desire to see the province of the Saïd [Upper Egypt] as far as the end of the land of Egypt, and my sole reason was to see so many superb buildings, churches, colossal statues, needles and columns.'[3]

Greater ease of access to the Nile Valley coincided with the first stirrings of Renaissance thought, with the result that sixteenth-century European travellers to Egypt did not just visit the country as idle tourists but also began to take an interest in its distinctive characteristics, especially its ancient monuments. This trend accelerated in the following decades. In 1610, George Sandys, the seventh and youngest son of the Archbishop of York, spent a year in Turkey, Egypt and Palestine as part of an extended grand tour. Like others before him, he climbed the Great Pyramid, but he also took pains to observe its interior, and to study the second and third pyramids at Giza. The account of his travels, *A Relation of a Journey begun An. Dom. 1610, in Four Books* (1615) is notable, not only for its astonished description of crocodiles, but also for the assertion that the pyramids were not built by the Jews, were not the granaries of Joseph, but were tombs built by the ancient Egyptians for their kings. He was thus perhaps the first European to deduce the true purpose of the pyramids, dismissing handed-down myths and medieval traditions and using his own first-hand observations to inform his conclusions.

This groundbreaking approach was built upon by another Englishman, the mathematician and astronomer John Greaves. Unlike many of his more dilettantish contemporaries, he was a serious and committed scholar, dedicated to advancing understanding of his chosen subjects. For example, in order to be able to read ancient Greek, Arab and Persian works on astronomy, he studied a number of oriental languages and travelled extensively in the Ottoman empire, collecting scientific manuscripts. During his trip in the 1630s, he went from Constantinople to Rhodes and thence to Egypt. Equipped with mathematical instruments, he travelled from Alexandria to Cairo to take accurate measurements of the pyramids. He formed his own opinion of their purpose, concurring with Sandys that they had been built as royal tombs; he too explored the interior of the Great Pyramid. He also measured the size of its stones, produced a remarkably accurate cross section of the monument above ground level, and correctly identified a neighbouring building as a funerary temple. Greaves published his results in a book entitled *Pyramidographia, or a Discourse on the Pyramids in Aegypt* (1646). It was heavily criticized by his contemporaries, but is lauded today as a landmark work, ahead of its time.

Under the tutored eyes of men like Sandys and Greaves, the study of ancient Egypt slowly began to emerge from the fog of myth and legend into the light of scientific enquiry. However, the more fanciful interpretations of pharaonic monuments had not quite had their day. Their undoubted champion in the seventeenth century was, on the face of it, an eminent scholar. Athanasius Kircher was a German priest and antiquarian, who had entered the Jesuit order and studied philosophy, mathematics and a host of oriental languages. In 1635 he was appointed professor of mathematics at the Roman College, but he was a true renaissance man, not confining his studies to a single subject. He could read Hebrew, Syriac and Arabic, and correctly surmised that Coptic – the liturgical language of the Egyptian Orthodox Church – was related to ancient Egyptian. But what might have provided the basis for an insightful study of pharaonic civilization was fatally undermined by Kircher's interest in, and adherence to, a school of religious philosophy popular at the time, known as Hermeticism.

In the early centuries AD, a community of Greek writers in Egypt, probably based at Alexandria, had adopted the collective name Hermes Trismegistus and, under this pseudonym, had composed a body of texts. The writings comprised religion and philosophy, magic and alchemy, and reflected the diverse cultural influences alive in Alexandria at the time. They were a mixture of Platonism, Stoicism and popular philosophy, spiced up with some Jewish and Near Eastern elements. To give this melange some semblance of authority, the writers claimed great antiquity for their work. Few of their Greek contemporaries in Alexandria would have fallen for such a ruse, but when the text reached the hands of the early church fathers, the authors' claims were believed. Hermes Trismegistus was acknowledged as a real person, and the collection of writings ascribed to him became known as the *Corpus Hermeticum*. Moreover, European theologians saw in the corpus prefigurations of the essential truths of Christianity. It gained a hallowed status and eventually, in 1460, was translated from Greek into Latin, and subsequently into many European languages.

Throughout the Middle Ages, Hermeticism, as it came to be known, had a profound influence on Western thought. Kircher's adherence to Hermeticism coloured his interpretation of the ancient Egyptian monuments he saw around him in Rome, which he published in his influential 1652 work, *Oedipus Aegyptiacus*. He felt certain that the hieroglyphs must express profound Hermetic truths, discernible only to initiates, and gave his imagination full rein when producing interpretations of what were, in truth, rather pedestrian inscriptions. Despite growing evidence that it was profoundly mistaken, Hermeticism remained stubbornly influential throughout the seventeenth and eighteenth centuries. The belief that Egypt was the source of occult wisdom was simply too enticing to abandon.

The problem for scholars like Sandys and Greaves was that ancient Egyptian civilization was too mysterious to be accepted on the same basis as ancient Greece or Rome. Had not Greek and Roman authors themselves, including Herodotus, Strabo and Diodorus Siculus, remarked on Egypt's magical, mystical characteristics? Other texts of equal repute seemed to confirm the view. Alongside the *Corpus Hermeticum*, another hugely influential work was the *Hieroglyphika* by the fifth-century author Horapollo. When rediscovered by scholars in fifteenth-century

Florence, it strongly reinforced the theory that ancient Egyptian writing encoded deeper, mystical truths. This view of pharaonic civilization would be inherited by the Rosicrucians and Freemasons.

During the European Enlightenment, the allure of ancient Egypt was thus due more to its association with esoteric knowledge and mystical insight than to any sense of wonder at the practical achievements of the pharaohs. A growing fashion for all things ancient Egyptian found expression not only in books but also in the widespread adoption of Egyptian architectural forms, in country houses and landscape gardens. As well as being aesthetically pleasing, they signalled that the owner was a free thinker, open to new and radical ideas.

In the eighteenth century, curiosity about Egypt and its ancient past began to grow. The Nile Valley's peculiar combination of biblical and classical resonances made Egypt a land at once familiar and strange. While no more than half a dozen or so first-hand accounts of Egypt were published by Europeans between 1500 and 1650, during the following century-and-a-half the number rose to over fifty. Frenchmen were the most frequent travellers to the Nile Valley with at least twenty-seven accounts, while the British were in second place with sixteen. Other nationalities making the journey to Egypt and recording their experiences included Germans, Dutch, Italians and Swiss.[4] Most of these books were little more than collections of exotic experiences and fanciful interpretations of the surviving monuments, written by adventurers to titillate their readers. But three European travellers to Egypt between 1712 and 1738 showed a keener interest in the country's antiquities, a genuine desire to understand as well as observe, and their writings made significant contributions to emergent Western understanding of the Egyptian past.

The first of these pioneers and proto-Egyptologists was, like

Athanasius Kircher, a Jesuit scholar. Claude Sicard travelled as a missionary to the Holy Land – first to Syria and then, from 1712, to Egypt, where he stayed for the rest of his life. His main purpose was to convert the Copts to Roman Catholicism, but he had also been ordered by the Regent of France, Philippe d'Orléans, to survey and record Egypt's ancient monuments. In pursuance of this task, Sicard made a series of extended tours from his base in Cairo: five to Upper Egypt, one to the Fayum, one to the Sinai peninsula, and one to Middle Egypt and the Delta. He became the best-travelled European in Egypt since Classical times and, after the anonymous Venetian of 1589, the first Westerner since the Romans to visit the temples of Upper Egypt and the first to reach as far south as Aswan. His diary entry for 17 December 1720 noted, 'we examined and measured at Edfu a famous temple of Apollo which is still almost intact'.[5] He went on to describe around eighty more temples.

Sicard did not merely travel and observe, he studied. As a result, he was the first modern tourist correctly to identify the ruins at Luxor as the 'Hundred-gated Thebes' of Classical legend, and the Valley of the Kings as a royal cemetery. He sensed that, in the tomb inscriptions of Thebes, 'we have there the story of the lives, virtues, acts, combats and victories of the princes who are buried there, but it is impossible for us to decipher them for the present'.[6] After his first visit to Luxor, in 1718, he decided to embark on a hugely ambitious project: the creation of a comprehensive map of the Nile Valley, accompanied by a description of every location, ancient and modern. The map, published in 1722, was the first accurate chart of the Nile Valley ever produced in the West, with Arabic place names correctly transcribed. Sicard referred to it, presciently, as the *Description de l'Egypte*. The accompanying gazetteer was never completed, and only a single, partial copy survives. Sicard's original papers were also lost, and the surviving fragments of the gazetteer were published only in 1982.

Had Sicard been able to publish his work during his lifetime, he would undoubtedly have been regarded today as one of the founding fathers of Egyptology. The first glimmerings of the nascent discipline are ascribed, instead, to two slightly later travellers, an Englishman and a Dane; though nowhere near as curious or studious as Sicard, they were more diligent in printing and promulgating their accounts. Richard Pococke (1704–65) was typical of the small breed of English travellers who ventured as far as Egypt during the eighteenth century. A clergyman by vocation (he later became Bishop of Ossory, then of Meath), he was primarily interested in Egypt for its biblical connections. Although the Nile Valley seemed distant and exotic in the European imagination, it was, in fact, relatively accessible for an adventurous traveller willing to set sail from a Mediterranean port. As Pococke recounted: 'Having embark'd at Leghorn on the seventh of September, one thousand seven hundred thirty-seven, old style, we arrived at Alexandria on the twenty-ninth of the same month, being only a week in the voyage, from the time we lost sight of Sicily.'[7]

During his six months in Egypt, Pocoke visited Giza and 'the famous sphynx,'[8] and became the first Briton to travel south of Cairo, exploring tombs in the Valley of the Kings and journeying as far south as Philae and the First Cataract. After his return to England, he joined the newly founded Egyptian Society in 1741, and the following year was elected as its secretary. At the same time, he was moved, 'by the persuasion of some friends, to give an account of his travels, and of several accidents, that might give an insight into the customs and manners of people so different from our own'.[9]

His two-volume *A Description of the East and some other countries* (1743–5) was, in many respects, a typical product of mid-eighteenth-century English scholarship. It was dedicated to Pococke's patron, the Earl of Chesterfield, while many of the individual plates were dedicated to other notable personages who had contributed towards the cost of publication.[10] But, in other respects, Pococke's work was pioneering. The first volume was arranged in five sections, devoted respectively to the Delta; the Nile Valley; the Sinai peninsula; government, customs and natural history; and 'Miscellaneous subjects, chiefly relating to the Antiquities and Natural History of Egypt'. The last included detailed and comprehensive descriptions of sites and places which had not yet been touched by tourism. Pococke's *Description* was to remain *the* indispensable guide to the pharaonic monuments for nearly seven decades.

At exactly the same time as Pococke was exploring Egypt, a Danish naval captain named Frederik Norden (1708–42) was also travelling up the Nile. He had been sent by his king, Christian VI, on a mission to obtain a full and accurate account of Egypt, and he stayed in the country for about a year. By the time of his journey, travellers' accounts of the Egyptian capital were so numerous that Norden glossed over Cairo's sights. He later wrote: 'This city is so well known, by such a number of relations and descriptions, as have been published of it, that I flatter myself, the reader will be pleased with my forbearing to enter into circumstantial details.'[11]

Instead, he was primarily interested in the relics of the pharaonic era: 'Before I quit Cairo, and its adjacent parts, I cannot forbear speaking of the monuments that are the most worthy of the curiosity of those, who travel into Egypt: I mean the PYRAMIDS.'[12]

Entering the Great Pyramid was an adventure: 'After these necessary preliminaries, you must have the precaution to strip yourself entirely, and undress even to your shirt, on account of the excessive heat . . . Afterwards, when you have regained your natural heat, you mount up to the top of the pyramid, in order to have a prospect from thence of the country round about, which is charming to behold.'[13]

But Norden's interest in the Giza monuments went much further than mere touristic curiosity. By careful observation, he came to a developed understanding of their purpose and age: 'They have all been raised with the same intention; that is to say, to serve for sepultures . . . we must absolutely throw back the first epoch of the pyramids into times so remote in antiquity, that vulgar chronology would find a difficulty to fix the era of them.'[14]

Indeed, noting the absence of hieroglyphic inscriptions, he deduced that the pyramids must have been built before the invention of writing. (He was wrong on this point, but his reasoning was sound.) Norden even dared to critique Greaves's *Pyramidographia*, then the last word on the Giza monuments.

On Norden's journey up the Nile, he visited most of the major sites. Luxor Temple was buried in sand up to the shoulders of the seated colossi of Ramesses II flanking the entrance,[15] but Norden could see enough to describe the monument as 'these superb ruins'.[16] At Karnak, like generations of travellers since, he was plagued by crowds asking for *bakhshish*.[17] He was fascinated, not only by the monuments, but by the manners and customs of the ancient Egyptians, making a particular study of mummification 'in order to render the art of Egyptian embalmings more intelligible'.[18]

Norden and Pococke may well have passed each other on the river, or in the backstreets of Cairo, but it is not known if they actually met during their sojourn in the land of the pharaohs. They certainly encountered each other afterwards; for, on returning from Egypt, Norden was attached to the British navy and settled in London where he, like Pococke, joined the short-lived Egyptian Society. It had been established, under the presidency of Lord Sandwich, with the aim of 'promoting and preserving Egyptian and other ancient learning'.[19] Another of its members was the antiquarian and pioneer of archaeological surveys, William Stukeley. But it met for less than a year-and-a-half before falling into abeyance when the interest of its aristocratic patrons waned.

Norden, however, was not finished with ancient Egypt. He set to work writing up his *Travels in Egypt*, which appeared posthumously in 1757, more than a decade after Pococke's *Description*. Norden's book was, if anything, even more influential. Its lively and observant text was illustrated by a fine series of plates. The book was translated at once from Danish into English, French and German, becoming one of the most widely read accounts of Egypt and its monuments. Moreover, it made an implicit claim that would shape Western engagement with Egypt for the next two centuries: in the English edition, the engraved frontispiece shows a standing classical figure, holding a staff topped with the Christian Chi-Rho monogram and pointing towards the image of a chained crocodile, surrounded by pharaonic ruins, while a lion rests at the figure's feet. The symbolism was clear: by re-discovering Egypt, Western civilization had also mastered it. Norden's English editor, Peter Templeman, made the claim even more explicitly. In his dedication to the British monarch George II, he reflected: 'In reading the following account of a country, that was once the model to other nations, but is now sunk through tyranny into the greatest ignorance and brutality, one cannot but reflect with transport on our own happiness in this country, under the reign of a wise, just, and beneficent Prince.'[20]

No other travellers of the eighteenth century came close to Pococke and Norden in terms of careful observation and accurate description of pharaonic monuments. European visits to Egypt in the second half of the century slowed to a trickle, as disturbances in the south of the country put off all but the most adventurous of tourists. Those who did sail across the Mediterranean and up the Nile either met with misfortune or left little by way of intelligent accounts. For example, a scientific expedition sent to the Middle East in 1761 by King Frederik V of Denmark stayed in Egypt for over a year (while avoiding Upper Egypt); all but one of the members died from disease within months of leaving Alexandria. An eccentric English member of parliament and traveller, Edward Montagu, sailed from Livorno to Egypt (following in Pococke's footsteps) in April 1763, returning three years later to make a brief study of Pompey's Pillar. He carried out a series of cursory excavations, the finds from which eventually passed to the nascent British Museum. But, despite making two further trips to Egypt in the 1770s, he added little to contemporary understanding of the country or its history. A British diplomat, Nathaniel Davison, who accompanied Montagu on his first visit, later returned to Giza with a pair of French companions to explore the Great Pyramid. He discovered the lowest set of relieving chambers above the burial chamber, which were duly named after him; to this day, they are known as Davison's chambers. But, on being posted to Algiers, his interests turned to other matters. Finally, in 1768, the Scottish traveller James Bruce braved danger and discomfort to visit Thebes, and was rewarded for his efforts by discovering the tomb of Ramesses III in the Valley of the Kings (which is still known as 'Bruce's Tomb'). But the subsequent account of his discovery 'inspired disbelief, not interest'.[21]

By the last quarter of the eighteenth century, advances in the study of ancient Egypt had ground to a halt. The Nile Valley, like the rest of the 'Orient', remained, for most Europeans, a remote and inaccessible land of myth. To wake Western scholarship from its torpor and to bring Egypt from semi-obscurity into the light of understanding would require a determined effort: a proper scientific expedition, well planned and well resourced, with the profile to focus Western attention on Egypt as never before.

⊲⊙⊳

From the Renaissance onwards, the East was regarded by Europeans as a source of wisdom – as expressed in the Latin motto *ex oriente lux*, 'light from the East'. People looked to the East, and to the ancient East in particular, for new concepts of divinity, and for new answers to humanity's problems.[22] This concept of 'orientation' gained particular popularity during the French revolution. Of all the oriental civilizations, ancient Egypt seemed to provide inspiration for a different model of society, be it theistic, pantheistic, cosmotheistic or secular.[23] One of the most influential books of the late eighteenth century was a treatise by the French aristocrat, Constantin-François Chasseboeuf, comte de Volney, entitled *Les Ruines, ou Méditation sur révolutions des empires* (1791). Inspired by Volney's travels in Syria and Egypt in the mid-1780s,[24] *Les Ruines* blended science, philosophy and theology, attacked orthodox religion, and championed atheistic humanism as the foundation for future human happiness. It helped to shape revolutionary thought, and not just in Volney's own country. Within a year of publication, *Les Ruines* was translated into English (as *Ruins of Empires*), where it chimed with the nascent spirit of Romanticism.

Volney's view of Egypt, as a source of wisdom, found expression in other artistic creations of the time. Mozart's operas *Zaïde* (1779–80) and *The Magic Flute* (1789–91) are replete with pharaonic symbolism, in the latter case blended with Masonic influences. In a similar vein, Charles Monnet's painting *The Fountain of Youth*, which was widely distributed as an engraving from 1793, shows a crowd of people surrounding a fountain in the form of the goddess Isis, with water flowing from her breasts. One of the worshippers raises a goblet to drink from the water of wisdom.[25] There was thus a philosophical impetus at the end of the eighteenth century – and especially in revolutionary France – to learn more about ancient Egyptian civilization. For, as a contemporary commentator put it, Egypt stood 'at the beginning of sacred and profane antiquity'.[26]

There were also more mundane, political reasons why French revolutionary leaders took a particular interest in the Nile Valley. France had been stung by its loss of influence in India during the Seven Years War. Pushed into second place in the subcontinent by the British, France was not about to suffer the same indignity in the Mediterranean, its own backyard. Moreover, French merchants had well-developed commercial interests along the coast of North Africa, and French scholarship boasted an impressive tradition of oriental studies. In short, France felt that North Africa in general, and Egypt in particular, were its by right. Action to assert this claim was not a spur-of-the-moment decision: Leibnitz had proposed the French annexation of Egypt as far back as 1672.[27] Furthermore, the leaders of the French revolution saw their movement in historic, epochal terms: they were not simply forming a new government in France, but ushering in a new era for Europe. Looking to ancient Rome as a model, their objective was to restore the power and purpose of the Roman republic in a new republic, centred on Paris. In a memoir to the Directorate of 13 February 1798, the French foreign minister Talleyrand explained his government's thinking in the clearest possible terms: 'Egypt was a province of the Roman Republic; she must become a province of the French Republic. Roman rule saw the decadence of this beautiful country; French rule will bring it prosperity.

The Romans wrested Egypt from kings distinguished in arts and science; the French will lift it from the hands of the most appalling tyrants who have ever existed.'[28]

Whereas the British in India had simply replaced native despotism with its colonial equivalent, French rule in Egypt, Talleyrand asserted, would be a liberation, benefiting both parties.

Persuaded by the force of such arguments – and perhaps goaded into action by the gathering momentum of British exploration – the Directorate, in March 1798, authorized a French expedition to Egypt. Its purpose would be twofold. Military conquest would annex Egypt to the French republic, and have the added benefit of undermining British interests in the Mediterranean and, ultimately, India. At the same time, scientific study would facilitate the intellectual acquisition of Egypt, its people, its monuments, and its illustrious past.[29] A successful expedition to Egypt would thus make France both the dominant military power in Europe and its leading cultural force.

While Talleyrand was the spokesperson for the enterprise, its guiding force was the man who had emerged from the chaos of the revolution as France's new strongman: Napoleon Bonaparte. He certainly understood and espoused the strategic arguments for an expedition to Egypt, but his motivations were as much personal as political. Napoleon saw his leadership in dynastic terms, consciously emulating figures from Europe's classical past. While the French republic might model itself on its Roman forebear, Bonaparte looked further back for his personal inspiration, to another military leader who had over-thrown the established order and reshaped the world: Alexander the Great. At the apogee of his power, Alexander had conquered the land of the pharaohs; twenty centuries later, Napoleon would liberate the Nile Valley from generations of barbarism.[30]

Napoleon's expedition was planned in conditions of great secrecy, under the code name 'the Left Wing of the Army of England'.[31] Throughout the late spring of 1798, its members were recruited, and its materials assembled, from across France. Alongside the levying of troops, great pains were taken over the selection of the five hundred or so civilian members of the expedition. Among their number were 151 savants (experts). They were mostly young men (the youngest was just fifteen, and their average age was twenty-five), for whom the prospect of making new discoveries and establishing a new outpost of France represented the adventure, and the opportunity, of a lifetime. They were led by five established scientists, chief among them the thirty-year-old mathematician Jean-Baptiste Joseph Fourier. A teacher at the Ecole polytechnique, he was charged by Napoleon with recruiting suitable students for the Egyptian expedition. Among those who signed up were two young engineers, Edmé-François Jomard and Jacques-Marie Le Père. Both would go on to make signal contributions to the expedition's scientific aims, and to the rediscovery of ancient Egypt.

The veritable army of experts assembled by Fourier embraced all the disciplines required to meet the expedition's scientific and cultural aspirations. The relative numbers of different professions are revealing of Bonaparte's intentions. Most numerous of all were the printers (twenty-seven of them, together with three of their wives), for Napoleon and his fellow revolutionaries understood the power of the written word: to describe and publish was to master and control. Next came the surveyors and civil engineers (fourteen of each), for a country could only be brought under effective control and made economically productive if it was properly mapped and equipped with an effective infrastructure – roads, bridges and canals. Joining the printers, surveyors and engineers were nine mechanics and three shipbuilders (to keep the new infrastructure running); five mining engineers and three mechanical engineers (to develop Egypt's economy); four architects, an equal number of mathematicians, seven naturalists and three astronomers (to observe, record and study the natural wonders of Egypt); three gunpowder-makers (to assist the mining engineers as well as the army); eight interpreters and eight artists (to facilitate and record the expedition's achievements); seven surgeons and three pharmacists (to keep the whole company in good health); and two archaeologists. Although antiquarianism was already a popular pastime in late eighteenth-century Europe, the scientific study of the past was still in its infancy. The inclusion of two archaeologists in the Napoleonic expedition, whilst relatively insignificant compared with the large number of printers and engineers, was thus a pivotal moment in the emergence of the discipline. Indeed, it is ironic that the expedition's archaeological achievements would far outweigh its other accomplishments. What was launched as primarily a military, political and economic venture would gain a lasting reputation as the crucible of Egyptology.

After two months of feverish activity, everything was ready. The main flotilla set sail from the port of Toulon on 19 May 1798. It comprised thirteen ships of the line; forty-two frigates, brigs and corsairs; and 130 transport vessels. On board were 17,000 soldiers, an equal number of sailors and marines, and 500-odd civilians, including the 151 experts. The armed forces had at their disposal over a thousand artillery pieces and 700 horses, while the experts had measuring instruments, scientific equipment, and a large library comprising just about every book on Egypt then available in France.[32] Once at sea, the flotilla was joined by three smaller convoys sailing from Genoa, Ajaccio and Civita Vecchia; they brought the strength of the entire armada to 400 ships and 36,000 men. It was the largest expeditionary force destined for Egypt since the days of ancient Rome.

At the head of his expedition, Napoleon landed at Alexandria on 1 July 1798. One of his first acts on disembarking was formally to establish a commission of science and arts, comprising the 151 savants. His cultural ambitions were matched by his military prowess, and Alexandria fell to the overwhelming French forces on the first morning. Less than three weeks later, after marching his army southwards, Napoleon won the decisive Battle of the Pyramids – against the forces of Egypt's Mamluk rulers – and on 25 July he entered Cairo as the country's conqueror. But his victory was short-lived. On 1 August, a British fleet under the command of Horatio Nelson defeated the French navy in the Battle of the Nile at Abukir Bay; Nelson was ennobled (as Lord Nelson of the Nile) and Napoleon found himself stranded in Egypt, with no obvious escape route. However, the British had not landed any forces, so the French still had control of the country, and Napoleon set about pursuing the scientific purposes of the expedition with gusto. By an order of 22 August, he created the Institut d'Egypte, modelled on the Institut de France, and appointed Fourier as its permanent secretary. It met for the first time on 23 August and represented the ideals of the French Enlightenment. Its membership was drawn from the commission and the expedition's leading military and administrative personnel. The number of members was restricted to just forty-eight, divided evenly between representatives of four branches of science: mathematics, physical sciences, political economy, and arts and letters. A captured Mamluk palace was adapted as the institute's headquarters, equipped with meeting rooms and laboratories, and furnished with the reference library brought from France.[33]

While the institute's members set about their work in Cairo, the study of ancient monuments further upstream fell to Napoleon's friend and colleague, Dominique Vivant, Baron

Denon (1747–1825), who attached himself to a section of the French invasion force, under the command of General Desaix, that left Cairo on 25 August in pursuit of one of the deposed Mamluk rulers, Murad Bey. For the next ten months, Desaix's army, with Denon firmly embedded in the ranks, marched southwards, stopping only to marvel at the sites they encountered on the way. They were enthralled by what they found. The ruins of ancient Thebes, in particular, made a profound impression. On 26 January 1799, Denon himself recalled: 'The army came to a stop by itself and spontaneously burst into applause, as if occupying the ruins of this capital had been the goal of our glorious mission and had completed the conquest of Egypt.'[34]

By contrast, the Egyptians who observed these strangers were probably somewhat perplexed by their obsession with dusty ruins, for Arabic interest in Egypt's antiquities had long since waned.[35] Nor were the European invaders always prepared for the conditions they encountered: when Desaix first reconnoitered the Valley of the Kings in the blistering summer heat of 1799, two of his soldiers died of sunstroke.[36]

In the late summer of 1798, the physicist (and head of the French ballooning corps) Jean-Marie-Joseph Coutelle and the expedition's chief civil engineer, Le Père, with a guard of a hundred soldiers, hired 150 local workers to clear the inner chambers and descending passage of the Great Pyramid at Giza. The mission was able to take accurate measurements of the pyramid's exterior, including the height of each course of masonry, while the architect François-Charles Cécile measured and drew the interior grand gallery. On 24 September 1798, worked paused briefly when Napoleon himself visited Giza. Inside the Great Pyramid, he asked to be left alone for a while in the King's Chamber – perhaps consciously emulating Alexander the Great at the Siwa oracle. Bonaparte never revealed what he experienced in that moment of solitude,[37] but he was certainly struck by the sheer scale of Giza. His architects and engineers calculated that there was enough stone in the three main pyramids to build a wall half a metre thick and three metres high all the way around France; or that, if laid end to end, the stones would reach two-thirds of the way around the earth. The institute's surveyor and cartographer Pierre Jacotin produced a large-scale map of Giza that remains useful two centuries later. Equally influential, though in a different way, was the conclusion of Jomard, who was so awestruck by the pyramids that he felt they must incorporate a deeper, mystical truth.[38] The workmen had begun clearing sand from around the Sphinx when the soldiers accompanying the mission were called away on military duties. The institute's investigations thus came to a halt, but not before they had carried out the most detailed, comprehensive documentation of Giza yet attempted.

Elsewhere in Egypt members of the commission were busy surveying the country and planning its economic renaissance as a province of the French Republic. One of the most significant pieces of work was the survey of Lake Manzala undertaken by Le Père, part of a programme to explore the possibility of opening a canal from Suez to link the Mediterranean with the Red Sea. That particular project planted a seed very firmly in the French consciousness that would lie dormant, but not forgotten, until brought to fruition under a future Napoleon (Bonaparte's nephew, Emperor Napoleon III). Bonaparte, however, had realized that his primary dream of annexing Egypt to France was destined to fail. The British Minister of War, Lord Dundas, had warned that: 'The possession of Egypt by any independent Power would be a fatal circumstance to the interests of this country,'[39] signalling that Britain was determined to thwart France's territorial ambitions. On 25 July 1799,

Napoleon won the second Battle of Abukir Bay, buying him enough time to plan his escape. One of his last decisions made on Egyptian soil was to instruct the commission to continue and complete the systematic inventory of Egypt's antiquities begun by Denon. A decree of 13 August appointed two subcommissions to carry out the task. Nine days later, Napoleon and Denon slipped through the British naval blockade of Alexandria and made their way back to Paris. Bonaparte arrived in the French capital on 16 October and seized power as first consul three weeks later.

The remaining story of the French expedition is the story of the commission members, left to their own devices while their erstwhile leader busied himself with other matters in far-off France. As instructed, they continued their research, gathering material for the official expedition publication. But their days in Egypt were numbered. To guarantee British hegemony, troops under Sir Ralph Abercromby landed in Egypt on 18 March 1801; Cairo surrendered on 18 June and Alexandria on 3 September. The remaining members of the commission made a series of attempts to escape, eventually breaking through the British stranglehold and finding their way back to Paris.[40] Theirs was a sorry reckoning: of the 151 savants who had accompanied Napoleon, nearly a quarter were dead within eight years. This included five killed in battle and five who were assassinated; ten who died of plague, five of dysentery, and one from drowning; and five who died back home in Europe from the ill-effects of their time in Egypt.

Militarily, too, the Napoleonic expedition was a disaster. But its long-term repercussions, for Egypt as well as for Egyptology, were profound. The introduction of the printing press, and the ideas that the commission brought with them from France to the Nile Valley, stirred the beginnings of Egypt's political awakening, for good and for ill. An Egyptian eyewitness of Napoleon's

invasion, Sheikh Abdel Rahman el Djabarty, commented laconically that 'it was the beginning of a series of great misfortunes'.[41]

Indeed, the brief French occupation swept away the old order,
without putting anything in its place. Into the political vacuum
stepped a young officer in the Ottoman army by the name of
Mehmet Ali. Born in 1769 in Macedonia (present-day Greece),
to an Albanian family, Mehmet Ali had risen to be commanding
officer of an Albanian unit loyal to the Ottoman sultan. In
spring 1801, following the retreat of Napoleon's army, Mehmet
Ali's unit was ordered by Constantinople to reoccupy Egypt. It
landed at Abukir Bay, site of Nelson's victory less than three
years earlier. Across Egypt, Mehmet Ali found a power struggle
raging between the former rulers of Egypt, the Mamluks (who
had regrouped after the French withdrawal), and the forces loyal
to the Ottoman sultan. Mehmet Ali managed to work with
both sides while steadily building up popular support for himself.
Eventually, in May 1805 (exactly a year after Napoleon
proclaimed himself Emperor of France), he was able to engineer
the downfall of the Ottoman viceroy and his own elevation to
the post. The sultan in Constantinople had little choice but to
acquiesce, confirming Mehmet Ali (his name now Egyptianized
as Muhammad Ali) as Pasha of Egypt in 1806.

He consolidated his power by defeating a small British
invasion the following year, and set the seal on his absolute
rule with an act of the greatest barbarity. On 1 March 1811,
Muhammad Ali invited the surviving Mamluk leaders to a
great celebration in the Citadel of Cairo. As soon as they had
entered the fortress, he had them surrounded and killed, before
sending his army to round up the remaining Mamluk forces
throughout the country. Thus did an Albanian army officer
become viceroy of Egypt and founder of a dynasty that would
rule the Nile Valley – often with an iron fist – for the next
century and a half.

Not only did the Napoleonic expedition – the first major imperialist incursion into the Middle East in modern times – play unwitting midwife to the birth of Muhammad Ali's dynasty: it also confirmed Egypt as the focus of Anglo-French political rivalry for the next hundred years.[42] Moreover, the excitement generated by the expedition and the resulting publication awakened a public interest in ancient Egypt across the Western world that has never abated. Napoleon's enduring legacy in Egypt was the genesis of a new nation and the birth of a new science. Each would prove a mixed blessing.

⬥

The French may have lost the military advantage in Egypt, but thanks to the work of Napoleon's savants it was France, not Britain, that emerged victorious in the battle for cultural supremacy. By the mid-1810s, the French representative in Egypt exercised a virtual monopoly on the acquisition of antiquities throughout the Nile Valley. Indeed, for Bernardino Drovetti, who participated in the Napoleonic campaign and later served as French consul-general in Cairo between 1810 and 1829, collecting ancient art and artefacts was his primary concern and occupation. A popular saying in early nineteenth-century Cairo was: 'The riches of Egypt are for the foreigners therein.'[43]

The head start gained by the French in amassing antiquities for the great national collection at the Louvre did not go unnoticed in London. In 1815, buoyed by Wellington's victory over Napoleon at Waterloo, the British Foreign Office urged its diplomats around the world to start collecting for the British Museum. Never mind advances in knowledge, national pride was at stake: 'Whatever the expense of the undertaking, whether successful or otherwise, it would be most cheerfully supported by an enlightened nation, eager to anticipate its

Rivals in the prosecution of the best interests of science and literature.'[44]

Britain's response to French cultural hegemony in Egypt was to appoint its own consul-general. In 1815, the government announced that its new chief representative in Cairo would be Henry Salt. He arrived in Cairo in April 1816 with his wife and, over the next decade, devoted most of his energies to collecting antiquities – not only for the British Museum, but also to sell at a profit to supplement his meagre diplomatic salary. A posting in Egypt was not merely an opportunity to get one over on the French, it was also a chance to get rich – an irresistible combination.

The rivalry between Drovetti and Salt dominated the exploration – or, more often, the ransacking – of Egypt's ancient sites throughout the second and third decades of the nineteenth century. As a later observer put it, 'the archaeological field became a battle plain for two armies of Dragomans and Fellah-navvies. One was headed by the redoubtable Salt; the other owned the command of Drovetti.'[45] Salt lost no time in ingratiating himself with Muhammad Ali, believing that good relations with Egypt's new ruler would greatly facilitate the collection of antiquities. But Muhammad Ali was nothing if not an adept political operator. He used antiquities (or the promise of them) to play the Western powers off against each other.[46] At first, Salt was regularly outsmarted and outmanoeuvred by Drovetti, who had built up a network of loyal – and ruthless – agents throughout Egypt. Salt's response – and his stroke of luck – was to appoint as his own agent a man whose determination and resourcefulness, not to mention physical abilities, were more than a match for any rival.

Giovanni Battista Belzoni (1778–1823) emerges from the early annals of Egyptology as a giant in every sense. Born into poverty in the Italian city of Padua, as a teenager he made his way to Rome, intent upon a career in holy orders. But the Napoleonic invasion in 1798 forced Belzoni to leave the city, and he wandered for a time around Europe as a travelling pedlar, before landing up in London in 1802. There, he put his extraordinary physical stature to good use, taking to the stage in a series of show-stopping acts: as a weightlifter dubbed, first, 'the Patagonian Sampson', then 'the French Hercules'; as the eponymous giant in the pantomime *Jack the Giant-killer* (better known today as *Jack and the Beanstalk*); and finally, under his own name, as 'the Great Belzoni', actor, conjuror and strongman. After marrying an Englishwoman, Sarah, Belzoni sought new adventures and travelled to Malta. There, by good fortune, he met a representative of Muhammad Ali's, who was scouting Europe for engineers and other experts to assist in the modernization of the Egyptian economy. Belzoni argued that, with a background in theatrical hydraulics, he was just the man to improve Egypt's irrigation system. Remarkably, the envoy took Belzoni at his word, and invited him to Cairo, to present his ideas to the pasha himself. Muhammad Ali's thinking was simple: as he is reported to have told a visitor, 'I know that among fifty men who come from Europe to offer me their services, forty-nine are only to be compared to false stones. Without testing them, I cannot discover the only genuine diamond that may be among them. I begin by buying them all and when I discover the one, he often repays me by a hundred-fold for the loss I have incurred by the others.'[47]

Belzoni was to be a major beneficiary of this thinking. 'We sailed from Malta on the 19th of May, 1815,' he wrote, 'and arrived at Alexandria on the 9th of June following; Mrs Belzoni, myself, and James Curtain, a lad, whom I brought with me from Ireland, formed our party. The principal cause of my going to Egypt was the project of constructing hydraulic machines, to irrigate the fields, by a system much easier and more economical than what is in use in that country.'[48] Even for a man who had seen much of Europe, Egypt was terra incognita, and presented unexpected challenges: 'On entering the harbour of Alexandria, the pilot informed us, that the plague was in town. To a European, who had never been in that country, this was alarming intelligence.'[49]

After making his way from Alexandria to Cairo, Belzoni soon got to know other Europeans living in the Egyptian capital. One of his first acquaintances was the Swiss explorer Johann Ludwig Burckhardt, who had studied Arabic at Cambridge, travelled extensively in the Middle East, discovered Petra in 1812, and, later that year, settled in Cairo, living as a Muslim under the name Sheikh Ibrahim ibn Abdullah. Since arriving in the land of the pharaohs, Burckhardt had become fascinated by the country's antiquities. (He was the first European to see the rock-cut temples at Abu Simbel, in March 1813.) One in particular intrigued him. On the plain of western Thebes, opposite Luxor, there stood a ruined edifice, characterized by towering columns, tumbledown walls, and the remains of colossal statues. Napoleon's savants had studied the building, and, inspired by the writings of the first-century BC Greek historian Diodorus Siculus, had named it the 'Tomb of Ozymandias'.[50] Other Europeans referred to it as the 'Palace of Memnon'. By whichever name it was known, its most notable features were a gigantic royal statue that lay prone on the sand and, nearby, two colossal royal heads.[51] The larger and more spectacular of the two, a bust measuring 2.7 metres high and 2 metres wide, cut from a single block of granite, was nicknamed the 'Young Memnon'. It had attracted the attention of the Napoleonic expedition, which had tried, unsuccessfully, to remove it.[52] Now Burckhardt decided that it would make a wonderful addition to a European museum – but the British Museum, not the Louvre. According to Belzoni: 'Mr Burckhardt had for a long time premeditated the removal of the colossal head, or rather bust, known by the name of Young Memnon, to England, and had often endeavoured to persuade the Bashaw [Pasha] to send it as a present to the Prince Regent; but as it must have appeared to a Turk too trifling an article to send to so great a personage, no steps were taken for this purpose.'[53]

Burckhardt was supported in his scheme by another traveller and antiquarian, William John Bankes, who had come to Egypt in 1815 and had voyaged upstream as far as Wadi Halfa. He was an avid collector of antiquities, and the idea of transporting the Young Memnon to England, to stand as the centrepiece of the British Museum, greatly appealed to him. Together, Burckhardt and Bankes pressed their case with the newly arrived British consul-general, Henry Salt.

By a fortuitous combination of circumstances, Belzoni arrived in Cairo just as Salt was considering the proposal. The Italian giant – doughty, fearless and uncannily experienced in moving heavy objects – presented the perfect solution. On 28 June 1816, Salt wrote in a letter: 'Mr. Belzoni is requested to prepare the necessary implements, at Boolak, for the purpose of raising the head of the statue of the younger Memnon, and carrying it down the Nile.'[54] According to Belzoni, the decision was not quite so straightforward. He claimed that 'The consul seemed inclined to comply, but was indecisive for some time, saying he would think about it'. Belzoni also categorically denied having been engaged or employed by Salt, claiming instead to have acted in his own capacity for the British Museum.[55] Whatever the truth – and the difference in accounts was symptomatic of the tempestuous relations between the two men, which ultimately broke down completely[56] – Belzoni accepted the commission and set off for Thebes. On arrival, he recruited eighty local Arab men, and they began work on 27 July 1816.

Brute force proved its worth, and 'On the 3d [August] we went on extremely well, and advanced nearly four hundred yards'.[57] By 12 August, the colossal bust had been dragged all the way to the west bank of the Nile. This remarkable feat must have been the talk of Luxor. News even reached the ears of a professor at al-Azhar, Abd al-Rahman al-Jabarti, who in a 1817 commentary on European collecting activities made special reference to the Young Memnon; he did not condemn its removal, but he did not entirely understand the Western fascination for Egypt's ancient relics.[58] The Young Memnon's journey downstream to Cairo took a further twenty-four days, and the torso eventually docked at the port of Bulaq on 15 December 1816. After a break for the Christmas and New Year festivities, the torso embarked on a second river journey, arriving at the port of Rosetta, at the mouth of the Nile, on 10 January 1817.

Mission accomplished, Belzoni turned his attention to some of Egypt's other ancient sites. According to his own account: 'I had the good fortune to be the discoverer of many remains of antiquity of that primitive nation. I succeeded in opening one of the two famous Pyramids of Ghizeh, as well as several of the tombs of the Kings at Thebes.'[59] Foremost of these was the spectacular tomb of Seti I, father of the Young Memnon's creator, Ramesses II.[60]

Meanwhile, the Young Memnon was stuck in quarantine in the port of Rosetta. Only on 17 October 1817 was Salt able to inform the foreign secretary, Lord Castlereagh, that the artefact had finally been embarked on the transport ship *Nearchus* and was bound for Malta. There, it was transferred to a Royal Navy store ship, HMS *Weymouth* (laden with antiquities from Leptis Magna), for the final journey to England. Throughout the torso's long voyage from Luxor to London, news of its progress was eagerly covered by the European press. In January 1818, the *Quarterly Review*, looking forward to the statue's impending arrival, described it as 'without doubt the finest specimen of ancient Egyptian sculpture which has yet been discovered'.[61] Eventually, in March that year, the *Weymouth* anchored in the Thames and the Foreign Office and Admiralty were able, finally, to notify the British Museum that their prize acquisition had arrived. At a stroke, the Museum became 'the first repository in the world of Egyptian art and antiquity'.[62] The scope and ambition of its collections both reflected and proclaimed the scale and reach of the growing British Empire. The torso, now its star attraction, went on permanent display towards the end of 1818. One of its early admirers was the poet John Keats. His great friend and fellow poet, Percy Bysshe Shelley – a man who 'perused with more than ordinary eagerness the relations of travellers in the East'[63] – was inspired to write his sonnet 'Ozymandias'.[64] The poem – the most famous meditation in the English language on the fragility of human power – was published on 11 January 1818, just as the torso was making its way up the English Channel.

In the autumn of that same year, Bankes, Salt and a Prussian naturalist Albert von Sack set sail from Cairo for Upper Egypt. At Luxor, they were joined by the Italian explorer Alessandro Ricci, who had made drawings for Belzoni in the tomb of Seti I, and the Greek merchant Giovanni Anastasi, who had succeeded Belzoni as Salt's agent in Upper Egypt and who would later serve as consul-general for Norway-Sweden. Proceeding southwards to the island of Philae, the party met up with four more travellers, including Thomas Wyse, leader of Irish Catholic emancipation, and the architect Charles Barry, who would go on to work at Bankes' country seat, Kingston Lacy in Dorset, design the Houses of Parliament, and remodel Highclere Castle, home of the earls of Carnarvon. Such was the interconnected and multinational nature of European travel in Egypt in the years immediately following Waterloo.[65] Ever the eagle-eyed collector, Bankes took a particular fancy to an obelisk among the picturesque ruins of Philae and determined to remove it. The French agent Drovetti tried to stop him, but Salt asserted Britain's prior claim. Bankes succeeded in having the obelisk shipped to England and erected at Kingston Lacy, where it would play a key role in the decipherment of hieroglyphics.

As for Belzoni, after his falling-out with Salt, he had turned his attention to Giza, where he succeeded in entering the pyramid of Khafra on 2 March 1818.[66] The following year he returned to England and published the account of his adventures. In 1821, he opened an exhibition of some of his finds – together with a scale model of the tomb of Seti I – in the appropriate surroundings of the Egyptian Hall, Piccadilly. It attracted 1,900 visitors on its first day and ran for a year. (By contrast, when he took it to Paris in 1822, it was not a success: national rivalries were not so easily forgotten.) Eager for new adventures, Belzoni left England again in 1822 on an expedition to locate the source of the River Niger. On his way to Timbuktu, he succumbed to dysentery and died, at Gwato in present-day Benin, in 1823, at the age of just forty-five.

While Salt's motives for archaeology may have been questionable, he certainly possessed an uncanny ability to spot talent. Another of his employees was Giovanni Battista Caviglia who began his career as a ship's captain and eventually found his way to Egypt. In 1817, while Belzoni was off digging in the Valley of the Kings, Caviglia was hired by Salt to excavate the Great Sphinx. Caviglia spent over two decades at Giza, clearing the sand from around the Sphinx, thus fully revealing it for the first time since antiquity, and also studying the pyramids, which, he was convinced, concealed mysteries of great religious significance.[67] Around the Sphinx, digging down through the encroaching sand dunes, he uncovered a Roman staircase and esplanade, fragments of the statue's missing beard and the cobra from its forehead, and – between its paws – the Dream Stela, the translation of which would have to await the decipherment of hieroglyphics.[68] In the Great Pyramid, he descended by means of ropes, burning sulphur in an attempt to clear the fetid air.[69] His pains were rewarded by the discovery of a previously unknown underground chamber directly beneath the centre of the monument. Energetic and enterprising, the two Giovanni Battistas, Belzoni and Caviglia, epitomize the adventure and derring-do of early nineteenth-century Egyptian exploration.

⊲◧⊳

In the wake of the Napoleonic expedition, the acquisition of artefacts became, for the nations of Europe, a measure of success and a matter of pride. Among the myriad antiquities pilfered from the Nile Valley during and after Bonaparte's Egyptian adventure, two in particular shaped the birth of Egyptology and defined its role in the wider cultural politics of Europe.

In the middle of July 1799, a detachment of Napoleonic troops under the command of General Menou was busy strengthening the defences of Fort Julien (known today as Borg Rashid), the medieval fortress of Rosetta, in preparation for the second Battle of Abukir Bay. As they laboured under the watchful eye of engineer and Commission member Pierre François Xavier Bouchard, they discovered an irregularly shaped slab of granite, weighing three-quarters of a ton, embedded in the walls of the fortress. Bouchard knew at once that this was no ordinary piece of re-used stone, for one face of the slab was covered with a lengthy inscription. The inscription clearly fell into three sections. The uppermost part was written in ancient Egyptian hieroglyphics, the lower part in Greek characters, and the middle part in a strange, cursive script. Like all members of the Commission, even those employed on military and civil engineering tasks, Bouchard was alert and alive to the discovery of Egyptian antiquities. He immediately reported the discovery of the stone slab to General Menou, who arranged for it to be sent to the Institut d'Egypte in Cairo for further study.

There, the savants could scarcely believe their eyes or their luck. What the soldiers had discovered was an amazing survival: the same text, inscribed in three scripts. Any reasonably well-educated scholar could read the lowermost section, written in the ancient Greek language. The uppermost section must therefore record the self-same content, but rendered in the ancient Egyptian language of the pharaohs. Indeed, the last sentence of the inscription, translated from the Greek, confirmed the nature of the monument as a whole: 'This decree shall be inscribed on a stela of granite, in hieroglyphic, demotic and Greek writing.'[70] The *Courier de l'Egypte*, the official journal of the Napoleonic expedition, which was published in Cairo using the imported French printing presses, reported the discovery in its edition of 29 July 1799: 'This stone offers great interest for the study of hieroglyphic characters; perhaps it will give us the key at last.'[71]

Recognizing the importance of the discovery, members of the Institute took prints of the stone – both as a lithograph (by applying printer's ink to the surface, leaving the engraved inscriptions un-inked) and as a copper plate (filling the inscriptions with ink to give a black-on-white copy) – and sent copies to Paris. From there, they were distributed to scholars around Europe, who began work on the fiendish challenge of deciphering the hieroglyphic section. Among their number were a patrician English polymath, Thomas Young (1773–1829), and a revolutionary French obsessive, Jean-François Champollion (1790–1832). Their respective efforts were to shape the next two decades of Egyptological inquiry, and perpetuate the intense Anglo-French rivalry that had been present at the subject's birth.

As for the slab itself, now dubbed the Rosetta Stone after its place of discovery, it was sent in 1801 from Cairo to Alexandria, to await shipment back to Paris for display at the Louvre. However, following the surrender of the French army to the British expeditionary force, the antiquities collected by the commission were declared spoils of war.[72] The Rosetta Stone would now go to London, not Paris. With delicious irony, its chosen conveyance was a captured French frigate named *L'Egyptienne.* The ship docked at Portsmouth in February 1802, and the stone was sent at once to the Library of the Society of Antiquaries of London, before being presented by the society's royal patron, King George III, to the British Museum. The Rosetta Stone thus became one of the first Egyptian antiquities acquired by the Museum (a department of antiquities was only established five years later), and a centrepiece of its collection.

Two decades later, the situation had changed. Britain had won the battle for military supremacy, but France had undoubtedly gained the upper hand where cultural matters were concerned. Notwithstanding the successful shipment of the Young Memnon to London, Salt was finding himself regularly bested by his arch-rival Drovetti. After frequent run-ins between their respective agents in the field, the two consuls-general came to a gentleman's agreement. A British visitor, Sir Frederick Henniker, observing for himself the result of this compromise, was not impressed: 'The whole of ancient Thebes is the private property of the English and French consuls; a line of demarcation is drawn through every temple, and these buildings that have hitherto withstood the attacks of *Barbarians*, will not resist the speculation of civilized cupidity, virtuosi, and antiquarians.'[73]

By contrast, the French patron of an expedition to Egypt in 1821, Sébastien Louis Saulnier, was especially pleased with Muhammad Ali's policy on antiquities: 'Among other means employed, by the government of Egypt, to allure Europeans thither, is the permission granted to all comers to search for and carry away antiquities, whether on the surface or under-ground.'[74]

This was no mere casual observation, for Saulnier, antiquarian and collector, had sponsored an expedition to Egypt with only one thing in mind: acquiring for France an artefact even more renowned than the by-now famous Rosetta Stone.

Back in 1798–9, when the French army under General Desaix – with Denon in tow – had marched through Upper Egypt in pursuit of the fugitive Mamluk, a highlight of their journey (for Denon at least) had been the temple of Dendera. There, standing proud among the lone and level sands of the surrounding desert, was a spectacular Roman temple dedicated to the Egyptian mother-goddess Hathor.[75] Among the many colourfully decorated and beautifully preserved reliefs inside the temple, one had caused a particular stir: a ceiling block inside a small roof chapel, carved with a fine circular representation of a zodiac, complete with constellations and astronomical figures, supported at four corners by slender Egyptian goddesses. Denon had made an accurate drawing on the spot, and, ever since, the zodiac had been coveted by France. Fortunately (from a French perspective): 'its removal was not attempted at that period, as it must have fallen into the hands of the English, like the inscription of Rosetta, the sarcophagus of Alexander, and other monuments collected by the Institute of Egypt'.[76]

Now, France regarded 'the acquisition of the Zodiac as, in some measure, compensating for the absence of these noble monuments'.[77] Saulnier's account tells the story of the patriotic endeavour, undertaken by the expedition leader, Jean-Baptiste

Lelorrain:[78] 'His first intention was for bringing away the zigzag borders, but the weight of the great stone was found to be so enormous, that it would be impossible to convey it. It was, moreover, of ornament rather than utility, and hence M. L. [Monsieur Lelorrain] contented himself with removing the planisphere, and the square wherein it was inclosed.'[79]

Lelorrain's exploits were discovered by an American diplomat, Luther Bradish, who happened to be visiting Dendera as operations were proceeding. Bradish carried the news to Cairo, where it reached the ears of Henry Salt. Saulnier picks up the story:

> No attempts were made at Cairo to dispossess M. Lelorrain of his treasure, but the British consul-general had repaired to Alexandria to renew his solicitations with the Pacha. Fortunately for M.L. he was not long held in suspense, for, on the Pacha enquiring whether he had been duly authorized, and an answer being given in the affirmative, he pronounced at once in his favour . . . The decision of the Pacha was speedily forwarded to him, and he lost no time in embarking the Zodiac on-board a vessel that was bound for Marseilles, and which set sail July 18th. It has thus been rescued from destruction and danger, to which it was exposed, not only on the part of the natives, but of certain Europeans that appear zealous for the preservation of antiquities.[80]

The zodiac was brought ashore in Marseilles on 27 November 1821 and sent to Paris for immediate display, where it caused even more of a stir than had the arrival of the Rosetta Stone in London twenty years earlier.

Just about the only Frenchman to question the removal of the zodiac from its original context was the author of an anonymous letter to the *Revue encyclopédique* in October 1821.

While the writer was proud that so important a monument should have been acquired by France (and not Britain), he deeply lamented the resulting damage to one of Egypt's greatest temples:

> We applaud the patriotic sentiments which guided this, our two compatriots' bold project, carried out so skilfully and successfully . . . But in congratulating Messrs Saulnier and Lelorrain on having, so carefully, transported the circular zodiac of Dendera from the banks of the Nile to those of the Seine, and not the Thames, we cannot, however, refrain from expressing a certain regret that this magnificent temple has been deprived of one of its finest monuments . . . Should we, in France, follow the example of Lord Elgin? Certainly not.[81]

The author of that letter was none other than Jean-François Champollion. Less than a year later – and thanks to the Rosetta Stone in London, not the zodiac in the Louvre – he would become the most famous name in the history of Egyptology.

ONE

Description and decipherment

The Rosetta Stone, key to the decipherment of hieroglyphics.

Mr Champollion, junior . . . has lately been making some steps in Egyptian literature, which really appear to be *gigantic*.[1]

THOMAS YOUNG, 1822

After a fortnight of late summer heat, with daytime temperatures nudging twenty-seven degrees, the morning of Saturday 14 September 1822 brought a welcome break for the citizens of Paris. The sky was overcast, there was a light wind, and the thermometer at the Royal Observatory had fallen to a more pleasant thirteen degrees.[2] In his brother's house at 28 rue Mazarine, just a few minutes' walk from the Pont Neuf on the south bank of the Seine, Jean-François Champollion once again took up his papers, and, with the oppressive heat of recent days lifted, applied himself afresh to his task. For the past fourteen months, ever since arriving in the French capital, he had devoted himself single-mindedly to the greatest intellectual challenge of the age: cracking the code of ancient Egyptian writing. There had been promising avenues and blind alleys in equal measure, and any number of wrong turns. Now, finally, armed with a crucial piece of new evidence, the path opened up once again. This time, there would be no turning back: the prize lay ahead.

Shortly before noon, Champollion sprang from his study, rushed out of the house and 200 metres down the street to the imposing domed building which, since the beginning of the century, had housed the Académie Royale des Inscriptions et Belles-Lettres, one of the five national academies of France. Bursting into his brother's office at the *académie*, he flung a sheaf of papers onto the desk and exclaimed: *'Je tiens mon affaire!'* ('I've done it!') Overcome with emotion and exhausted by the mental effort, he promptly collapsed to the floor, unconscious. As Eureka moments go, it was suitably dramatic. After being taken back home, for five days Champollion was confined to his room, completely incapacitated, watched over by his anxious relatives. When he finally regained his strength, on the Thursday evening, he immediately resumed his feverish studies.

Just one week later, on Friday 27 September, he was strong enough to deliver a formal lecture at the *académie*, announcing his breakthrough. Addressed, as was the custom, to the *académie's* permanent secretary, a certain Bon-Joseph Dacier, the lecture was published the following month by Didot Father & Son, booksellers of 24 rue Jacob, under the title *'Lettre à M. Dacier, Secrétaire Perpétuel de l'Académie Royale des Inscriptions et Belles-Lettres, relative à l'alphabet des hiéroglyphes phonétiques employés par les Egyptiens pour inscrire sur leurs monuments les titres, les noms et les surnoms des souverains grecs et romains'*.[3] The *Lettre à M. Dacier*, as it is universally known, announced to the world the decipherment of hieroglyphics. It was, and remains, one of the greatest feats of philology. By lifting the civilization of the pharaohs out of the shadows of mythology into the light of history, it marked the birth of Egyptology.

Champollion is still revered for his scholarly achievement. Yet the history of Egyptology is rarely uncontested, rarely straightforward. Champollion may have been a lone scholar, but his breakthrough did not occur in isolation. It drew upon a series of insights by other scholars, and was ultimately born out of one of the great academic rivalries of the nineteenth century. The full, circuitous story of decipherment began two

decades before that momentous autumn of 1822, in the immediate aftermath of the Napoleonic expedition.

⊲◦▷

As Bonaparte's soldiers were licking the wounds of defeat, their
scholarly compatriots, the savants who had accompanied
Napoleon to Egypt, were busy mapping and studying the
country and its antiquities. The British might have won the
day on the battlefield, but it was the French who had conquered
Egypt for science. From that moment on, France held to an
unerring belief that the study of ancient Egypt was its hard-
earned, irrevocable prerogative. From that moment on, too,
successive French governments, and successive generations of
French scholars, would look with ill-concealed disdain on the
footling attempts of the British to understand the civilization
of the pharaohs. The Napoleonic expedition and its aftermath
thus set the tone for the next century and a half of discovery
in the Nile Valley. Whilst, for the British, Egyptology would
begin, and largely continue, as an interesting diversion for well-
heeled dilettantes and minor academics, for the French it was,
and would ever remain, an important part of their self-image
as a nation.

The first great blow for French Egyptological pre-eminence
was struck by a member of Napoleon's entourage, a man who,
though largely forgotten in the annals of archaeology, ranks as
one of the most colourful figures in the entire history of the
subject. Dominique Vivant, Baron Denon, was born into a
family of landed gentry near the provincial town of Chalon-
sur-Saône. At the age of sixteen he went to Paris to make his
fortune, and succeeded in being appointed a *gentilhomme
ordinaire* – an aristocratic hanger-on – at the court of Louis
XV. Like many of his ambitious contemporaries, Denon recognized that the seduction of influential women could prove just

as potent a recipe for political and financial advancement as any amount of flattery of the monarch himself. Using his position at court – he was curator of the royal collection of antique gems – Denon caught the eye of Louis XV's mistress, Madame de Pompadour, and became one of her favourites.

Popular for his quick wit and lively conversation, Denon possessed abundant charm, refinement and powers of persuasion. His talents did not go unnoticed, and the king duly appointed him to the French diplomatic service. It was the perfect career for a man of Denon's talents and interests. In St Petersburg he used his social contacts to 'ferret out State secrets and boudoir intrigues that were of great service to his ambassador'.[4] On a secret mission to Switzerland in 1775, he was a frequent guest of Voltaire's and penned a remarkable series of sketches of the ageing philosopher. During a subsequent posting in Naples, which was rather lacking in diplomatic intrigue, Denon amused himself instead by indulging his love of drawing and his interest in antiquities. He visited the Roman ruins of Herculaneum and Pompeii, and amassed a valuable collection of Etruscan vases which he subsequently sold to the new king, Louis XVI (and which were sent to the royal porcelain factory at Sèvres to be copied). Denon's wanderings further afield, in Sicily, formed the basis of his first book, *Voyage en Sicile*, published in 1788. It was a charmed life. France's interests and Denon's were in perfect alignment. But it was not to last.

The French revolution of 1789 brought the ancien régime crashing down. The aristocracy fled or were guillotined, their lands confiscated and privileges abolished. Denon only escaped with his life because he was in Venice, on a study tour of its paintings and art treasures (having been elected to the Académie Royale des Beaux-Arts in 1787, he had resigned from the diplomatic service to pursue a full-time career as an artist); but all his property, hard won over the previous two decades, was confiscated. While awaiting a restoration of his fortunes, Denon put his skills as an engraver and his abundant experience of sexual liaisons to good use, publishing a titillating volume of erotic scenes, inspired by the pornographic frescoes at Pompeii, entitled *Œuvre priapique* (1793). It hardly marked him out as a future authority on ancient Egypt. Yet Denon's wide and cultured circle of friends now came to his rescue, and conspired to launch him on his second, unexpected career.

That same year, Denon took the brave decision to return to Paris and try to use his diplomatic skills to recover his fortune. Through his contacts in the art world, he secured the patronage of the revolutionary painter Jacques-Louis David. With such an influential supporter, Denon was able successfully to petition Robespierre, who now rescinded his banishment and restored his confiscated properties. As Denon's biographer has put it, 'Not the least of Vivant Denon's talents was his adaptability to changing political regimes.'[5] Once again a free and wealthy man, Denon resumed his favourite pastime and, before long, had charmed his way into the favour of an attractive young widow and socialite, Marie-Josèphe-Rose Tascher de la Pagerie. Rose, as her friends knew her, had had a lucky escape of her own. Her husband, Alexandre Viscomte de Beauharnais, had, like so many of his class, been arrested as an enemy of the people, and guillotined in the Place de la Révolution in 1794, leaving Rose impoverished and with two young children. She had herself been imprisoned in Paris's Carmes gaol, only to be released five days after her husband's execution following Robespierre's fall from grace and the end of his Reign of Terror. Rose and Denon were thrown together by the shared experience of loss and reprieve. For Denon, it was a singularly lucky meeting; for Rose had done the only thing a woman in her position could do: wooing leading politicians in order to provide some measure of security for herself and her children. In

1795, having recovered her late husband's property, she met a young revolutionary, six years her junior, by the name of Napoleon Bonaparte. She became his mistress and, the following year, his wife. In place of 'Rose', Napoleon preferred to call her by the diminutive of her middle name, Joséphine. Denon now found himself back in favour, and back at the centre of power. His personal history had come full circle.

So it was that Denon joined Napoleon on his campaign to Egypt in 1798, as one of the expedition's official artists. Travelling up the Nile with the French soldiers, Denon amazed them with his resilience and determination. It is said that, 'even while he ate his scanty meals his sketch pad was beside him'.[6] This was not the pampered aristocrat his battle-hardened compatriots might have been expecting, but a dedicated servant of the expedition and its revolutionary aims. Be that as it may, Denon had not lost his entrepreneurial flair. Within a year of his return to France, he followed up his earlier foray into travel-writing by publishing his own, highly personal account of the Egyptian expedition, the two-volume *Voyages dans la Basse et la Haute Egypte* (1802). It was an instant bestseller, an eyewit-ness record of Bonaparte's audacious journey through the land of the pharaohs. Translated into English and German, *Voyages* reawakened European public interest in ancient Egypt and influenced the course of nineteenth-century scholarship. It remained in print for nearly 150 years, something of a record in the annals of Egyptology. One of the great historians of archaeology has summed up Denon's achievement thus: 'Napoleon conquered Egypt with bayonets, and held it for one short year. But Denon conquered the land of the Pharaohs with his crayon, and held it permanently.'[7] In recognition of his contribution to scholarship, Denon (along with Napoleon) was elected to honorary membership of the American Academy of Arts in its first year. The French government made him director general of museums, a post he held until the downfall of his patron in 1815. (In the meantime, Denon would travel with Napoleon's army across Europe, amassing works of art for the Louvre, and establishing it as one of the great collections of the world.)

Denon's *Voyages* had, as he knew it would, the benefit of a considerable head start on the official publication of the Napoleonic expedition. But then the latter was an altogether more monumental undertaking. The *Description de l'Egypte*, published with the endorsement of Napoleon himself, was the first great work of Egyptology. Its publication was announced by a consular decree in February 1802, which also confirmed that the (considerable) expense would be borne by the government. The editor-in-chief would report directly to the minister of the interior. Bonaparte saw in the publication the opportunity to salvage the reputation of his ill-fated mission, and restore French pride. (The preface, written by the mathematician Fourier but personally approved by Napoleon, asserted that Egypt, a country 'which has transmitted its knowledge to so many nations, is today plunged into barbarism', effectively justifying the French expedition.) Moreover, the *Description* would serve to assert France's claim to the cultural riches of Egypt.

In time, three editors-in-chief would work on the *Description*. The third, and longest-serving, Jomard, devoted over two decades of his life to the project, seeing it through to completion. (A grateful French government duly appointed him curator of the Bibliothèque Nationale: the reward for good behaviour was, it seems, further punishment.) Although planned as a celebration of Napoleonic endeavour, only about half the entire work was published before Bonaparte's downfall and exile. The restored monarchy under Louis XVIII might have abandoned the project, but, recognizing the opportunity to bolster France's reputation, decided to proceed. The finished work did not disappoint. It comprised eight huge folio volumes of text (four on antiquities, two on modern Egypt, and two on natural history) and nine accompanying folio volumes of plates on the same topics (five, two and two respectively). A coloured plate of the Dendera zodiac took pride of place in the second volume.

Indeed, it is the plates – all 974 of them – for which the *Description* remains most famous, and which have stood the test of time. Although the artists failed to reproduce many of the hieroglyphic inscriptions accurately, not knowing what they were copying, the images of monuments are much more reliable; in some cases, they are the only record of buildings which were subsequently damaged or destroyed. Nearly four hundred engravers were involved in the project; Denon himself contributed 140 drawings. The magnificent frontispiece to the first volume (dated 1809 but published the following year) was a masterpiece of propaganda, which both 'framed and claimed Egyptian antiquity'.[8] It shows a composite, mythical scene of pharaonic ruins: a winding road leads from an obelisk in the foreground, past sphinxes, a pyramid, temples, colonnades and columned halls into the far distance. The frame, under the protection of an Egyptian winged disc, captures the heroic nature of the expedition in a classical idiom. Along the top, Napoleon is shown in the guise of Alexander the Great, mounted on a chariot, spear in hand, and preceded by the French imperial eagle, bearing down on a group of hapless enemies. The sides, surmounted by further eagles, comprise a series of trophies bearing the names of the 'conquered' locations – from Alexandria via the pyramids and Thebes all the way to Abukir (the site of Napoleon's defeat at the Battle of the Nile, but included, nonetheless, without a hint of irony). The bottom register shows supplicant groups of Egyptians, complete with their horses and camels, parading before

Napoleon's imperial monogram. And, to complete the symbolism, a pair of cartouches – the oval rings within which pharaohs wrote their names – appear, each containing a star and Napoleon's personal emblem, the bee.

By the time the final volume of the *Description* was published, in 1828, the emperor had been deposed, the Bourbon monarchy had been restored and was itself on the way to abolition. But the *Description* stood as a testament to France's cultural superiority, proof of France's ownership of Egypt's ancient past. Champollion's breakthrough of September 1822 merely confirmed that conviction.

⊲IOI▷

Even before the last hieroglyphic inscription was carved, on 15 August AD 394, detailed understanding of the script had all but died out in the Nile Valley. Beyond Egypt's borders, knowledge gave way to speculation, and all sorts of fanciful theories began to spring up about the meaning of the signs. As early as the first century BC, the Greek historian Diodorus Siculus had adumbrated that Egyptian writing was 'not built up from syllables to express the underlying meaning, but from the appearance of things drawn and by their metaphorical meaning learned by heart'.[9] Thus began the erroneous belief that hieroglyphic was a symbolic rather than a phonetic script; while this may have been true of some of the Ptolemaic-era signs, it was a fundamental misconception, a red herring which would deflect scholars from the path of successful decipherment for the next nineteen centuries.

European interest in the writing of the ancient Egyptians was revived at the beginning of the Renaissance, when a manuscript of the fourth-century work, Horapollo's *Hieroglyphika*, was discovered on a Greek island and subsequently published in Italy in 1505. It caused a stir, and went through thirty editions (one of them with accompanying illustrations by Albrecht Dürer); but its whole approach, influenced by Neoplatonic mysticism, only served to obfuscate rather than illuminate the inner workings of the hieroglyphic script. Indeed, Horapollo's readings were 'more like a collection of conceits and enigmas than an exploration of a real system of serious literature'.[10] Nonetheless, the idea that the key to Egyptian writing lay in mythology, not philology, became firmly lodged in European consciousness. The first post-classical work on the subject, the influential 1556 book *Hieroglyphica* (full title *Hieroglyphica, sive, De sacris Aegyptiorum literis commentarii,* 'Hieroglyphics, or, Commentaries on the Sacred Letters of the Egyptians') by the Venetian scholar Pierio Valeriano, followed the same, flawed approach, as did the wildly speculative publication by Kircher, a century later, of the inscription on a Roman obelisk. The bald truth was that, for over forty generations, no living soul had been able accurately to read an ancient Egyptian text.

Scholars began to think the task impossible. By the early eighteenth century, the English antiquarian, William Stukeley, could confidently assert that: 'The hieroglyphics of the Egyptians is a sacred character . . . The characters cut on the Egyptian monuments are purely symbolical . . . The perfect knowledge of 'em is irrecoverable.'[11] Pococke, in the 1743 account of his journey to Egypt, made the important realization that: 'As far, therefore, as hieroglyphics are emblematical, they seem to stand for things; but as they are inscriptions, they stand for words or sounds as well as things, and might be read in the vulgar language by the children of the priests.'[12] Two decades later, a French cleric, Jean-Jacques Barthélemy, correctly surmised that the cartouches might contain royal or divine names. But these were pinpricks of insight in an enveloping fog of misapprehension. Even the great French orientalist, Antoine Silvestre de Sacy, regrettably concluded that full decipherment was 'too complicated, scientifically insoluble'.[13]

Only at the very end of the eighteenth century did a brave Danish scholar, Georg Zoëga, dare to suggest, against received wisdom, that some hieroglyphs might be phonetic after all. In the foreword to his book *De origine et usu obeliscorum* ('On the origin and purpose of obelisks'), published in 1797, Zoëga suggested that: 'When Egypt is better known to scholars, and when the numerous ancient remains still to be seen there have been accurately explored and published, it will perhaps be possible to learn to read the hieroglyphs and more intimately to understand the meaning of the Egyptian monuments.'[14] It was a prescient statement. Just a year later, Napoleon launched his expedition to Egypt, exploring and publishing the country's ancient remains and, in the discovery of the Rosetta Stone, providing scholars with the key that would finally unlock the mysteries of Egyptian writing.

In Cairo, one of Napoleon's savants, the engineer Jean-Joseph Marcel, recognized the script in the middle section of the stone as demotic and correctly identified the royal name 'Ptolemy', by comparison with the Greek text where it occurred eleven times. He also guessed that the first two signs in the group must therefore be the letters 'P' and 'T'; but was unable to take this hunch any further.[15] So, when copies of the stone's inscription began to circulate in Europe, it was a happy circumstance that they came to the attention of two of the most brilliant minds of the age – two men who could not have been more different in talent or temperament. One was a dazzling polymath, the other a single-minded obsessive; one a man of easy, self-effacing erudition, the other a self-conscious and jealous intellectual; for added piquancy, one was English, the other French. The rivalrous race to decipherment had begun.

Thomas Young was a man of his time. Born into a prosperous

Quaker family that placed a high value on learning, he showed an early aptitude for languages alongside a fascination for science. By all accounts, he was able to read by the time he was two years old, and by the age of fourteen had gained some proficiency in French and Italian, Latin and Greek, Hebrew and Syriac, Arabic and Persian, Turkish and Ethiopic, as well as the obscure ancient languages Chaldaean and Samarian. He was encouraged in his studies by a great-uncle who moved in London's fashionable intellectual circles. However, Young was not wealthy, and needed a profession to support himself. Medicine seemed to offer a socially respectable and financially rewarding career; so he enrolled, first at the University of Edinburgh, then at Göttingen (renowned in the eighteenth century for its outstanding library). A paper on the workings of the human eye gained him election to a fellowship of the Royal Society at the precocious age of twenty-one. (He would later serve as the society's foreign secretary.) Finally, to gain the MD needed to practise as a doctor, he went up to Emmanuel College, Cambridge in 1797 (a move which also required him to renounce his Quaker faith and join the Church of England), where his fellow students nicknamed him 'Phenomenon Young'. It was a barbed compliment. Absorbed in his studies, Young attended few lectures, remaining instead in his room, carrying out his own experiments in the exciting new field of physics.

The year he entered Cambridge was a bittersweet one for Young. His great-uncle died, depriving Young of an influential and supportive mentor, but giving him financial independence thanks to a large legacy of property and money. Young was now able to pursue his own passions. Moving to London in 1799, he began practising as a doctor, but science remained his passion. An autodidact – while still at Cambridge, he had written to one of his brothers that, 'Masters and mistresses are very necessary to compensate for want of inclination and exertion: but whoever would arrive at excellence must be self-taught'[16] – he nonetheless achieved remarkable insights and breakthroughs. Alongside his observations on the human eye – explaining how the lens accommodates, describing astigmatism, and proposing a theory of colour vision – he also demonstrated the wave theory of light, an insight which Einstein regarded, after Newton's *Opticks*, as 'the next great theoretical advance' in the subject.[17] Among many other accomplishments, Young formulated the modulus of elasticity (still used by engineers), advised the Admiralty on shipbuilding, served as secretary of the Board of Longitude, and was an expert on life insurance. In 1802–3, when still only in his late twenties, Young gave a series of lectures at the Royal Institution in London, covering virtually every aspect of science; for sheer breadth of knowledge, it has never been surpassed. Also that year, during a brief lull in the Napoleonic Wars, Young was able to visit France and to hear Napoleon – fresh from his Egyptian adventures – speak at the Institut National in Paris. Little did either man know that Young would soon come closer than anyone else to snatching the crown of Egyptology from the French.

With his prodigious knowledge of languages, ancient and modern, and his supreme gifts as a linguist, it is not, perhaps, surprising that Young should have become interested in *the* philological conundrum of the age, the decipherment of hieroglyphics. In his own words, he could not resist 'an attempt to unveil the mystery, in which Egyptian literature has been involved for nearly twenty centuries'.[18] The challenge seems first to have piqued his curiosity in 1814 when he reviewed a recent German publication on the history of languages, Johann Christoph Adelung's *Mithridates, oder allgemeine Sprachkunde*. At the same time, Young began studying a copy of the Rosetta Stone inscription. Blessed with an almost photographic memory, he started to discern patterns and resemblances that had escaped other, less punctilious observers. In particular, he noticed similarities between some of the signs in the demotic and hieroglyphic scripts (until then believed to be unrelated). His intuition was confirmed the following year when he consulted a borrowed copy of an early volume of the *Description* which included facsimiles of ancient Egyptian papyri. Young thus became the first scholar to suggest, correctly, that monumental hieroglyphs, cursive hieroglyphs and demotic were closely connected. Not only did this insight require an extraordinary combination of gifts, it also demanded a leap of imagination and the abandonment of centuries of false theories about ancient Egyptian writing. Young did not demur from rejecting Horapollo's readings as 'puerile', nor from pouring scorn on Kircher's attempts at translation: 'according to his interpretation, which succeeded equally well, whether he happened to begin at the beginning, or at the end of each of the lines, they all contain some mysterious doctrines of religion or of metaphysics'.[19] As for Kircher's famous drawings of Egyptian obelisks, Young damned with faint praise, calling them 'tolerably faithful, though inelegant, representations of the principal monuments of Egyptian art, which had before his days been brought to Europe'.[20] Young also broke with received wisdom by correctly proposing that demotic combined both symbolic and phonetic signs. By contrast, other scholars working on the Rosetta Stone at the time, notably Champollion's teacher Silvestre de Sacy and the Swedish diplomat Johan Åkerblad, wrongly concluded that demotic was entirely alphabetic. However, not even Young made the logical step of realizing that hieroglyphic, too, was a hybrid script. That breakthrough would have to wait for the laser-like brilliance of Champollion.

In common with many gentleman scholars of the early nineteenth century, Young kept up a lively correspondence with his contemporaries, in Britain and beyond, sharing observations and theories, and keeping abreast of new discoveries. However, Young never corresponded directly with Champollion. The reason was a remarkable letter, written by Silvestre de Sacy to Young on 20 July 1815. In it the French orientalist warned: 'If I might venture to advise you, I would recommend you not to be too communicative of your discoveries to M. Champollion. It may happen that he may hereafter make pretension to the priority.'[21]

The teacher evidently knew his former pupil well, and his prediction would come true. As a result of Silvestre de Sacy's letter – probably prompted by a political row with Champollion; the latter was a Bonapartist, while the teacher was a royalist, and Louis XVIII had been restored to the throne less than a month earlier – Young never shared his work on hieroglyphics with the only other scholar who could have truly appreciated it.

Alongside his scholarship on Egypt, Young's research continued to be prodigious in its scope. His contributions to the 1816 edition of the *Encyclopaedia Britannica* ranged from annuities to waves. His article on languages was the first to use the term 'Indo-European', for Young recognized that languages as diverse as English, Latin and Greek all belonged to the same family. (He had achieved this insight while still in his teens, by comparing the key features of hundreds of languages.) But, naturally reserved and conditioned by his Quaker upbringing to value modesty, Young rarely wrote under his own name. Most of his articles, groundbreaking as they were, were published anonymously. For Young, the intellectual adventure was reward enough. All through 1816 and 1817, he continued to work on decipherment, eagerly studying any new publications of Egyptian manuscripts he could lay his hands on. Indeed, in 1817 he founded the Egyptian Society of London, for the express purpose of publishing pharaonic texts.

Ever the gentleman scholar, he had no intention of following in Belzoni's footsteps and going to Egypt to secure manuscripts himself. Instead, he appealed for funds 'for employing some poor Italian or Maltese to scramble over Egypt in search of more'.[22]

In 1818, Young summed up his knowledge of hieroglyphic and demotic scripts in a further article for the *Encyclopaedia Britannica*, published the following year in a supplement to the fourth edition. It was entitled, simply, 'Egypt'. In it, he correctly established the phonetic values of some demotic signs, and a number of correspondences between the demotic and hieroglyphic scripts. Once again, the article was anonymous; Young did not publish it under his own name until 1823, a year after Champollion's *Lettre à M. Dacier*. However, Young's authorship of 'Egypt' was well known and recognized at the time of publication by those in his intellectual circle (which of course excluded Champollion). Henry Salt used the article to read the cartouches of Ptolemy on the temple of Dakka in Nubia, and mentioned the fact in a letter written to William Hamilton from Cairo on 1 May 1819.[23] In 1820, Belzoni wrote of Young's 'discovery of the alphabet of the Egyptians'[24] and included the article 'Egypt' as an appendix to his own work: 'An Explanation of some of the principal Hieroglyphics, extracted from the Article Egypt in the supplement of the Encylopædia Britannica; with additional Notes'. However, the anonymity of the published article would subsequently allow Champollion to claim all the credit for decipherment, just as Silvestre de Sacy had predicted.

Champollion was seventeen years Young's junior. Born in the town of Figeac, in the Lot, to a bookseller and his wife, Champollion grew up surrounded by writings and displayed a precocious genius for languages. Until the age of eleven, Jean-François was educated at home by his elder brother, Jacques-Joseph, himself a gifted scholar and linguist.[25] In 1798,

Jacques-Joseph asked to participate in the Napleonic expedition
to Egypt, reflecting his established interest in the subject, but
his request was turned down. Despite this disappointment, he
continued to take an interest in the emerging discipline of
Egyptology, and evidently transmitted his enthusiasm to his
younger brother. When Jean-François turned eleven, he enrolled
in the lycée in the city of Grenoble, 500 km from the family
home, and renowned as a centre of learning. According to
legend, it was during a visit to Grenoble in April 1802 by
Fourier, eminent mathematician and participant in the
Napoleonic expedition, that the young Champollion was invited
to see the great scholar's private collection of antiquities,
sparking a lifelong fascination for ancient Egypt. Sadly, the
known historical facts do not support the story; but it is likely
that both Champollion brothers attended the soirées held by
Fourier at his official residence in Grenoble between 1804 and
1806. (Fourier had been appointed prefect of the *département*
of Isère by Napoleon on their return from Egypt in 1801.)
Certainly, Jean-François first saw a copy of the Rosetta Stone
in 1804, and started to learn Coptic the following year. In 1806,
he presented a paper to the Grenoble Academy in which he
(correctly) argued that Coptic was a direct descendant of ancient
Egyptian; it was this insight, and his later fluency in Coptic,
that would prove decisive in the decipherment of hieroglyphics.
That same summer, the mayor of Grenoble is reported to have
asked Champollion if he intended to study the fashionable
natural sciences. 'No, Monsieur,' Jean-François is said to have
replied. 'I wish to devote my life to knowledge of ancient
Egypt.'[26]

For a young man with such an ambition, there was only one
place to go: Paris, the centre and beacon of French scholarship.
So, in 1807, he enrolled at the Ecole Spéciale des Langues
Orientales Vivantes where his teachers included Silvestre de

Sacy. During two years in Paris, Champollion not only vigorously pursued his studies, but also wrote a major part of his first book, *Introduction à l'Egypte sous les Pharaons* (1811) and completed a second, *L'Egypte sous les Pharaons, ou Recherches sur la géographie, la religion, la langue, les écritures et l'histoire de l'Egypte avant l'invasion de Cambyse. Description géographique* (1814). On completing his studies in Paris, Champollion returned home to take up a teaching post in history and politics at Grenoble, being promoted to a chair at the town's Collège Royal in 1818. This brought a measure of professional and financial security, and finally allowed Champollion to devote more of his time to the serious study of ancient Egypt. At exactly the same time, across the Channel in England, Thomas Young was writing his seminal article on 'Egypt'. Almost entirely unaware of each other's work, the two greatest minds of the age were engaged in a race to crack the code of hieroglyphic writing.

In a curious twist of fate, the spur to Champollion's decisive breakthrough was an incident which nearly ended his career entirely. Having grown up in revolutionary France, imbibed the radical promise of liberty, equality and brotherhood, and followed Napoleon's meteoric rise, it was perhaps no surprise that Champollion should have shared the anti-monarchist sentiment of the age. It must have come as a bitter disappointment, indeed a betrayal, therefore, when, following Napoleon's defeat and exile in 1815, France restored the Bourbons to the throne. For a man as fixed in his views and as certain of his own rightness as Champollion, such a reversal was never going to be taken lying down. In March 1821, Bonapartists in Grenoble staged a rebellion, raising the revolutionary tricolour in place of the white flag of the Bourbon monarchy. Champollion was accused of being the ringleader; the new arch-royalist prefect of Isère, Baron de Haussez, attempted to indict

Champollion on a charge of high treason. Had this succeeded, and Champollion been found guilty, he could have faced the death penalty. Fortunately for Champollion, his academic brilliance had not gone unnoticed in Paris, and supporters in the French capital intervened to have him tried in a civil rather than criminal court. He was acquitted of all charges, but would remain forever tainted, in the eyes of political opponents and jealous rivals, as a dangerous revolutionary. De Haussez may have failed to have Champollion tried for treason, but he saw to it that he lost his positions and income at the Collège Royal in Grenoble. Without a job, without a salary, and persona non grata in his home region, Champollion returned to Paris to stay with his ever-dependable elder brother. So it was that, on 20 July 1821, Champollion arrived at 28 rue Mazarine. With nothing else to occupy his time, and with the benefit of his brother's extensive library, he devoted himself wholeheartedly to the challenge that, within fourteen months, would result in his seminal achievement.

Three months before his arrival in Paris, Champollion had published his first significant work on ancient Egyptian writing, *De l'écriture hiératique des anciens Egyptiens*; focussing on the cursive form of hieroglyphics (known as 'hieratic'), the study was apparently produced in total ignorance of Young's *Encyclopaedia Britannica* article. Consequently, Champollion maintained that both hieratic and demotic were entirely symbolic, an error he soon realized and regretted. (So much so, that he tried to suppress his own text and to withdraw all copies from circulation.) Over the course of the next year, Champollion read Young's article, and changed his mind: against all accepted wisdom, he now concluded that there was indeed a phonetic element to ancient Egyptian scripts.

In the meantime, Young had not been idle. On a grand tour of Italy in the summer of 1821, he studied obelisks in Rome, and discovered a second bilingual inscription in the Drovetti collection of antiquities, temporarily stored in a warehouse in Livorno. Copies of the inscription on the obelisk removed from Philae by William Bankes now began to circulate, but Young's copy contained an error which threw him off the scent. By contrast, Champollion's copy, which he received in January 1822, was accurate, and enabled him to make further progress. The cartouche of Cleopatra, alongside that of Ptolemy, was to prove decisive in assigning phonetic values to individual hieroglyphic signs. By applying these equivalences to other cartouches on surviving Ptolemaic and Roman monuments, Champollion was able to read the names of further rulers from Egypt's classical past: Alexander and Berenice, Trajan and Caesar. Certain that he was making rapid progress, Champollion drew up a table showing the demotic and hieroglyphic equivalents to the letters of the Greek alphabet. (He would publish this *Tableau des signes phonétiques* later the same year, as part of his *Lettre à M. Dacier*, with a cheeky cartouche of his own name in demotic at the foot of the page.)

Others, too, were trying their hand at decipherment. Salt wrote from Cairo on 26 April 1822: 'At Philae, where I did not hope to do much, after the long stay of Mr Bankes there, I found and excavated the front of a small temple with an inscription upon it in Greek, which proves that it was dedicated by Ptolomeus Epiphanus to Esculapius. I have made some progress in the hieroglyphics, though not much.'[27] Salt could at least take pride in the growing fame of his greatest achievement, the acquisition by the British Museum of the Young Memnon. The year 1822 saw the first scientific publication about the statue,[28] which acknowledged it, not merely as a trophy of antiquarian treasure-hunting, but as an art-historical object in its own right. France, by contrast, marked the year 1822 with the issue of a bronze portrait medal of Denon, now retired from his position at the Louvre. A decade earlier, French scholarship had achieved international renown by describing ancient Egypt. Now, surely, it could do the same with decipherment.

The final breakthrough came on the morning of 14 September 1822 when Champollion received a new hieroglyphic inscription: it showed cartouches from the temple of Abu Simbel, and had been copied by a French architect Jean-Nicolas Hugot who had recently travelled to Egypt with Bankes. Champollion applied his familiarity with the Rosetta Stone, with the value of certain hieroglyphic signs, with the Coptic language, and with pharaonic history – all the elements of knowledge that he had laboured so long and so assiduously to aquire – to read the royal name contained in the cartouches as that of Ramesses. Encouraged by this success to accept that hieroglyphics might, after all, be a hybrid system, comprising both symbolic and phonetic signs – at least in the writing of names – Champollion applied the same approach to the second half of the long cartouche of Ptolemy on the Rosetta Stone, and was able to decipher the royal epithets 'beloved of Ptah, who lives forever'. By the end of the morning, he needed no further proof that his system was the right one; papers in hand, he sprinted down the rue Mazarine to his brother's office in the Académie des Inscriptions to announce his discovery.

◁◦▷

By an extrordinary coincidence, Thomas Young happened to be in Paris two weeks later, and attended the meeting of the *académie* on 27 September at which Champollion presented his *Lettre à M. Dacier*. Moreover, Young was invited to sit next to Champollion while he read out his discoveries.

Another member of the *académie*, the physicist François Arago, introduced Young and Champollion to each other at the end of the session. It was their first meeting. In a letter written two days later, Young acknowledged the Frenchman's extraordinary achievement: 'Mr Champollion, junior . . . has lately been making some steps in Egyptian literature, which really appear to be *gigantic*. It may be said that he has found the key in England which has opened the gate for him, and it is often observed that *c'est le premier pas qui coûte*; but if he did borrow an English key, the lock was so dreadfully rusty, that no common arm would have had strength enough to turn it.'[29]

But this outward magnanimity concealed a deeper hurt that Champollion had failed to acknowledge Young's contribution to decipherment. (As Young would put it shortly afterwards, with characteristic understatement: 'I did certainly expect to find the chronology of my own researches a little more distinctly stated.'[30]) Quietly determined to set the record straight, he eschewed his customary anonymity, and within a few months, published his own work, under his own name. It was entitled, rather pointedly, *An Account of Some Recent Discoveries in Hieroglyphical Literature and Egyptian Antiquities, Including the Author's Original Alphabet, As Extended by Mr Champollion*. Young dedicated it to his friend, the Prussian scholar Alexander von Humboldt (1769–1859), who had also attended Champollion's presentation at the *académie* that late September day.

Young's *Account* is surprisingly personal in tone, and allows us a rare insight into the workings of his mind and conscience. In the preface, he admitted to a desire for public acknowledgement of his efforts: 'I cannot resist the natural inclination, to make a public claim to whatever credit may be my due, for the labour that I have bestowed, on an attempt to unveil the mystery, in which Egyptian literature has been involved for nearly twenty centuries.'[31] But in case the reading public should think him a narrow-minded, peevish scholar, he affected a more modest air a few pages later: 'I think myself fully justified in endeavouring . . . to obtain, while I have yet a few years more to live and to learn, whatever respect may be thought due to the discoveries, which have constituted the amusement of a few of my leisure hours.'[32] (This was disingenuous. In fact, Young was a workaholic, having admitted to a friend: 'I have learned more or less perfectly a tolerable variety of things in this world: but there are two things that I have never yet learned, and I suppose I never shall – to get up and to go to bed.'[33]) Even in describing the heights of his scholarly achievements, Young nonetheless wished to present himself as a dilettante gentleman scholar. It was a view of British Egyptology that was to be perpetuated, for good and ill, throughout the nineteenth century.

Young was especially put out that Champollion, not content with claiming unique insight into hieroglyphics, had also meddled in the middle section of the Rosetta Stone, which Young had rather thought his specialist subject. Worse, Champollion had decided to cast aside Young's nomenclature for the cursive script and replace it with his own. As Young reminded readers: 'I have called these characters enchoric, or rather *enchorial*: Mr. Champollion has chosen to distinguish them by the term *demotic* . . . in my opinion, the priority of my publication ought to have induced him to adopt my term, and to suppress his own.'[34] A natural self-publicist, Champollion won the argument. Today, if Young is remembered at all in the annals of philology, it is as the decipherer of demotic, not of enchorial.

Warming to his theme in the *Account*, Young made a few last, brave attempts at magnanimity:

I fully and sincerely acquit Mr Champollion of any intentions actually dishonourable: and if I have hinted, that I
have received an impression of something like a want of
liberality in his conduct, I have only thrown out this
intimation, as an apology for being obliged to plead my
own cause . . . however Mr Champollion may have arrived
at his conclusions, I admit them, with the greatest pleasure
and gratitude, not by any means as superseding my system,
but as fully confirming and extending it.[35]

But, eventually, as he wrote more about his own discoveries,
his natural reserve deserted him and he launched into fifteen
pages of barbed comment. One piece of advice, directed at
Champollion, summed up Young's feelings:

in fact, the further that he advances by the exertion of
his own talents and ingenuity, the more easily he will be
able to admit, without any exorbitant sacrifice of his fame,
the claim that I have advanced to a priority with respect
to the first elements of all his researches . . . and I cannot
help thinking that he will ultimately feel it most for his
own substantial honour and reputation, to be more
anxious to admit the just claims of others than they can
be to advance them.[36]

The Frenchman was not about to take such sentiments lying
down. In an angry letter to Young, dated 23 March 1823,
Champollion retorted: 'I shall never consent to recognize any
other original alphabet than my own . . . and the unanimous
opinion of scholars on this point will be more and more
confirmed by the public examination of any other claim.'[37]
Young's friends were outraged by this slight, but failed to
make headway against Champollion's version of events. Whilst

the Frenchman was adept at self-promotion, his English rival Young 'could not bear, in the most common conversation, the slightest degree of exaggeration, or even of colouring'.[38] Even Young's friend, François Arago, supported Champollion's claims; nationalism, it seems, took precedence over friendship. Thereafter, Young largely lost interest in hieroglyphics, turning his prodigious mind to other matters.

Not so Champollion. In January 1823, a chance encounter in a Paris sale room introduced him to the Duke of Blacas d'Aulps, an influential courtier of Louis XVIII's. The duke was to become Champollion's benefactor, supporting his studies and protecting him from his jealous rivals and political opponents. The acquaintance soon bore fruit. In February, the duke presented Champollion with a gold box from the king, encrusted with the royal cipher in diamonds, and bearing the inscription 'King Louis XVIII to Mr Champollion on the occasion of his discovery of the alphabet of hieroglyphs'.[39] Even for a Bonapartist like Champollion, this royal recognition of his breakthrough must have felt like a vindication. Buoyed up and encouraged by such praise, he continued to work on decipherment. It led him to a second, vital realization. In his *Lettre à M. Dacier*, Champollion had asserted that hieroglyphics were only used phonetically in the writing of proper names. Over the following seven months, he completely changed his mind. In April 1823, Champollion announced to the Académie des Inscriptions that hieroglyphic writing was, after all, a fully hybrid system, and had been so throughout Egyptian history. He showed that his new system could be applied successfully to read pharaonic names, such as that of Ramesses, and could equally be applied to texts as well, using Coptic as a guide to the meaning of ancient Egyptian words. (For example, the Coptic word *pnoute* gave the meaning of the Egyptian *pa-netjer*, 'god'.)

This, rather than Champollion's initial breakthrough, marked the real moment at which ancient Egyptian once again became a readable language. The full extent of his system was revealed in his magnum opus, published in early 1824 and dedicated (thanks to the Duke of Blacas's efforts) to Louis XVIII, who received Champollion in a private audience. In the *Précis du système hiéroglyphique des anciens Egyptiens*, Champollion summed up the character of ancient Egyptian: 'Hieroglyphic writing is a complex system, a script at once figurative, symbolic, and phonetic, in the same text, in the same sentence, and, I might almost say, in the same word.'[40]

His place in history now secure beyond challenge, Champollion even felt able to acknowledge his great rival, albeit grudgingly:

> I recognize that he was the first to publish some correct ideas about the ancient writings of Egypt; that he was also the first to establish some correct distinctions concerning the general nature of these writings, by determining, through a substantial comparison of texts, the value of several groups of characters. I even recognize that he published before me his ideas on the possibility of the existence of several sound-signs, which would have been used to write foreign proper names in Egypt in hieroglyphs; finally that M. Young was also the first to try, but without complete success, to give a phonetic value to the hieroglyphs making up the two names Ptolemy and Berenice.[41]

In the end, despite their radically different characters and temperaments, Young and Champollion both made essential, if not quite equal, contributions to decipherment. Young developed the conceptual framework, recognizing the hybrid nature of the demotic script and its connection with hieroglyphics.

Had he stuck at the task, and not been distracted by his numerous other scientific interests, he might well have cracked the problem. Instead, it took Champollion's linguistic abilities and his single-minded focus to solve the riddle.

In 1825, with Champollion now basking in the glory of decipherment, Young moved to a new, grand house in Regent's Park where 'he led the life of a philosopher, surrounded by every domestic comfort, and enjoying the pleasures of an extensive and cultivated society, who knew how to appreciate him'.[42] He might easily have left his Egyptological studies entirely behind, had it not been for a letter he received in June 1827 from a Coptic scholar in Turin, Amadeo Peyron. Peyron wrote:

> You write that from time to time you will publish new material which will increase our knowledge of Egyptian matters. I am very glad to hear this and I urge you to keep your word . . . there is universal regret that your versatility is so widely engaged in the sciences . . . that you are unable to press on with your discoveries and bring them to that pitch of perfection . . . for you are constantly being drawn from one science to another.[43]

Young had been beaten to the decipherment of hieroglyphics; he wasn't about to let the same thing happen again with his beloved demotic. So, from that moment on until the day of his death, he worked assiduously on the problem. He even sought out Champollion's assistance, perhaps confident that the Frenchman was now too busy with other responsibilities (he had been appointed a curator at the Louvre) to pose a serious challenge in this particular scholarly endeavour. Indeed, Young seems to have forgiven Champollion for any earlier slights. In the summer of 1828, when Young travelled to Paris to accept the honour of election as a foreign associate of the Institut

National, he told a friend that Champollion had 'shown me far more attention that I ever showed or could show, to any living being: he devoted seven whole hours at once to looking over with me his papers and the magnificent collection which is committed to his care'.[44] Champollion was far less magnanimous. The following spring, he wrote to his brother: 'The Brit can do whatever he wants – *it* will remain *ours*: and all of *old* England will learn from *young* France how to spell hieroglyphs using an entirely different method.'[45]

Six weeks later, on 10 May 1829, Thomas Young died, just short of his fifty-sixth birthday. On his deathbed, pencil in hand (he was too weak to wield a pen), he was still working on the proofs of his landmark publication, his answer to Champollion's *Précis*, the modestly titled *Rudiments of an Egyptian Dictionary in the Ancient Enchorial Character; Containing All the Words of Which the Sense Has Been Ascertained*. It was published posthumously and remains a milestone in the history of Egyptian philology. But, like Young's achievements, his passing scarcely attracted any attention from his contemporaries. A brief news item in the *Lancet* noted the death of Thomas Young the respected physician; an address by the president of the Royal Society marked the demise of a devoted servant of science. There was little else. Eventually, five years after his death, Young was honoured with a memorial plaque of white marble in St Andrew's chapel, Westminster Abbey, paid for by his friend Hudson Gurney. Beneath a profile portrait medallion by the noted sculptor Sir Francis Chantrey, the epitaph (composed by Gurney) reads:

Sacred to the memory of Thomas Young M.D. Fellow and Foreign Secretary of the Royal Society Member of the National Institute of France. A man alike eminent in almost every department of human learning. Who, equally distinguished in the most abstruse investigations of letters and science, first established the undulatory theory of light and first penetrated the obscurity which had veiled for ages the hieroglyphicks of Egypt. Endeared to his friends by his domestic virtues, honoured by the World for his unrivalled acquirements, he died in the hopes of the Resurrection of the just. Born at Milverton in Somersetshire June 13th 1773, died in Park Square London May 10th 1829, in the 56th year of his age.[46]

A more poignant acknowledgement had to wait nearly a century and a half, for the 1972 exhibition in Paris marking the 150th anniversary of decipherment. In a unique act of scholarly cooperation, the British Museum lent France the Rosetta Stone. In a reciprocal gesture, Paris displayed the stone next to pictures of Champollion *and* Young – both of equal size.[47]

TWO

In the footsteps of Napoleon

Frontispiece of the Napoleonic *Description de l'Egypte*, which 'framed and claimed' the Nile Valley for European scholarship.

A single column from Karnak is more of a monument
on its own than all four facades of the courtyard of
the Louvre.[1]

JEAN-FRANÇOIS CHAMPOLLION, 1829

In the summer of 1824, Jean-François Champollion was
riding high. His breakthrough *Lettre à M. Dacier*, followed
two years later by his landmark *Précis du système hiéroglyphique*,
had firmly (if not fairly) established his reputation as the undisputed decipherer of ancient Egyptian. By means of his scholarly exertions, he had also done a great service to his country
and, most gratifyingly of all, bested the British. As his nephew
was to put it in a later biography, Champollion's discovery
belonged 'not only to him, ultimately to France'.[2] In return for
such a patriotic achievement, Champollion's aristocratic patron,
the Duke of Blacas, saw to it that appropriate rewards were
forthcoming. He successfully petitioned the king to finance a
study tour of Italy, to enable Champollion to examine, at first
hand, the antiquities brought back from Egypt since the days
of the Roman emperors.

Setting off from Paris that same summer, Champollion
travelled first to Turin, capital of the Kingdom of Sardinia and
seat of the House of Savoy. Thanks to his connections in Paris,
the Frenchman came armed with letters of introduction from
the Duke and Duchess of Orléans to the King and Queen of
Sardinia. Turin's Museo Egizio (Egyptian Museum) was a

magnet for scholars, as it housed one of the longest-established collections of Egyptian antiquities anywhere in Europe. Seven decades earlier, in 1753, King Carlo Emanuele III (r.1730–73) had sent a botanist, Vitaliano Donati, on an expedition to Egypt to bring back objects for the royal collection. Donati had returned with 300 antiquities, largely from Karnak and Coptos, and these still formed the nucleus of the Museum's holdings. Then, only a few months before Champollion's arrival, the current King of Sardinia, Carlo Felice (r.1821–31), had greatly augmented the collection by purchasing part of the vast hoard of antiquities amassed by the French consul Drovetti. The sale comprised over five thousand objects, including a hundred statues, stelae, mummies and 170 papyri. When Champollion arrived in Turin, many of the treasures were still in their boxes, waiting to be unpacked.

As well as studying the objects, he was also keen to test his skills at decipherment on a whole host of new inscriptions. One papyrus, in particular, promised exciting new revelations for someone who could read the hieratic script in which it was written: the so-called Royal Canon of Turin dated from ancient Egypt's New Kingdom and contained not one, but two extensive texts. One side of the papyrus listed tax returns from various districts along the Nile Valley; but – of far greater interest to scholars like Champollion – the other side was inscribed with eleven columns listing all the rulers of Egypt from the time of the gods down to the threshold of the New Kingdom. When the papyrus had been acquired by Drovetti, it was virtually complete. Champollion eagerly looked forward to reading it and discovering hitherto unknown details of ancient Egyptian chronology. When he came to unpack it, however, he was utterly dismayed and bitterly disappointed. During its long transit from Egypt to Turin, the papyrus had crumbled into pieces. Champollion was faced, not with a roll, but with a mass of jumbled fragments.[3] He lamented: 'I confess that the greatest disappointment of my literary life is to have discovered the manuscript in such a desperate condition. I shall never get over it – it is a wound that will bleed for a long time.'[4]

The condition of the Turin Canon, and Champollion's attempts to piece it back together, weighed altogether more heavily on his mind than the death, during his stay in Turin, of the French king Louis XVIII. Despite Champollion's revolutionary past, he had found royal favour, which both protected him from his enemies and enabled him to undertake his study tour. Indeed, feted by Turin's nobility and invited by the King of Sardinia to catalogue the Drovetti collection, Champollion's republican sympathies seem to have faded somewhat. He was enjoying his fame as the decipherer of hieroglyphics, and only too happy to accept invitations into the aristocratic salons of Piedmont. A still more exalted audience awaited him on the next leg of his tour, in Rome.

Ever since the days of Julius Caesar, the eternal city had been home to a glittering collection of Egyptian monuments, most notably obelisks. At least fifteen of these stone needles had been transported to the city during the Roman empire, of which thirteen still remained. A century and a half before Champollion's arrival, Athanasius Kircher had copied (badly) and interpreted (fancifully) the hieroglyphic inscriptions on the most prominent obelisks. Now, as the first scholar truly able to read the inscriptions since Roman times, Champollion embarked on a systematic study. Very quickly he realized the deficiencies in Kircher's work, and determined to produce accurate copies that would stand the test of time. (This would become something of a theme for the remainder of Champollion's career.) However, before he could complete his study, Champollion – not usually one to be deflected from his scholarship – had to break off from his work. In June 1825, he was faced with an altogether more delicate assignment; for he had been summoned by the pope, Leo XII (r.1823–9), to a private audience at the Vatican.

Best known for his reactionary views, Leo XII was not particularly interested in Egyptology. He was, however, concerned with the infallibility of Church doctrine, and was therefore acutely aware of a debate that had raged over the date of the Dendera zodiac ever since its discovery by Napoleon's expedition and subsequent removal to Paris by Lelorrain in 1821. By studying the positions of the stars portrayed in the inscription, no less a scholar than Jomard, the editor-in-chief of the *Description de l'Egypte*, had proposed a date of 15,000 BC. This was anathema to the Catholic Church which still held that the world had been created in 4004 BC. Louis XVIII, with his traditional views, had been scandalized, the arch-conservative Leo XII, appalled. A rival astronomer had suggested a much later date, 747 BC, and this scholarly dispute had come to epitomize the clash between religion and science. In the end Champollion had shown that the answer lay not in the position of the zodiac's stars, but in the hieroglyphs of its accompanying text. In the summer of 1822, as he was finalizing his system of decipherment, he had read the cartouche in the lower right-hand corner of the zodiac as the title 'autocrator', firmly dating the monument to the Roman period. (The zodiac, along with the foundation of the temple of Dendera, is now dated to the reign of Cleopatra VII, shortly before the Roman conquest of Egypt). Jomard was incandescent, and would remain Champollion's implacable opponent, frustrating his ambitions whenever he had the chance. But the Church was delighted, and relieved: the traditional date of creation could stand, unchallenged. When Champollion presented himself before a grateful pontiff in Rome, Leo XII is said to have repeated, three times and in perfect French, that the scholar had rendered 'a beautiful, great and good service to the Church'.[5] He even offered to make him a cardinal. Champollion politely declined. Insistent that so valuable a service demanded official recognition, the pope instead suggested to the French government that Champollion be admitted to the Légion d'honneur. What the scientific and political revolutionary made of all this is not recorded. It was certainly one of the strangest moments in Champollion's illustrious career.

Escaping Rome two days later, and moving on to Florence, Champollion found himself in more familiar territory. Not to be outdone by the King of Sardinia, the Grand Duke of Tuscany, Leopoldo II (r.1824–59), had also recently acquired a large collection of Egyptian antiquities. This one had been amassed by an Italian diplomat, Giuseppe di Nizzoli, who had served for seven years as chancellor of the Austrian consulate in Cairo. He had sold the first part of his collection in 1821 to the Austrian government. Three years later, he put a second part on the market, taking advantage of the interest (and high prices) generated by the Drovetti sale. Leopoldo II seized his chance and secured the collection for Tuscany. And who better to catalogue the objects than the greatest and most famous scholar of ancient Egypt in all of Europe, Jean-François Champollion? It was a relationship that would prove crucial for the next phase of Champollion's studies.

On this first visit, however, Champollion stayed in Florence for only two weeks. He was anxious to head back to Turin to immerse himself for a second time in the spectacular Drovetti collection. En route, he received word that a further collection, amassed by Drovetti's great rival Henry Salt, had been sent to Europe for sale and currently lay in store at the Livorno docks. Champollion's interest was piqued, so in July 1825 he made a detour via Livorno to see Salt's antiquities for himself. What he found more than lived up to expectations. The British consul had clearly enjoyed a flair for acquiring rare and important artefacts. With the Drovetti and di Nizzoli collections having been snapped up by ambitious rulers in Turin, Vienna and Florence, Champollion determined, there and then, that the Salt collection should come to Paris. Champollion's motives were not entirely unselfish. If Paris were to acquire a significant collection of Egyptian antiquities, then the Louvre would have to appoint a curator to look after them; and Champollion saw himself firmly in the frame for such a prestigious appointment. All he needed to do was to persuade the French government, and, in particular, France's new king, Charles X (r.1824–30).

In November 1825, just before the route across the Alps became impassable with the winter snows, Champollion made the journey from Turin to stay with his family in Grenoble, before returning to Paris to begin his lobbying. Unfortunately, the Salt collection was not the only one on the market; nor, Champollion discovered, was he the only plausible candidate for the Louvre curatorship. One by one, hoards of antiquities amassed by European collectors were being auctioned off to rival European courts, taking advantage of the newfound fashion for all things ancient Egyptian that the *Description* and decipherment had prompted. The latest collection to come onto the market was an extensive group of objects formed by an Italian horse-dealer-turned-excavator, Giuseppe Passalacqua. Among those advocating its purchase by the French state was Champollion's arch-nemesis, Jomard, who rather fancied himself as inaugural curator of Egyptian antiquities at the Louvre. Once again, the Duke of Blacas came to Champollion's rescue. Thanks to the duke's powers of persuasion, Charles X issued a royal grant in February 1826 which enabled Champollion to return to Livorno to make a full study of the Salt collection and estimate its value. Champollion's assessment was sufficiently favourable that, just two months later, after further intervention by Blacas, the French king approved the purchase of the Salt collection, and, a few weeks later, confirmed Champollion's appointment to the plum new job at France's national museum.

Champollion stayed in Livorno for a full six months, to supervise the shipment of the collection to Le Havre. Even this enforced delay turned out to be another stroke of luck. For Grand Duke Leopoldo II of Tuscany had sent a young scholar, a professor of oriental languages at the University of Pisa named Ippolito Rosellini (1800–43), to meet Champollion, hoping the great man might take the twenty-five-year-old under his wing. Rosellini asked Champollion directly if he would take him as his pupil. As Rosellini later recalled: 'I immediately determined to follow him wherever he should go.'[6] Not only did the two get on famously, beginning a lasting friendship and collaboration, but together they hatched an audacious plan: for a joint Franco-Tuscan expedition to Egypt, following in the footsteps of Napoleon but with all the advantages that decipherment had brought to the study of pharaonic civilization. It seemed fitting that a medal had recently been struck in France to celebrate the second edition of the *Description de l'Egypte*. The obverse showed a conqueror in Gaulish-Roman attire unveiling a voluptuous female personification of Egypt.[7] If Egypt were to be uncovered anew, it was only right that it should fall to a Frenchman and an Italian to accomplish the task. Rosellini joined Champollion in Paris at the end of the year to discuss their plan in more detail.

For Champollion, who had devoted his entire adult life to the study of ancient Egypt, the prospect of actually visiting the land of the pharaohs, rather than reading about it in books, now lodged itself firmly in his imagination. But, on a more prosaic level, there was the overwhelming task of his day job. The Salt collection of 5,000 objects was followed, in 1827, by the second Drovetti collection. As a consequence of these two purchases, the Louvre now had the best holdings of ancient Egyptian antiquities outside Egypt itself. It fell to Champollion, as curator, to sort, study and arrange the objects in the new Egyptian galleries. Breaking with tradition, he determined to present the collection not as mere objets d'art but in historical order, to chart the development of pharaonic culture. It was an immense undertaking, not helped by his many enemies in the French capital and the vested interests at the Louvre. The old Parisian courtiers did not take kindly to this upstart scholar from the provinces with his radical ideas, and they worked to frustrate him at every turn. Already in November 1826, Champollion had written to Rosellini:

> My life has become a fight . . . My arrival at the Museum has disturbed the whole place, and all my colleagues are conspiring against me, because instead of treating my position as a sinecure, I busy myself with my department, which inevitably makes it appear that they are doing nothing with theirs . . . Fortunately the minister is on my side, but I regret having constantly to involve him and weary him with all these political manoeuvres. How I long to be camped on the deserted plain of Thebes! Only there will it be possible for me to find at the same time both pleasure and rest.[8]

To add insult to injury, in 1827 Champollion was blocked from election to the Académie des Inscriptions; his radical views on politics and history seemed increasingly out of favour with the deeply conservative bent of Charles X's government. Beset with frustrations and disappointments on every side, Champollion found Egypt calling him ever more loudly.

⊲○▷

While the *Description* had brought the monuments of the Nile Valley to the forefront of European consciousness, in truth it had recorded an Egypt that was fast disappearing. Muhammad Ali's modernization of Egypt gathered momentum throughout the 1820s and, as more land was brought under cultivation and factories began to spring up along the riverbanks, it was Egypt's ancient monuments that bore the brunt. In the quarter century following the Napoleonic expedition, the Young Memnon and the sarcophagus of Seti I had been shipped to London, the Philae obelisk to Kingston Lacy, and the Dendera zodiac to Paris. Great quantities of smaller objects had been ruthlessly collected, then sold at a tidy profit, by European consuls and adventurers. Many of the antiquities that remained in Egypt fared even worse. At Aswan, the pillared chapel on the island of Elephantine was dismantled in 1822 to build barracks and warehouses; other monuments were demolished to feed lime kilns, while ancient mud brick made excellent fertilizer to support an increase in agricultural production. Between 1810 and 1828, thirteen whole temples were lost. Muhammad Ali even encouraged his engineers to use the Giza Pyramids as a convenient source of stone for the construction of new dams across the Nile. Little by little, Egypt's archaeological sites were being cannibalized to feed its industrial revolution. And what economic development spared, treasure-hunting and slapdash excavation often claimed. The burial site of an ancient Egyptian hero, General Djehuty, was discovered by Drovetti in 1824, but the sumptuous contents were dispersed, unrecorded, and even the location of the tomb was lost.

As reports of this orgy of destruction began to reach Europe, scholars became increasingly concerned. A desire to record and preserve Egypt's ancient patrimony before it was lost forever became a key motivation for nineteenth-century Egyptologists, starting with Champollion. In his case, a further spur to action may have been the sense of growing British activity in Egypt, as witnessed by the burgeoning number of travellers' accounts. France may have lost the Battle of the Nile, but it wasn't about to lose the battle of ideas or of science – not if Champollion had anything to do with it.

Rosellini's patron, Grand Duke Leopoldo II, supported the idea of a Franco-Tuscan joint expedition from the outset. It would bring glory to his dynasty – then vying with the House of Savoy for pre-eminence in Italy – and promised to enrich his Florentine collection with further treasures. Charles X of France was rather less enthusiastic. However, the prospect of closer political ties with Tuscany and the opportunity to split the cost (a French-led expedition at half the price), coupled, no doubt, with further persuasion by the tenacious Duke of Blacas, finally won over the king. Royal permission for the expedition to proceed was granted on 26 April 1828 at an audience secured by La Rochefoucauld, minister of the royal household.

In accordance with the proposal, first drawn up by Champollion and Rosellini in the middle of the previous year, the expedition would build on the foundations laid by Napoleon and his savants, and would extend the work of the *Description* (the final volume of which had still not been published). Now was the time, Champollion argued, to use the breakthrough of decipherment to advance the study of ancient Egypt – in situ. It was agreed that Champollion, as the elder and more eminent scholar, would be expedition leader, with Rosellini as assistant director. Reflecting the fifty-fifty division of costs, each side would include seven members. On the French side, alongside Champollion, were Charles Lenormant (inspector general); Antoine Bibent (architect); Alexandre Duchesne, Pierre-François Lehoux and Edouard Bertin (painters); and Nestor L'Hôte (artist-cum-customs officer). Joining Rosellini on the

Tuscan side were his uncle Gaetano Rosellini (architect), his brother-in-law Cherubini (artist), Giuseppe Angelelli (painter), Giuseppe Raddi and Gaetano Galastri (naturalists), and Alessandro Ricci (doctor). The last was a practical addition to the party, who would more than justify his inclusion. All seemed set fair. There was just one final detail to iron out: permission from the Egyptian ruler, Muhammad Ali.

Unfortunately, political events in the Eastern Mediterranean, and with them, relations between Egypt and the European powers, were suddenly plunged into crisis. Things had started to simmer in 1821 when the Greek provinces rebelled against Ottoman rule and agitated for independence. In the months that followed, the Ottoman army had been unable to quell the uprising, and intercommunal violence between Greeks and Turks had spread to Constantinople. With Britain, France and Russia all united in support of the Greek cause, the Ottoman sultan cast around elsewhere for military assistance. With heavy irony, the wayward province of Egypt seemed to offer an answer. For, in 1822, as part of Muhammad Ali's modernization plans, and to cement and enhance his own power, he had created a new Egyptian army. His 'new order' (*nizam jadid*) was consciously modelled on the Napoleonic regime, and brought all barracks, military schools and training camps under a single code of instruction and discipline.[9] Up to 200,000 men were drafted from communities large and small throughout Egypt, often for years at a time, and garrisons for them and their families were built near all the country's major towns. Muhammad Ali's policies ushered in nothing less than the thorough militarization of Egyptian society; it was to be perhaps the most durable of his reforms. And it meant that, when the appeal came from Constantinople for military assistance, Muhammad Ali was ready to respond – at a price. In exchange for the offer of Crete as an addition to Egyptian territory, he eventually sent 16,000 soldiers and sixty-three naval vessels under the command of his son, Ibrahim. If the intervention had succeeded, the Ottoman sultan would have retained his authority, and the ruler of Egypt greatly enhanced his. Unfortunately for both men, the combined forces of Britain, France and Russia proved too resolute and powerful an enemy. The ensuing confrontation culminated in October 1827 at the Battle of Navarino, when the entire Egyptian fleet, alongside many Ottoman ships, was sunk. Humbled and hopelessly exposed, Muhammad Ali had to sue for terms with the European powers. Never again would he risk the Egyptian army defending his nominal suzerain in far-off Constantinople. From now on, Egypt's foreign policy would be resolutely in pursuance of its own interests.

Against such a backdrop, a European expedition to Egypt headed by a Frenchman was unlikely to be welcomed by the Egyptian government. To make matters worse, Champollion had detractors closer to home: ever since the death of Henry Salt in October 1827, the French consul Drovetti had enjoyed a near monopoly on collecting antiquities in the Nile Valley; when news of the proposed Franco-Tuscan expedition reached him, he was aghast at the prospect of a state-backed, scientific mission encroaching on his lucrative activities, and lost no time in trying to prevent it. No matter that, back in 1824, he had promised Champollion assistance with any future Egyptian expedition. To safeguard his own position and income, Drovetti now wrote to Champollion in terms carefully calculated to frighten and dissuade: 'I suffer, more than any other, from the circumstances which prevent me from encouraging this project to go ahead in the current year . . . There reigns in Egypt, as in all the other parts of the Ottoman empire, a spirit of animosity towards Europeans which, in certain cases, could produce ferment and seditious acts against the personal safety of those domiciled or who find themselves travelling there.' He continued, at his most disingenuous: 'Please be assured that I could not be more sorry for not being able to facilitate your wishes.'[10]

The expedition might have been stopped in its tracks there and then, had not the French king, Charles X, already given permission for it to proceed, exactly one week before Drovetti's letter. Upon receiving royal approval, Champollion wasted no time in departing Paris for Toulon, eager to embark as soon as possible. On his way south, Champollion must have crossed with Drovetti's letter, winging its way to his Paris address. There, it was opened by Champollion's brother, who, smelling a rat, deliberately delayed forwarding it to Toulon. By the time it arrived at the port, prompting a request by the French government to the local prefect to detain the expedition, Champollion had set sail. (He only learned of the letter upon arrival in Alexandria, and commented: 'It is the hand of Amun that diverted it.'[11]) His parting words to his brother were: 'Goodbye, my dear friend; do not worry, the gods of Egypt watch over us.'[12]

Champollion and his companions sailed out of Toulon harbour on 31 July 1828 – thirty years after Napoleon – and first set eyes on the Egyptian coast eighteen days later. Champollion had waited all his life for this moment, and felt as if he had come home. In the first of a regular series of letters to his brother which, together with his journal, provide a vivid and invaluable account of the whole expedition, he wrote: 'It's as if I had been born in this country, and the Europeans have already concluded that I look like a Copt . . . Moreover, I have adopted the manners and customs of the country.'[13]

Indeed, his swarthy complexion and excellent Arabic meant that he could easily pass for a native. (He later adopted local dress and grew a long beard, completing the transformation.) With the monuments of ancient Egypt now at his fingertips, he set straight to work. On his first full day in the country, he visited the most famous sight in Alexandria, Cleopatra's Needles, and concluded from their inscriptions that they had nothing at all to do with Cleopatra but, instead, dated back to pharaonic times. In a similar vein, he established that another famous Alexandrian monument, Pompey's Pillar, had been erected by the emperor Diocletian, 300 years after Pompey's visit. Thus, in the space of a few hours, thanks to his ability to read the ancient Egyptian texts, Champollion cut a swathe through the accumulated myths, legends and misunderstandings of centuries. For the first time since the Roman empire, the monuments of ancient Egypt could once again speak for themselves.

Memories of a more recent empire stirred patriotic thoughts in Champollion's mind, as he toured places visited by Napoleon and his savants three decades earlier. 'Everything in this city', he wrote to his brother on 23 August 1828, 'breathes the memory of our former power and shows how easily French influence exerts itself on the Egyptian population.'[14] But Champollion's ambitions extended far beyond Alexandria. If he were to follow in the footsteps of his childhood hero and explore the Nile Valley in its entirety, he would need permission from the Egyptian ruler. Fortunately, in the weeks since Champollion had left France, the political situation in Egypt had calmed. Britain had signed a treaty with Muhammad Ali, permitting the evacuation of Egyptian troops from Greece. As a result, the pasha was now less ill-disposed towards Europeans and might, after all, be persuaded to grant the expedition a royal firman (official permit).

Just six days after landing in Alexandria, Champollion was granted the all-important audience with Muhammad Ali, and must have been surprised and delighted at the outcome: not only was the expedition given permission to travel as far south as the Egyptian border with Sudan, it was also allocated two Egyptian guards for its protection. A furious Drovetti tried to intervene, but Champollion had established his own direct line to the French consulate; Muhammad Ali's firman arrived on 10 September. It even gave the Franco-Tuscan expedition permission to visit sites formerly reserved for Drovetti and his fellow antiquities collector Anastasi. It was a total victory for Champollion. Ecstatic and relieved, he wrote to his brother:

I have had to use all my diplomatic skills (all this letter is absolutely confidential). You have seen in Drovetti's letter that the reasons for preventing my voyage to Egypt were exaggerated. It was, at root, simply a calculation of personal interest. The antiquities dealers were all squirming at the news of my arrival in Egypt with the intention of excavating.[15]

When Muhammad Ali put a large sailing boat, the *Isis*, at the expedition's disposal, Drovetti made the gallant gesture of supplying it with bottles of fine French wine. But he would not forget the indignity of having his monopoly so rudely and completely snatched away, and would take his revenge by failing to forward Champollion's post from France during the course of the expedition. Champollion would later write of Drovetti:

He should be ashamed for his conduct towards me regarding the excavations and the firman which I had to extract from the authorities . . . I have not the least confidence in him, and I am not impressed by his politicking and his conduct in Egypt, where he is only concerned for his own interests . . . All the French despise him, and I wouldn't dare say that they are wrong.[16]

Through a combination of his intellectual reputation and political connections, Champollion had bested his rival. On

the eve of departure from Alexandria, 13 September 1828, the
founder of Egyptology was full of anticipation: 'In forty-eight
hours *I will have seen* the sacred river of which, until now, I
have only *drunk*; and this land of Egypt, about which I have
dreamt for so long.'[17]

⊲ɪoɪ⊳

Champollion came to Egypt as a devotee, fulfilling the ambition of a lifetime. He drank Nile water as a matter of pride
(despite concerns about the plague), and felt more at home in
the backstreets of Cairo than in the boulevards of Paris. He
certainly found the Egyptian capital remarkably clean compared
with the filth of its French counterpart. However, his love affair
with the land of the pharaohs did not blind him to the harsh
realities of life under its modern masters. Only a few days after
arriving in Cairo, he wrote in his journal: 'The pace of civilization would march very quickly here, if a well-intentioned
government presided over the affairs of unhappy Egypt. But a
totalitarian spirit devours or dries up everything.'[18]

If the state of contemporary Egypt was depressing, the
ancient monuments presented an equally dispiriting picture.
Champollion was particularly disappointed by Saqqara, with
its confusing mass of spoil heaps and ruins. 'The vast expanse
interrupted by pyramids was riddled with hillocks of sand
covered in debris,' he wrote. 'All these hillocks are the result of
excavations in search of mummies and antiquities, and the
number of shafts or tombs at Saqqara must be enormous, if
you consider that the sand thrown up in discovering one shaft
must itself hide the openings to several other shafts.'[19]

In the early nineteenth century, ancient Egypt was still
buried beneath the sands. That was especially true at Giza,
which Champollion had first glimpsed in the distance on 19
September 1828 and which he began to explore in earnest

three weeks later. As he wrote on 8 October: 'I wanted to clear the sand covering the inscription of Thutmose IV which is engraved on the [Sphinx's] chest; but the Arabs who descended upon us from the heights crowned by the Pyramids told me that it would require forty men and eight days to accomplish. So I had to give it up.'[20]

Strangely, there is a gap in Champollion's otherwise comprehensive journal corresponding to the next three days, which he spent at Giza. Whether he was dumbstruck by the sheer magnificence of the pyramids, overcome by mental and physical exhaustion, or simply too preoccupied by the ancient ruins to commit his observations to paper, it is an unexplained hiatus in an otherwise detailed record of his Egyptian expedition.

Following in the footsteps of Napoleon, Champollion felt a heavy responsibility: not just to study the monuments recorded in the *Description*, but to improve upon that great work by making accurate drawings of the inscriptions – aided by his ability to read them – and to correct other inaccuracies so as to present the most authoritative study of pharaonic civilization ever undertaken. He was certainly uniquely qualified to undertake such a task. Indeed, his reputation as the decipherer of hieroglyphics preceded him, as he had discovered when preparing to set sail from the port of Cairo on his journey upstream: 'I met here Lord Prudhoe, Mr Burton and Major Felix, Englishmen, committed hieroglyphicists, who showered me with attention as if I were the head of a sect.'[21] Nothing, however, could have prepared Champollion for the sheer number of monuments and quantity of inscriptions to be studied and copied when he reached the great southern city of Thebes. The temples were on a grand scale – 'Suffice to say . . . that we in Europe are mere Lilliputians and that no people, ancient or modern, has conceived the art of architecture on a scale so sublime, massive and awe-inspiring as did the ancient Egyptians'[22] – and he quickly realized that to do the site justice would require months, not days. But far from being overwhelmed by the task, he felt newly energized. He wrote to his brother: 'My health is excellent; the climate suits me, and I am much better than in Paris.'[23] Indeed, Egypt had transformed not only Champollion's health but his whole outlook. He felt moved to declare: 'I belong entirely to Egypt – she is everything to me and I must seek consolation from her, because I will receive none from Europe.'[24]

With each new site he visited, this reaction grew stronger. At Dendera, once home to the famous zodiac now displayed in Paris, Champollion and his companions 'spent two hours in ecstasy, running through the great halls with our poor torch, trying to read the exterior inscriptions by the light of the moon'.[25] No inconvenience or danger would be allowed to stand in the way of scientific examination. At Abu Simbel, where two great temples were hewn from the living rock face – a recent visitor had declared the site 'the ne-plus-ultra of Egyptian labour, and . . . the noblest monument of antiquity that is to be found on the banks of the Nile'[26] – the challenges were especially daunting. When Burckhardt had rediscovered the site fifteen years before, in 1813, the whole of the main entrance and most of the four flanking colossi had been completely covered by sand, the accumulation of twenty-five centuries. Bankes had visited in 1815, but was unable to enter. It took Belzoni, with his engineering expertise, to clear the sand and open the temple in 1817; Bankes had returned two years later to find drifts once again threatening access. Now, another decade on, the desert had reclaimed its prize, and the portal was completely blocked. It took a huge effort just to clear a hole big enough for a man to squeeze through. But Champollion was undaunted:

I undressed almost completely, down to my Arab shirt and long linen underpants, and pushed myself flat on my stomach through the small opening in the doorway that, if cleared of sand, would be at least 25 feet in height. I thought I was entering the mouth of a furnace, and, when I had slid entirely into the temple, I found myself in an atmosphere heated to 52 degrees: we went through this astonishing excavation, Rosellini, Ricci, I and one of the Arabs holding a candle in his hand . . . After two and a half hours of admiration, and having seen all the bas-reliefs, the need to breathe a little fresh air made itself felt, and we had to regain the mouth of the furnace.[27]

During two intense weeks at Abu Simbel, the expedition succeeded in making copies of all the temple reliefs; it was a heroic effort. As Champollion remarked to his brother: 'Thus has been our memorable Abu Simbel campaign: it is the bitterest and the most glorious we have accomplished during the entire voyage. Frenchmen and Tuscans have been rivals in zeal and devotion.'[28]

As they prepared to leave, the men took the scaffolding away from the entrance, whereupon the sand collapsed, recovering the doorway to a depth of two metres above the cornice. Having yielded up its secrets, the temple fell silent again. Champollion knew he would never return.

The mammoth campaign at Abu Simbel exhausted the exped-ition both physically and materially. By the time Champollion and his companions reached Wadi Halfa, on Egypt's southern border with Sudan and the furthest point of their journey, they were surviving on dry biscuits brought from Aswan. After replenishing their stores in the town's *souk*, they celebrated New Year's Day 1829, and the beginning of the return journey, with a Nubian dinner washed down with two bottles of Saint-Georges wine. Reaching the Second Nile Cataract without incident and copying the inscriptions at Abu Simbel were not the only causes for celebration. The expedition had also vindicated Champollion's theory of decipherment and proved the accuracy of his system. He wrote triumphantly to his old friend and mentor, Bon-Joseph Dacier:

> I am proud that, having followed the course of the Nile from its mouth to the second cataract, I am able to announce to you that there is nothing to modify in our *Lettre sur l'alphabet hiéroglyphes*. Our alphabet is good: it can be applied with equal success to Egyptian monuments of Roman and Ptolemaic times and, which is of greater interest, to the inscriptions in all the temples, palaces and tombs of pharaonic date. Everything justifies, therefore, the encouragement that you so kindly gave to my hieroglyphic work at a time when nobody was disposed to favour it.[29]

Glowing with justification and pride, Champollion allowed personal thoughts to invade his mind for the briefest of moments, asking his brother in a postscript: 'Send me news of my wife.'[30] He also displayed glimpses of humour, writing in his journal, after an unsuccessful hunting trip: 'Thus deprived, for the twentieth time, of the sweet hope of eating grilled crocodile, we continued downriver.'[31] Then he plunged back into his studies.

As he embarked on the return journey and looked ahead to the successful conclusion of the expedition, Champollion began to think about establishing a more permanent connection between Egypt and France. One idea, in particular, started to fix itself in his mind. As the *Isis* sailed between Aswan and Kom Ombo, he wondered: 'Will we see, at last, an Egyptian obelisk in one of the squares of Paris? That would be nice!'[32] Of all the obelisks still standing in Egypt, the pair in front of the temple at Luxor had attracted particular admiration. Thirty years earlier, during the Napoleonic expedition, Denon had remarked that 'there is nothing on earth to compare with them'.[33] Champollion was rather of the same opinion, musing: 'Why toy with transporting the one in Alexandria when one could have one of these for the modest expense of 400,000 francs at most? The minister who erected one of these admirable monoliths in one of the squares of Paris would immortalize himself with little effort.'[34]

While Champollion's ability to read the ancient texts may have shattered earlier theories about the obelisk inscriptions – 'far from confirming what people have for so long thought – profound religious mysteries, high philosophical speculations, secrets of occult science, or astronomical observations – they are simply dedications, more or less fatuous, of the buildings in front of which these monuments are erected'[35] – the appeal of the monuments themselves remained undimmed. As the date of his departure from Egypt grew ever nearer, Champollion began to agitate to have one of the Luxor obelisks transported to the French capital: 'If we are to see an obelisk in Paris, let it be one of these at Luxor. Ancient Thebes will have to console itself in keeping the Karnak one, the finest and most beautiful of all . . . Without spending three hundred thousand francs in preliminary preparations, one of the two Luxor obelisks could be transported by river, on a big raft . . . It would be possible. If it was really wished for, it could be done.'[36]

In the meantime, there was the work of the expedition to finish. Thebes, with its countless monuments, was even more daunting a site than Abu Simbel. In the Valley of the Kings, Champollion worked relentlessly, recording no fewer than sixteen tombs. He insisted on working alone, telling his fellow expedition members: 'I need absolute silence in order to hear the voice of history.'[37] On more than one occasion, they found him lying unconscious from exhaustion, in a chamber deep underground. Whilst his sense of duty and destiny drove him ever onwards, his companions struggled to keep up, and began to wilt. One by one, citing various excuses, they melted away, leaving Champollion to his own devices. By the time the expedition formally departed western Thebes, only half the French members were left. Thanks to the more resilient local labour, and his good relations with the Theban villagers and the Ababda Bedouin, Champollion was able to continue his excavations during the blistering summer months of June, July and August. He complained about the lack of extra funds, convinced that they had been withheld deliberately, but still managed to hack two life-sized reliefs from the walls of the tomb of Seti I: 'big and beautiful things' for the expedition's royal patrons.[38] To this day, one is in Paris, the other in Florence.

By the time Champollion left Thebes, he, too, was exhausted, and ready to head home. But his ordeals were not over. In Alexandria, the Tuscan members of the expedition departed on one of their own ships, but Champollion was left stranded for two months while awaiting a French naval vessel. He put the time to good use, writing a brief history of ancient Egypt at Muhammad Ali's request. In return, the Egyptian ruler gifted the two Luxor obelisks to France. (One of them was finally transported to Paris in 1836, and erected in the Place de la Concorde, where it still stands.) Emboldened by this show of royal generosity, Champollion decided to intervene on behalf of the hard-pressed peasantry and ask Muhammad Ali to improve the education system in Egypt; but the presumptuous request was met with a stony silence. Champollion might have been master of the pharaonic past, but Muhammad Ali was firmly in control of Egypt's future. Champollion was sanguine. After all, he remarked: 'There is enough of the old Egypt, without occupying myself with the new.'[39]

Egypt under Muhammad Ali was determinedly forward-looking, anxious to throw off centuries of economic stagnation and political indifference to chart its own, bold course. From the very beginning of his reign, Muhammad Ali had realized that modernization of the economy would be the key to national prosperity and, ultimately, self-determination. Major improvements to the country's irrigation and transportation network paved the way for the introduction of cotton production and the development of new international markets. In tandem with this revolution in agriculture, Egypt embarked on an industrial revolution. Europe had shown that the production of raw materials was not the passport to wealth: advanced economies were built on the manufacture and export of processed, higher-value products. Egypt needed to do the same, and reduce its dependence on imported goods (a dependence which merely underlined and reinforced its colonial status). So it was that in the 1820s, and subsequent decades, the Nile Valley reverberated to the sound of construction projects, on a scale not witnessed since the days of the pharaohs. In place of temples and palaces there were engineering projects – dams and bridges, canals and railways – and industrial buildings: cotton mills, sugar mills and rice mills, factories for textiles and munitions.[40]

As a result of all this activity, the face of Egypt changed more in the first two decades of Muhammad Ali's rule than in perhaps the previous thousand years. Champollion was the first traveller since Roman times to be able to read the ancient Egyptian monuments, yet also one of the last to see the sites as they had been preserved since antiquity. By the end of his expedition, he was under no illusions that the country's precious patrimony was at risk of disappearing. He tried to use his scientific renown to persuade Muhammad Ali of the need for preservation, arguing that: 'all of Europe will take notice [if] . . . His Highness would . . . assure the conservation of temples, palaces, tombs, and all kinds of monuments which still attest to the power and grandeur of ancient Egypt, and which are at the same time the most beautiful ornaments of Modern Egypt.'[41]

In a nod to this sentiment, Muhammad Ali chose a pyramid as the masthead of his new journal, *Al-Ahram* (The Pyramids), which remains the official organ of the Egyptian government to this day. But the ruler of Modern Egypt was much more interested in European technology than in lectures about conservation, much more focussed on Egypt's industrial potential than on the sentimental value of a bunch of old ruins. If Europe was interested in acquiring antiquities, Muhammad Ali was only too happy to supply them in exchange for political favours and technological know-how. Hence, when he presented the Luxor obelisks to France, he declared: 'I give her the relic of an old civilization; it is in exchange for the new civilization of which she had spread the seeds in the Orient.'[42]

On 28 November 1829, fifteen months after setting foot in Egypt, Champollion bid farewell to the land of his dreams. His last words written on Egyptian soil, in a letter to his ever-faithful brother, were tinged with sadness, but also with a sense of accomplishment: 'So goodbye . . . The end of my drama will, I hope, be as happy as the four preceding acts. Goodbye, yours with heart and soul . . . Vive la France!'[43]

Landing at Toulon on 23 December, his thirty-ninth birthday, he had to endure a month's quarantine before being allowed to travel back to Paris. On his arrival, on 4 March 1830, he wrote: 'I have amassed enough work for an entire lifetime.'[44]

Thomas Young was a brilliant linguist and polymath, Ippolito Rosellini an accomplished scholar and excavator; but

Champollion is justly remembered as the founder of Egyptology. Though his adversaries continued to frustrate his advancement and belittle his achievements to the very end (and beyond), he was eventually, if belatedly, recognized with appointment to the world's first chair in Egyptology (at the Collège de France) and election – the third time around – to the Académie des Inscriptions et Belles-Lettres, the institution which had launched his career on that mild September day in 1822.

As for his great expedition, the first since Roman times to be able to engage with the monuments on their own terms, its impact was less than it should have been. Two years, to the very hour, after arriving back in Paris, Champollion died from a stroke, aged just forty-one. His untimely death precipitated a breakdown in the relationship between the French and Tuscan teams. As a result, two competing works were published, a ten-volume Italian account, *Monumenti dell'Egitto e della Nubia* (1832–40), and a four-volume one in French, *Monuments de l'Egypte et de la Nubie* (1835–45). Without a mentor, Rosellini's career spluttered and faded. And, even after the posthumous publication of Champollion's *Grammaire égyptienne* (1836), detractors continued to decry his whole system of decipherment, calling it 'a great humbug'.[45] Champollion had predicted as much, writing to Rosellini from quarantine in the south of France in January 1830, 'My *Grammar* will appear at the end of this year . . . It won't convert those who oppose my system and deprecate my work, because they don't want to be converted.'[46]

Eventually, the weight of Champollion's scholarship and the abundant proof of his system silenced all opposition. Today, in honour of his achievements, a huge replica of the Rosetta Stone has been installed in the courtyard of his family home in Figeac; one of the roads radiating out from Cairo's Tahrir Square is named Sharia Champollion ('Champollion Street'), and the

Egyptian Museum itself, standing proudly at the edge of the square, bears Champollion's engraved name in pride of place. His tomb, in Paris's Père Lachaise cemetery, is marked with an Egyptian-style obelisk. Fittingly, for one who dedicated his entire working life to unravelling the mysteries of Egypt's ancient civilization, his last words are said to have been: 'And now for the afterlife, on to Egypt, on to Thebes!'[47] But perhaps the most appropriate epitaph for this most dedicated and gifted of pioneer scholars is his simple credo: 'Enthusiasm, that is the only life!'[48]

THREE

Englishmen abroad

John Gardner Wilkinson, a quintessential Englishman in Turkish dress.

It is so difficult to tear myself away from this place & from Egypt altogether. One seems tied down to it for life.[1]

JOHN GARDNER WILKINSON, 1832

The birth of Egyptology in the wake of the Napoleonic expedition was felt not just in France, but also in her long-time foe and arch-rival, England. Ever since the publication of Pococke's and Norden's travelogues in the mid-eighteenth century, Egypt had exerted an increasingly powerful allure on the English imagination. Napoleon's exploits and his savants' scientific accomplishments fully reawakened public interest in pharaonic civilization, both across continental Europe and across the Channel. Throughout the British Isles, the early nineteenth century was the era of historical and antiquarian societies, with groups springing up at local and national levels to cater to the growing fascination with the past. In London, a close-knit circle of gentleman scholars, mostly well-educated men of private means, met and corresponded frequently, assisting each other's research as they attempted to make sense of the new information coming from excavation and exploration in the Mediterranean lands and further afield.[2]

At the same time, two ramifications of Bonaparte's imperial ambitions unexpectedly turned Egypt into one of the most popular destinations for adventurous British travellers. First, the Napoleonic Wars that raged during the first decade and a half of the nineteenth century effectively closed Western Europe to tourists, forcing those in search of adventure to travel further afield, to the Eastern Mediterranean and beyond. Second, Muhammad Ali's rise to power as ruler of Egypt, in the wake of the French occupation and subsequent defeat, led to a marked improvement in the security situation throughout the Nile Valley. As a result, Egypt was not just accessible but also safe. Indeed, as one British traveller remarked: 'I do not know of any European country where one may travel with greater safety than in Egypt.'[3] All this meant that, from the beginning of the nineteenth century onwards, Egypt became a favoured destination for Britons seeking diversion, enlightenment or fortune abroad.

Some, like William Bankes, travelled to collect antiquities for their country houses back home. Others, like Frederick Catherwood, went to Egypt as artists, drawn by the spectacular ruins, the cloudless climes and starry skies.[4] A few went to escape their past and forge a new future, like William Thomson who, after being involved in a brawl in Inverness, joined the British army and went to Egypt. Taken prisoner and faced with the choice of death or conversion to Islam as a slave, he chose the latter, and adopted Turkish dress and customs for the rest of his life, changing his name to Osman Effendi. He served in Muhammad Ali's army in Arabia, where he met the great traveller Johann Burckhardt. At Burckhardt's prompting, and with the intervention of the British consul-general Henry Salt, Osman was freed from slavery in 1815 and settled in Cairo, where he rendered great service to countless British travellers until his death from dysentery twenty years later.

Some British visitors to Egypt in the early nineteenth century simply wanted to make money by feeding the public appetite for travel-writing. (British authors published over a hundred such accounts of visits to Egypt between 1798 and 1850, more than twice as many as their French counterparts.[5])

There were also those who travelled to Egypt to experience the picturesque and romantic thrill of a country still associated in the European imagination with the Bible story and the *Arabian Nights*. Frederick Henniker was typical, writing in his travel account, 'my delight was rather in nature than in works of art'. Indeed, the monuments of ancient Egypt interested him little: the Great Pyramid he ignored, noting that: 'The excellent description by Denon of this the largest pyramid in the world, renders further observations almost unnecessary'; the pyramids of Saqqara and Dahshur were 'uninteresting after those of Ghiseh'; Luxor temple, he remarked, 'swarms with dogs, Arabs, houses, and other filth'; in Thebes, 'the city of the hundred gates, the inhabitants on the east bank live in mud hovels, on the west they live underground'; while Elephantine he found 'part covered with palm trees and corn, partly with ruins', adding 'the mud cottages of the natives add to the picturesque'.[6]

In November 1822, just one month after the publication of Champollion's *Lettre à M. Dacier*, a British periodical, the *Eclectic Review*, noted presciently that 'in every point of view, Egypt is an object of the highest interest, and is likely to become increasingly such'.[7] Eighteen months later, it could assert 'no-one can now pretend to have seen the world who has not made one of a party of pleasure up the Nile'.[8] Indeed, by 1824, travellers' accounts of Egypt had become so common that the author of yet another, *Scenes and Impressions in Egypt and in Italy*, felt obliged to concede, 'the ground over which I would conduct my reader, has been trodden, and described by a hundred travellers, and is . . . as well known, perhaps, as any road or province in our native country'.[9] Families travelling overland between Britain and India swelled the numbers of visitors to Egypt; and, by the time Champollion first visited Egypt, in 1828, it was apparently 'scarcely possible to turn the corner of a street without meeting an Englishman recently arrived, either from the borders of the Red Sea, the cataracts of the Nile, or the ruins of Palmyra'.[10]

The French sneered at all this tourism, ascribing it to *maladie du pays* engendered by Britain's own failings.[11] The Egyptians, in whose midst all these strange travellers now appeared, were suspicious, believing that foreigners must be in search of treasure or political advantage (they were correct on both counts). Fortunately, for the history of Egyptology, there were at least some Englishmen (and one or two women) whose interest in the Nile Valley was more benign – who sought neither gold nor power, but knowledge; and whose dedicated scholarship and detailed accounts would secure the study of Egypt as a proper scientific pursuit.

⋖⊙⊳

If he had been asked to describe himself, John Gardner Wilkinson (1797–1875) would have laid claim to the titles of gentleman scholar, traveller and antiquarian, but not, one suspects, of scientist. Yet his position in the pantheon of great Egyptologists rests on secure foundations. He studied virtually every archaeological site of importance, and in his copious writings did more than anyone else, before or since, to make the civilization of the pharaohs accessible to the general public. His work was a far cry from Champollion's determinedly academic publications, but no less influential.

Wilkinson was born into a comfortable, middle-class, educated family which fully embraced the ideals and opportun-ities of the Enlightenment. His clergyman father was a fellow of the Society of Antiquaries and a member of the African Exploration Society (later the Royal Geographical Society), and his friends included the traveller James Grey Jackson; Jackson's stories of travelling through Morocco thrilled the young Wilkinson and left a deep impression, planting in him a seed and a desire to pursue his own foreign adventures.

Meanwhile, Mrs Wilkinson, every bit as erudite as her husband, taught her son French, Latin and Greek while he was still in the nursery. But it was a childhood touched by loss as well as by learning. When Wilkinson was just six his mother died, followed two years later by his father. Their untimely demise left Wilkinson an orphan, but a wealthy one. The combination of means and motivation propelled him to follow his interests, which, in the spirit of the times, centred on ancient history. At the age of sixteen, Wilkinson entered Harrow School to complete his education and prepare for university. It was either a careful or a lucky choice, for the headmaster, George Butcher, was a friend of Thomas Young and had studied hieroglyphics alongside the great polymath. Spotting the young Wilkinson's interest in the ancient world, Butcher probably introduced his new pupil to the study of pharaonic Egypt. (Wilkinson would remember this early inspiration, bequeathing his collection of Egyptian antiquities to his old school, where it remains to this day.)

After Harrow, three years at Oxford were the norm for a man of Wilkinson's background, but they did little to advance his scholarship. Like many of his contemporaries, he decided that a grand tour would rectify the situation, and so, on 25 June 1819, just weeks after leaving university, he embarked on a European odyssey, intending to return before the end of the year to take up a commission in the army. However, once entered upon the life of a leisured tourist, all thoughts of the military quickly disappeared. Wilkinson would, in fact, spend the next fourteen years abroad, twelve of them in Egypt. His first destination, however, which he reached via France and Germany, was Geneva, where he spent the winter of 1819–20. From there, he travelled to Rome and Florence, then back to

Geneva, before returning to Rome for the following winter. It was during one of his sojourns in the Eternal City that Wilkinson first encountered the man who was to change the course of his life: the classical scholar, bibliophile and avid correspondent, Sir William Gell.

Gell was one of those remarkable, early nineteenth-century figures who not only excelled as a scholar in his own right (he was a fellow both of the Royal Society and of the Society of Antiquaries, and was knighted for his services to archaeology), but also maintained a vigorous correspondence with virtually every other serious scholar in his field, the length and breadth of Europe. He has been memorably described as 'a sort of Egyptological clearing-house. He gathered ideas from all sides, and communicated everybody's discoveries to everybody else.'[12] He corresponded regularly with Thomas Young and Henry Salt, and with Champollion. He had read every work published to date on Egyptology, ancient as well as modern. He knew the Hermetic and Neoplatonic writings. And he sensed, in 1820, that the study of ancient Egypt was on the brink of a major breakthrough, 'poised between a rich tradition of antiquarian scholarship and unprecedented opportunities'.[13]

He must, therefore, have been more than usually interested in the latest traveller to cross his path in Rome. Here was a young man who combined an enquiring mind with a deep interest in the ancient world and was an accomplished artist to boot. Gell duly invited Wilkinson to visit him in his book-filled house in Naples. There, in the summer of 1821, just a few weeks after Napoleon's death on St Helena, Gell offered to teach Wilkinson everything he knew – which was everything then known – about ancient Egypt. From the transliteration of hieroglyphics being developed by Young to the collections of Egyptian antiquities just beginning to reach the museums of Europe, Gell shared all the latest insights and discoveries with his protégé. By the time Wilkinson left Naples for Egypt – for the land of the pharaohs was, inevitably, to be the next destination on his grand tour – he was better prepared than any previous traveller to the Nile Valley.

Travelling by sea from Malta to Alexandria, Wilkinson caught his first glimpse of the Egyptian coast on 22 November 1821. On coming ashore, as instructed by Gell, he dutifully visited the classical monuments of Alexandria; but what he really wanted to see were the pharaonic ruins further south, in the Nile Valley proper. Within three weeks of arrival, he was on his way to Cairo. In the Egyptian capital, still largely untouched by Muhammad Ali's accelerating reforms, Wilkinson was granted an audience with the ruler, thanks to an introduction by Salt (and no doubt at Gell's urging). Osman Effendi, then working as a translator at the British consulate-general, took Wilkinson off to buy Ottoman clothes and showed him how to deport himself as a Turk. By February 1822, everything was ready. Joined by his friend James Samuel Wiggett, Wilkinson set sail from Cairo, bound for Upper Egypt and its manifold splendours.

While British travellers before Wilkinson had written any number of books about Egypt, few had published anything that could be reliably used as a guide. Armed only with a copy of Norden's *Travels in Egypt and Nubia*, Wilkinson and Wiggett made their way upstream, via Thebes and Aswan, as far south as Semna, at the foot of the Second Nile Cataract. Before turning around to begin the return journey, Wilkinson, like a few other visitors before and many since, carved his name on the rock of Abusir, overlooking the cataract, together with the date, 14 April 1822. A little under three months later, the friends were back in Thebes – where the Nile nearly claimed them both. Wiggett contracted dysentery from contaminated water, and Wilkinson, sailing by night to fetch Salt's doctor, nearly drowned. Thankfully, Wiggett recovered, but understandably chose to return home to England. Wilkinson, however, had been well and truly ensnared. Giving up all thoughts of an army career, he chose to stay in Egypt and immerse himself in its antiquities. Salt reported back to Gell: 'The interest he takes in our Egyptian antiquities far exceeds that of ordinary travelers.'[14] That letter was written on 16 September 1822. Two days earlier, in Paris, Champollion had declared: *'Je tiens mon affaire!'* Gell's intuition had been proved right, on both counts.

Wilkinson decided to take a house in Cairo, but not in the Frankish quarter, frequented by Europeans (who had a reputation for squalor and thieving). Instead, he chose to live in the Turkish districts of the city, first Hasanain, then the more fashionable Ezbekiya. Like his friend Osman Effendi, he wore Turkish clothes, ate in the Turkish style (to the distress of some of his English acquaintances) and, to all intents and purposes, lived like a Turk. This was not merely a romantic gesture on Wilkinson's part: Egypt was still very much an Ottoman possession, and the Turks were a privileged class of society. So to adopt Turkish manners and customs guaranteed a measure of respect and protection. Moreover, Wilkinson displayed a combination of European prejudice and Ottoman haughtiness when it came to Egypt's long-suffering peasantry. He wrote: 'The fellah, born in slavery, is consequently the most degraded of human beings, devoid of gratitude & every kind of virtue, he sees none in those around him; tyranny is to him a mark of superiority, & this alone he respects.'[15]

Like so many European travellers of the nineteenth century, Wilkinson was enamoured of Egypt's ancient rulers but felt little sympathy for its modern inhabitants. Impressed by Muhammad Ali's modernization programme, he expressed the faint hope, if not the expectation, that 'if the present Pasha continues to govern here the condition of the people may be considerably improved'.[16]

One of the most remarkable features of Wilkinson's long sojourn in Cairo was the circle of friends and fellow artists with whom he shared his houses, his interests, and his women. Besides Osman Effendi, there was James Burton, who had first met Wilkinson in Naples, at Gell's house, in 1821.[17] Burton subsequently obtained a position as a mineralogist in the government of Muhammad Ali (one of many European advisers employed by the Pasha) and arrived in Egypt, with his private secretary Charles Humphreys (d.1839), four months after Wilkinson. Unlike Wilkinson, who kept and discarded sexual companions, Burton bought a Greek woman at a slave auction in Cairo and married her. During his career for the Geological Survey of Egypt, he travelled with Wilkinson in the Eastern Desert and located the mines which had supplied ancient Rome with imperial porphyry. Taking up archaeology, he cleared the sand from the temples of Medinet Habu and Karnak, and excavated several tombs in the Valley of the Kings.

Another member of the circle was Robert Hay,[18] who had first visited Alexandria in 1818 as a midshipman in the Royal Navy. After inheriting a large estate from his brother, he had been drawn back to Egypt, inspired by Belzoni's books. He spent two long periods there (1824–8 and 1829–34), during which he, too, married a Greek woman he had 'rescued' from a slave market. During the Greek war of independence, Greek Christian women from defeated rebel villages were regarded by many Egyptian troops as part of the spoils of war. Captured and sold into slavery, they commanded high prices in the slave markets of Cairo: a white-skinned Greek could fetch between three and ten times the price of a black-skinned Abyssinian. Wealthy European men living in Cairo often bought Greek women as wives. Hay purchased a number of them in order to educate and resettle them. (He showed no such concern for their non-white counterparts.)

Wilkinson's friends in Egypt numbered military men like Major Orlando Felix, aristocrats like Lord Prudhoe, and businessmen with useful commercial contacts. Then there was the artist Frederick Catherwood, and the remarkable Edward Lane (1801–76), who, as we shall see, was Wilkinson's equal in every respect. Last, but not least, there was the sculptor and draughtsman Joseph Bonomi. He worked as Hay's assistant, but also with Wilkinson, Lane, and even Rosellini. Later in his long career, he accompanied Karl Richard Lepsius's expedition to Egypt in the 1840s, set up the Egyptian Court at the Crystal Palace in the 1850s, secured Hay's collection for the British Museum in the 1860s, and corresponded with Amelia Edwards as she prepared her landmark book on Egypt in the 1870s. The first keeper of Egyptian antiquities at the British Museum, Samuel Birch (1813–85), who knew all the Egyptologists of the mid-nineteenth century, ascribed to Bonomi 'greater knowledge and experience of Egypt than anyone else of the period save Wilkinson'.[19] Whether or not this praise was justified, Bonomi would provide the unique, personal link between many of the greatest figures in the nineteenth-century story of Egyptology.

Each of these men did their own thing, but they corresponded frequently and met up as they travelled the Nile. Wilkinson, from his first arrival in Egypt, was also guided from afar by his mentor Gell, a steady stream of letters from Naples suggesting sites worthy of exploration and instructing Wilkinson where to dig. As early as July 1822, Gell was suggesting Abydos as a promising location, based solely on its renown in later antiquity: 'Abydus was so famous a burying place that I have little doubt a great deal might be done by excavating the sands which have filled it up.'[20] (His hunch would prove correct: among the antiquities subsequently unearthed at Abydos – the cult centre of Osiris, god of the underworld – were two spectacular temples, built by Seti I and his son Ramesses II, the tombs of Egypt's earliest kings, later royal cenotaphs, and countless private burials.) Without ever having visited Egypt, Gell's encyclopaedic knowledge of the relevant literature, both ancient and modern, was unparalleled. Wilkinson, for his part, was diligent and enthusiastic, and had an artist's eye for detail. The two men made a perfect team. Moreover, unlike the bookish Gell, Wilkinson was always ready for an adventure. In 1823, for example, he undertook an arduous and epic expedition deep into the Red Sea Hills of the Eastern Desert with a caravan of sixty-six camels and twenty dromedaries, to locate two of the most famous quarries of the ancient world, Mons Claudianus and Mons Porphyrites, remote and desolate sites which had supplied the Roman emperors with sandstone and imperial porphyry respectively.

But events back in Europe were soon to turn Wilkinson's efforts in a different direction. Once again, Gell, with his finger firmly on the pulse of Western scholarship, was the first to spread the news. He had been predicting a breakthrough in decipherment, and when it came, he was certain of Champollion's achievement, telling Wilkinson: 'I cannot give you a dissertation on it but the thing is quite settled.'[21] Gell even sent some of Champollion's transcriptions, so that Wilkinson might learn the system for himself. Soon, armed with this new knowledge, Wilkinson began to apply decipherment to the ancient Egyptian monuments in situ, five years before the decipherer himself would have the opportunity to do so. Gentleman scholar he might have been, but nobody else in Egypt in the early 1820s had the knowledge to advance the study of pharaonic civilization as Wilkinson did. Among his many achievements was to date the Giza pyramids correctly to the Fourth Dynasty, years before the discovery of a royal name proved their antiquity.

Muhammad Ali may have improved Egypt's internal security, but, for Egyptians and Europeans alike, life in the Nile

Valley in the early 1820s was still beset with dangers. At that time, crocodiles lived in the river at Thebes; shortly after Hay's arrival in 1824, a child who had gone down to the river to fetch water was snatched, followed a few days later by a woman. Then there were regular outbreaks of plague – Henry Salt's wife died during one virulent epidemic in 1824 – and dysentery was rife. The latter disease killed both Salt (in 1827) and Osman Effendi (in 1835). Conjunctivitis was another common ailment, one from which Wilkinson suffered at regular intervals. In nineteenth-century Egypt, as in ancient times, villages were 'full of the bleary-eyed, the one-eyed, and the blind, with inflamed and festering eyelids, of all ages'.[22]

The worsening diplomatic situation between Egypt and the European powers during the mid-1820s added to the stresses and strains, especially in the capital. When Hay arrived from Europe (carrying the inevitable letter of introduction from Gell), he was only too glad to leave the city after a short stay for the relative quietude (crocodiles excepted) of Thebes. Even Wilkinson seriously considered leaving Egypt for India. But his own relentless curiosity and Gell's encouragement proved too strong, and Wilkinson soon embarked on further voyages of discovery into Upper Egypt and beyond. He visited the tombs at Beni Hasan, four years before Champollion and Rosellini, and was able to make copies of the reliefs when they were still almost pristine. He was probably the first European to visit the tombs at nearby Amarna, in 1824, but was puzzled by the strange style of the decoration (characteristic of the reign of the 'heretic pharaoh' Akhenaten) and thought it might be Persian in origin. Wilkinson certainly knew he had found something important, and swore his travelling companion, Burton, to secrecy in case another antiquarian or treasure-hunter should claim Amarna as his own.

With the means as well as the motivation, Wilkinson's years

in Egypt were immensely productive. He briefly thought of returning home – once, in 1826, when relations between Egypt and Britain reached a nadir following the sinking of the Egyptian fleet at the Battle of Navarino. He even went so far as to send his papers back home, whither he planned to follow. But, ironically, the same conflict prevented him from making the Mediterranean voyage, so he decided to stay. In any case, his heart was in Egypt, and he was tireless in his determination to explore and record it as thoroughly as possible. In a series of expeditions, he covered the length and breadth of the country, visiting far-flung corners where scarcely any European had set foot before, including the oases of the Western Desert and the wadis of the Eastern Desert. His curiosity was insatiable, extending not just to the ancient monuments but also to the landscape and the modern inhabitants. Indeed, the connection between people and culture fascinated him, as it did his friend Edward Lane, and would shape both men's seminal works.

In the first six years of his stay in Egypt, Wilkinson largely had the country to himself as far as serious antiquarian exploration was concerned. All that changed in 1828 with the arrival of Champollion and Rosellini and their Franco-Tuscan expedition. Despite a shared passion for Egyptian antiquity, and a shared acquaintance with the arch-interlocutor, William Gell, it is remarkable that Wilkinson and Champollion never met. Perhaps there was more than a touch of rivalry between them. Perhaps Wilkinson, like many of his compatriots, was aggrieved at Champollion's sidelining and disparagement of Thomas Young. Whatever the reason, Wilkinson never even corresponded with Champollion, although he did exchange letters with his brother in Paris. Rather pointedly, for much of the duration of the Franco-Tuscan expedition, Wilkinson 'withdrew for a lengthy stay in the Eastern Desert'[23] and depended on his friends in Cairo, several of whom met Champollion, to give him their impressions. They were by no means flattering. The Frenchman's boastfulness and his Italian colleagues' ebullience rankled with British reserve. Orlando Felix, for one (a veteran of Waterloo who could, therefore, have been forgiven for a little Francophobia), reported that 'the whole party are perfectly disgusting'.[24]

Two years after Champollion's departure, Wilkinson was still in Egypt, and had a very different experience with the French expedition sent to remove one of the Luxor obelisks. He struck up cordial relations with the engineer in charge, Jean-Baptiste Apollinaire Lebas, and even made a drawing of the operation. Another visitor to Thebes that same year, 1831, was the young Benjamin Disraeli, at the age of twenty-seven still finding his way in the world. With his sister's fiancé, William Meredith, he journeyed to Egypt via Europe on a grand tour partly financed by the success of his novel *The Young Duke*, published the year before. While in Thebes, the pair stayed at Wilkinson's dig house, built on the hillside above one of the Tombs of the Nobles, and marked by an ancient sycamore tree. Disraeli later wrote in his memoirs: 'We were a week at Thebes with the advantage of the society of Mr. Wilkinson, an Englishman of vast learning, who has devoted ten years to the study of hieroglyphics and Egyptian antiquity, and who can read you the side of an obelisk, or the front of a pylon, as we would the last number of the Quarterly.'[25] (Wilkinson's house would become a local landmark, a favourite sight for later generations of British tourists, and a convenient base for archaeologists passing through. Lepsius would stay there during his expedition of 1842–5, and scholars stayed there as late as 1909.)

Despite being a fully paid-up member of the establishment, who could count among his friends a future prime minister (Disraeli) and the future Duke of Northumberland (Prudhoe), Wilkinson was not always predictable in his views. His apparent animosity towards Champollion does not seem to have been motivated by prejudice against the French in general, as his friendship with Lebas proves. Moreover, despite the long-standing animosity between the agents of British and French consuls – one of Salt's employees lived just down the hill from Wilkinson's house, while an Italian working for Drovetti had a house nearby; the two men argued frequently over the precise boundaries of their adjoining concessions, and distributed generous bribes to local officials to advance their respective cases – Wilkinson remained neutral. He seems not to have been especially bothered by the removal of the Luxor obelisk to Paris. He happily left his workmen unsupervised, allowing them to steal artefacts and sell them to collectors; yet he took great pains in his own investigations not to damage the delicate reliefs inside the tomb of Seti I. (Champollion, by contrast, 'cut away the sections that pleased him most and carried them away'.[26]) Wilkinson approved of his friends' purchase of women from the Cairo slave market, yet intervened to help the local Theban villagers in their disputes with the overbearing government authorities; they, in gratitude, looked after his house while he was away, and long after he had left Egypt. Perhaps most surprising of all, Wilkinson expressed his public backing for Muhammad Ali's conquest of Syria in 1831, despite a strong, independent Egypt posing a threat to British economic and political interests, and despite fierce opposition from the British government which feared that the premature break-up of the moribund Ottoman empire would be to the advantage of Russia.

A man of inherent contradictions, Wilkinson was nonetheless a dedicated and accomplished surveyor, draughtsman and scholar. Thebes was his special passion, in particular the Tombs of the Nobles with their scenes showing daily life in ancient Egypt. As he later wrote: 'Here, manners and customs, historical events and religious ceremonies, carry us back, as it were, to the society of those to whom they refer; and we are enabled to study the amusements and occupations of the ancient Egyptians, almost as though we were spectators of the scenes represented.'[27]

Among his many lasting achievements, he produced the first comprehensive plan of western Thebes, introduced a numbering system (still used today) for the tombs in the Valley of the Kings, and copied scenes that have subsequently been damaged or destroyed, providing later generations of scholars with an invaluable record of now lost masterpieces of ancient Egyptian art.

Just a year after Wilkinson played host to Disraeli, the world of Egyptology changed suddenly and unexpectedly. Young had died in 1829 and now, in 1832, Champollion was dead, too. The future of the new discipline looked deeply uncertain. On hearing the bad news from Paris, Wilkinson wrote to Hay: 'What a loss – there is an end to hieroglyphics – for say what they like no one knew anything about the subject but himself, though wrong – as must necessarily happen in a similar study – in some instances.'[28]

More alarming still, Wilkinson found himself single-handedly bearing the torch of ancient Egyptian scholarship. Gell wrote to him: 'We must depend upon you for what is to be learned in the future.'[29] Wilkinson was not so sure, replying to Gell: 'He [Champollion] had great self-confidence & much ingenuity. I do not expect to see another like him for this study.'[30] Gell kept sending Wilkinson suggestions for new avenues of enquiry, but the pressure of expectation seems eventually to have become too much for a man who had stumbled on Egyptology quite by accident, and had travelled to Egypt as an extension of his grand tour. Eventually, after nearly twelve years in the country – very probably the longest continuous sojourn of any European since Roman times – he took the momentous decision to return to England, and sailed from Alexandria on 1 June 1833, with a box of mummified heads. (They were duly quarantined on arrival in Livorno.)

Having left Egypt in the throes of Muhammad Ali's reforms, Wilkinson found the country of his birth in no less a state of transition. Since he had been away, Britain had been transformed economically, physically and socially. The first passenger railway had opened between Stockton and Darlington, and the Menai suspension bridge linking Anglesey with the mainland. The Combination Acts forbidding trades unions had been repealed, and the first Factory Act, improving conditions for child workers, passed. Catholic emancipation had been followed by the Great Reform Act. The Metropolitan Police had been established, and the first government grant made to English schools. Morse had invented the electric telegraph, and the Georgian era had come to an end with the death of 'Prinny' and the accession of William IV.

Of more immediate concern to Wilkinson was the change in public attitudes to ancient Egypt. Fashions had moved on, and the manuscript of Wilkinson's travels – the most important ever undertaken by an Englishman – did not find a publisher. Wilkinson lamented to Gell: 'No one cares about Egypt.'[31] This was not entirely fair. The new Egyptian Sculpture Gallery at the British Museum was completed in 1833, the year Wilkinson returned from Egypt, and opened to great popular acclaim. Also that year, Wilkinson's friend, the doctor and antiquarian Thomas Pettigrew, who had known Belzoni and had recently purchased Egyptian antiquities from Salt's collection, conducted a public unwrapping of a mummy in the anatomy theatre at Charing Cross Hospital. According to the *Literary Gazette*, 'the room was attended by many men of literature and science, who warmly greeted the able lecturer when he had concluded his interesting work'.[32] (Over the next eighteen years, the doctor would preside over dozens of similar events, earning himself the nickname 'Mummy Pettigrew'.[33] In 1834, he published his *History of Egyptian Mummies*, which has been called 'the first British scientific contribution to Egyptian archaeology'.[34]) Although no English publisher would take Wilkinson's book, he managed through a friend to have it printed by the government press in Malta. His understanding of ancient Egyptian history was the most accurate yet published, and an advance on Champollion's work.

While the British public's appetite for books on ancient Egypt and for travellers' tales may have waned, the upsurge in the number of tourists visiting Egypt itself showed no signs of abating. The enterprising publishers John Murray spotted a gap in the market and commissioned Wilkinson – for there was none better – to write a travel guide to the Nile Valley. (The first modern guidebook had been published in French a few years earlier.[35]) Now firmly ensconced back in London high society, Wilkinson fitted in his writing around his other social commitments, often working in the early hours of the morning, after returning home from a party. Despite the perils of such an approach, the resulting book, entitled *Topography of Thebes* (1835), was a triumph. Alongside a guide to the major monuments, it included – a first – a handy English–Arabic vocabulary. Wilkinson gave full rein to his views on pharaonic civilization, for example noting with approval that 'the stern regulations of Egypt withheld her monarchs from the fatal allurements of effeminate luxury' and that, 'though riches and splendor took the place of the early simplicity of the Egyptians, they still continued to reject the enervating habits of the East'.[36]

Having spent over a decade in Egypt, Wilkinson knew, better than anyone, the trials and tribulations facing a European visitor, so thoughtfully provided his readers with an appendix listing: 'Things required for travelling in Egypt, and general instructions to those who visit it either from Europe or India.' Nearly two centuries later, Wilkinson's list provides an illuminating, often entertaining, snapshot of those early, pioneering days of Egyptian tourism. It began:

> I shall merely point out the most necessary: – as a camp-bedstead, bedding, and musquito curtain; a camp stool and drawing table; umbrella, double or lined; drawing paper, pencils, and Indian rubber; and if he intends to follow European customs a plentiful supply of tea, wine,[†] cognac, aromatic and distilled vinegar, and as many luxuries as he may think proper.
> [†] I believe white to be better in a hot climate than red.[37]

Falling ill was an ever-present worry for the foreign traveller, and the lack of even the most basic medical facilities in Egypt meant that a European tourist needed to take a full medicine chest. Wilkinson recommended the basic necessities: 'a lancet, diachylon and blistering plaster, salts, rhubarb, cream of tartar, ipecacuanha, sulphate of bark, James's powders, calomel, laudanum, sugar of lead, or sulphate of zink, nitre, oil of peppermint, and other common medicines'.[38] Alongside medicaments, a decent library was the other prerequisite for the serious traveller, and here Wilkinson displayed both his erudition and his familiarity with sources ancient and modern, recommending Herodotus, Champollion's *Phonetic System of Hieroglyphics*, Pococke, Denon, Hamilton's *Ægyptiaca*, *Modern Traveller*, and Colonel Leake's or his own map of Egypt. Other suggestions included works by Browne, Belzoni, Burckhardt, Ptolemy, Strabo and Pliny.[39]

Through the interest and encouragement of his mentor, William Gell, Wilkinson had been transformed from a dilettante into a serious scholar; indeed, after the deaths of Young and Champollion he was the foremost living expert on ancient

Egypt. But, at root, Egyptology had never been a calling for Wilkinson, only a curiosity (albeit one that absorbed him for a decade and a half). When Gell died in February 1836, just a few months after the publication of *Topography of Thebes*, the guiding hand was taken away from Wilkinson's academic pursuits, and he soon found himself without either direction or momentum. His last great Egyptological undertaking, his magnum opus, and in many ways the reflection of his own – rather than Gell's – interests, was a comprehensive study of daily life in ancient Egypt, inspired and illustrated by the scenes in the Tombs of the Nobles which he had studied and copied so meticulously during those long stays in Thebes.

By the 1830s, the fashion for subjective travelogues had given way to more objective ethnographic studies of foreign cultures; Wilkinson's genius was to apply this new anthropological approach to the past. His *Manners and Customs of the Ancient Egyptians* (1837) was an instant success. It was the first book to use ancient Egyptian (as opposed to classical or biblical) evidence to illuminate pharaonic civilization, the first to present the ancient Egyptians as real people rather than figures of myth and legend. Above all, it made Egyptology accessible to a general readership, both creating and feeding an appetite for popular history. (Fortunately for Wilkinson, those scholars who might have sneered at his populist approach had all died.) The book was printed in a handy size and sold at an affordable price (unlike the huge and expensive folio volumes of the *Description de l'Egypte*). Published in the year of Queen Victoria's accession, it remained the definitive account of ancient Egypt throughout her long reign. In a richly ironic gesture, Wilkinson even travelled to Paris to present a copy to King Louis Philippe – a polite two-fingered salute to the late Jean-François Champollion.

⋖○▷

As Wilkinson was writing his *Manners and Customs of the Ancient Egyptians*, one of his friends from his years in Cairo, Edward Lane, was busy with a landmark study of contemporary Egypt entitled *Manners and Customs of the Modern Egyptians* (1836). Taking the same approach to describing a foreign culture, the two became companion volumes; the plans for Lane's book were altered before its publication so that it would appear in the same size, format and style as Wilkinson's. However, while subsequent scholarship has largely rendered *Ancient Egyptians* obsolete (if still an historical curiosity), *Modern Egyptians* has stood the test of time and remains a key text for historians of the Arab world. The story of its conception and creation is an important chapter in the Western rediscovery of Egypt, and an illuminating counterpoint to Wilkinson's adventures.

Little is known about Lane's early life, before he visited Egypt. Like Wilkinson, he came from an educated and cultured middle-class family: his father was a prebendary of Hereford Cathedral, his mother a niece of the painter Thomas Gainsborough. Edward seems to have inherited his great-uncle's artistic talents, and was apprenticed to an engraver in London. Here it was that he first developed an interest in Egypt. When Lane arrived in the capital, one of the city's most famous new landmarks was the Egyptian Hall in Piccadilly, which had opened in 1812 and hosted Belzoni's exhibition of Egyptian antiquities in 1821. Lane, like many others of his generation, was fascinated by Egypt and resolved to visit the country for himself. Unlike most of his contemporaries, however, he prepared for the trip with the greatest scholarly dedication, studying Arabic language and culture for three long years. By the time he set sail, he was as well prepared to study modern Egypt as Wilkinson had been to study its ancient civilization, three years earlier. Anchoring off Alexandria on 19 September 1825, Lane wrote:

As I approached the shore, I felt like an Eastern bride-groom, about to lift the veil of his bride . . . I was not visiting Egypt merely as a traveller, to examine its pyramids and temples and grottoes, and, after satisfying my curiosity, to quit it for other scenes and other pleasures: but I was about to throw myself entirely among strangers; to adopt their language, their customs and their dress; and in associating almost exclusively with the natives, to prosecute the study of their literature.[40]

He stayed first at the house of Henry Salt. The British consul welcomed Lane like an old friend (though the two had never met) and was impressed by his qualities, writing: 'In Lane's praise I cannot say too much.'[41] On closer inspection, however, Alexandria proved to be a disappointment: 'A scene of more complete desolation can scarcely be conceived. Mounds of rubbish and drifted sand occupy nearly the whole site of the ancient city.'[42] So Lane travelled on to Cairo, where he met up with Wilkinson and his circle of friends. Like all new arrivals, Lane lost no time in heading for the pyramids, but, unlike most visitors, he stayed for two weeks to draw the site. In the cool of the evening, he would sit, smoking his pipe, looking out across the Mokattam Hills, the minarets of Cairo hazy in the distance. He slept in a nearby tomb (as would another great English scholar, Flinders Petrie, sixty-five years later). Lane later wrote, 'never did I spend a more happy time'.[43]

In Cairo's close-knit community of English ex-patriots, Lane and Wilkinson became firm friends. They called each other by Arabic nicknames: Lane was Mansoor, Wilkinson Ismail. Yet the two were, in many ways, very different characters. Wilkinson was gregarious, while Lane preferred to work alone. Wilkinson had adopted the dress and customs of Egypt's Turkish ruling class, while Lane lived as a native Egyptian. Even with local dress, excellent Arabic and an open mind, travel in Egypt was still a hazardous affair for a European in the first quarter of the nineteenth century, as Lane and Hay discovered when they decided to visit the pyramids and tombs at Saqqara, about thirty miles south of Cairo. They set off one afternoon on donkeys, with a baggage train for their equipment. By sunset, they had only travelled half the distance to Saqqara, and had already been separated from their luggage and servants. They stopped by a Muslim cemetery, but baulked at sleeping among the tombs, so carried on to a nearby village. Unfortunately, the villagers were wary of strangers, having been attacked the previous night by marauding Bedouin, and would not let Lane and Hay enter. They eventually persuaded them of their good intentions by throwing bread over the walls. Continuing onwards the following morning, they were reunited with the rest of their party. Lane wrote, with characteristic sangfroid: 'our troubles thus ended: our mattresses were spread; and we passed the night very comfortably'.[44] On a subsequent trip to the Fayum, Lane and his companions had forgotten to fill their water flasks; seized with violent thirst, in desperation they drank from a stagnant pool and ate cucumbers from the fields. The result was chronic dysentery that would plague Lane for years to come, even after his return to England.

Despite such hazards, Lane began an extended trip up the Nile in March 1826. Over the course of the next two years, he made copious drawings with the aid of a camera lucida (a device for projecting an image onto a drawing surface) and immersed himself in the Egyptian way of life. Indeed, by the time he returned to England in 1828, he had become so thoroughly Egyptianized – he was, for example, addicted to the hookah – that he found it hard to adjust back into polite London society. He tried to have his drawings published, but the cost of the plates made his proposal for a *Description of*

Egypt unaffordable. Lacking funds, he was unable to accompany his friend Hay back to Egypt in 1830. 'As long as the climate and language of Egypt remain the same,' lamented Lane, 'it will always be the country for me.'[45] Eventually, his deep knowledge and love of the country persuaded a publisher to commission him to write a book about modern Egypt, and he was able to return in December 1833 to undertake further research. Living an exemplary life according to the Islamic code, he was fully accepted in Cairo as an Arab poet and scholar in his own right. Within two years, he had finished the manuscript of *Modern Egyptians*, which was published in December 1836 – a few months before Wilkinson's *Ancient Egyptians* – with his own woodcut illustrations.

Lane's book was a seminal publication. It redefined Egypt as part of the Arab world, and reshaped the Western view of Islamic civilization. While Europeans had long admired the relics of the pharaohs, they had also nurtured a deep-seated Islamophobia, a hangover from stories of the Crusades and the fight for Christendom, which had coloured their view of Egypt. Early nineteenth-century travellers to Cairo marvelled at 'the pyramid and the mosque, the obelisk and the minaret; the sublimest monuments of human industry, amidst the mouldering reliques of Saracenic power'.[46] Other commentators expressed their views more virulently, describing Egypt as 'that nation of sages, and of savages; the source of philosophic illumination, and the sink of barbarous ignorance; the mistress of the mightiest and the tributary of the meanest; earth's palace of splendour, and her hospital of wretchedness'.[47] Lane's *Modern Egyptians*, to the surprise of its readers, dispensed with this lazy, ingrained prejudice, instead portraying Arabic society as complex, coherent and subtle. Even more revolutionary was Lane's insider's view, which helped to foster the notion that the world of Islam might offer an alternative to, even a refuge from, the Western world.⁴⁸ Reviewers were astonished to read a book about Egypt that did not focus on the country's antiquities. One wrote: 'We verily believe the words obelisk, pyramid, temple, never once occur . . . not a mummy crosses his path.'⁴⁹ After reading Lane's book, Thomas Carlyle gave his famous lecture on the underpinnings of Islam, 'the first strong affirmation in European literature of the sincerity of Mohammed'.⁵⁰

Following hard on the heels of *Modern Egyptians*, Lane plunged into another ambitious project, a translation of the *Arabian Nights*, which appeared in monthly instalments between 1838 and 1840. This was followed by a translation of passages from the Qur'an. But Lane's chronic illness, contracted in Egypt, began to reassert itself soon after the death of his mother, and his doctors urged him to move to a warmer climate. It was just the excuse he needed. In 1842 he set off once again for Egypt to begin work on his final magnum opus, a comprehensive Arabic–English lexicon. This time, he was supported by a grant of £150 a year from his old friend, Lord Prudhoe. (This was not as generous as it sounds: the funds had to support not just Lane, but also Lane's wife, sister, two nephews and an Arab translator.) As on his first trip, Lane went fully prepared. He took with him his private library of 130 volumes, housed in bookcases, and a portable writing table.

Lane's sister, Sophia Poole, stayed with him in Cairo for two years, during which time she carried out her own research, visiting harems to observe at first hand the lives of Egyptian women. Like her brother, she was a dispassionate and objective scholar, not bound by the prejudices of many of her contemporaries. She recorded the everyday cruelties suffered by wives, children and slaves, but also the maternal tenderness she witnessed. Her observations of Egyptian women were nuanced and balanced: 'In some cases I have been amused by their familiarity, and in many fascinated by the natural grace of their deportment.'[51] The resulting book, *The Englishwoman in Egypt* (1851), is a feminine counterpart to *Manners and Customs of the Modern Egyptians*, and every bit as remarkable; yet it is little known today.

⊲OĐ⊳

The lot of Egyptian women may not have improved during the early decades of Muhammad Ali's rule, but the country at large was undergoing profound changes. 'Cairo is rapidly becoming more and more unlike what it was,' observed Lane. 'An order was lately issued for extensive "improvements".'[52] This latest wave of modernization had begun back in December 1829, shortly after Lane's first visit, when the Egyptian government had published a sixty-page booklet entitled *Programme for Successful Cultivation by the Peasant and the Application of Government Regulations*. The outcome of a meeting of 400 provincial, military and central officials called to address the problem of declining government revenues, the booklet set out how Egypt's fields were to be worked and which crops were to be grown. It also mandated the confinement of peasants to their villages, where they were to be inspected and guarded.[53] Any peasant who failed to perform his duties would be punishable with twenty-five lashes; the penalty for a second offence was fifty lashes, and a hundred for a third. Sheikhs would also be punished if they neglected their responsibilities. The booklet was followed swiftly by a government order of January 1830, which required all Egyptians to obtain an official permit and identification papers to travel outside their home district. Even the spies were spied upon by those further up the chain of command, all the way to the Central Bureau of Inspection. The result of this oppressive regime was that tens of thousands of peasants ran away and became outlaws, which simply made matters in the countryside worse, heaping yet more burdens and more misery on those who remained.

Yet English commentators, wilfully blind to the sufferings of Egypt's ordinary people, generally approved of Muhammad Ali because he had 'manifested the design, not merely to found a dynasty . . . but at the same time to regenerate and conduct into the track of European civilization a people demoralized and degraded by a thousand years of political servitude'.[54] Even more to his perceived credit, he had done so by studying European methods and hiring European experts. In the 1820s, for example, he had sent a group of twenty young Egyptians to study at Joseph Lancaster's Central School in London, which was organized with military discipline, and a further group of forty-four students from Al-Azhar to Paris to learn modern skills. The latter group travelled with an imam, Rifa'a Rafi el-Tahtawi (1801–73), who, on his return to Egypt, was to become a major figure in the country's nineteenth-century renaissance.[55]

European acquiescence merely encouraged Muhammad Ali to bolder measures to bolster his personal power and his country's independence. Throughout the 1830s, Egypt's efforts at territorial expansion – as we have seen, first an invasion of Syria to compensate for losses at the Battle of Navarino, then a full-scale assault on Constantinople – had to be reined in through protracted diplomatic negotiations. Eventually in 1840, in the face of further Egyptian confrontation with the Ottoman Empire, the European powers called the Convention of London. They offered Muhammad Ali a deal: if he withdrew his forces from Lebanon and Syria, they would grant him and his dynasty hereditary rule over Egypt. His brinksmanship had worked. He had to accept a limit on the size of the Egyptian army, but he had gained his independence from the sultan and established himself as the unquestioned ruler of the Nile Valley.

His political goals achieved, Muhammad Ali duly set about transforming Egypt's economy. His agricultural reforms brought an additional one million acres of land under cultivation, in turn leading to a rapid expansion of the population – from 2.5 million to 4.5 million within the space of twenty-five years. Political stability also led to a surge in Europeans travelling to, and through, Egypt. Within eight years, the number of travellers taking the overland route between Britain and India increased by a factor of ten. The Peninsular & Oriental Steam Navigation Company won the contract to deliver mail to India, and operated on both sides of the isthmus of Suez. In the process, the P&O steamer service via Gibraltar and Malta gave British travellers a faster, more frequent route to Egypt. To cater to this burgeoning number of transit passengers, two English entrepreneurs named Hill and Raven set up a series of rest houses between Cairo and Suez. Each had its own well to supply fresh water, and was stocked with food and drink: beer and ale at a shilling a bottle, and even a modest range of wines. However, even with such comforts, Suez, never mind the Eastern Desert, could not compete with the attractions of Cairo. As a result, hotels run by and for Europeans began to spring up across the capital during the 1830s. A certain Samuel Shepheard was employed to run Hill's hotels, including the one in central Cairo that would later bear his name and become a central fixture in the European experience of Egypt. Passengers bound for India could remain in Cairo until their steamer for India was ready, its arrival at Suez announced by a semaphore relay across the desert.[56]

All this economic development put Egypt's heritage in an increasingly vulnerable position. As early as 1829, Champollion had appealed to Muhammad Ali to protect his country's patrimony. Eventually, six years later, the Egyptian government passed its first piece of antiquities legislation. It blamed

Europeans (with some justification) for the destruction of Egypt's monuments, but also cited European precedents for introducing an export ban on antiquities and the establishment of a national collection. The latter, named the *Antiqakhana*, was initially set up in the Ezbekiya district, under the direction of the imam Tahtawi. However, within a few years, it was already in a parlous condition: 'nothing but a confused mass of broken mummies and cases, some imperfect tablets, and various fragments, which, had they been capable of being spoilt, would have been rendered valueless by the damp of the place'.[57] (Just two decades after its establishment, the collection had disappeared entirely, through a combination of neglect and indifference; the final pieces were presented to Archduke Maximilian of Austria in 1855 as a diplomatic gift.[58])

At the same time as the Egyptian government was passing a law to protect its ancient monuments, Muhammad Ali was giving an order to build eighteen new saltpetre factories, one of them constructed from blocks dynamited from the ninth pylon at Karnak. The thoughtless neglect and wanton destruction of Egypt's pharaonic inheritance provoked a mixture of despair and anger among Western observers. The French claimed the moral high ground, asserting that: 'France, snatching an obelisk from the ever-heightening mud of the Nile, or the savage ignorance of the Turks . . . earns a right to the thanks of the learned of Europe, to whom belong all the monuments of antiquity, because they know how to appreciate them. Antiquity is a garden that belongs by natural right to those who cultivate and harvest its fruits.'[59]

The American consul in Cairo, George Gliddon, was even more outspoken, claiming that 'in destroying the Ancient Monuments of Egypt, the present government of that country has been influenced by avarice, wantonness and negligence'.[60]

He praised Champollion for delivering antiquities 'out of the house of bondage'[61] to the safety of European museums, and launched a vitriolic attack on Muhammad Ali for neglecting, not just pharaonic but also Islamic monuments: 'besides destroying the Monuments of remote Egyptian antiquity, the civilizing and praise-bespattered ruler of Egypt has not erected any substitutes worthy of the slightest notice, nor has he preserved those great and noble Edifices belonging to the religion, of which he is so erroneously termed the Defender and Representative'.[62]

Gliddon painted a bleak picture of what would happen if no action were taken – 'Great will be the disappointment of the traveler . . . to find, – a mound, where a Temple existed – a crater, where a sculptured Pylon but lately stood – a heap of broken stones on the site of a gigantic Portico – a yawning abyss, instead of a Hemi-speos – a powder-blasted cavern, in lieu of a Monarch's tomb!'[63] – in each case citing a real example of a site where this had already happened or was about to occur. He appealed to his readers to intervene before it was too late: 'Let therefore all those parties, individuals, or Societies, who are anxious to save Egypt's remaining Antiquities, from a destruction that will otherwise be swift and inevitable, apply to their respective Governments, and urge the subject upon their enlightened notice.'[64]

As for the handful of Egyptians actively interested in their country's pre-Islamic past, people like Tahtawi conceded the pre-eminence of European scholarship but did not believe this gave foreigners the right to remove Egyptian antiquities at will.[65]

It was in this febrile atmosphere of destruction and mutual recrimination that a third Englishman abroad came to Egypt, with literally explosive consequences.

In contrast to Wilkinson and Lane, Richard William Howard Vyse (1784–1853) was no scholar or aesthete. He was an army man through and through. His father had been a general, his grandfather a field marshal. Following in the family tradition, Vyse joined the British army in 1800 at the age of sixteen and won rapid promotion up the ranks: lieutenant in 1801, captain in 1802, major in 1813.[66] He combined his military duties with two terms as a Member of Parliament for Beverley and then for Honiton (this, of course, was before the Great Reform Act).

Vyse arrived in Egypt at the end of December 1835, intending to visit the major sites, satisfy his curiosity, and prove the historical veracity of the Bible. He later wrote: 'Among the many objects of interest . . . the Pyramids, particularly those of Gizeh, attracted my attention.'[67] He was intrigued by their age, purpose and construction, and determined to break open their secrets. True to his military instincts, Vyse first carried out reconnaissance on the Giza plateau, before commencing 'operations' in November 1836. There had been previous half-hearted attempts to explore the pyramids. By contrast, Vyse was resolved to leave no stone unturned. His account of the expedition is peppered with references to 'blasting': 'Two quarrymen were employed in blasting the stones in the lower entrance of the Second Pyramid';[68] 'Daoud was sent to blast in Davison's Chamber; and small charges of gunpowder were used in the other works wherever they could be applied.'[69] The pyramid of Menkaura, with its lower courses of granite casing, had proved particularly intractable to earlier investigators, but Vyse was not going to be deterred: 'I was resolved to examine every part of the pavement, and even to take down the face of the building; in short, to leave no expedient untried, with whatever expense of money or time it might be attended, to find the mysterious entrance';[70] 'the mortar was nearly as hard as the stone itself, so that with Arab workmen, and common tools, it was a most tedious operation . . . Towards the end of this work gunpowder was used with great effect.'[71]

The impact on the monuments was matched by the deleterious effects on Vyse's workmen – 'Achmet, the Janissary, was sent to Cairo on account of ophthalmia . . . a circumstance not to be wondered at, considering the dust and heat to which he had been constantly exposed by night as well as by day in the bottom of the shaft of the Third Pyramid'[72] – but the pyramids duly yielded up their secrets. In the Great Pyramid, Vyse discovered a further set of relieving chambers above the burial chamber. These he named, without a hint of irony, after famous Britons of his day: the Duke of Wellington, Admiral Nelson, the now obscure Lady Arbuthnot, and the (long since forgotten) diplomat Patrick Campbell. In his diary entry for 28 April 1837, Vyse proudly recorded: 'Mr Hill inscribed Nelson's great name in the chamber lately discovered.'[73] In the pyramid of Menkaura, Vyse located the burial chamber which still housed the king's basalt sarcophagus. This was promptly extracted and sent to the British Museum in London, but was lost at sea when the ship carrying it, the *Beatrice*, sank off the coast of Spain. (It still awaits recovery.) Vyse also bored into the back of the Great Sphinx, attempting to find a hidden chamber. The great statue put up stiff resistance to the assault – 'The boring rods were broken owing to the carelessness of the Arabs, at the depth of twenty-seven feet in the back of the Sphinx. Various attempts were made to get them out, and on the 21st of July gunpowder was used for that purpose'[74] – but eventually yielded. Nothing was found.

Vyse was utterly confident of his own abilities and secure in his own views. Unsurprisingly, he fell out with his first assistant, Caviglia. Vyse subsequently hired a civil engineer from Lincolnshire, John Shae Perring, lately arrived in Egypt as manager of public works for Muhammad Ali. Vyse left

Perring to complete the work at the pyramids, and returned to England to resume his military career.[75] Despite its (numerous) shortcomings, Vyse's work at the pyramids was, nonetheless, the most important undertaken at Giza during the nineteenth century, and the resulting publication remained a standard work well into the twentieth. Having travelled to Egypt to prove the veracity of the Bible (which attributed the pyramids to the Shepherd Kings), Vyse returned to England having definitively shown that they were, in fact, royal tombs of the Old Kingdom. It was a small but significant victory for archaeology over ideology.

Even as Vyse was working at Giza with his sticks of dynamite and boring rods, two important developments signalled the dawning of a new era for the study and conservation of Egypt's cultural heritage. In Cairo, European residents with a serious interest in antiquity founded the Egyptian Society. Inspired by memories of Napoleon's short-lived Institut d'Egypte, its objective was to serve as 'a rendezvous for Travellers, with the view of associating literary and scientific men, who may from time to time visit Egypt'.[76] Membership grew steadily, from an initial dozen or so to over a hundred within seven years. The society acquired a good working library, and conferred honorary membership on all the distinguished European figures of Egyptian scholarship: Jomard and Rosellini, Wilkinson and Lane. In London, at the same time, another future member, Samuel Birch, began his long and distinguished career at the British Museum. Over the next half-century, he would establish the museum as a leading centre of scholarship on ancient Egypt, bringing a new professionalism to the work of cataloguing and studying its growing collections. Every scholar interested in Egypt, from Lepsius to Budge, would beat a path to Birch's door. He would go on to found the influential Society of Biblical Archaeology; and he would assist both with the publication of Vyse's expedition report and with the revisions to Wilkinson's *Manners and Customs*.

As for Wilkinson himself, after *Manners and Customs* was published in 1837, his considerable energies increasingly took him in different directions. When he had left Egypt, back in 1833, he had told his friend Hay that he planned to return within two years. But he was soon diverted by other interests. He spent much of his time visiting his wide circle of well-read and well-heeled friends, painting refined watercolours of their country houses, indulging his love of conversation and debate. He corresponded with the scientist Charles Babbage, and with Byron's daughter, the mathematician Ada Lovelace. He joined the Oriental Club and the Athenaeum; the latter was housed in a new building designed by James Burton's younger brother, Decimus, and hosted the Cabinet for dinner most Wednesdays. Wilkinson's two clubs, along with the Royal Society and the Royal Society of Literature – he had been elected a fellow of both – and the Royal Geographical Society – where he became a member of the council – provided intellectual stimulation aplenty. He enjoyed his role as a public intellectual, his opinion being sought on the great issues of the day, and he was knighted in 1839 (he chose to be known as 'Sir Gardner' rather than 'Sir John').

Wilkinson maintained more than a passing interest in Egyptology, advising the British Museum, to which he had donated some of his collection of antiquities, on further acquisitions. In 1841, he finally returned to Egypt to gather material for a second edition of his *Topography of Thebes* (renamed *Modern Egypt and Thebes* (1843)). He did not like what he found. He wrote to Ada Lovelace: 'Egypt is much spoilt since I saw it before . . . the travellers who go up the Nile will I fear soon be like Rhine tourists & Cheapside will pour out its legions upon Egypt.'[77] Of course, these very travellers were the people for whom he was writing *Modern Egypt and Thebes*, just as they would be the readers of its successor volume, Murray's *A Handbook for Egypt* (1847), one of a series that set the pattern for all subsequent tourist guides.

Wilkinson returned to Egypt and Nubia for a third time in the winter of 1848–9, sailing upstream as far south as the temple of Gebel Barkal, a site that only a handful of Europeans had visited. From his close study of pharaonic monuments, Wilkinson had developed a keen interest in ancient Egyptian architecture; but, when it came to publishing the material, he had chosen to leave the field clear for his friend Hay. Only when it became apparent that Hay was never going to deliver did Wilkinson complete his own study, publishing it privately by subscription. *The Architecture of Ancient Egypt* (1850) appeared in the same year as David Roberts's six influential volumes of lithographs of *The Holy Land, Syria, Egypt and Nubia*.[78] Wilkinson's book may not have had such a wide circulation, but its impact on mid-nineteenth-century architecture was profound. Suddenly, Egyptianizing forms became all the rage, often in the most unlikely contexts. John Marshall's flax mill in Leeds had a facade modelled on the temple of Edfu, and a smokestack disguised as an obelisk. The architects of the Albert Memorial even briefly considered an Egyptian design.

In October 1855, suffering from ill-health, Wilkinson sailed again to Egypt for the fourth and last time, but sunstroke kept him confined to his cabin for much of his stay. Egyptological scholarship, which he had done so much to foster, had come on in leaps and bounds, and a new generation of scholars had left him behind. Edward Lane's nephew, Reginald Stuart Poole, kept him abreast of new developments; but Wilkinson was now an observer rather than an active participant. On his return to Britain in 1856, he married Caroline Lucas, a woman twenty-four years his junior to whom he had been introduced by a mutual friend, the Welsh heiress Lady Llanover. In Caroline's company, he spent his final years living on the Gower Peninsula, his interests focussed on Welsh culture and British antiquities. He died in 1875 and was buried at Llandovery in a grave marked by a monument of his own design, in the shape of an obelisk.

Meanwhile, Lane – the only one of Wilkinson's friends who maintained a lasting interest in Egypt – had struggled to find a publisher for his monumental *Arabic–English Lexicon*. The Prussian government had promised to cover the costs of printing, but the 1848 revolutions in Europe scuppered the plan. Eventually, Lane persuaded his friend Lord Prudhoe (who had succeeded to the dukedom of Northumberland in 1847) to finance the work, while Lane and his family had to subsist on a modest annual grant from the British Government Fund for Special Service. After 1849, he never returned to Egypt, but continued to work on the *Lexicon* for the rest of his life, devoting himself to it nearly every day. It remains supreme in its field. Lane died in 1876, just ten months after Wilkinson.

Back in their youth, in the 1830s, Wilkinson and Lane, together with their group of friends and fellow-travellers, had transformed the West's engagement with Egypt. The pharaonic past, which under Champollion had been the preserve of erudite specialists, was made accessible to an interested public. And Arab Egypt, for so long seen through the lens of Crusader tales and the *Arabian Nights*, was revealed as a vibrant, complex and rapidly modernizing society. Above all, through their companion volumes of *Manners and Customs*, Wilkinson and Lane had given life to the people of Egypt, past and present. Dismissed by later generations as amateurs and dilettantes, Wilkinson and his colleagues are only now finally gaining recognition for their lasting contribution to Egyptology.[79]

FOUR

The Prussian project

Richard Lepsius and members of his Prussian expedition atop the Great
Pyramid at Giza, in an illustration by the expedition artist Johann Frey.

My next plan: a scientific expedition to Egypt and
the copper-rich lands in Arabia.[1]

RICHARD LEPSIUS, 1840

Napoleon and Nelson, Salt and Drovetti, Young and
Champollion: during the first three decades of the nineteenth century, the scramble for Egypt – to describe, acquire,
understand and control – was a two-horse race between France
and Britain. Champollion made it possible to understand
pharaonic culture in its own words, on its own terms; Wilkinson
and Lane opened up new avenues of enquiry, and made
Egyptian civilization, ancient and modern, accessible to the
general reading public. But after Champollion's death in 1832,
none of his associates or pupils had the same depth of learning,
the same drive or determination, to take his linguistic studies
any further. After the death of Gell in 1836, Wilkinson's
research on ancient Egypt lacked direction, and Britain's leadership in Egyptian archaeology and history waned. The infant
discipline of Egyptology could have died there and then. With
France convulsed by the aftermath of the July revolution of
1830, and Britain preoccupied with political, social and industrial upheavals, the world of ancient Egypt struggled to compete
for attention. Moreover, French and British archaeologists had
found a new arena for their rivalry: Mesopotamia.[2] What was
needed, if the study of Egypt's ancient past was to take the
next leap forward, was a new force, and a new champion.

The changes that swept Europe in the 1830s, challenging and transforming the old powers of Britain and France, also provided a window of opportunity for a new power to assert itself, on the continent and further afield. The kingdom of Prussia had been born in the early eighteenth century from the union of Brandenburg and territories to the east, and had come through a series of conflicts – the War of the Spanish Succession, the Seven Years War, the Napoleonic Wars – with its territories intact and its position strengthened. A German customs union was established on 1 January 1834, largely at Prussian behest, ushering in a new era of prosperity and economic opportunity.[3] When French forces crossed the Rhine in 1840–1, a wave of German nationalism was unleashed which Prussia was able to ride and exploit. The result was that, by 1842, Prussia had emerged, unchallenged, as the engine of German power in Europe, and a serious rival to the colonial ambitions of Britain and France.

Ever since the days of ancient Rome, upstart nations had turned to the past to legitimize their power: by appropriating the cultural glories of an illustrious predecessor, a new polity might lay claim to the mantle of leadership and assert its place on the world stage. France had done it with the Napoleonic expedition, and with the subsequent transport of one of the Luxor obelisks to Paris. (Charles X had been assured that if Paris gained an obelisk, 'it would no longer have any reason to envy Rome'.[4]) Britain had done it by claiming the Rosetta Stone as war booty, and by the transport of the Young Memnon to London. Now Prussia, as the new European power, looked to the past to seize the present and assert its future.

Cometh the hour, cometh the man. By a remarkable coincidence, Karl Richard Lepsius (1810–84) was born exactly twenty years to the day after Champollion, and was destined to pick up the torch he had lit so brightly. Lepsius, too, showed an early genius for languages, studying Sanskrit, comparative philology and archaeology at the universities of Leipzig and Göttingen, and gaining his doctorate in 1833 with a dissertation on ancient Italian dialects. He could have taken his studies in any direction. The fact that he chose Egypt was due to three other towering figures of nineteenth-century German scholarship, men who were to act as mentors, advocates and supporters throughout Lepsius's career, guiding his energies and directing his enthusiasms to the benefit of Egyptology. The first, and eldest, was Alexander von Humboldt, polymath and scientific adviser to successive Prussian monarchs. Humboldt's interests were extraordinarily wide-ranging and he personally knew most of the leading European intellectuals of the age. (As we have seen, he attended the landmark session of the Académie des Inscriptions et Belles-Lettres in 1822 at which Champollion announced the decipherment of hieroglyphics; Humboldt would act as a pall-bearer at Champollion's funeral ten years later.) The second of Lepsius's mentors was Carl Josias von Bunsen, another scholar of astonishing range and ability. Besides being a noted expert in oriental languages, philology, theology and ancient history, Bunsen was also an accomplished diplomat, serving for the best part of two decades (1824–41) as Prussian minister-resident in Rome, and then for a further fourteen years (1841–54) as Prussian ambassador in London (where his circle of acquaintances included Wilkinson and Birch). Completing the triumvirate was the archaeologist Eduard Gerhard, who spent most of his time in Rome where he and Bunsen had founded the Institute of Archaeological Correspondence in 1829 under the patronage of the then crown prince of Prussia.

During his years in Italy, Bunsen surrounded himself with a brilliant intellectual circle, akin to Gell's in Naples, welcoming visiting scholars to discuss and debate the latest discoveries and ideas. It was in this context that Bunsen was introduced to Champollion (when the latter visited Rome in April/May 1825) and thus to the emergent discipline of Egyptology. For the rest of his career, Bunsen eagerly followed the development of the subject, corresponding with its leading practitioners. The publication of Rosellini's *Monumenti dell'Egitto e della Nubia* in 1832 confirmed the importance of Egyptian civilization. The following year, Gerhard encountered Lepsius in Berlin and recommended him at once to Bunsen: here was the man to spearhead Egyptological studies in Prussia. At Gerhard's encouragement, Lepsius travelled to Paris to spend three years learning about Champollion's system of decipherment and conducting his own private research. Champollion had died the year before Lepsius's arrival, but it was as if the standard of Egyptological scholarship passed seamlessly from one man to the other, Lepsius picking up where Champollion had left off. Lepsius's studies not only confirmed the correctness of Champollion's system, but took Egyptian philology to the next stage, enabling, for the first time, the translation of running hieroglyphic texts as opposed to mere names and epithets.[5]

With such an auspicious start to Prussian Egyptology, Humboldt suggested to the Berlin Academy of Sciences that it should formally adopt the new discipline as one of its areas of research; and who better to lead it than Lepsius? After initial reservations about devoting his career to a still nascent field, Lepsius agreed, and set about learning Coptic, gathering copies of ancient texts, and immersing himself in hieroglyphics. In 1836, a grant from the academy – again facilitated by Humboldt, Bunsen and Gerhard – allowed Lepsius to make an extended study trip to Italy. His itinerary followed closely that of Champollion a decade earlier. In Turin, he made copies of the *Book of the Dead* and the Turin Royal Canon; in Pisa, he met, and received encouragement from, Champollion's pupil and co-director of the Franco-Tuscan expedition, Rosellini; in Livorno, he studied Egyptian artefacts being held in storage; and in Rome, he met members of Bunsen's circle, including the chaplain to the Prussian diplomatic mission, Hermann Abeken, and the Swiss artist Johann Frey, who made engravings for Lepsius of the hieroglyphic inscriptions on Roman monuments. Bunsen and Gerhard showed their faith in Lepsius by appointing him secretary of the Institute for Archaeological Correspondence, and he established its periodical, the *Annali dell' Istituto*, as a major vehicle for Egyptological scholarship. The result of this first intensive period of study was the publication, in 1837, of Lepsius's *Lettre à M. le Professeur H. Rosellini sur l'alphabet hiéroglyphique* – a conscious homage to Champollion, which both championed his illustrious predecessor's system and extended it by demonstrating the existence of syllabic as well as phonetic signs. Lepsius left Rome in 1838, prepared for the second phase of his career, which, like Champollion's, would take him to Egypt itself.

⊲⊙⊳

Back in 1820–1, before Champollion or Wilkinson had set foot on Egyptian soil, the Berlin Academy had sent an expedition to the Nile Valley to collect antiquities. In the absence of an archaeological expert, it had been led by a Prussian army officer, Johann Heinrich von Minutoli, accompanied by two doctors-cum-naturalists, Christian Gottfried Ehrenberg and Wilhelm Friedrich Hemprich. They had visited distant Siwa, reached as far south as Dongola (Hemprich died in Abyssinia), and collected antiquities, as well as specimens of flora, fauna and minerals. Some of the pharaonic objects they brought back were sold in Paris and seen by Champollion; others were acquired for the Berlin Museum. Perhaps the most important outcome of the expedition was the interest in Egypt that it sparked in the young crown prince of Prussia, an interest which Minutoli encouraged and which Humboldt and Bunsen nurtured. As a result, in 1827, the prince bought the collection of Egyptian antiquities amassed by Passalacqua, which had been offered to but rejected by the French government. It formed the core of the new Berlin Museum, and Passalacqua duly had himself appointed as the first curator of Prussia's Egyptian collections.

On 7 June 1840, the old Prussian king died, and was succeeded by his eldest son, the crown prince, as Friedrich Wilhelm IV (r.1840–61). The scholars of the Berlin Academy seized their moment. Just six months later, on 21 December, Humboldt sent the new king a formal proposal for an Egyptian expedition, suggesting Lepsius as its leader. The expedition needed a proven scholar with expertise in hieroglyphics as well as pharaonic civilization; Lepsius, in financial difficulties and struggling to establish himself in Berlin, needed the expedition to advance his career. It was a mutually beneficial arrangement. To advance the cause, Lepsius wrote directly to the royal palace, pleading for this chance to secure his own and his family's prospects. He noted: 'Your Royal Majesty has so favourably and graciously deigned to express yourself regarding the truly confidential advice of Humboldt about my next plan: a scientific expedition to Egypt and the copper-rich lands in Arabia,' and undertook to obtain 'insights not accessible to Champollion' if the king would only authorize the expedition to commence 'next autumn for 1½ to 2 years at the state's expense'.[6] The antiquarian monarch could not resist, and, before the year was out, granted funds for a major expedition to depart for the Nile Valley the following autumn.

Planning started at once. The king appointed his minister for religious, educational and medical affairs, Johann Albrecht Friedrich Eichhorn, to oversee preparations. The first task was to identify the expedition members. Lepsius had specifically requested an architect, in order to make accurate measurements of all the monuments, something that neither the Napoleonic nor the Franco-Tuscan expedition had undertaken. He explained: 'It is especially desirable for me to have the assistance of a technician to pursue the architectural objectives of the expedition which have, until now, been so unfairly neglected given that they constitute so important a part of Egyptian cultural history.'[7]

A suitable candidate soon presented himself, in the form of the Berlin-based architect and surveyor, Georg Erbkam. However, within days of Erbkam's appointment, Lepsius began to have doubts that the rest of the preparations could be accomplished in the allotted time. If his was to be a properly scientific expedition, not just another antiquarian voyage up the Nile, it would need meticulous planning, and a great deal of advance research. He had already begun to formulate in his mind the questions he wanted the expedition to solve. Foremost among them were various unexplained intricacies of ancient Egyptian chronology. To make serious strides in this area, Lepsius realized, would require a detailed knowledge of the extant sources, notably the Turin Royal Canon. There was no way he could master the document, as well as make all the other arrangements, in a few short months. Reluctantly, he shared his doubts with his mentors. They were in agreement. In March 1841, Bunsen wrote to Eichhorn, asking for the expedition to be postponed. A few weeks later, Humboldt wrote to the king in the same vein. The financial uncertainty created by a year's delay would be more than compensated for by the extra time for preparations.

Lepsius set to work on the Turin Royal Canon, and on the *Book of the Dead* in the same collection. Embarrassingly, two of his academic mentors, Bunsen and the classicist August

Boeckh, favoured radically different approaches to ancient Egyptian history; Lepsius could not afford to upset either, so he produced only a handwritten manuscript of the Canon. But he was able to publish his edition of the *Book of the Dead* (*Todtenbuch der Aegypter nach dem hieroglyphischen Papyrus in Turin*), a copy of which he proudly sent to the Prussian king as a new year's gift on 3 January 1842. Lepsius also took advantage of the expedition's postponement to visit the most important European collections of Egyptian antiquities, in Paris, Leiden and London, leading to a second publication, *Auswahl der wichtigsten Urkunden des Aegyptischen Altherthums.* His scholarship was now making significant strides, and before the spring was out, the king controversially appointed Lepsius to an extraordinary professorship in the faculty of philosophy at Berlin University. (The faculty already had twenty-three extraordinary professors, against a budget for only fourteen, and had argued against creating a post in Egyptology; but Eichhorn successfully persuaded the king that an official government expedition should be led by someone with professorial status. Prussian pride prevailed.)

His major pieces of philological and cultural research accomplished, on 24 May 1842 Lepsius sent a formal prospectus to Eichhorn, setting the context and outlining his proposals for the forthcoming expedition: 'In the twenty years since Champollion's *Lettre à M. Dacier*, Egyptian history has been revealed, at first back to the time of Moses and Jacob, now back to the first flowering of the Old Kingdom.'[8] He went on to chart the main achievements of Egyptology to date, including the Franco-Tuscan expedition; to laud Young as the forerunner of Champollion; to praise Wilkinson's recently published *Manners and Customs*; and to note the zeal with which antiquities were being acquired in England through private as well as government enterprise, so that the British Museum now possessed the greatest collection of sculpture and manuscripts after Turin. The prospectus was carefully calculated to press all the right buttons: by praising the achievements of French and British scholars, it shone a light on the notable absence of comparable German scholarship; by referring to the impressive Egyptian collections in London and Turin, it highlighted the second-rate status of Berlin's collection.

Having piqued Prussia's sense of its own destiny, Lepsius proceeded to elaborate the goals of his expedition: 'to investigate and collect, with an historical and antiquarian view, the ancient Egyptian monuments in the Nile Valley, and upon the Peninsula of Sinai'.[9] The few living Egyptologists (Rosellini, Wilkinson, Birch, and Leemans[10] in Leiden) were either focussed on philology or busy curating museum collections; nobody was pursuing the study of pharaonic history. That would be Lepsius's task, and his opportunity. He wanted to understand ancient Egyptian culture, as represented through art, mythology and language, not only in its own terms but also in relation to other cultures and to world history. The expedition would systematically collect the material for such a study. It would also fill in the gaps left by the Napoleonic and Franco-Tuscan expeditions, especially in relation to ancient Egyptian architecture.

Thanks to his meticulous research, Lepsius knew exactly which sites he would need to visit to solve the chronology of the Old Kingdom (a term first coined by Bunsen to refer to the first great flowering of pharaonic civilization during the Pyramid Age, *c.*2575–2175 BC). He had identified Memphis, the Fayum, the Delta, Abydos and the Wadi Hammamat – sites largely ignored by Champollion – as the most promising. He also intended to reach the oases of the Libyan Desert and the copper mines of Sinai. The expedition would seek to understand the relationship between Egypt and Nubia, and to locate the Ramesside monuments in Asia Minor, Syria and Palestine.

Lepsius further suspected that there were more eighteenth-dynasty royal tombs awaiting discovery in the Valley of the Kings. The expedition would set itself the task of taking paper squeezes (applying wet papier maché to the surface of a relief to create a durable impression) and making copies of every significant relief and inscription from pharaonic Egypt. Finally, if all this were not enough, Lepsius would target the removal of key antiquities for the Berlin Museum, to make the Prussian state collection the equal of those in London, Paris, Leiden and Turin. Specifically, he had in mind the carved list of kings from Karnak (the British Museum had a version from Abydos); the scene of desert tribespeople bringing tribute, from the tomb of Khnumhotep at Beni Hasan; the scene of brickmakers (believed to be Hebrews in bondage) and the figures of Amenhotep I and Queen Ahmose-Nefertari from the tomb of Rekhmira at Thebes; either or both of the small obelisks of Senusret I at Heliopolis and Crocodilopolis; and a representative selection of historical papyri and Coptic manuscripts. All in all, it was a colossal set of objectives.

The members of the Berlin Academy were impressed by Lepsius's ambition, but rather doubted that so many goals could be achieved in just two years. They also thought his proposed budget (of 19,000 thaler) wholly inadequate. Going for broke, on 19 June they authorized Eichhorn to forward the proposal, supported by copious expert testimony, to the king, but with a total budget of 33,100 thaler – 25,000 thaler for the expedition, 1,000 thaler for purchases, 3,000 thaler for transport (which Lepsius had completely forgotten to include), and 1,100 thaler for final preparations. To everyone's relief, the sum was granted. The expedition would go ahead. (In the final account, it cost 34,600 thaler – an overspend, but not a large one.)

There followed feverish activity to identify the remaining members, who would contribute so much to the endeavour's success. Lepsius wanted not one, but two draughtsmen, explaining that 'a second draughtsman for sculpture and sites is almost essential, for when the first is busy copying inscriptions'.[11] Two brothers currently in Berlin, Ernst and Max Weidenbach, came highly recommended, but Max (then aged nineteen) was due to begin his military service the following year. Lepsius wrote to the ministry of foreign affairs to request a deferment. He had already signed up an old friend from his Rome days, Johann Frey, but he also wanted a moulder who could make plaster casts of important statues, and had in mind a sculptor from his home town of Naumburg, Carl Franke. The Prussian government agreed to fund all six participants – Lepsius, Erbkam, the Weidenbachs, Frey and Franke – and to send Abeken (another of Lepsius's Roman contacts) as expedition chaplain 'who in various ways promoted the antiquarian objects of the journey'.[12] Two further members would join the party in London before departure: a second architect, James Wild, and Joseph Bonomi, a trusted and experienced Egypt hand, who had been part of Wilkinson's circle in Cairo.

Following the London Convention of 1840, the Prussian diplomatic presence in Egypt had been sharply reduced, leaving the country's interests in the hands of the Swedish consul-general, Anastasi. This turned out to be a blessing in disguise, since Anastasi was well known to Muhammad Ali. Nonetheless, Lepsius was taking no chances in preparing for his expedition. In early July 1842, he wrote to the Prussian foreign minister, Heinrich von Bülow, asking him to seek a firman from the Ottoman sultan in Constantinople, and another from Muhammad Ali, together with letters of recommendation from the foreign ministers of Austria, Britain and France to their agents in Egypt making clear the antiquarian nature of the expedition: Lepsius wanted not only to obtain official permission, but also to avoid potential conflict with other countries' agents employed to collect antiquities. Finally, to oil the wheels, the Prussian king wrote to Muhammad Ali to add his personal seal of approval to the endeavour, and sent a pair of vases from the royal porcelain factory as a gift. The pasha was delighted with the present, proclaiming the Prussian porcelain superior in quality to the French dinner service he had received from Louis Philippe of France a decade earlier.[13] The reciprocal diplomatic niceties were appreciated on both sides.

In one last request, Lepsius – conscious that the Egyptian collections in Berlin were under the direction of Passalacqua – asked that, while all antiquities brought back from Egypt would be the property of the Prussian state, he should be granted unfettered access to them for his lifetime. It would prove a canny move. With this request granted, everything was in place. Lepsius set sail from Southampton on 1 September 1842 on the greatest, and best-prepared, scientific expedition to Egypt that had ever been attempted. As he noted afterwards: 'It was fitted out and maintained for more than three years by the munificence of the King, and enjoyed uninterruptedly his gracious favour and sympathy, as well as the most active and kind attention from Alexander v. Humboldt, and by a rare union of fortunate circumstances, it attained the purposes they had in view, as completely as could be expected.'[14]

After 'a stormy passage through the Bay of Biscay and a short stay in Gibraltar and Malta',[15] Lepsius landed in Egypt on 18 September, to rendezvous with the other members of the expedition who had arrived via different routes. Despite the assistance of Anastasi, Lepsius was concerned at the lack of Prussian diplomatic support on the ground, noting to his friend Graf Usedom that: 'The Turks set great store by protocol, good recommendations, and an introduction by an important person.'[16] Not only was Prussia without representation, nobody in Alexandria believed that the head of the Prussian legation in Constantinople, von Wagner, would ever visit Egypt, let alone take up residence. Lepsius pleaded for a Prussian representative to be based permanently in the country.[17] In the event, Lepsius need not have worried. Still smarting from the London Convention, Muhammad Ali was casting around for a friendly European nation. The rising power of Prussia fitted the bill perfectly. As a result, Muhammad Ali's firman, when it arrived, was unusually generous, giving Lepsius 'unlimited permission to make all the excavations which I might think desirable, and with instructions to the local authorities to render me assistance'.[18] Furthermore, the recent legislation prohibiting the export of antiquities was waived in Lepsius's favour. So it was with confidence and a sense of possibility that the expedition left Alexandria, bound for Cairo and the start of an epic programme of work.

Egypt's capital had changed considerably since Champollion's expedition fourteen years earlier. Most noticeable, perhaps, was the huge increase in the number of resident Europeans. What had been a relatively small community of around 3,000 in 1836 had grown to a sizeable population of 50,000 by the end of the 1840s.[19] To accommodate the burgeoning number of Western visitors, Cairo's tourist infrastructure was also undergoing something of a transformation. Wilkinson noted the changes in his 1843 *Modern Egypt and Thebes*: 'The first hotel for some years has been Hill's, or the Eastern Hotel. But its place is now taken by the Hôtel d'Orient . . . which is said to be very comfortable.'[20] He was full of admiration for the entrepreneurs – 'In a place like Cairo, where the houses are badly suited for hotels, where European comforts are unknown, and where every thing has to be created afresh to suit the convenience of travellers, great praise is due to any one who has sufficient enterprise to set up one of these large establishments'[21] – but they were simply responding to a growing market. Among the tourists who passed through Cairo in the 1840s were Gustave Flaubert and Florence Nightingale; indeed, they arrived within two days of each other, but stayed in different hotels. Flaubert was attracted by the exoticism of the Orient and the easy availability of prostitutes. Nightingale, on the other hand, was horrified by the poverty and squalor she encountered in the backstreets of Egypt. She wrote to her parents: 'No European can have the least idea of the misery of an African village; if he has not seen it, no description brings it home.'[22]

It was not just the poverty that appalled Nightingale. For many in Muhammad Ali's Egypt of the 1840s, life was nasty, brutish and short. While the London Convention had reined in the pasha's territorial ambitions abroad, it had done nothing to constrain his use of military force at home. Although much reduced in number, the Egyptian army was being put to good use to round up deserters from Muhammad Ali's harsh economic regime and return them forcibly to their villages. On the large private estates set up to produce cash crops for the European market, the workers were treated little better than slaves. As the situation deteriorated, a new law of April 1844 laid down the death penalty for anyone found harbouring outlaws. In such a climate, desertion from the army spiralled, and men resorted to self-mutilation to avoid conscription. Muhammad Ali's answer was further repression, and a ruthless emphasis on obedience and discipline. The Egyptian government even set up a school in Paris, run by the French ministry of war, to inculcate these values in young Egyptians who, it was intended, would return to Egypt equipped to become the country's future leaders.

By contrast with the increasingly despotic Muhammad Ali, Lepsius's royal patron, Friedrich Wilhelm IV of Prussia, was a benevolent monarch. Moreover, he was actively interested in ancient Egypt and had made the whole expedition possible. Not since the days of Napoleon had a European ruler shown such a commitment to antiquarian and archaeological study. For this reason, perhaps, Lepsius decided that 15 October 1842, the king's birthday, should be marked in style with the expedition's first visit to the pyramids at Giza. It was a memorable occasion, laden with patriotic feeling:

> The morning was beautiful beyond description, fresh and festive. We rode in a long procession through the yet quiet city, and through the green avenues and gardens which are now laid out before it . . . It is impossible to describe the scene that met our view when we emerged from the avenues of date-trees and acacias; the sun rose on the left behind the Moqattam hills, and illuminated the summits of the Pyramids in front, which lay before us in the plain like gigantic rock crystals. All were overpowered, and felt the solemn influence of the splendour and grandeur of this morning scene . . . What a spectacle, and what recollections did it call forth! When Abraham came to Egypt for the first time, he saw these very Pyramids, which had been already built many centuries before.[23]

To celebrate the occasion, the expedition members climbed to the top of the Great Pyramid and unfurled the Prussian flag. (Frey made a memorable drawing of the scene, which now rests in the department of drawings in the National Gallery in Berlin.) They also sang the Prussian royal hymn inside the burial chamber. Finally, as a more permanent gesture, they carved and set up a commemorative inscription on a stone tablet, five feet wide and four feet high, painted in bright colours. Carefully composed in hieroglyphics, the text was probably the first extensive translation into ancient Egyptian for fifteen centuries. It ran:

> Thus speak the servants of the King, whose name is the Sun and Rock of Prussia, Lepsius the scribe, Erbkam the architect, the Brothers Weidenbach the painters, Frey the painter, Franke the moulder, Bonomi the sculptor, Wild the architect: All hail to the Eagle, the Protector of the Cross, to the King the Sun and Rock of Prussia, to the Son of the Sun, who freed his Fatherland, Frederick William IV, the Philopator, the Father of his Country, the Gracious One, the Favourite of Wisdom and History, the Guardian of the Rhine, whom Germany has chosen, the Dispenser of Life. May the most high God grant the king, and his Consort, the Queen Elizabeth, the Rich in Life, the Philometor, the Mother of her Country, the Gracious One, an ever new and long life on Earth, and a blessed habitation in Heaven through all Eternity. In the year of our Saviour, 1842, in the tenth month, on the fifteenth day, on the forty-seventh Birthday of his Majesty, on the Pyramid of King Cheops.[24]

It was a composition worthy of a pharaoh. In a sign of his easy mastery of the principles of ancient Egyptian script, Lepsius substituted the Prussian eagle for the usual falcon in the king's title, and used it to stand for 'Prussia', while a double-headed eagle signified 'Germany'. The inscription duly installed, Lepsius swelled with pride – young Prussia had left its mark on the greatest monument from antiquity. Others were less impressed; back in England, Wilkinson wrote to a friend: 'You have of course read Dr Lepsius's letters from Egypt & I dare say have wondered as I have how people could be so silly as to put that inscription in hieroglyphs on the great Pyramid about the King of Prussia & the rest. The English have been laughed at for scribbling their names but this far exceeds in folly any thing done by them.'[25] One may detect just a hint of jealousy.

Returning to Giza for a second visit on 9 November, Lepsius's expedition set up camp to start its systematic exploration of the site. It would take more than six months. As Lepsius noted, Champollion and Rosellini 'did little more than pass through' and, other than the recent 'operations' by Vyse and Perring, 'little had been done to promote a more minute investigation of this remarkable spot'.[26] New Year's Eve 1842 was marked with the lighting of bonfires on the tops of the pyramids, but Lepsius and his team kept at it: 'Still always here! in full activity since the 9th November, and perhaps for several weeks longer in the new year. But yet, how could I suspect from the accounts that have hitherto been given by travellers what a harvest we had to gather on this spot.'[27]

Upwards of forty workmen were employed to clear the sand and rubble from around the monuments, but not everything went to plan. In the first few months of 1843, the expedition was visited by a succession of disasters, some of them almost biblical in scale. First, a sudden rainstorm and flash flood destroyed the camp, washing away belongings 'into the muddy, foam covered, slimy lake, our books, our drawings, sketches, linen, instruments of all kinds'; dripping wet, the men had to wade waist-deep to retrieve their possessions, or rather 'what the sand had not yet swallowed'.[28] Then, a few weeks later, a swarm of locusts ravaged the country for miles around. The following month, an armed mob attacked the camp one night, plundering it for anything of monetary value. Lepsius was sanguine, recording 'none of our party were seriously injured, and nothing that is irreparable was lost. The affair, therefore, is over, and the consequences may only prove a useful lesson to us.'[29] Thereafter, the camp was patrolled each night by eight watchmen, permanently on guard against attacks by Arabs or Bedouin. Finally, to add insult to injury, Lepsius was struck down by a violent cold and had to return to Cairo to recover. 'It is to be hoped that my state of health will not detain me long here,' he lamented, 'for my impatience daily increases to return from the living city of the Mamelukes into the solemn Death-city of the old Pharaohs.'[30]

Lepsius summed up the various trials and tribulations suffered by the expedition in its first six months:

> It appears that we are to have a taste of all the plagues of Egypt. Our experience began with the inundation at the Great Pyramids; then came the locusts . . . which, combined with the previous cattle disease, is indeed sufficient to cause a famine; then occurred the hostile attack which was preceded by a daring robbery. Nor has even a conflagration been wholly wanting. By an incautious salute, Wild's tent was set on fire and partly burned in Saqâra . . . Now comes, in addition, to this, the annoyance of mice . . . they gnaw, play, and squeak away in my tent . . . During the night they run over my bed, and over my face . . . In spite of all these annoyances, however, we continue to keep up a good and cheerful spirit.[31]

To cap it all, Frey was taken seriously ill and had to return to Europe. (It may have had something to do with the expedition's drinking habits: Lepsius had declared 'the Nile water is pleasant to the taste, and may be enjoyed in great abundance without any detriment'.[32]) Lepsius certainly felt responsible, and asked the Prussian government for extra funds to support both Frey and his elderly mother. Archaeology in Egypt in the 1840s was no walk in the park.

Lepsius's expedition may have set new standards in the study of individual sites and monuments, but it took a retrograde step where preservation was concerned. Armed with a royal firman, it plundered with abandon, sending statues, stelae and even entire tomb chapels back to Berlin to grace the city's museum. A train of ten camels was needed to transport the loot from Giza to Cairo. Yet, with no hint of irony, Lepsius complained about the quarrying of monuments: 'It is really shocking to see how every day whole trains of camels come here from the neighbouring villages, and march back again in long files, laden with building stones.'[33] A decade earlier, Wilkinson had baulked at hacking reliefs out of tomb walls, but Lepsius felt no such qualms. Certainly, the parlous state of the official government collection of antiquities did nothing to persuade him to leave priceless artefacts in situ. Muhammad Ali had talked about founding a national museum, but even enlightened European scholars like Wilkinson had scoffed at the notion, declaring that: 'the formation of a Museum in Egypt is purely Utopian; and while the impediments raised against the removal of antiquities from Egypt does an injury to the world, Egypt is not a gainer. The excavations are made without knowledge or energy, the Pasha is cheated by those who work, and no one there takes any interest in a museum.'[34]

One of the objects Lepsius especially wanted to acquire was the Karnak king list. But his rivals had other ideas. In the summer of 1843, as Lepsius was making his way upstream, the French adventurer, Achilles Prisse d'Avennes, whom Muhammad Ali had appointed as an engineer and lecturer in military schools, cut the block from the temple, working secretly at night, right under Lepsius's nose, and loaded it onto his boat to take down the Nile, and onwards to Paris. As the two men passed on the river, Prisse d'Avennes invited Lepsius aboard and sat him down on a crate which, unbeknownst to Lepsius, contained the priceless relic.[35] It was a typically extravagant and pointed gesture by the Frenchman, and a reminder to the Prussians that national rivalries were alive and kicking in the race for Egypt's past.

Stopping only briefly at Thebes, Lepsius's expedition pressed on southwards, 'impatient to commence immediately our second fresh task, which consisted of the investigation of the Ethiopian countries, situated higher up the river'.[36] This was Lepsius's chance to get one up on the French (and the British), given that: 'The French-Tuscan expedition did not go beyond Wadi Halfa, [while] Wilkinson's careful description of the Nile land and its monuments . . . only extends a little higher up, as far as Semneh.'[37] Lepsius's patriotism, and his eagerness to best the French, did not however affect his deep admiration for Champollion, with whom he felt a special connection, given the coincidence of their birthdays. On 23 December 1843, Lepsius's thirty-third birthday, and what would have been Champollion's fifty-third, the Prussian composed a rather clumsy, if heartfelt, poem to his hero, and committed it to his journal:

Champollion! Champollion!	*Champollion! Champollion!*
Erklingt ihr Gläser, ting, tang, tong!	*Let your glasses ring out, ting, tang, tong!*
Daß er's im Grab erfahre!	*That he may experience it in the grave!*
Ihm gilt der heutige Ehrentag,	*To him belongs today's auspicious day,*
Ich kam ihm weit, weit hinten nach,	*I came far, far, behind him,*
Fast 21 Jahre.	*Almost 21 years.*
Champollion! Champollion!	*Champollion! Champollion!*
Erklingt ihr Gläser, ting, tang, tong!	*Let your glasses ring out, ting, tang, tong!*
Champollion soll leben!	*Champollion shall live!*
Vermöcht'ich was auf seinem Pfad,	*Might I do something on his path,*

Wie gern wollt'ich in Wort und Tat,	*How much would I like, in word and deed,*
Ihm gern die Ehre geben.[38]	*To do him the honour.*

The study of Upper Nubia and its native languages was, in many respects, the expedition's most groundbreaking and lasting achievement. Knowledge of the Nile Valley beyond the Second Cataract was still very limited; few Europeans had travelled that far south, and the conditions were extremely difficult and dangerous. But Lepsius was not easily disheartened (as the series of disasters earlier in the year had shown). At Korosko, the expedition had to wait for two months for camels to take them on to Meroë. One of the beasts was subsequently killed by a lion.[39] The party eventually reached Khartoum on 5 February 1844, and spent the next five months carefully exploring all the sites downstream to Wadi Halfa. The political crisis that erupted between Muhammad Ali and his son in July that year – though word of it reached Europe and prompted Lepsius's concerned father to write a letter, asking after his son's safety – scarcely touched the distant reaches of the Nile. By the time Lepsius and his colleagues had regained civilization, the crisis had passed.

The expedition's next major sojourn was at Thebes, where Lepsius and his colleagues spent a total of seven months, four on the west bank and three at Karnak on the east. The effect of the city's magnificent monuments was energizing. Lepsius wrote: 'Here, where the Homeric figures of the mighty Pharaohs of the eighteenth and nineteenth dynasties meet me in all their splendour and magnificence, I feel once more as fresh as at the beginning of my journey.'[40] He certainly needed abundant reserves of energy, for, as he soon realized: 'The number of monuments of all kinds, both above and below ground, at Thebes, is so great that they may be truly called inexhaustible, even for a combined power like ours.'[41] A complete survey and record of every Theban monument being an impossibility, the expedition selected those it believed most important to achieve its stated goals, and focussed its efforts accordingly. The team stayed in Wilkinson's house while carrying out excavations nearby, and Lepsius recorded his thanks to the Englishman for having 'rendered an essential service to later travellers by building up the habitable rooms, which, from our being desirous of spending a long time in Thebes, we have profited by'.[42]

By March 1845, the end of the expedition was fast approaching, and Lepsius was anxious to finish the collection of major antiquities for the Berlin Museum. Of his original targets, neither the scene of desert tribespeople nor the scene of brickmakers could be removed without damage; the obelisk of Senusret I at Crocodilopolis turned out to be not an obelisk at all, but 'more an obelisk-like elongated stela';[43] while the obelisk at Heliopolis, which was indeed a true obelisk, was rumoured to have been promised by Muhammad Ali to the pope. It wasn't a great start. Lepsius knew he needed antiquities that were truly monumental, befitting a royal expedition and a national collection. What he had in mind was nothing less than an entire wall of the Ramesseum, and he wrote back to Berlin seeking permission to begin the deconstruction work. But the Prussian government, not wanting to jeopardize its newfound favour with Muhammad Ali, baulked. The Ramesseum, Ramesses the Great's 'temple of a million years', remained intact. A sequence of Old Kingdom funerary chapels at Giza and Saqqara was not so lucky. Before an export licence had even been granted, workers were sent in secret to dismantle three chapels.[44] Only when the blocks had been taken down and packed did Wagner seek the pasha's permission to ship them to Berlin. As it was, on 9 September, Lepsius had to report that the chapels could not yet be dispatched because winter ice would prevent the ships entering German harbours, and storage costs in England or Holland were much higher than in Alexandria. Wagner, by now thoroughly fed up with Egypt and no doubt regretting his move from Constantinople, left for a holiday in Berlin and expressed the hope that he would never have to return. He took one of the expedition members with him, while the others made their own way. Lepsius remained in Alexandria, watching over his precious cargo.

Eventually, Lepsius left Egypt at the beginning of October, over three years since his arrival in the country, and, after a brief detour to his home town of Naumburg, was back in Berlin in January 1846 to start work on publishing his results. And what results they were.

⊲⊙⊳

The success of the expedition exceeded all expectations, and fully justified the trust placed in Lepsius as its leader. As he had hoped from the outset, the most important results were in the fields of history and chronology. Careful study of the monuments of the Old Kingdom, a period largely neglected by Champollion and Wilkinson, pushed the origins of Egyptian civilization back by a millennium, and situated them firmly within the Nile Valley. (Earlier generations of scholars had sought them in Ethiopia or even India; Lepsius's knowledge of comparative linguistics, and his careful exploration of Nubia, disproved both hypotheses.)

The historical existence of the Old Kingdom, and the order of succession of the twelfth dynasty rulers were conclusively demonstrated, and the hiatus of the Amarna Period – when the 'heretic pharaoh' Akhenaten brought in sweeping changes to Egyptian religion, art and architecture – was revealed for the first time. At Thebes, Lepsius identified a previously unknown ruler of the eighteenth dynasty, the female pharaoh, Hatshepsut; and by systematic study of inscriptions, correctly established the chronology of the thirteenth, fifteenth, seventeenth and twentieth dynasties of kings.

In others areas of enquiry, the results were no less impressive. Thousands of paper squeezes and copies of inscriptions brought new insights into ancient Egyptian – 'The lexicon has been increased by our becoming acquainted with several hundred signs, or groups, and the grammar has received a great many corrections'[45] – while Lepsius's study of Nilotic languages (spoken by peoples of the Upper Nile, and distantly related to ancient Egyptian) was truly groundbreaking. He revealed the different canons of proportions (the rules laid down for the depiction of the human body) used at different periods of Egyptian history, so that: 'The different epochs of Egyptian art now first appeared clear and distinct, each marked by its peculiar character . . . They had so frequently been misunderstood, that no one believed in their existence; they were lost in the general uniformity.'[46]

The expedition brought back maps and plans of the Nile Valley, and of individual sites, 'more perfect and exact than any hitherto made',[47] as well as stone and soil samples from 'the more remarkable localities'.[48] And then there were the antiquities. Before leaving Alexandria, Lepsius had received a firman authorizing the removal of the collection, which was to be regarded as a gift from Muhammad Ali to the Prussian king. In total, there were 15,000 antiquities and plaster casts. Once the winter ice had melted, they arrived in Hamburg on 23 May 1846, marking the official end of the expedition. Unloaded and brought to Berlin, they made the city's museum, at a single stroke, a serious rival to those in Paris, London and Turin. In recognition of Lepsius's superlative contributions to science and the fatherland, he was named, by royal appointment, professor of Egyptology at Berlin University with a salary of 1,500 thaler.

There was, however, a fly in the ointment. Lepsius had transformed the Egyptian collection in Berlin, but another man, Passalacqua, controlled it. Lepsius wanted to create a dramatic new display, which would stand as a permanent monument to his expedition, showing the development of Egyptian art and culture. The objects would be arranged chronologically, replacing the old 'cabinet of curiosities' with a modern, scientific layout. In Lepsius's view, this was no more than Berlin deserved. After all, since the beginning of the decade, Egyptian antiquities had formed the centre and the main attraction of the British Museum's collection in London; moreover, the museum's guide explicitly recognized Egyptian art as standing at the head of the Western art tradition, 'the source from which the arts of Sculpture and of Painting, and perhaps even the Sciences, were handed to the Greeks – and from the Greeks to us'.[49] The new displays Lepsius had in mind for Berlin would demonstrate the point even more clearly. He also had firm views about the decoration of the galleries themselves, favouring coloured scenes from Egyptian temples and tombs as the most suitable backdrop for pharaonic artefacts. Not everyone agreed. As one commentator put it diplomatically, 'the decoration of the rooms in the Berlin museum by no means meets with such universal approbation'.[50] But Passalacqua, out-argued and out of his depth, had to give way. Lepsius got his new display, and the Egyptian galleries opened to public acclaim in 1850. Lepsius became co-director of the museum in 1855, and director on Passalacqua's death ten years later.

The Berlin Museum has since been redesigned more than once, and Lepsius's colourful, neo-pharaonic decorative scheme has been swept away. The most enduring memorial to his expedition is to be found, not in bricks and mortar, but in paper and ink – in the form of the most massive Egyptological publication ever produced (or ever likely to be). Lepsius's ambition in this respect was clear and straightforward: to publish the results of the expedition 'in a style corresponding with the magnificence of the treasures we brought away with us'.[51] He wrote to his father in March 1847: 'The proposal for the great atlas, which I have set forth in 1000 folio plates, is now before the king, or nearly . . . The sums are significant, and must, of necessity, come from the public purse . . . So it is possible that the Minister of Finance may strike out the budget, unless the king himself approves it.'[52]

It fell to Lepsius's most trusted mentor, Humboldt, to plead the case. The Prussian king needed little persuasion, however, and immediately granted 15,000 thalers as a first instalment, giving Lepsius the green light to proceed. The finished work, *Denkmäler aus Aegypten und Aethiopien*, eventually ran to 894 folio plates, published in twelve enormous volumes. As another Egyptologist remarked: 'One needs a corporal and four soldiers to use your Lepsius' *Monuments*.'[53] It was, and remains, astonishing both for the quantity and quality of the contents. According to Lepsius's pupil and biographer, the *Denkmäler* 'is, and must ever remain, the chief and most fundamental work for the study of Egyptology'.[54] As a record of the last major expedition to Egypt before the advent of photography,[55] the work effectively sums up the heroic efforts of the early nineteenth-century antiquarians and archaeologists. Wilkinson had in his private library a copy of the *Denkmäler*, given to him by the German emperor. Lepsius's great work is still the most prized publication in the history of Egyptology.

To accompany the *Denkmäler*, Lepsius also published his letters from Egypt, which he had written to Eichhorn, to his academic colleagues, and especially to his father. He dedicated them to Humboldt 'with the profoundest veneration and gratitude'. Unlike the monumental official tomes, they were aimed not just at antiquarians and scholars, but also at the general public:

> to offer a picture to a larger circle of interested readers of the external features of the Expedition, the personal cooperation of the different members belonging to it, the obstacles, or the fortunate circumstances of the journey, the condition of the countries that we traversed, and the influence they exercised on the immediate objects of our understanding; finally, a series of remarks on the individual sites of the monuments in that most historical of all countries . . . which may also excite an increased sympathy in others who have acknowledged the great importance of this newly established science.[56]

Like Wilkinson before him, Lepsius hoped to win converts to the emergent discipline of Egyptology. Unlike Wilkinson, the end of Lepsius's great adventure in Egypt was not accompanied by any diminution of his scholarly output. Quite the reverse. Over the remaining forty years of his career, he published essays on the construction of the pyramids, the Nile height measurements at Semna, and the language and culture of the Ethiopians; the first scientific study of ancient Egyptian chronology, *Die Chronologie der Aegypter* (1849), which sparked criticism from theologians because it challenged biblical orthodoxy, but laid the foundations for all subsequent studies; a comprehensive king list of Egyptian rulers; a Nubian grammar; and a study of measurements and proportions in the ancient world. He discovered a bilingual inscription, the Canopus Decree, which proved Champollion's system of decipherment beyond doubt, and he was the first to tackle the question of Egypt's prehistoric past. At the opening of the Suez Canal in

1869, Lepsius led the new Prussian crown prince (later Emperor Friedrich III) on a Nile cruise, and from 1874 until his death he was director of the Royal Library.

Few others in the history of Egyptology – not even Champollion – can claim so many achievements. In 1850, the Berlin Academy, where Lepsius's career had begun, elected him a full member (he had been made a corresponding member in 1844, during the expedition to Egypt), thus publicly recognizing that the study of ancient Egypt stood alongside theology, philology and all the branches of learning, on its own merits. Champollion cracked the code, Wilkinson gave the ancient Egyptians a human face, but it was Lepsius, through his meticulous and systematic approach, who separated Egyptology from classical antiquity and founded it as an independent, scientific discipline.

FIVE

French foundations

A seated statue of King Khafra, found in situ in
his valley temple at Giza by Auguste Mariette.

This was like taking possession of Egypt for the cause of science.[1]

AUGUSTE MARIETTE, 1858

Eighteen forty-eight was the year of revolutionaries and revolutions across Europe and beyond. In London Marx and Engels published their *Communist Manifesto*. In Bohemia and Hungary there were nationalist risings, forcing the Hapsburg emperor Ferdinand to abdicate. In France, King Louis Philippe was overthrown, ushering in the Second Republic. Egypt, too, experienced its own dramatic political change with the deposition of Muhammad Ali on grounds of senility. The Albanian soldier who had murdered the Mamluks, thumbed his nose at the Ottoman empire, and played the European powers off against each other, had not only won recognition for himself as the de facto independent ruler of Egypt and for his heirs and successors as hereditary viceroys: he had also, during the course of his forty-three-year reign, transformed Egypt from a pre-industrial, feudal society into a thrusting country with a vibrant economy in a headlong rush into the modern age. Through force of will and of arms, he had imposed a planned economy, revolutionized agricultural production, introduced cash crops to boost exports, built factories and mills to reduce Egypt's dependence on imports, and improved transport and communications through the construction of roads and bridges, canals and dams. As regular visitors could not fail to notice, Egypt in 1848 was almost unrecognizable compared to the country Muhammad Ali had inherited.

But, as commentators were also quick to point out, all this modernization had been achieved at a heavy cost. The long-suffering fellahin, backbone of Egypt's rural economy, were especially hard pressed. A combination of demanding production targets, heavy taxes, military conscription and the dreaded corvée (conscripted labour, levied as a form of taxation) made life for an average Egyptian peasant tough and unrelenting. Not just the general population but also Egypt's patrimony bore the brunt of Muhammad Ali's development. From Champollion's in the 1820s to Gliddon's in the 1830s, there had been no shortage of appeals to the Egyptian ruler to protect the country's ancient monuments before any more damage was done. But these appeals had fallen on deaf ears. As far as the pasha was concerned, portable antiquities were a handy currency, while larger monuments like obelisks were powerful bargaining chips that could be used to buy support and influence. If Westerners were passionate about the relics of Egypt's past, that merely gave Egypt's present ruler greater leverage. The fate of the first national collection of antiquities was a case in point: it had been neglected, given away as trinkets, and the remaining pieces presented to an Austrian archduke as a diplomatic gift. While Muhammad Ali had introduced a few pieces of antiquities legislation, they had been more honoured in the breach than in the observance, and were customarily waived at the ruler's whim. Antiquarians and archaeologists with a genuine concern for pharaonic civilization were either despondent, angry or resigned: there seemed little prospect of change, little likelihood of a comprehensive package of measures to protect Egypt's heritage, at least while Muhammad Ali remained in charge.

So his removal from office in July 1848, and the succession, in short order, of his eldest son Ibrahim (who reigned for only four months) and then his nephew, Abbas Hilmi I (r.1848–54), offered the prospect of change. At the same time, thanks to the stunning achievements of Lepsius's expedition and the popularity of his public lectures, the recent publication of Champollion's *Monuments de l'Egypte et de la Nubie*, and the runaway success of Wilkinson's *Manners and Customs*, the study of ancient Egypt had regained the popularity it had previously enjoyed in the time of Belzoni. Indeed, the subject now had its own name: the word *égyptologie* first appeared in a French dictionary in 1850. (It would take another nine years before its English equivalent, 'Egyptology', made it into the *Oxford English Dictionary*; when it came to matters Egyptological, the French always got there first.) As for the French authorities, newly energized by the overthrow of a repressive and moribund monarchy and the return to Napoleonic values (the man who emerged, rather swiftly, as president of the new Constituent Assembly was none other than Bonaparte's nephew, Prince Louis-Napoleon), and no doubt inspired by memories of Bonaparte's achievements during the First Republic, they looked again to Egypt to secure their national pride. Since the death of Champollion, the baton of Egyptology had been surrendered to France's fierce rivals, Britain and Prussia. It was time to take it back.

The man appointed for the task was not an obvious choice. Auguste Mariette (1821–81) had nurtured an interest in ancient Egypt since childhood, prompted by visits to the local museum in his home town of Boulogne-sur-Mer. The museum's Egyptian collection was small, but choice. It had been formed in 1824, and supplemented with further acquisitions during the 1830s. The object that particularly gripped the young Mariette's imagination was a sarcophagus that had once belonged to Vivant Denon, leading member of the Napoleonic expedition and doyen of early nineteenth-century Egyptology.

When Mariette was nine years old, his mother died and he was largely thrown back on his own devices, spending hours at the museum, learning all he could about ancient Egypt. However, for someone of limited means and provincial background, the study of ancient Egypt hardly provided good prospects. So, at the age of eighteen, Mariette crossed the Channel to take up a job as a teacher of French and drawing at the Shakespeare House Academy in Stratford-upon-Avon. It didn't suit him. After a year, he moved to Coventry to be apprenticed to a ribbon maker, but struggled to make ends meet. England had let him down, so he returned to Boulogne to finish his studies and seek a career.

It was shortly after Mariette's graduation, with a master of studies from the Collège de Boulogne, that another death in the family changed the whole direction of his life. In 1842, a distant relation, Nestor L'Hôte, who had been a member of the Franco-Tuscan expedition to Egypt under Champollion, died, bequeathing to his relatives in Boulogne all his papers. They included a huge number of notes and drawings made during a total of three visits to Egypt. Mariette devoured them, learning the hieroglyphic alphabet and the principles of decipherment. He had found his calling. As he would later explain: 'The Egyptian bug is a formidable creature. Once you've been bitten by it, it won't let you go.'[2] For seven long years he immersed himself in private study while holding down a series of more or less dull, provincial jobs. He studied the plates in the *Description de l'Egypte* (unaware of the many errors), learned Coptic (as a prerequisite for the serious philological study of ancient Egyptian), and published an analytical catalogue of the Egyptian antiquities in the Boulgone museum. In 1849, he managed to secure a minor post at the Louvre, allowing him to devote himself full-time to Egyptology; but he found it difficult to survive in the French capital on a lowly salary. Nonetheless, the museum authorities were impressed by his diligence and dedication, especially after he succeeded, in little more than twelve months, in transcribing all the inscriptions then in the Louvre's collection – an enormous feat.

The opening in 1850 of Lepsius's new Egyptian galleries at the Berlin Museum, to great public acclaim, reignited the competition between European capitals to acquire and display the best Egyptian artefacts. The Louvre, which since the time of Champollion's directorship had enjoyed a position (real or perceived) of pre-eminence, suddenly felt threatened. The museum authorities therefore decided it was time to boost their collection in areas not hitherto well represented. Above all they wanted to acquire manuscripts of the early Christian period, in Coptic, Ethiopic and Syriac, to compete with the remarkable Papyrussammlung (Papyrus Collection) in Berlin. As for the best person to accomplish such a task, their thoughts turned naturally to the young employee who had single-handedly transcribed all the existing inscriptions, and who knew Coptic as well as hieroglyphics. So it was that, in the late summer of 1850, they agreed to send Mariette to Egypt, with a modest budget of 6,000 francs, on a mission of acquisition.

Mariette embarked at Marseille on 4 September 1850, on the aptly named *Osiris*, a post steamer in service across the Mediterranean, and landed in Egypt six weeks later. Like many a European traveller before him, he was immediately struck by the quality of the light, and by the heat and smells of Egypt. Like other antiquarians of his time, he was also struck by the wholesale destruction of monuments taking place all around him. He wrote to his brother: 'Every day, I witness a new loss to science; every day, I learn of a further catastrophe.'[3] But as a twenty-nine-year-old employee of a foreign government, he was powerless to intervene. The best he could hope for was a chance to excavate and record those monuments still surviving, before it was too late.

First, however, before he could have any chance of securing a dig, he had to satisfy his employers back in Paris. So he installed himself at the Hôtel d'Orient in Cairo, a favourite haunt of French expatriates and tourists, where Gustave Flaubert and his friend and fellow writer Maxime du Camp had stayed the previous year, and made his introductions to the Coptic patriarch, in the hope of securing a good haul of ancient manuscripts. But, as he was soon to discover, in the competitive antiquities market there were losers as well as winners. Back in the 1830s, two English collectors, Robert, Lord Curzon, and the Reverend Henry Tattam, had gone to Egypt in search of early Christian manuscripts, and had stripped the monasteries of their prize collections. Not surprisingly, when another 'collector' arrived eleven years later, seeking further manuscripts, the Coptic patriarch was unwilling to cooperate.[4] Mariette was rebuffed, and it looked as though his mission was doomed from the outset.

It turned out to be a blessing in disguise. With no prospect of achieving what he had come for, Mariette decided to follow his own instincts, and to gamble the Louvre's funds and his own career on an excavation. And not just any excavation. For Mariette had decided he was going to try to find the long-lost Serapeum. The monument sacred to the god Serapis had been famous in classical times as one of the wonders of Egypt. In the first century BC, Strabo had written: 'There is also a Sarapium at Memphis, in a place so very sandy that dunes of sand are heaped up by the winds; and by these some of the sphinxes which I saw were buried even to the head and others were only half-visible; from which one might guess the danger if a sand-storm should fall upon a man travelling on foot towards the temple.'[5]

Mariette would have been familiar with the description,[6] but it was not enough, on its own, to pinpoint the location. After all, the Memphite necropolis stretched over a distance of some thirty miles of desert, and was dotted with pyramids, tombs, and sand dunes. However, Mariette was blessed with a photographic memory, and a rare ability to make connections in his mind. With his eagle eyes he had spotted clues that had apparently escaped others' notice. On first landing in Alexandria, he had seen a number of small stone sphinxes, and had thought little of it. But when he noticed two similar statues in the garden of the Ecole Polytechnique in Cairo, he began to wonder. He traced them to the antiquities dealer Salomon Fernandez, whose valuable collection had attracted the attention of both Wilkinson and Lepsius. It turned out that Fernandez still had three identical sphinxes in his storeroom. Moreover, they all came from the same part of the Memphite necropolis, close to the Step Pyramid. Mariette had his lead, and he set off at once for Saqqara, with his trusty assistant Marius François Joseph Bonnefoy, a friend from Boulogne.

Mariette's first task was to produce a detailed map of the site. (He was unaware of the results of Lepsius's expedition, as the *Denkmäler* had not yet been published.) It seemed like an almost impossible task. The jumble of tombs and shrines, of damaged and reused monuments, of subterranean galleries and hidden shafts, combined with the ever-shifting dunes, presented a daunting picture. To make matters worse, carrying out any sort of antiquarian or archaeological work at Saqqara meant first negotiating access with local Bedouin tribes who regarded the site as their property. Fortunately for Mariette, his imposing figure (1.8 metres tall, with ginger hair), gave him a forbidding presence – local villagers nicknamed him 'the red giant' – and he was able to secure their agreement. Setting straight to work, his systematic approach soon bore fruit. As he later recalled:

'One day, walking across the necropolis, metre-rule in hand, seeking to disentangle the plans of the tombs, my eye fell on another of these sphinxes. It was a revelation. Although three-quarters buried, it was clear that this sphinx was in its original location. The avenue which had furnished the collectors of Cairo and Alexandria with so many monuments was therefore found.'[7]

Hurried excavations around the buried sphinx revealed an offering table inscribed with a prayer to Osiris-Apis. The pieces of the puzzle were coming together: Mariette knew that the fabled Serapeum must lie nearby. Without permission from his employers at the Louvre, and without an Egyptian government permit, on 1 November 1850 he traced out on the sand the line of what would be his first excavation. He soon discovered a second sphinx – just twenty feet from the first, but buried sixteen feet deep in sand – then another, and another. By late December, after two months' work, he had revealed no less than 134 sphinxes. Then the avenue disappeared.

A less dedicated scholar might have given up, there and then. Not Mariette. On Christmas Eve he found the 135th sphinx on an axis perpendicular to the first part of the avenue. The race to locate the Serapeum was back on. Along the new axis, the discovery of a chapel dedicated to the sacred Apis bull by the pharaoh Nectanebo II, a statue of the household deity Bes, and a perfectly preserved sculpture of a seated scribe[8] reassured Mariette that he was on track. But the conditions made large-scale excavation almost impossible. The sand simply poured back in as quickly as it could be removed. Working in such unpleasant conditions brought on an acute eye infection, and Mariette had to return to Cairo for medical treatment. By the time he got back to Saqqara, a sandstorm had blown away his tent. Mariette was undeterred. In any case, he travelled light – all his belongings fitted into two cases and an iron trunk –

and he had only a single book with him, being blessed with a prodigious memory. (If he needed a precise reference he could consult a friend's library in Cairo.)

Mariette continued digging, uncovering dozens of bronze statuettes that pilgrims to the Serapeum in pharaonic and Classical times had left behind as votive offerings. Most were in poor condition, but any discovery of a metal object from beneath the sands of Egypt soon had tongues wagging. Rumours of buried treasure started circulating, and a government inspector was sent from Cairo to investigate. But still Mariette perservered, digging without a permit, working by night to avoid detection, and resting by day in a rough shelter he had erected nearby that was marginally more robust and comfortable than his erstwhile tent.

At last, after a year's toiling in the longest and deepest trench ever dug through the sands of Egypt,[9] his labours bore fruit. At three o'clock in the morning, the coldest time of night, on 12 November 1851, he came upon a lintel of polished white limestone. He knew it must be part of a doorway, a doorway to the Serapeum, but what might lie beyond? Before he could satisfy his curiosity, dawn began to break. At this of all moments, he could not afford to be discovered excavating illegally. So he ordered his workmen to cover up all traces of the lintel, fill in the trench, and erase their footprints as they retreated. The following night, as soon as darkness had fallen and the antiquities inspectors had clocked off, Mariette began again where he had left off, exposing the lintel and clearing away the fallen stones that blocked the doorway. A rush of stale air emanating from the gap indicated a void beyond, and a lighted candle put through the hole went out immediately. He enlarged the opening to allow in some fresh air, and to give him room to wriggle through. Then, with a rope tied around his waist, he climbed into the hole and descended into the darkness. After a drop of about six feet, his feet touched the floor. Before his candle was extinguished by the asphyxiating atmosphere, he had just enough time to look around and take in his surroundings. In the gloom, he could make out the lines of a vaulted gallery, cut into the rock, some ten feet high and around twice as wide. It looked endless. The floor was covered with the debris of centuries: broken stelae, statues, votive objects, *shabti*s (servant figurines), and *ostraca* (flakes of limestone used for jottings). In a side chamber, he glimpsed an enormous stone sarcophagus. Other than a few robbers, it seemed probable that he was the first person to enter the catacomb for twenty centuries. But he had precious little time to savour the moment: almost on the point of suffocation, he reluctantly called to his workers above to haul him back up. Having regained the fresh air, he whispered to his co-conspirator Bonnefoy, 'I was right.'[10] Mariette's months of toil, '*à la recherche du temple perdu*,'[11] had paid off. He had discovered the Serapeum.

It was not only the find of the century, but indeed the first great archaeological discovery in the history of Egyptology. Yet, for the moment at least, it had to be kept quiet. The only people Mariette entrusted with the news were the French consul-general in Egypt, Arnaut Lemoyne, and the engineer and explorer, Louis Linant de Bellefonds who had worked with Bankes, Belzoni and Champollion, and had been the first European to explore the Upper Nile. It fell to Lemoyne to reach a diplomatic agreement with the pasha's court, and to clear matters with the authorities back in Paris. The French were first off the mark, recognizing the importance of the discovery and the glory it would bring, not to mention the 230 cases of antiquities excavated by Mariette that were destined for the Louvre. The French parliament voted funds to transport the finds to Paris, but they had jumped the gun: the pasha had not yet agreed to an export licence and he promptly sent guards to stop further excavations. Mariette simply did what he had done before, digging secretly at night; he also had one of his assistants produce fake antiquities to fob off the inspectors.[12]

European rivalries in the scramble for ancient Egypt, for so long at work behind the scenes, now came out into the open. Under Abbas's rule, the British could have been forgiven for believing they were winning the race for influence in Egypt. For example, in July 1851, the pasha had signed an agreement with Robert Stephenson (son of the *Rocket*'s inventor) to build a railway between Alexandria and Cairo – not merely the first line in Egypt, but the first anywhere to the east of continental Europe. Stephenson went on to be confirmed as chief engineer of the Egyptian railways, and another Briton, an army officer from India, was appointed director. While British engineering was busy transforming modern Egypt, reconstructions of the country's ancient monuments, made for the Crystal Palace, were having a profound influence on British art and scholarship.[13] The authorities in London must have felt they had Egypt in their pocket. So Mariette's arrival on the scene, and the resurgence of French archaeological prowess, came as an unwelcome wake-up call.

Both the British and the Austrian consuls lobbied Abbas to take a hard line against Mariette, but Lemoyne managed to broker a compromise: over a hundred objects found to date could be sent to the Louvre, and Mariette would be allowed to continue with his excavations, but all future finds would remain the property of the Egyptian state.[14] On 19 November 1852, the pasha formally relinquished his government's claim to the antiquities already discovered, but refused to sanction further excavations until his ownership of future finds was legally recognized. But possession was nine-tenths of the law, and Egyptian inspectors were no match for the wily Mariette. He continued to excavate clandestinely and hid his finds in a deep underground shaft before smuggling them out in grain sacks. With Lemoyne's complicity, they were loaded onto French ships and escorted by French navy frigates out of Egyptian territorial waters, and onwards to France. Mariette later defended his actions by pointing out that the objects that had been surrendered to the Egyptian government and sent to the Cairo Citadel were subsequently given away as presents. But Mariette's behaviour was, nonetheless, extraordinarily brazen for someone who, later in his career, would be in charge of preserving Egypt's antiquities.

Whatever his methods, the scale of his achievements cannot be overstated. The Greater Vaults of the Serapeum, Mariette's first discovery, contained twenty-four massive stone sarcophagi in which the sacred Apis bulls had been buried from the fourth to the first centuries BC. The continuity of burials enabled scholars to refine the chronology of the twenty-sixth to Ptolemaic dynasties, bringing a new measure of precision to the understanding of Egyptian history. The Lesser Vaults, discovered in spring 1852, contained yet more bull burials. De Bellefonds calculated that a single sarcophagus weighed up to 17,000 kilogrammes; none has ever been successfully removed, provoking awe and wonder at the ancient Egyptian workers who manoeuvred them into place without the aid of modern machinery. De Bellefonds also played a key role in clearing the galleries, taking a leaf out of Howard Vyse's book by using explosives (more than a hundred charges in total).

The later Apis burials had all been robbed in antiquity, but Mariette subsequently discovered an earlier, intact burial made in the reign of Ramesses II and overseen by his son, the High Priest of Ptah, Khaemwaset. In the thin layer of sand which covered the floor around the sarcophagus, the footprints of the ancient Egyptian workmen were still visible; and around the doorway were the fingerprints of the priest who had sealed the chamber more than three thousand years before. Mariette was deeply moved by this human thread stretching across so many centuries.[15]

What had started out as a short-term mission to acquire Coptic manuscripts had now, more than two years later, acquired the makings of a more or less permanent archaeological expedition. Back in Paris, Mariette's wife gave up waiting for him to return, and set sail for Egypt with their three daughters. They joined him at Saqqara where they settled down in a ramshackle construction dubbed 'the little house among the sands'. Mariette's employers at the Louvre forgave him his failure to procure any papyri, and were only too happy for him to continue his excavations. The Serapeum became the most celebrated discovery since the Rosetta Stone, and a favourite day trip for scholars and tourists from Cairo. By the time the thousands of finds from the Serapeum reached the Louvre, the President of the Second Republic's Constituent Assembly, Louis-Napoleon, had declared himself Emperor Napoleon III (r.1852–70). Mariette's discovery, and the cultural riches it brought his homeland, were thus celebrated as an auspicious harbinger of a new imperial age. With a confidence not seen since the days of the first Napoleon, France looked forward to regaining its rightful place as the leading Egyptological nation of the world.

The impact of Mariette's discoveries – bolstered by Maxime du Camp's photographic study, *Egypte, Nubie, Palestine et Syrie*, published the same year – spread across Europe, propelling the civilization of ancient Egypt back into the forefront of fashion. Two of the strangest manifestations of this new 'Egyptomania' were aristocratic follies: in Scotland, the newly deceased tenth Duke of Hamilton was mummified and buried in a Ptolemaic sarcophagus in the family vault, following his own carefully expressed wishes;[16] while, in Germany, the newly widowed

Prince of Pückler-Muskau began creating massive earthwork pyramids in his landscape garden, one of which was to serve as his final resting place, following funeral rites modelled on those of ancient Egypt.[17]

Having rediscovered the famed Serapeum beneath the sands of Saqqara, Mariette next turned his attention to the most iconic area of the Memphite necropolis, the Giza plateau. Vyse and Perring had been there a decade and a half earlier, and had blasted open the burial chambers of the three main pyramids; but, Mariette believed, they had only scratched the surface (or, more accurately, drilled the back) of the Great Sphinx. In 1817, Caviglia had made some discoveries – the flight of steps ascending the monument and the pavement between its paws – but the dunes had returned, covering both Caviglia's trench and the bulk of the great statue. As at Saqqara, the work required just to hold back the sand, let alone remove it, would be daunting . . . and expensive. The French government might have been delighted by the recent haul of antiquities from the Serapeum, but it baulked at financing a further flight of fancy. So, like Champollion and Lepsius before him, Mariette turned to an influential patron to advance his cause. Emmanuel, Vicomte de Rougé was ten years' Mariette's senior. A talented philologist and the first person to translate a running ancient Egyptian text, he had been appointed conservator of the Egyptian collection at the Louvre in 1849, the same year that Mariette had started work at the museum; the two had become firm friends. Through his aristocratic contacts, de Rougé secured for Mariette the interest and patronage of a noted collector, Honoré d'Albert, Duc de Luynes, who was keen to solve the riddles of the Sphinx. The duke sent the princely sum of 60,000 francs for Mariette's new mission, and on 15 September 1853 the work began.

It took fifty workmen to clear the sand, which covered the Sphinx up to its shoulders, and remove the dwellings on top of the statue. Clearing the northern face alone took nearly a month. In the process, Mariette was the first to reveal the full extent of the Sphinx enclosure. He relocated the chambers that Caviglia had found, and the well described by an earlier traveller, Father Vansleb, in the seventeenth century. Mariette hoped the shaft might lead to a hidden chamber, but after fifteen days of clearance, it turned out to be a natural fissure in the rock. As Giza's twenty-first century archaeologists have noted, not without sympathy: 'Mariette plunged into the sea of sand that had once again filled Caviglia's trench of 30 years earlier. The more he dug, the more sand would pour down into his trench, and there was no immediate flow of discoveries as in his excavation at the Serapeum. He soon lost patience.'[18]

The absence of discoveries, though dispiriting, was nonetheless important for what it disproved: there was no entrance to the Sphinx, no hidden chambers, no secret corridors; it was simply a natural knoll with masonry additions. While the Sphinx might hold no further secrets, Mariette had a hunch that an area to the south-east, where Wilkinson had noted a series of pits, might prove more promising. Once again, Mariette's intuition was rewarded. In June 1854, he discovered the valley temple of King Khafra's pyramid complex. It was filled with sand, up to twenty-six feet deep in places. Another mammoth clearance effort ensued but, with just three feet of sand to go, Mariette's funds ran out. He appealed to Paris, but to no avail. With great reluctance he had to abandon the work, leaving any hidden treasures (of which there turned out to be one very significant example) for another day.

Frustrated and elated in equal measure, Mariette prepared to leave Egypt and return home. With his wife and three children, he embarked at Alexandria at the end of July. Just two weeks earlier, Abbas had been assassinated by his bodyguard, leaving the throne to his son, the Francophile Said

(r. 1854–63). It was, as it turned out, a good omen for the future. Mariette's first visit to Egypt had been full of unexpected twists and turns, disappointments but also great discoveries. As he later summed it up: 'I left for Egypt in search of Coptic manuscripts. I didn't find any. But I brought back a temple.'[19]

⤙◦⤚

On his return to Paris, Mariette found that he had become something of a celebrity. His lectures at the Académie des Inscriptions were reported in *Le Figaro*. The discovery of the Serapeum was lauded by figures as eminent as Jomard (geographer to the Napoleonic expedition and arch-rival of Champollion), Louis de Saulcy (keeper of the Artillery Museum and senator), and Mariette's own friend and mentor, de Rougé. People queued to see the seated scribe on display at the Louvre. Indeed, Mariette's employers at the museum could count themselves well pleased with his achievements, and they promoted him to 'adjunct curator', his first substantive post in Egyptology. He wrote to his half-brother, Edouard: 'My destiny is set.'[20] He immediately began writing up his discoveries, but other duties soon supervened, and he only ever finished the first volume. He longed to return to Egypt, but instead the Louvre sent him on a study tour of other Egyptian collections across Europe (mindful, no doubt, of his skills as a copyist and cataloguer). A second trip to the land of the pharaohs seemed to be receding ever further into the distance when fate intervened a second time.

On 14 August 1857, Napoleon III visited the Louvre to open its new wings, and Mariette was present at the celebrations. A few weeks later he was unexpectedly ordered back to Cairo. The circumstances could not have been stranger. The emperor's cousin, Prince Napoleon, had expressed a desire to visit Egypt for himself, and not just as a tourist. The prince wished to discover some antiquities. For the sake of Franco-Egyptian relations the visit had to be a success. As the leading (indeed the only) Egyptian archaeologist in France, Mariette's job would be to unearth, and then rebury, a series of objects for the prince to 'discover'. This was just the opportunity Mariette was looking for. There was little prospect of further promotion at the Louvre, and he dearly wished to return to excavation.

Once back in Egypt, he presented his credentials to the new ruler. Said (now more often styled 'viceroy' rather than 'pasha') was suspicious of Mariette's motives, wondering if the real purpose of his visit was to advance French interests in the Suez Canal project. But he graciously made a steamer available for Mariette's personal use, and the Frenchman lost no time in initiating new digs throughout the Nile Valley: at his old stamping grounds of Saqqara and Giza, as well as the rich archaeological sites of Abydos, Thebes and Elephantine.[21] The results were immediate and impressive. At Saqqara, Mariette discovered the sarcophagus of the fourth dynasty king Shepseskaf, still in situ in the burial chamber of his coffin-shaped pyramid. Mariette celebrated with a winter cruise up the Nile with his close friend and fellow Egyptologist, Heinrich Brugsch. Ever the diplomat, Mariette dedicated his handsome folio publication of the Serapeum which appeared that year (*Le Sérapéum de Memphis*, 1857) to Prince Napoleon, with a foreword that consciously harked back to the Napoleonic expedition led by the prince's forebear half a century earlier: 'It is not only through the bravery of our soldiers and the genius of their commander that the Egyptian expedition has attracted the attention of posterity. Perhaps the prestige of this glorious campaign would be the less if science had not profited from our victories, and if Egypt, subject to our armies, had not at the same time been opened up to research by our scholars.'[22]

But then, quite unexpectedly, it was announced that the prince had postponed his visit indefinitely, and Mariette's mission was changed from one of archaeology to one of acquisition: instead of finding objects for the prince to unearth, he was now required to gather a representative sample of antiquities for the prince's personal collection, which Said would present as a diplomatic gift. Mariette did not demur. The objects were sent to Paris, and the prince was delighted. Mariette's good standing with Said was restored. In a fulsome letter of thanks to the viceroy, Prince Napoleon felt emboldened to make a suggestion: 'If Your Royal Highness were to ask of France the offices of a scholar to protect [Egypt's] heritage and create a museum, the government would designate no other man but [Mariette].'[23]

As with the original suggestion of sending Mariette back to Egypt, the influence of Ferdinand de Lesseps – who had known Said since their shared childhood days in Cairo, and was now an influential member of the viceroy's circle – can be detected. Said got the message. On 1 June 1858, by royal decree, the Egyptian Antiquities Service was founded; Mariette was appointed director of Egypt's historic monuments, at a generous salary of 18,000 francs per annum. The letter of appointment, signed by Said, stated: 'You will ensure the safety of the monuments; you will tell the governors of all the provinces that I forbid them to touch one single antique stone; you will imprison any peasant who sets foot inside a temple.'[24] Mariette summed up his feelings succinctly: 'This was like taking possession of Egypt for the cause of science.'[25]

To accompany his exclusive excavation rights throughout Egypt, the new director had extraordinary resources at his command. In addition to use of the royal steamer *Samannoud* (on which he had travelled up the Nile with Brugsch the previous winter) for his tours of inspection, Mariette was given the right to call upon the army and to levy corvée labour. In total, he had access to 7,000 workmen. He wasted no time in putting them to good use. His old friend Bonnefoy was named director of excavations in Upper Egypt, and digs were launched at many sites simultaneously. Mariette mobilized a hundred workers at Abydos, over three hundred at Giza, and up to five hundred at Thebes, where four new tombs were opened in the Valley of the Kings.[26] A young Egyptologist, Théodule Devéria, arriving in Cairo in early 1859 to be Mariette's assistant, wrote: 'They are removing the sand the entire length of the valley and around Cairo – a veritable army of diggers is at work.'[27]

With unprecedented effort directed at uncovering Egypt's ancient past, the discoveries came thick and fast:[28] the relief of the Queen of Punt in 1858;[29] the coffin and jewellery of Queen Ahhotep the following February; the leonine sphinxes of Amenemhat III from Tanis later that same year; the 'Sheikh el-Beled' wooden statue and the wooden panels of Hesira from Saqqara in 1860. One of the greatest finds, and for Mariette one of the most rewarding, was the magnificent seated statue of Khafra from his valley temple at Giza. Because lack of funds had forced Mariette to give up the excavation of the temple six years earlier, it was one of the first sites to be reopened when he took up the reins of the new Antiquities Service. Just as he had suspected, the temple had been abandoned in antiquity and there, in its inner hall, was a life-sized statue of its royal owner, carved from a single block of diorite, undamaged over the succeeding forty-three centuries. It was, and remains, one of the greatest masterpieces of ancient Egyptian art.

Mariette's results may have been impressive, but his methods were decidedly slipshod, even by the standards of the time. With work progressing on many fronts simultaneously, he left his workmen unsupervised, kept few records, paid no attention to stratigraphy, and happily split up groups of objects. It did not have to be so. In 1855, a Scotsman named Alexander Rhind, a lawyer rather than an archaeologist, had come to Thebes for his health and, while he was there, excavated several Theban tombs. He argued that ancient monuments and antiquities should be left intact and in situ, and that museums should display only casts and facsimiles. But his ideas were ahead of his time, and his death before his thirtieth birthday robbed archaeology of a visionary practitioner. Mariette, while not quite in the Vyse camp, definitely belonged to the old school. His excavations have, perhaps unfairly, been described as 'miseries inflicted by Europeans . . . without tangible benefit to the workers'.[30] Certainly, his foremen showed no mercy in the application of the corvée.

Early in his tenure at the Antiquities Service, Mariette realized that his future career now lay in Egypt. He returned to France to fetch his family, but his employers at the Louvre were not exactly thrilled to see him. They did not welcome one of their staff working for the Egyptian government – especially as one of Mariette's first actions had been to send inspectors to unauthorized digs, to seize any antiquities illegally excavated (highly ironic, given his own activities at the Serapeum, less than ten years earlier). A compromise was reached whereby Mariette resigned from his substantive position at the Louvre, accepting an honorary deputy keepership instead.[31] He and his wife, and their children – now numbering four daughters and a son – set up home in the port of Bulaq, in a house infested with rats, snakes and scorpions. It was even less comfortable than the 'little house among the sands'.

One of the most pressing issues resulting from the frenzy of archaeological activity was where to store all the resulting finds. Mariette had identified the former hangars of the Alexandria–Cairo Steamer Company at Bulaq (defunct since the arrival of the railway) as a suitable repository; but after just a few months, the storerooms were full. A permanent solution was clearly needed, and one was not long in coming. In 1859, Said agreed to establish a national museum with Mariette as director. The only question was where it should be located. Mariette's proposal was the valley temple of Khafra (also known as Armachis) at Giza, the site of his most spectacular discovery since the Serapeum. He wrote to Brugsch: 'As for the Museum, I firmly believe that it should be at the pyramids themselves, utilizing the temple of Armachis which I discovered previously. It is a good enough location, which has the huge advantage of being out of sight of the Turks, who are a little offended by Viceroy's European notion of founding a Museum.'[32]

Building modern Egypt's national museum at the site of ancient Egypt's greatest cultural achievement was a bold plan, but utterly impractical. Giza was still covered in sand dunes, difficult to reach, and distant from the Nile. (Mariette's vision of a Grand Egyptian Museum at Giza has only now been realized, over a century and a half later.) By contrast, Bulaq, the main port of Cairo, presented a more sensible option, given its location on the east bank of the Nile and its proximity to the centre of Cairo. So, while not giving up on his dream of a purpose-built museum, Mariette came up with a design for the Bulaq site.

Meanwhile, there was no let-up in the pace of excavations. Bonnefoy was struck down by exhaustion and malaria, but Mariette continued to dig even in the intense summer heat. Bonnefoy's death at Thebes, in August 1859, shook Mariette – the two had worked together since Mariette's first visit to Egypt – and he returned to France to recuperate. His reception was decidedly less warm than at his previous homecoming, five years earlier. He was accused by his former colleagues at the Louvre of betrayal by establishing a museum in Cairo, and by ending the practice of dividing finds between the excavator and the Egyptian state. Nonetheless, he was still a valuable asset for the French government in Egypt: on a subsequent visit to Paris, at a private audience with Napoleon III, the emperor asked him to act as a secret agent, to protect French interests against the schemes of the British.

The entente between Second Empire France and Said's Egypt was cemented in 1862 when the viceroy paid a state visit to France, with Mariette as his personal guide. Travelling from London, Said landed at Boulogne to a rapturous reception. In Mariette's home town, the viceroy announced to a delighted crowd that he had conferred on Mariette the status of bey, and placed him in charge of educating the royal children. In recognition of his achievements, the Académie des Inscriptions in Paris finally elected Mariette a member. But his moment of triumph was short-lived: just a few months later, Said's death, on 17 January 1863, dealt Mariette's plans a fatal blow and robbed him of a staunch ally (and France of a valued friend). He would have to build a new relationship, from scratch, with the new viceroy, Said's nephew Ismail (r.1863–79).

Fortunately for both Mariette and Egypt's antiquities, Ismail had grand ideas of his own status and equally grand plans for his reign. He lost no time in announcing his wish to establish a national museum for Egypt, comparable to the great museums of Europe, and in confirming Mariette as director, both of the Museum and of the Antiquities Service. Ismail's vision was of a monumental museum on Ezbekiya Square, in the heart of the capital; but he agreed that, in the short-term, work should continue at Bulaq. Construction work resumed without delay, and the Bulaq Museum opened its doors on 16 October 1863, in a ceremony presided over by Ismail himself. The British authorities were represented by their consul, and the French government by Ferdinand de Lesseps. The main museum building comprised four magnificent halls; the objects in each were arranged around a star attraction. These centrepieces included the wooden 'Sheikh el-Beled' statue from Saqqara, Queen Ahhotep's jewellery from Thebes, and the seated diorite statue of Khafra from Giza. Each of the artefacts on display had an accompanying description written by Mariette. Indeed, he was proud of the fact that, in stark contrast to the situation in European museums, the provenance of every object housed at Bulaq was properly recorded.

With its masterpieces of pharaonic art and its convenient location, close to the quay where *dahabiyas* departed for the journey up the Nile, the museum soon became a major tourist attraction. Ismail wrote to its founder-director: 'I am told, M. Mariette, that your museum is, after the pyramids, the most visited place in the capital. I am very glad of it.'[33] Mariette, however, in sentiments somewhat ahead of his time, expressed his wish that Egypt's second *Antiqakhana* should serve the Egyptian people as well as well-heeled Western visitors. In his guide to the collection, published five years after the official opening, he wrote: 'The Museum of Cairo is not only intended for European travellers. It is the Viceroy's intention that it should be above all accessible to the natives, to whom the Museum is entrusted in order to teach them the history of their country . . . Not long ago, Egypt destroyed its monuments; today, it respects them; tomorrow it shall love them.'[34]

Egyptian scholars responded positively to the sentiment, although some were sceptical of Ismail's motives in promoting a museum of antiquities, especially one that had reputedly cost the public purse hundreds of thousands of francs. (Mariette's biographer would later claim, loyally if not entirely plausibly, that the cost had been much lower, around sixty thousand francs, and that Mariette had contributed some of the funds out of his own pocket.) Abdullah Abu al-Su'ud, who produced the Arabic translation of Mariette's guidebook and championed a connection between the ancient and modern Egyptians as the same 'people of Egypt',[35] was more generous, asserting that Ismail wanted 'to waken us from this torpor by the study of the history of our ancestors so that we can revive the glorious virtues and follow their example in working together as true Egyptians and true patriots, for the renaissance of Egypt'.[36]

Despite Mariette's laudable aspirations, the Bulaq Museum was always more of an attraction for European tourists than for Egyptian natives. And because it housed the very latest antiquities dug from the sands of Egypt, with the benefit of accompanying documentation, the collection also became a valuable tool for Egyptologists. Mariette had intended as much, declaring that the museum was 'a museum arranged for the practical service of Egyptology'.[37] If casual observers queried the inclusion of damaged fragments, he would respond that 'there is not a single archaeologist who, with me, would not wish to see them to advantage'.[38] Indeed, his underlying philosophy, both of museum display and of the excavations that fed the museum, was avowedly scientific rather than antiquarian:

In effect, one does not have a proper idea of the value of excavations carried out in Egypt if one thinks these excavations have, as their only purpose, the discovery of monuments preserved in the museums of Europe. For every stela, for every statue, for every monument which the aforementioned collectors have included in their collections, there are twenty others that they have left on the ground . . . Now, it is impossible that among these fragments there are none with some scientific value.[39]

Following the lead of Lepsius a decade earlier, Mariette was transforming the excavation and display of Egyptian antiquities from a pastime for dilettantes into a proper academic discipline.

After 'taking possession of Egypt for the cause of science', Mariette looked forward to consolidating his achievements and safeguarding the country's patrimony. However, to his disappointment, it soon became clear that Ismail had supported the establishment of a national museum for reasons of personal pride, not out of any great interest in, or love for, Egypt's heritage. The viceroy temporarily took away Mariette's steamer, essential for his tours of inspection up and down the Nile, and sharply reduced his budget. By 1867, his excavation workforce of thousands had shrunk to only a few hundred.[40] But still he persisted. He may have been an absentee archaeologist, often leaving his workmen to their own, worst devices, but he was an assiduous and fiercely protective museum director. When Napoleon III's consort, Empress Eugénie, asked Ismail for Egypt's entire collection of antiquities, it was Mariette, not the viceroy, who refused the royal request. To safeguard the museum from thieves of a pettier kind, Mariette lived on site, in a wing of the building that served as his official residence. He even kept a pet gazelle in the garden. As he later commented: 'I don't say we will be lodged there like kings, but at least we will have an ensemble of galleries while we await the definitive museum.'[41]

⊲○▷

Mariette never gave up on his dream of a purpose-built museum, but it would always elude him. The best he managed to achieve was an extension to the Bulaq building, two extra halls, in 1869. All too predictably, Ismail had been persuaded, not by the necessity of further space to house Egypt's burgeoning collection of antiquities, but by the argument that an expanded museum would impress European dignitaries visiting Egypt that year.[42] The occasion was the inauguration of a third great monument to French influence which, alongside the Antiquities

Service and the Egyptian Museum, would shape Western engagement with the Nile Valley for generations to come.

At the very end of the eighteenth century, geographers and cartographers participating in the Napoleonic expedition to Egypt had discovered the remains of an ancient canal linking the Nile with the Red Sea. From the ceremonial stela erected near its southern terminus, it could be dated to the period of Persian domination in Egypt in the sixth century BC, and more specifically to the reign of Darius I. Darius's vision had been to link Egypt's great artery with 'the sea that begins in Persia' (i.e. the Arabian Sea and its extension, the Red Sea), thus uniting his extensive realm through waterborn trade. The discovery had given Bonaparte an even grander idea: a canal linking the Mediterranean and the Red Sea via the Gulf of Suez, in order to give France effective control of sea routes to India and thus deprive Britain of easy access to its empire in the east. But Napoleon's defeat at the Battle of the Nile shifted the balance of power in Egypt, and the dream of a Suez Canal remained just that, a dream. What it needed to turn it into reality was an Egyptian ruler as ambitious as Darius, a presiding genius with Napoleonic drive and determination, and a great deal of money.

Through a mixture of serendipity and planning, all the ingredients came together in the early 1830s, but it would take a further thirty-seven years – and several changes of ruler in the Nile Valley – before the project could be brought to fruition.

The presiding genius, and the name forever associated with the Suez Canal, was the Frenchman Ferdinand de Lesseps. Born in the year of Napoleon's self-elevation from consul to emperor, de Lesseps grew up with French patriotism and the French national interest as his guiding principles. After completing his education in Paris, he followed his father into the French diplomatic service, accompanying him in 1828 on a posting to Tunis:

de Lesseps *père* was consul-general, while de Lesseps *fils* served as an assistant vice-consul. The son quickly proved his worth, and was given a prestigious solo posting just four years later, as French vice-consul in Alexandria. De Lesseps set out on his voyage across the Mediterranean, eager to take up his duties in Egypt's great port city. While his ship was quarantined off the port of Alexandria, waiting for permission to disembark its passengers, de Lesseps used the time to prepare himself for his new post, avidly devouring books on various aspects of Egyptian history and culture sent out to his boat by the French consul-general in Alexandria. Among the volumes de Lesseps received, as he lay at anchor, was a memoir on the abandoned canal of Darius I by the French engineer Le Père. As chief civil engineer of the Napoleonic expedition, Le Père had undertaken a survey of the isthmus of Suez and had mused on the possibility of digging a canal from sea to sea. The notion fired de Lesseps's imagination, but any thoughts of realizing such a great feat of engineering were soon overwhelmed by other, more pressing priorities.

After landing in Alexandria, a second stroke of luck came de Lesseps's way. It just so happened that the ruler of Egypt at the time, Muhammad Ali, had reason to recognize the name de Lesseps: Ferdinand's father had been consul-general in Egypt at the time of Muhammad Ali's rise to power, and indeed had advised the French government to support the Albanian army commander's elevation to viceroy. Muhammad Ali may have been a ruthless autocrat, but he never forgot a favour, especially from a foreign power. De Lesseps junior duly received a warm welcome as the new French vice-consul, and was introduced to Muhammad Ali's own son, Said, then a boy of ten years old. The two became firm friends. De Lesseps's good standing with the Egyptian royal family did not go unnoticed back at the Ministry of Foreign Affairs in Paris, and promotions followed rapidly: to consul in Cairo in 1833, and a few months later to consul-general in Alexandria, at the head of the French diplomatic mission in Egypt. After four years of service to France's interests, de Lesseps left Egypt for other postings, before retiring from the diplomatic service in 1851. But he never forgot his friendship with Said, nor his interest in the idea of a canal linking the Mediterranean and Red Seas.

The elements came together with Said's accession to the viceregalty in July 1854. The new ruler of Egypt lost no time in inviting his old childhood friend to visit. De Lesseps arrived in Alexandria on 7 November that very year, and within a month had received a royal concession granting him the right to build a Suez Canal. A few months later, back in Paris, de Lesseps convened engineers from across Europe – he diplomatically included a representative from Britain, as well as French, Dutch, Italian, Spanish, Austrian and German members – to assess the different options. In 1856, the grandly titled 'Commission internationale pour le percement de l'isthme de Suez' (international commission for the piercing of the isthmus of Suez) agreed on plans drawn up by two French engineers (little surprise there), Louis Adolphe and Linant de Bellefonds, the latter fresh from his exploits with Mariette at Saqqara.

The reaction from Britain was predictably furious. The prime minister, Lord Palmerston, was fiercely resistant to any plan that might strengthen French influence in Egypt, and especially to a project that might threaten British access to India. He wrote to Lord Cowley, Britain's ambassador in Paris: 'We do not want Egypt or wish it for ourselves, any more than any rational man with an estate in the north of England and a residence in the south would have wished to possess the inns on the north road. All he could want would have been that the inns should be well-kept, always accessible, and furnishing him, when he came, with mutton-chops and post-horses.'[43]

Disraeli, who, of course, knew something of Egypt from his visit of 1831, was likewise against the plan. Sir Gardner Wilkinson, by now the grand old man of British Egyptology, declared his opposition to the Suez Canal on the grounds that 'it could obviously destroy our Indian trade & throw it into the hands of the Austrians, Greeks, French, Russians and all petty traders who can carry cheaper than the English'.[44] Only Gladstone offered a more measured and realistic assessment, asking: 'What would be more unwise than to present ourselves to the world as the opponents of a scheme on the face of it beneficial to mankind, on no better ground than remote and contingent danger to interests of our own?'[45] (In any case, British opposition to the canal rang a little hollow, given their continuing dominance of the Egyptian railway network: following the success of the Alexandria to Cairo route, a second line, from Cairo to Suez, was completed in 1858.)

Despite the voices of opposition from London, de Lesseps pressed ahead, raising the necessary funds by issuing shares in the newly formed Compagnie universelle du canal maritime de Suez (Suez Canal Company). On 25 April 1859, the first spadeful of earth was cut at the Mediterranean end of the canal's route – named Port Said in the viceroy's honour – by de Lesseps himself.

Work on the colossal project proceeded apace, thanks to the thousands of Egyptian peasants who were called up for the corvée and sent to labour in appalling conditions. Britain continued to oppose the whole scheme – and not out of any concern for the workers. But de Lesseps was having none of it. Nor was Said's successor as viceroy, Ismail, who, if anything, harboured even grander visions for Egypt than his uncle. Under mounting British pressure, the Ottoman sultan in Constantinople eventually agreed to issue an ultimatum to the Suez Canal Company, asserting that Said's concession had never been ratified by the Sublime Porte.[46] Britain and France, at loggerheads, agreed to the establishment of a Commission of Arbitration; but, headed as it was by Napoleon III, it was never going to be objective – especially as the emperor's wife, Eugénie, was a cousin of de Lesseps. Family ties and national loyalty won the day. The commission found in favour of the project continuing, but in a nod to British sensitivities, required the company to give up its land holdings and navigation rights in return for massive financial compensation of 130 million francs, payable by the Egyptian government. Not for the first time, nor for the last, the European powers were the ultimate winners, and Egypt the loser. The debt Egypt incurred to rescue the canal project would, within twenty years, doom it to colonial occupation. (In one of Egyptology's bitterest ironies, the first major history of Egypt up to the Arab conquest to be published in the country's own language, Tahtawi's *Anwar tawfiq al-jalil fi akhbar Misr wa-tawthiq Banu Ismail*, appeared in 1868, just a year before the completion of the canal.)

Altogether, the realization of de Lesseps's vision cost 453.6 million francs and involved the removal of 97 million cubic yards of spoil. During the course of construction, the population of Suez grew sevenfold. Finally, just ten years after the first sod of earth was cut, the canal was finished. From Port Said on the Mediterranean to Suez on the Red Sea via the Great Bitter Lake, it stretched for 193.3 kilometres. The travel entrepreneur Thomas Cook called it 'the greatest engineering feat of the present century',[47] and so it was. To celebrate such a stupendous achievement, Ismail (who had recently won both Ottoman and international recognition as hereditary 'khedive' of Egypt) arranged the most sumptuous of opening ceremonies. The guests of honour, headed by Empress Eugénie, included the Emperor of Austria and the Crown Prince of Prussia. Wilkinson, despite his opposition to the whole scheme, was flattered to receive an official invitation.

On 17 November 1869, five days of celebrations began with a great religious ceremony at Port Said. The Coptic Patriarch of Alexandria and the chaplain to the French imperial court (the *évêque aumônier des Tuileries*), celebrated a Mass and a Te Deum. Then the Grand Mufti of Cairo and the clerics of al-Azhar read verses from the Qur'an and recited prayers to Allah. The religious rites accomplished, guests were invited to a grand banquet in the government buildings: fifty courses, prepared by over five hundred European chefs and served by a thousand European waiters, brought over to Egypt specially for the occasion. After the feast, a great flotilla of ships set out down the canal towards the Red Sea. At the head was Empress Eugénie on board the imperial yacht *L'Aigle* ('The Eagle'), with de Lesseps at her side, and Mariette and de Bellefonds at a respectful distance behind; they were followed closely by Ismail in his royal yacht *Maroussia* ('Fiancée') and the boats of other guests, while a huge crowd watched from the banks. At Lake Timsah, Egyptian naval vessels that had come from the Red Sea joined the flotilla and fired a gun salute. The next day, in the newly founded city of Ismailia, Ismail threw a ball in the royal palace he had built for the occasion; Eugénie arrived in a carriage pulled by six white dromedaries. On the third day, the flotilla reached the Red Sea and anchored off Suez. Two days later, on 21 November, guests made the return journey to Port Said in just fifteen hours.

To set the seal on this great triumph of French diplomacy and engineering, France's leading Egyptologist, Mariette, escorted Eugénie on a trip up the Nile. She visited Abydos – riding a mule the four hours from the Nile to the temple of Seti I – and Dendera, Luxor and western Thebes,

Elephantine and Philae. She showed no signs of tiredness. Ismail was so delighted with the success of the trip that he showered Mariette with honours and promised funds for the education of the archaeologist's sons and dowries for his two eldest daughters.

Thanks to Mariette, de Lesseps and – in her own way – Empress Eugénie, the 1850s and 1860s were France's decades in the Egyptian sun. French scientific and cultural superiority were asserted over Britain and Prussia, and French foundations laid that would shape the future, not only of Egyptology, but of Western engagement with Egypt. But, just as the statue of the once-mighty Khafra had been swallowed up by the sands of Giza for over forty centuries, so events after 1869 were not kind to the French. Less than a year after Eugénie's triumphal progress along the Suez Canal and up the Nile, her husband was overthrown, bringing an end to the Second Empire and consigning the house of Napoleon to history. De Lesseps's great achievement, which should have secured French economic interests in Egypt, instead led to a rapid expansion of British trade through the Suez Canal.[48]

And as for Mariette, while he was lauded in Egypt, he found much less favour in his home country. It has been said that he 'sought no friends except the ruler, and he alienated both those who wanted to exploit the monuments of Egypt by denying them that privilege and those who wanted to support his work of conservation by his solitary gruffness'.[49] For all that he had founded and stewarded the Antiquities Service, established Egypt's first national museum, and discovered a host of major monuments and priceless artefacts, he was never taken entirely seriously by the scholarly community. He was sanguine about his academic reputation, writing: 'I know the truth, that during my scientific career, I have done only two things, the Serapeum and the Cairo Museum, that most people would regard as services to science. But I have published nothing further, except a few insignificant and incomplete articles.'[50]

The Académie des Inscriptions et Belles-Lettres finally appointed Mariette a permanent member in 1878, just three years before his death. A more fitting, and lasting, tribute may be found inscribed on his sarcophagus which lies, not in a Paris cemetery, but in the garden of the Egyptian Museum in Cairo. It reads, simply, *'L'Egypte reconnaissante'* – a grateful Egypt.

SIX

A thousand miles up the Nile

Lucie Duff Gordon, lady of letters and friend of the Egyptian poor.

The work of destruction, meanwhile, goes on apace. There is no one to prevent it; there is no one to discourage it.[1]

AMELIA EDWARDS, 1877

From the death of Cleopatra until the middle of the nineteenth century, the history of Egypt, and of Western engagement with Egypt, was written by men. Women played little or no public role in Roman, Byzantine, Arab or Ottoman rule over the Nile Valley; none of the early European travellers to Egypt was a woman; there were no female members of the Napoleonic expedition, nor of the subsequent expeditions led by Champollion or Lepsius. Only Sophia Lane Poole, with her first-hand account of life in the harems of Cairo, brought a female perspective to Western understanding of Egypt, and shone a light on the lot of Egyptian women. But the mores of the age demanded that her groundbreaking work be published semi-anonymously: her name is absent from the title page, which instead makes reference to her already famous brother: 'The Englishwoman in Egypt: letters from Cairo written during a residence there in 1842, 3, & 4, with E. W. Lane, Esq Author of the "Modern Egyptians". By his sister'. Sophia's own name only appears inside the book, at the foot of the preface.

Nineteen centuries of male-dominated encounters and experiences were finally brought to an end in the 1860s and 70s thanks to two remarkable women: women from very different backgrounds and with very different motivations, but who had the same passion, the same indomitable spirit, and an equal affection for Egypt. One developed a deep fascination for the modern Egyptians and found her calling as a friend of the downtrodden fellahin, bringing their plight to wider attention. The other was captivated by the ancient Egyptians, and, scandalized at the wholesale destruction of pharaonic monuments, launched a campaign to save Egypt's patrimony for future generations, in the process establishing Egyptian archaeology on a permanent footing. Lucie Duff Gordon and Amelia Edwards: while neither has achieved the worldwide fame of Champollion, Lepsius or Mariette, their names and contributions are writ large in the history of Egyptology, and their stories exemplify all the contradictions of European relations with Egypt in the mid-nineteenth century.

Born in 1821, the year before Champollion's decipherment of hieroglyphics, Duff Gordon was blessed with remarkable parents. Her father, John Austin, was a professor of jurisprudence and a noted intellectual. Her mother, Sarah, was unusually well educated for a woman of the time (Sarah's own mother had been a strong supporter of abolitionism, and had been used to discussing politics and literature on a par with men). The young Lucie inherited her parents' talents and, from an early age, developed an insatiable appetite for reading. A friend described her, with great perspicacity and not a little understatement, as 'a great reader, a great thinker, very original in her conclusions, very eager in impressing her opinions, her mind was not like those of many women'.[2] Lucie's natural inquisitiveness was fed by early exposure to foreign countries and cultures. The family lived in Boulogne-sur-Mer from 1834 to 1836, where Sarah was known as '*la belle anglaise*', and where Lucie's childhood neighbour and exact contemporary was none other than Auguste Mariette. Whether the two ever met is not known, but they are likely to have had friends in common.

When the Austin family returned to England, Lucie was on the verge of her 'coming out'. At her first society ball, at Lansdowne House – the London residence of the Marquess of Lansdowne, a leading Whig statesman, former Chancellor of the Exchequer and Home Secretary – her eyes fell upon a man more than ten years her senior. Sir Alexander Duff Gordon was of impeccable pedigree, being descended from Scottish nobility, and a baronet to boot. Despite the age difference, Alexander and Lucie fell in love and were married on 16 May 1840 – overcoming initial opposition from Alexander's mother, who disapproved of her son marrying a woman with no dowry. They made their home in Westminster, where, with Lucie's intellectual connections and Alexander's aristocratic cachet, they enjoyed a wide circle of friends. Tennyson used to come and read his poems at their house. Other visitors included the historian, Macaulay, and the novelists, Dickens and Thackeray; the prime minister, Lord Melbourne, and the future Emperor of France, Napoleon III, then in exile in London; the founder of the influential *Edinburgh Review*, Sydney Smith; and the travel writer, William Kinglake (whose first literary work, *Eothen; or Traces of Travel Brought Home from the East*, 1844, recounted his adventures in Egypt). To supplement the Duff Gordons' meagre income, Lucie put her academic and linguistic talents to good use by translating Niebuhr's *Stories of the Gods and Heroes of Greece* from German into English. She also demonstrated her concern for more distant lands and peoples when she took in a Nubian boy, who had been enslaved before being rescued by English missionaries, as her servant. Hassan el-Bakeet, always known as Hatty, remained a cherished member of the Duff Gordon household until his death from congestion of the lungs on Christmas Day 1850.

Indeed, a title and connections were certainly no protection against illness in mid-nineteenth-century London, and the Duff Gordons, like so many of the capital's families, were touched repeatedly by misfortune. Lucie's second child (her first, Janet, was born in 1842) died at only a few months old. Alexander nearly died of cholera in 1846. And, after the birth of their only surviving son, Maurice, in 1849, Lucie herself began to succumb to tuberculosis. She struggled against the disease, and gave birth to a second daughter, Urania, in 1858; but by the winter of 1861, Lucie was so ill that her doctors advised her to go abroad for a warmer, drier climate. Like many Britons, she headed first for the Cape, but then decided to try Egypt, newly fashionable as a winter resort, especially for consumptive Europeans.

She had read the Bible and Herodotus, the *Arabian Nights* and *Eothen*, but nothing could have prepared her for the grim realities of life in Said's Egypt. On her arrival in Alexandria in October 1862, she wrote 'what is not pleasant, is the absence of all brightness or gaiety, even from young and childish faces'.[3] From that moment on, her support for working-class politics back in Britain found an outlet as a champion of the hard-pressed peasantry of Egypt. Moreover, in her mother (if not in her husband), she knew she had a correspondent who shared her progressive views and who would not be shocked by her frequent scathing remarks about the British abroad. Duff Gordon's clear-sightedness and openness to other cultures made her an unusually sharp observer of colonial attitudes. 'Why do the English talk of the beautiful sentiment of the Bible and pretend to feel it so much,' she wondered, 'and when they come and see the same life before them, they ridicule it?'[4]

Lucie's dismay at the lives of ordinary Egyptians was compounded by her swift realization that the cost of living was far higher than she had expected, at least in Alexandria with its

growing European population. (By 1864, there were over 60,000
Europeans in Alexandria, one-third of the city's population;
fourteen years earlier, the entire European population in Egypt
had been just 50,000.[5]) Only days after her arrival, she wrote: 'I
regret more than I can say that I ever came here, for I fear it
will be utterly impossible to live as cheaply as I had hoped.'[6] But
she was nothing if not stoical in the face of adversity, and she
decided to make the best of her situation, travelling on to Cairo
where she found a more 'golden existence, all sunshine and poetry,
and, I must add, kindness and civility'.[7] There she took a servant,
Omar, known by his nickname Abu Halawy ('father of sweets'),
and, like all European visitors, set off on a journey upstream. 'If
this voyage does me as much good as it has done to others,' she
wrote, 'I shall be well enough for anything.'[8]

The Nile soon worked its magic. After just ten days on the
river, Duff Gordon began 'to eat and sleep again, and cough
less'.[9] As her health improved, so her fascination and sympathy
for the Egyptians themselves began to grow. She was struck
by their 'tolerant spirit'[10] and noted, with rare understanding,
that 'the much talked-of dirt is simply utter poverty. The poor
souls are as clean as Nile mud and water will make their bodies,
and they have not a second shirt, or any bed but dried mud.'[11]
By the time her boat reached Asyut, nearly three weeks into
the voyage, Egypt had her in its thrall. She wrote: 'I heard a
boy singing a *Zikr* (the ninety-nine attributes of God) to a
party of dervishes in a mosque, and I think I never heard
anything more beautiful and affecting.'[12]

But Egypt was changing: internal currents of political awakening were mixing with the external forces of nascent colonialism, and the results were often felt most acutely by the
ordinary people. On 17 January 1863, while Lucie was in Aswan,
the viceroy Said died and was succeeded by Ismail, a ruler who
wanted Egypt to be, and to be seen as, part of Europe – dynamic

and modern – not part of Africa (then cast as backward and primitive).[13] Yet one of Ismail's very first acts as viceroy was to receive, in an audience at the royal palace on Roda Island, the explorer John Hanning Speke, lately arrived from Khartoum having discovered the source of the Nile. By opening up Africa, Europe was preparing it for imperial subjugation. Indeed, a few years earlier, during a trip up the Nile, Flaubert had presciently remarked: 'It seems to me impossible that within a short time England won't become mistress of Egypt.'[14]

The sense of a country at a tipping point, poised precariously between a time-worn past and an uncertain future, comes across vividly in Duff Gordon's letters from Egypt. Unlike virtually every traveller to the Nile Valley before her, she was pointedly uninterested in the ancient monuments, declaring: 'It is of no use to talk of the ruins; everybody has said, I suppose, all that can be said . . .'[15] A visit to the greatest religious complex of the ancient world merited barely a mention: 'Yesterday I rode over to Karnac . . . Glorious hot sun and delicious air.'[16] Yet she could not be insensible to the layers of history visible at every turn, memorably describing Egypt as 'a palimpsest, in which the Bible is written over Herodotus, and the Koran over that'.[17] There were reminders of pharaonic civilization all around, and not just in the ruined temples and tombs. She observed that the Nubian women around Aswan still wore clothing and ornaments 'the same as those represented in the tombs',[18] while 'the ceremonies at births and burials are not Muslim, but ancient Egyptian'.[19] Away from 'the highroad and the backsheesh-hunting parasites'[20] life in the country was largely unchanged for millennia, and Lucie was greatly taken by 'the charm of the people',[21] declaring – for she was still, in her own mind, on a short-term visit – 'I shall say farewell to Egypt with real feeling.'[22]

Yet, even in the countryside, modernity was encroaching fast. The American Civil War, which had been raging for two years, had boosted the market for Egyptian cotton, and Ismail had responded, ordering vast new irrigation works in order to increase the acreage of cultivable land devoted to cash crops. Egypt's new-found prosperity did not escape the attention of the Ottoman sultan, Abdel Aziz. In 1863 he paid a visit to his upstart province (as Egypt still was, officially, if not in any practical sense), 'to see for himself a country which was stated to be more advanced than his own and where foreigners were investing money'.[23] One of Ismail's advisers was in no doubt what was going through the visitors' minds:

> The Sultan, and still more the Sultan's ministers, cannot bear to think that of the large revenues of Egypt not a tenth comes to his hands. They believe that if it were a completely dependent province, like Syria, they would have the spending and the plundering for themselves of the sums that are spent here for Egyptian purposes. They are continually intriguing against the Viceroy's quasi-independence. He is surrounded even in his hareem by Turkish agents and spies. This naturally throws him on foreign support.[24]

While Abbas had looked to England, Said and then Ismail turned to France. Nothing summed up the Franco-Egyptian relationship more powerfully than the Suez Canal project. But, in contrast to the wide-eyed wonder of most Western commentators, Lucie saw the human cost behind the impressive statistics. 'Everyone is cursing the French here,' she wrote. 'Forty thousand men always at work at the Suez Canal at starvation-point, does not endear them to the Arabs. There is great excitement as to what the new Pasha will do. If he ceases to give forced labour, the Canal, I suppose, must be given up.'[25]

But Ismail was too focussed on Egypt's modernization, and his own legacy, to listen to the grievances of his subjects; France's influence, and the canal project, continued without interruption.

Duff Gordon went back home to England in June 1863, but returned again to Egypt that October – not only for her health (which was failing month by month and year by year), but also because she was entranced by her adopted country. Despite missing her children, and pained by the anxiety her illness was causing her family, she freely admitted: 'The more I see of the back slums of Cairo, the more in love I am with them. The dirtiest lane of Cairo is far sweeter than the best street of Paris . . . I am in love with the Arab ways and I have contrived to see and know more of family life than many Europeans who have lived here for years.'[26]

Cairo, however, was too cold and damp in the winter months for a consumptive, so Lucie headed back to Upper Egypt and persuaded the French consul-general to let her take up residence in 'the French house' on the roof of Luxor Temple. The ramshackle dwelling had been built around 1815 by Henry Salt. Belzoni had lived there while supervising the removal of the 'Young Memnon', and Rosellini had stayed during the Franco-Tuscan expedition in 1829. But the moniker 'French House' had been acquired in 1831 when the dwelling was used as a base for the French naval officers who had come to Luxor to remove one of the obelisks and take it to Paris. Duff Gordon found the house charming: 'The view all round my house is magnificent on every side, over the Nile in front facing north-west, and over a splendid range of green and distant orange buff hills to the south-east, where I have a spacious covered terrace.'[27]

With 'glass windows and doors to some of the rooms'[28] and a few items of second-hand furniture, it became Lucie's 'Theban palace', and her home for the next six years.

With her bird's-eye view and her lucid prose, she would chart the transformation of Egypt during Ismail's reign, not so much through his *grands projets* as through their impact on Egypt's ordinary inhabitants. Back in 1855, Said had issued an edict compelling every master to free any slave who asked for freedom,[29] but a decade later the rural population was still effectively enslaved by the demands of the corvée: 'the poor fellaheen are marched off in gangs like convicts, and their families starve'. 'No wonder,' Lucie observed, 'the cry is, "Let the English Queen come and take us"'.[30] Having inherited a radical streak from her grandmother, Duff Gordon had found her voice as a champion of the Egyptian poor. She became increasingly outspoken against Ismail's profligacy, lamenting the fact that 'money is constantly wasted more than if it were thrown into the Nile, for then the fellaheen would not have to spend their time, so much wanted for agriculture, in building hideous barrack-like so-called palaces'.[31]

This was dangerous talk in a country swarming with spies and informers. Lucie's letters were intercepted by government agents – she discovered only later that many never reached England[32] – and on one occasion Ismail tried to bribe her boatman into drowning her; but her popularity locally saved her. Because of her fair-mindedness and caring attitude – 'I am, perhaps, not quite impartial, because I am *sympathique* to the Arabs and they to me, and I am inclined to be "kind" to their virtues if not "blind" to their faults'[33] – she gained a reputation among the people of Luxor and the surrounding villages as a trusted friend and advocate. When an epidemic swept the land in the spring of 1864, people preferred to visit her, not the government clinics, travelling up to twenty miles for treatment. She soon gained a reputation for having a 'lucky eye', and was asked for all sorts of favours, 'to go and look at young brides, visit houses that are building, inspect cattle, etc., as a bringer of good luck'.[34]

But even Duff Gordon's magic touch could not dispel the growing deprivation and oppression caused by the government's policy of rash, unbridled development. By January 1865, there was 'hunger, and pain, and labour without hope and without reward, and the constant bitterness of impotent resentment'.[35] Lucie felt that: 'The system of wholesale extortion and spoliation has reached a point beyond which it would be difficult to go'[36] and reported the mood among the townspeople of Luxor: 'The discontent is growing stronger every day. Last week the people were cursing the Pasha in the streets of Aswan, and every one talks aloud of what they think . . . The whole place is in desolation.'[37]

Hers, however, was a lone voice. Most European commentators – from the safety of their comfortable drawing rooms – were wholly supportive of Ismail's 'reforms'. British diplomats rarely ventured beyond the cities, and all were wilfully blind to the seething resentment building up beneath the surface. Duff Gordon alone could see what was coming, and wrote to her husband: 'I wish you to publish these facts; they are no secret to any but those Europeans whose interests keep their eyes tightly shut, and they will soon have them opened.'[38] She would, of course, be proved right, but only when it was too late.

⊲⊡⊳

While modern Egypt was lurching towards repression and revolution, the study of ancient Egypt was experiencing its own transformation under Mariette and the recently established Antiquities Service. Duff Gordon was no stranger to the world of oriental archaeology – Sir Henry Layard, discoverer of Nimrud and Nineveh, was a family friend – and every Egyptologist passing through Luxor could not fail to make her acquaintance. In February 1864, de Rougé and Mariette arrived by steamer; Lucie's main concern was that 'they will turn out good company'.[39] A more permanent companion was the American adventurer and antiquities dealer Edwin Smith, who was also living at Luxor, and for whom Duff Gordon procured the latest archaeological books from England.[40] As late as the 1860s, a few surviving links with Napoleonic Egyptology could still be found in a place like Luxor; one of Lucie's Egyptian acquaintances, whom she fondly referred to as 'my old "great-grandfather"', had been Belzoni's guide, and 'his eldest child was born seven days before the French under Bonaparte marched into Luxor'.[41]

Alongside these echoes from the past, new rivalries were beginning to shape the discipline. Lepsius's pupil, Johannes Dümichen, was in Egypt to copy inscriptions, and got to hear about a king list that Mariette's workers had uncovered at Abydos. He dutifully sent a copy to Lepsius, back in Berlin, who published it without even acknowledging Mariette. In the resulting furore, with national pride at stake, Dümichen and Mariette almost came to blows.[42] In truth, since Lepsius's expedition and the foundation of the Antiquities Service, German scholars had largely been shut out of fieldwork in Egypt.[43] Not even popular novels, with titles like *An Egyptian Princess* (1864), published by the Leipzig professor, Georg Ebers, could mask the sidelining of German Egyptology.

Mariette, meanwhile, was unstoppable, opening up excavations throughout Egypt and, to Duff Gordon's disgust, 'forcing the people to work'.[44] With all his power and authority, he was not immune to thinking himself above the law. On one occasion, no doubt after a heated argument about access to antiquities and fired by competing national interests, he struck the British consular agent at Luxor, Mustafa Agha Ayat, before flatly denying any wrongdoing. With her sense of fair play, Lucie was incensed, and wrote to the British authorities who sent a Foreign Office official to conduct an enquiry.[45] The Austro-Prussian War of 1866 led to a weakening of the French position in Europe, and the strengthening of Prussia under Bismarck; but none of this seemed to affect Mariette, secure in his position and master of all he surveyed. Duff Gordon, though, continued to cock a snook at her childhood neighbour: 'A man has stolen a very nice silver antique ring for me out of the last excavations – don't tell Mariette . . . My fellah friend said "better thou have it than Mariette sell it to the French and pocket the money; if I didn't steal it, he would" – so I received the stolen property calmly.'[46]

Well may Lucie have pocketed the odd illicitly acquired antique, for she was constantly worried about money, and struggled to make ends meet, even with her frugal lifestyle. An outbreak of murrain had swept Egypt in the autumn of 1863, killing large numbers of livestock and raising prices still further. Duff Gordon was forced to eke out an increasingly precarious existence: 'I live in the open air altogether. The bats and the swallows are quite sociable; I hope the serpents and scorpions will be more reserved.'[47] In the summer months, the heat could be unbearable; the only solution was to drop her European reserve and opt for something more practical: 'It has been so "awfully" hot that I have not had pluck to go on with my letter, or indeed to do anything but lie on a mat in the passage with a minimum of clothes quite indescribable in English.'[48]

Despite being settled in Luxor, Duff Gordon experienced bouts of terrible homesickness, still missing her children, and feeling she was gradually losing them. But by July 1864 she had begun to accept that she would never return to England. She wrote to her husband: 'I do not feel at all like breathing cold damp air again. This depresses me very much as you may suppose. You will have to divorce me.'[49] Far from damaging her reputation, however, her heroic existence in a distant land captured imaginations at home, and the publication of her *Letters from Egypt* in 1865 cemented her fame.

The Egyptian climate may have been beneficial for those suffering from tuberculosis, but other diseases were rampant. On a journey down the Nile in May 1865, Lucie nearly died of pleurisy, and had to be nursed back to health by her faithful servant Omar. (After recovering, she wrote to her husband: 'I beg you won't ever forget Omar's truly filial care and affection for me.'[50]) A few months later, in Bulaq, Mariette's wife was not so fortunate, and succumbed to cholera. Meanwhile, the plight of ordinary Egyptians continued to worsen. When desperate peasants had vented their anger by attacking a Prussian boat on the Nile, Ismail himself had paid a visit and 'taken a broom and swept them clean, *i.e.* – exterminated the inhabitants'.[51] One Egyptian had confided in Duff Gordon: 'I only pray for Europeans to rule us – now the fellaheen are worse off than any slaves.'[52] In Lucie's own view, a combination of factors had conspired to make life intolerable: 'The country is a waste for want of water, the animals are skeletons, the people are hungry, the heat has set in like June, and there is some sickness, and, above all the massacres . . . have embittered all hearts.'[53]

Ismail, however, carried on as if the day of reckoning would never arrive. In April 1866, he visited Constantinople and obtained from the Sultan, for a large sum, the right to pass the title of viceroy to his son, rather than to the eldest surviving relative, thus breaking with Turkish custom and effectively establishing his own dynasty. (The following year, the Sultan recognized the new reality and granted Ismail the title of khedive – also in return for a hefty payment.) By July, the Egyptian government was nearly bankrupt; Duff Gordon's own son-in-law, Henry Ross, was hit hard when his employer, the

Egyptian Commercial and Trading Company, suffered losses. But Ismail, instead of reining in his spending, merely clamped down on dissent 'The espionage is becoming more and more close and jealous,' Lucie wrote, 'and I have been warned to be very careful.'[54] Farmers were beaten to pay taxes for the following year, which they were unable to pay. Fellahin were conscripted to fight alongside Turkish troops to put down a rebellion on Crete. And, all the while, able-bodied men were plucked from the fields to work on government construction projects. The combined results were calamitous:

> The hand of the Government is awfully heavy upon us. All this week the people have been working night and day cutting their unripe corn, because three hundred and ten men are to go tomorrow to work on the railroad below Assiut. This green corn is, of course, valueless to sell and unwholesome to eat; so the magnificent harvest of this year is turned to bitterness at the last moment. From a neighbouring village all the men are gone, and seven more are wanted to make up the *corvée*.[55]

In the summer of 1867, Ismail accompanied his new best friend, the Ottoman sultan, to Europe, where they were feted by their hosts. The first stop was Paris, to view the Exposition Universelle. Duff Gordon remarked tartly: 'The universal prayer now is, "may he not return in safety, may he die in France and be buried in the graves of unbelievers".'[56] The khedive's next port of call was London, where Ismail was made a Knight Grand Cross of the Order of the Bath and the Sultan received the Order of the Garter. Egyptian officials who accompanied the royal visit were not just there to bask in the reflected glory: Ismail wanted them to learn about the modern developments taking place in Europe – for example, the remodelling of Paris under Hausmann – and copy them back in Egypt. Ali Mubarak, an engineer, was made Minister of Public Works and Minister of Schools on his return from France, and duly set about transforming the city of Cairo and establishing government schools throughout the country. Cairo witnessed its greatest construction boom since the Middle Ages as waste land was levelled and filled, new avenues and public squares laid out, dirt roads surfaced, and sewers dug. The unifying philosophy was *tanzim*: organization, regulation and modernization, an extension of military order into every aspect of civilian life.[57] It was also a deliberate attempt to turn Egypt into a Western nation. Plots in the new quarter of Cairo were made available to anyone who promised to build a building with a European facade. Ismail's eyes were fixed firmly on modernity, even if, in a nod to the growth of tourism, he adopted a pyramid-and-sphinx design for his country's new postage stamps.

Just as tourists expecting a scene from the *Arabian Nights* were disappointed by the remodelling of Cairo, so tourism itself was reshaping Egypt. In 1867, the year that Mark Twain first visited the country (to climb the Great Pyramid), Duff Gordon wrote 'Americans swarm in the steamboats, and a good many in *dahabiehs*'[58] and added: 'This year I'll bolt the doors when I see a steamer coming.'[59] No longer a quiet backwater, Thebes had been transformed into 'an English watering-place. There are now nine boats lying here, and the great object is to *do the Nile* as fast as possible.'[60] In January she entertained the writer Edward Lear, and in the autumn her mood was greatly lightened by a visit from her son, Maurice, who seems to have spent most of his time shooting water fowl. But time was catching up with Duff Gordon and her way of life. In December that year, she wrote laconically: 'Half of the old house at Luxor fell down into the temple beneath six days before I arrived; so there is an end of the

Maison de France, I suppose.'[61] Lucie's mother, Sarah Austin, had passed away in August 1867, and Duff Gordon's own health continued to worsen. By January 1869, she wrote to her daughter: 'I am more ill, I believe, than you quite suppose. I do not like your father to be worried, but I may tell *you* that I think it hardly possible I can last much longer . . . I think Maurice had better go home soon . . . I wish I could hope to see any of you once more, but I do not see any possibility of reaching Europe.'[62]

Later that month, she sent Maurice home, with the tart observation that: 'He ought to be doing something.'[63] In February, she was just about well enough to receive a visit from the Prince and Princess of Wales, during their trip up the Nile. (Since the publication of Duff Gordon's *Letters from Egypt* she had become something of a celebrity.) But, by the late spring, she knew the end was coming. Cairo would provide better terminal care, so she left Luxor amidst much weeping. She almost immediately regretted it, writing to her husband: 'If I live till September I will go up to Esneh, where the air is softer and I cough less. I would rather die among my own people in the Said [Upper Egypt] than here.' (She added, with just a hint of maternal exasperation: 'Don't think please of sending Maurice out again, he must begin to work now or he will never be good for anything.')[64]

Duff Gordon's final letter, written to her husband on 9 July 1869 from the spa resort of Helwan, just south of Cairo, ends: 'God bless you, my dearest of all loves . . . Kiss my darlings all . . . Forgive me all my faults toward you. I wish I had seen your dear face once more – but not now. I would not have you here now on any account.'[65]

She died in the early morning five days later, aged just forty-eight. The faithful Omar was by her side until the very end. In an obituary in *The Times*, Lucie's friend, Caroline

Norton, summed up her life and legacy succinctly: 'Lady Duff Gordon lived in Egypt, and in Egypt she has died, leaving a memory of her greatness and goodness such as no other European woman ever acquired in that country.'[66]

━◁○▷━

Khedive Ismail has been described as 'an ugly man of the greatest charm'.[67] His subjects may have begged to differ, at least on the latter point. Charming or not, he certainly had a taste for opulence (Sauternes was his drink of choice), and his extravagance was notorious, especially when it came to entertaining foreign guests. When Empress Eugénie visited Egypt in 1869, for the official opening of the Suez Canal, Ismail ordered an eight-mile long road to be laid from central Cairo to enable her 'to drive out to the Pyramids without fatigue (she perversely rode out there every morning on horseback) and had built under their shadow a stone mansion in which she might repose for a single night'.[68] As for his own palace at Giza, its gardens were intersected by mosaic pavements laid by craftsmen brought from Italy, all at a reputed cost of 30,000 Egyptian pounds. It was his love of European fashion and progress that caused him to remodel and modernize not just central Cairo, but virtually the whole of Egypt. In addition to his greatest project, the Suez Canal, opened in the year of Duff Gordon's death, he presided over the reclamation of 1.25 million acres of desert land, and the construction of 8,400 miles of irrigation canals, 1,185 miles of railways, 500 miles of telegraph, 4,500 primary schools, 430 bridges, sixty-four sugar mills, fifteen lighthouses, the Suez docks and a new harbour at Alexandria.

In Cairo, many of the buildings were jerry-built – outwardly ostentatious, but lacking in structural solidity. None demonstrated his love of indulgence and his obsession with European culture more than the Opera House. Built on one side of the Ezbekiya Gardens, facing Shepheard's Hotel, it was a monument to Western taste par excellence. Modelled on the Paris Opera, it was decorated inside with crimson hangings and an abundance of gold brocade; an opulent royal box included screened pews for the ladies of the king's harem. The first performance, a production of Verdi's *Rigoletto*, took place on 1 November 1869. Had Duff Gordon still been alive, she would no doubt have excoriated this latest demonstration of the khedive's vanity. Empress Eugénie sat in the royal box between Ismail and Emperor Franz Josef of Austria. Few Egyptians were invited that evening, and few would attend in the years to come. Instead, the Cairo Opera House became a favourite haunt for Western expatriates, where they could cocoon themselves from the harsh realities of life beyond the marble foyer.

Another of Verdi's works had been intended for the Opera's opening night, but was not ready in time. *Aïda* received its premiere two years late, on Christmas Day 1871, to great critical acclaim. In typical Ismailian fashion, the first performance featured 3,000 performers, including Nubians and slaves 'bearing in procession statues and figures of the ancient gods borrowed out of the museum for the occasion'.[69] As befitted an opera set in the time of the pharaohs, the libretto of *Aïda* had been commissioned from the greatest Egyptologist of the day, Mariette. Having presided over the Antiquities Service and Egyptian Museum for over a decade, he was at the height of his reputation and influence. But events far from the banks of the Nile soon threatened not just Mariette's position, but his very life.

Throughout the mid- and late 1860s, the rivalry between France and Prussia had been building, in Egypt and across the continent of Europe. The spat between Mariette and Dümichen was a symptom of a wider malaise. While Germans may not have been actively involved in excavations, they were impressively productive in other areas of scholarship, building on Lepsius's achievements a generation earlier. One of the leading lights of this second generation of German Egyptologists was Mariette's friend, Heinrich Brugsch. He had studied under Lepsius and assisted Mariette at the Serapeum. In 1863, he founded a learned periodical, the *Zeitschrift für Ägyptische Sprache und Altertumskunde*; it remains to this day one of the discipline's most respected organs, and arguably the premier journal for ancient Egyptian philology. In 1864, Brugsch served briefly as Prussian consul in Cairo, before returning home to take up a professorship at the University of Göttingen. In 1869, at the apogee of Ismail's flirtation with Europe, Brugsch was invited back to Cairo to be head of a new Khedivial School of Egyptology. Mariette had considered Brugsch a friend; now the two looked like rivals. The Frenchman opposed the School of Egyptology from the start: not only was it run by a German, it also threatened to create an alternative centre of scholarship in competition with the Egyptian Museum. Under Brugsch's leadership, the school gave back to German Egyptology a prestige it had not enjoyed since Lepsius's expedition. For Mariette, this was anathema.

Worse was to come. On 16 July 1870, the French parliament, fearing the spectre of German unification and the growing assertiveness of its neighbour, declared war on Prussia. It was a disastrous mistake. The Prussian-led coalition of German forces mobilized quickly and invaded north-eastern France. A series of rapid German victories culminated in the siege of Metz and the battle of Sedan. The French army was defeated and Napoleon III captured. In Paris, on 4 September, the empire was abolished and the Third Republic declared; but it was not enough to assuage German wrath. Two weeks later, German troops surrounded the capital and began to draw the noose tight. After a four-month siege, the French capital fell on 28 January 1871. France's defeat paved the way for what it had most feared: German unification under an all-powerful Prussia. Worse still, the Treaty of Frankfurt which brought the war to an end gave most of Alsace and part of Lorraine to Germany, upsetting the balance of power in Europe that had prevailed since the defeat of the first Napoleon in 1815.

By a stroke of singularly bad luck, Mariette had returned to Paris for his summer vacation when the siege broke out, and found himself trapped in the city for months. This was not just a personal misfortune: in his absence, rivals in Egypt started plotting to replace him. Brugsch was mentioned as a candidate for a possible German takeover of the Antiquities Service, but was loath to move against a former colleague, and Mariette's enemies failed to press their advantage. As soon as the siege of Paris was lifted, Mariette hurried back to Bulaq to reassert his own position, and, with it, France's leadership of the Museum and Service. He bore no ill will towards Brugsch, telling him: 'For me you are not a German, you are Brugsch . . . I love you as a true friend.'[70] Two years later, Mariette appointed Heinrich's younger brother Emile Brugsch, who had joined the School of Egyptology as his brother's assistant, to a post in the Museum, where he served loyally for the next forty years.

Mariette reaped the rewards of determination and magnanimity with a series of spectacular discoveries during the course of 1871. The painted fresco of geese, and the statues of Rahotep and Nofret (still some of the greatest treasures of the Egyptian Museum), were uncovered at Meidum, while the sands of Saqqara yielded the spectacular decorated tomb of Ti. But France's grasp on the levers of archaeological and cultural influence had been weakened, and no amount of digging for antiquities could change that fact. Following the Franco-Prussian War, the study of German was introduced into

Egyptian government schools alongside French, as Ismail and his ministers sought to hedge their bets on which European power would ultimately triumph.[71] Mariette had other concerns too. Not only was the Khedivial School of Egyptology under German control (in the person of Heinrich Brugsch), so too was the new Khedivial Library. Ludwig Stern became director in 1873, and was followed in post by four more German orientalists, the Library remaining a bastion of German influence until the outbreak of the First World War. When the Egyptian Society, founded in 1836, disbanded in 1873–4, its remaining books were donated to the Khedivial Library, bolstering the latter's position as one of the leading academic institutions of Cairo.

In Europe, too, Germany was challenging French preeminence in Egyptology, with a series of chairs established in all the leading universities: Göttingen in 1868 (created for Brugsch), Strasbourg – under German control since the Franco-Prussian War – and Heidelberg in 1872, and Leipzig in 1875 joined Lepsius's chair at Berlin as major seats of learning. What made matters worse, as far as French sensibilities were concerned, were the close ties between German and British Egyptology, dating back to the participation of Bonomi and Wild in the Lepsius expedition.

The long-standing competition between France and Britain for control of Egypt was thus replaced during the 1870s by a keenly felt Franco-German rivalry. So, when senior vacancies arose at France's two most prestigious institutions, the Collège de France and the Louvre, Mariette declined the chance to return home. Although Egypt had carried off his beloved daughter Josephine in March that year, following the death of his wife in 1865, he knew that his destiny – and his national duty – lay in Cairo, not Paris. As his biographer would later write, Mariette, 'had the choice once more between Egypt and

France, and he chose Egypt: he remained faithful until his death'.[72]

It was into this heady mix of major-power rivalry, old-fashioned digging and newfangled scholarship that one woman sailed in the autumn of 1873, rather by accident than design. She had no academic training and no governmental support. Yet her brief sojourn in Egypt would change her life and alter the course of Egyptology forever.

⊲⊙⊳

Amelia Blandford Edwards (1831–92), known to her family and friends as Amy, was born into a comfortable middle-class home in London, almost ten years to the day after Lucie Duff Gordon. Edwards's father was a bank clerk, who had previously served as an army officer under the Duke of Wellington in the Peninsular War against Napoleon. But it was Edwards's mother who encouraged the little girl to indulge her love of reading. Educated at home, like most young women of her generation, Amy developed an independent mind and a lively imagination, fired by travel books and the *Arabian Nights*. When she was six, Wilkinson's *Manners and Customs of the Ancient Egyptians* was published, and she devoured it from cover to cover. She later recalled: 'I had read every line of the old six-volume edition over and over again. I knew every one of the six hundred illustrations by heart.'[73] Inspired by such accounts of life in far-off days, she wrote a poem at the age of seven called 'The Knights of Old', which was reproduced in a penny weekly. It was her first published work. Beside reading and writing, another passion was drama, encouraged, once again, by her mother who took her on trips to the theatre at Sadler's Wells. Amy had a carefree childhood, combining cultural experiences in London with summers in the country, staying with her uncle and aunt in their Suffolk farmhouse.

There, she showed an early aptitude for painting, decorating the whitewashed walls of her room with a mural she titled 'The Landing of the Romans in Britain'. The combination of artistic skill, a vigorous and confident hand, and a love of historical drama would serve her well.

Alongside this wide range of accomplishments, Edwards's principal passion was music. She had natural talent, a good voice, and clear enunciation, and she hoped to make a career as a singer. When illness thwarted her attempts, she tried her hand as an organist, but found it insufficiently creative. With a career in music thus ruled out, she would have liked to become an artist, but that was considered entirely unsuitable for a respectable young woman in early Victorian England. So she fell back on writing, and into a career as a journalist, contributing to the *Saturday Review* and the *Morning Post*. The job was steady but not lucrative, so Edwards supplemented her income by publishing history and fiction. Perhaps to her surprise, she turned out to be rather good at it. Her writing was filled with an extraordinary range of information, reflecting her catholic interests, a sharp eye for contemporary customs, and a satirical wit.

In the early 1850s, Edwards travelled to France, Germany and Switzerland, developing a love of foreign travel and a receptiveness to other cultures – not to mention a connoisseur's knowledge of wine. More intriguingly, her visits to Paris seem to have brought her into contact with a Bohemian circle of artists and political radicals from whom she learned a determined, if largely concealed, sense of social justice. Armed with a host of experiences and a wealth of insight, she published her first novel, *My Brother's Wife*, in 1855, to favourable reviews. A second novel, *The Ladder of Life*, followed in 1857, and a further six novels together with a series of short stories in subsequent years. Meanwhile, Edwards's personal circumstances were not without incident. In 1860, in what she would later describe as 'the great misfortune of my life',[74] both her parents died, within four days of each other. She had been especially close to her mother, and, seeking company, decided to move in with friends, Mr and Mrs Braysher. They introduced her to upper-middle-class society, providing abundant material for a satirical novelist. When Mr Braysher died in 1863, Edwards and Mrs Braysher decided to set up home together, moving to a house in Westbury-on-Trym, which they shared for the rest of their lives.

By the late 1860s, Amy was settled and successful, but restless for new adventures. Remembering fondly her youthful excursions to the continent, she decided once again to travel. In the summer of 1871, she set out for Switzerland and Italy. She wintered in Rome, spent the spring in southern Italy, and moved on to the Italian lakes for the summer. So far, so conventional. Then, on a whim, she decided to explore the Dolomites, a region still largely unknown to tourists, accompanied by her friend Lucy Renshawe. The two women travelled alone, exploring the dramatic scenery and isolated mountain villages. The result was Edwards's first extensive travel book, touchingly entitled *A Midsummer Ramble in the Dolomites* (later reissued with the more romantic title *Untravelled Peaks and Unfrequented Valleys*). The trip to Italy was such a success that Edwards and Miss Renshawe set out again the following summer, for a walking tour of France. But, thwarted by bad weather, they decided to follow the footsteps of countless travellers before them and embark on a journey up the Nile instead. They braved a storm-tossed crossing from Brindisi to Alexandria and forty-eight hours in Egyptian quarantine before finally arriving in Cairo on 29 November 1873. As Edwards put it: 'In simple truth we had drifted hither by accident; with no excuse of health or business, or any serious object whatever; and had just taken refuge in Egypt as one might turn aside into Burlington Arcade or the Passage des Panoramas – to get out of the rain.'[75]

As soon as her publisher, Longman's, heard that she was in Egypt, they commissioned a book, giving the trip a purpose. With her novelist's eye for detail and her openness to new experiences, Edwards set out on her journey through Egypt and Nubia, a thousand miles up the Nile.

Egypt had changed a great deal during the first decade of Ismail's reign. The rebuilding of Cairo had swept away much of the traditional Islamic architecture, replacing it with modern constructions in the European style. New factories had sprung up in the towns, while extensive irrigation works and land reclamation had transformed the countryside. Tourism, too, had changed. Thomas Cook had conducted his first escorted tour up the Nile in 1869, using two hired steamers for 'the first publicly advertised party to the First Cataract and back'.[76] The following year, Thomas Cook's son John negotiated the use of the khedivial steamer *Beherah* to take forty-four guests up the Nile, 'the largest party of English and American tourists that had to date ascended the river as one party'.[77] It was said that, 'at every village landing-stage he scattered largesse, from great sacks of copper coins' to ingratiate himself with local people and trinket-sellers.[78] By the autumn of 1870, Cook's had been granted the sole agency for a passenger service by Nile steamer. The resulting explosion in tourism meant that, by the time Edwards and her companion arrived in Egypt, all the items that Wilkinson had listed in his 1847 *Handbook* as difficult to obtain were readily available in both Cairo and Alexandria.[79]

Eschewing the rapid steamer, Amy opted instead for the more traditional *dahabiya*, a more leisurely way to see the sights. She and Miss Renshawe were joined by twenty-three fellow-travellers. During the course of the next few months, as they sailed upstream, through the First Cataract and into Nubia as far as the rock of Abusir, they encountered all the hazards faced by shipping on the Nile: headwinds and periods when they were becalmed, sandbanks and rapids, sandstorms and a hurricane. For Edwards, these merely added to the adventure. So did the trials and tribulations involved in visiting some of the archaeological sites: 'It might be necessary to crawl into a tomb or slide down into the darkness on one's stomach.'[80] A further touch of spice was provided by a sense of competiton, for sailing alongside Edwards and her party in another *dahabiya* were the diarist Marianne Brocklehurst and her companion Miss Booth. Brocklehurst and Edwards were firm friends and fierce publishing rivals. As it turned out, Amy had nothing to worry about. For while Miss Brocklehurst was dismissive of the ancient monuments and contemptuous of the modern Egyptians, Edwards was entranced. All those well-thumbed illustrations in Wilkinson's *Manners and Customs* had come to life in front of her eyes. She knew she was gathering the material for a bestseller.

Like many a traveller before her, Edwards was captivated by the climate and scenery – 'the skies are always cloudless, the days warm, the evenings exquisite'[81] – but she was no mere tourist. From her earlier travels in Europe, she understood that 'the mere sight-seeing of the Nile demands some little reading and organizing, if only to be enjoyed',[82] and indeed believed that 'To "see" Egypt is to be required to learn'.[83] To this end, she took in every detail and sought out information on every tomb and temple she visited. At Saqqara, she took lunch on the terrace of Mariette's former dig house, and made a point of visiting Memphis, but was disappointed to find it reduced to 'a few huge rubbish-heaps, a dozen or so of broken statues, and a name!'[84] In general, though, with her romantic bent and love of the dramatic, Edwards could not fail to be moved by the antiquity and mystery of Egypt's pharaonic past. At Philae, she felt: 'If a sound of antique chanting were to be borne along the quiet air – if a procession of white-robed priests bearing aloft the veiled ark of the God, were to come sweeping round between the palms and the pylons – we should not think it strange.'[85] She was also unusually sensitive to ancient Egyptian religion, writing: 'One cannot but come away with a profound impression of the splendour and power of a religion which could command for its myths such faith, such homage, and such public works.'[86]

This open-mindedness did not, however, extend to sympathy for the modern Egyptians. Despite Edwards's political radicalism in a European setting, she was wilfully blind to the sufferings of the fellahin, arguing that 'there is another side to this question of forced labour . . . How, then, are these necessary public works to be carried out, unless by means of the *corvée*?'[87] When confronted by grinding poverty, her usual insight seems to have deserted her, and she fell back on European stereotypes: 'It seemed to us that the wives of the Fellahin were in truth the happiest women in Egypt. They work hard and are bitterly poor; but they have the free use of their limbs, and they at least know the fresh air, the sunshine, and the open fields.'[88]

From the vantage point of a comfortable *dahabiya* – 'our Noah's Ark life, pleasant, peaceful, and patriarchal'[89] – it was all too easy for the pampered to slip into prejudice. Edwards's description of ordinary Egyptians is as cruel as it is colourful: 'A more unprepossessing population I would never wish to see – the men half stealthy, half insolent; the women bold and fierce; the children filthy, sickly, stunted, and stolid.'[90]

It was ironic, therefore, that in Luxor, she made a point of visiting the house lately occupied by Lucie Duff Gordon, remarking that 'her couch, her rug, her folding chair were there still', and noting that 'every Arab in Luxor cherishes the memory of Lady Duff Gordon in his heart of hearts, and speaks of her with blessings'.[91]

On Edwards's return to England in the spring of 1874, she spent two years writing up her notes and preparing her book. Although intended for a popular readership, she wanted it to be accurate and informative. So she consulted specialist journals and sought advice from leading scholars, including Wilkinson's friend and member of Lepsius's expedition, Joseph Bonomi; Edward Lane's nephew Reginald Stuart Poole; and Samuel Birch at the British Museum. The result of all this research was both a triumph of scholarship and a captivating travelogue. European experiences of Egypt had, of course, for well over a century, provided fertile ground for writers of all sorts, 'soil already so heavily tilled, soil which has yielded literature of every grade down to the lowest level of banality'.[92] Not so Edwards's book. Published in 1877 to great critical acclaim, *A Thousand Miles Up the Nile* was both colourful and clever. It began diffidently, prefaced with a witty French epigram and a throwaway line: '"A donkey-ride and a boating-trip interspersed with ruins" does, in fact, sum up in a single line the whole experience of the Nile traveler.'[93] The opening sentence was carefully calculated to draw in the casual reader: 'It is the traveller's lot to dine in many table-d'hôtes in the course of many wanderings; but it seldom befalls him to make one of a more miscellaneous gathering than that which over-fills the great dining-room at Shepheard's Hotel in Cairo during the beginning and height of the regular Egyptian season';[94] and there were further nods in the direction of carefree travel-writing: 'Happy are the Nile travellers who start thus with a fair breeze on a brilliant afternoon.'[95] A tart put-down of the Paris obelisk – 'already scaling away by imperceptible degrees under the skyey influences of an alien climate, looks

1. Napoleon Bonaparte, whose expedition to Egypt in 1798 laid the foundations for the birth of Egyptology.

2. Giovanni Battista Belzoni, travelling salesman, circus strongman and amateur archaeologist.

3. A stone bust of pharaoh Ramesses II, nicknamed the 'Young Memnon', which Belzoni succeeded in removing in 1816 and acquiring for the British Museum.

4.   Jean-François Champollion, decipherer of hieroglyphics and founding
     father of Egyptology.

5. The temple of the goddess Hathor at Dendera; the zodiac from the ceiling of one of the roof chapels was removed in 1821 and taken to the Louvre.

6. A watercolour by David Roberts of the great temple at Abu Simbel, showing its appearance in the first half of the nineteenth century.

7. A wall decoration from one of the Tombs of the Nobles at Thebes; copying and recording such scenes was one of John Gardner Wilkinson's major contributions to Egyptology.

8. Muhammad Ali, the Albanian mercenary who founded a dynasty and presided over the modernization of Egypt.

9. A statue of a seated scribe discovered by Auguste Mariette while he
   was searching for the Serapeum at Saqqara.

10. A relief of the queen of Punt, from the temple of Hatshepsut at Thebes, one of many monuments excavated by the Antiquities Service in the 1860s under Mariette's direction.
11. The tomb of Mariette in the garden of the Egyptian Museum, Cairo.

12. Amelia Edwards, Victorian novelist, traveller, founder of the Egypt Exploration Society, and indefatigable champion of Egypt's ancient heritage.

13. A painted mummy mask from Hawara; dug from the sand by Flinders Petrie, this and other portrait masks shed new light on Egyptian culture during the Ptolemaic and Roman periods.

14. The Hypostyle Hall in the temple of Amun-Ra at Karnak; its partial collapse in 1899 brought home the need for better protection of Egypt's monuments.

15. The Egyptian Museum, Cairo; designed by a Frenchman, its facade bears the names of the great European Egyptologists of the nineteenth century.

16. The great temple at Abu Simbel: for many travellers, the ultimate destination and the highlight of a Nile cruise.

17. A triad of King Menkaura flanked by two goddesses; one of the masterpieces of ancient Egyptian sculpture discovered by George Reisner at Giza.

18. The portable furniture (bed, chair and canopy) of gilded wood made for Queen Hetepheres in the fourth dynasty and unearthed by Reisner some 4,400 years later.

19. The gilded mask of Tjuyu from the Valley of the Kings; discovered in 1905 by Theodore Davis, it formed part of the greatest treasure found in Egypt to that date.

20. Evelyn Baring, Lord Cromer, de facto ruler of Egypt for a quarter of a century until his retirement in 1907.

21. The mortuary temple of Hatshepsut at Deir el-Bahri, western Thebes, one of the sites where Howard Carter cut his teeth as a young archaeologist.

22. The painted limestone bust of Nefertiti, icon of ancient art, discovered in 1912 by Ludwig Borchardt in the ruins of the abandoned capital city of Amarna.

23. The golden mask of Tutankhamun; thanks to Howard Carter and Lord Carnarvon, a once-obscure boy-king has become the most famous of all Egyptian pharaohs.

down with melancholy indifference upon the petty revolutions and counter-revolutions of the Place de la Concorde'[96] – was designed to have her anglophone readership smiling with approval. But, slowly, almost stealthily, Edwards's true interests began to make themselves apparent. Liberally sprinkled throughout the text were quotes from Wilkinson, Lepsius, Mariette and even Duff Gordon. An entire chapter was devoted to the life and reign of Ramesses II. The Egyptian Museum was described in detail, and it was deemed worth the journey from Europe even if 'there was nothing else to tempt the traveller to Cairo'.[97]

Edwards's unique, intoxicating blend of romance and scholarship reached its culmination in her description of the great stone-hewn temples at Abu Simbel. Following in the footsteps of Burckhardt, Bankes and Belzoni, she detailed the various historical inscriptions, but reserved her most vivid and quotable prose for the special magic of seeing the colossal stone statues of the temple's facade at sunrise: 'Every morning I waked in time to witness that daily miracle. Every morning I saw those awful brethren pass from death to life, from life to sculptured stone. I brought myself almost to believe at last there must sooner or later come some one sunrise when the ancient chasm would snap asunder, and the giants must arise and speak.'[98]

But all this was a mere preamble to the main point of the chapter, the closing peroration which forms the spiritual heart of the book. Having thrilled her readers with her fabulous description of Abu Simbel, she brought them down to earth with a bump: 'The work of destruction, meanwhile, goes on apace. There is no one to prevent it; there is no one to discourage it. Every day more inscriptions are mutilated – more tombs are rifled – more paintings and sculptures are defaced. The Louvre contains a full-length portrait of Seti I, cut out bodily from the walls of his sepulchre in the Valley of the Tombs of the Kings. The Museums of Berlin, of Turin, of Florence, are rich in spoils which tell their own lamentable tale. When science leads the way, is it wonderful that ignorance should follow?'[99]

Edwards's true purpose was thus revealed: an appeal to scholarship to set an example – 'students in their libraries, excavators under Egyptian skies, toiling along different paths towards a common goal'[100] – and to rescue Egyptian archaeology from the clutches of treasure-hunting and national rivalries. She had found her calling at last: her journey to Egypt had turned her, unwittingly, into an Egyptologist. Following the publication of *A Thousand Miles*, Edwards abandoned fiction and reoriented her whole life. Her new mission would be to establish a society to undertake scientific excavations in Egypt, to record and publish its surviving antiquities more accurately than ever before, to protect them for future generations, and to win the public's backing for the task.

As if to confirm the dawn of a new age, Baedeker's published its first guide to Egypt in the same year as *A Thousand Miles Up the Nile* appeared. Tourism to Egypt was now a truly international, mass-market affair. The year 1877 also witnessed another milestone in the British affair with Egypt. One of the two small obelisks in Alexandria, known erroneously as Cleopatra's Needles, had been given to Britain by the Ottoman authorities soon after the expulsion of Bonaparte's troops in 1801. At the time, the government in London was unenthusiastic about the prospect, never mind the expense, of bringing a piece of old stone to London. Two decades later, in the excitement surrounding the decipherment of hieroglyphics, George IV had ordered the Foreign Office to reconsider the plan, but once again Parliament had baulked at the cost. From time to time, Egyptian rulers, from Muhammad Ali to Ismail, reminded the British that the obelisk was theirs for the taking, but there was little public appetite.

Interest in bringing the obelisk to London was temporarily piqued when Prince Albert heard rumours that the French might be about to steal a march and add it to their collection of Egyptian monuments. Fearing a national disgrace, the prince consort wrote to the prime minister, Lord John Russell, asking him to take swift action. Questions were duly asked in Parliament, and the government decided to act. The cost of transport was estimated at £15,000. The politicians bit the bullet, but instead of receiving a chorus of approval, they found their decision criticized by the very people they might have expected to support it, the small but vocal Egyptological community in Britain. The objections were led by Wilkinson, supported by a group of his scholar friends. Hay, for example, argued that Cleopatra's Needle was so inferior to the Luxor obelisk that it would be a national disgrace to bring it to London. Wilkinson's criticism of the plan was motivated more by aesthetics; he wrote to Birch: 'I do think it is a great mistake bringing obelisks to this country . . . we always place them in a position ill suited to them.'[101] (By contrast, Wilkinson had lobbied hard in the 1830s for the colossus of Ramesses II at Memphis to be brought to England; perhaps he felt it was easier to site a statue.) With such eminent figures expressing vocal opposition to the proposal, it was killed stone dead. Cleopatra's Needle remained on the Corniche in Alexandria.

It was only in 1877, a few years after Wilkinson's death, that the prospect of another calamity reopened the question of bringing the obelisk to London. This time it was not the perfidious French who forced Britain's hand, but a Greek land-owner who planned to cut up the monument for building stone. With slim prospects of Parliament voting the necessary funds, a wealthy businessman, Erasmus Wilson, offered to pay for the whole project. A barge, aptly named the *Cleopatra*, was dispatched to Alexandria, and the obelisk carefully lifted aboard from the quayside. Slowly but surely, the tow ship *Olga* began to pull the *Cleopatra* and its precious cargo out into the Mediterranean. Along the North African coast, past Malta, and through the Straits of Gibraltar: everything went smoothly until the ships entered the Bay of Biscay. There they hit a storm, and the *Cleopatra* began rolling uncontrollably. It looked as if it might capsize, sending its monolith to the bottom of the Atlantic. The *Olga* sent a rescue boat, crewed by volunteers, but it foundered in the waves, drowning all six onboard. With the *Cleopatra* drifting helplessly and threatening to sink at any moment, it had to be rescued by a Glasgow steamer and taken to a Spanish port for essential repairs. Eventually, it was towed around the Breton peninsula and up the English Channel, arriving at the mouth of the Thames on 21 January 1878.

Eight months later, amid great ceremony, Cleopatra's Needle was erected on the Victoria Embankment – where it, too, is now 'scaling away by imperceptible degrees under the skyey influences of an alien climate'. It may have been incongruous to see this monument from a sunny Mediterranean land on the banks of the cold, grey Thames, but the obelisk's symbolism was what mattered. Since the days of Julius Caesar, new empires had announced their arrival on the world stage and proclaimed their might by usurping the monuments of earlier empires, especially the empire of the pharaohs. Rome, Constantinople, Paris all had their obelisks; now it was London's turn. By bringing Cleopatra's needle to London, 'Britain signalled its inheritance of world power. London would thus become virtually a "New Rome".'[102] Those who had cried out to Lucie Duff Gordon: 'Let the English Queen come and take us!' were about to be granted their wish.

SEVEN

A permanent occupation

Flinders Petrie outside a rock-cut tomb at Giza (which served as his home)
on the first of his many archaeological expeditions to Egypt.

I believe the true line lies as much in the careful noting and comparison of small details, as in more wholesale and off-hand clearances.[1]

FLINDERS PETRIE, 1882

The early 1880s were perhaps the most momentous years in the entire history of Egyptology and of Egypt's entanglement with the West. They stand, alongside the Napoleonic expedition of 1798–1801, as a turning point in the European discovery of Egypt, and Egypt's discovery of itself. In the space of eighteen months, between January 1881 and July 1882, three unrelated yet inextricably intertwined events shook the comfortable worlds of the khedivial court and European scholarship. By the time the events had played out, the Egypt of Muhammad Ali, Said and Ismail, and the Egyptology of Champollion, Wilkinson and Lepsius would be irrevocably consigned to history. Neither the country nor the subject would ever be the same again.

For Ismail, it had all started so well. His recognition as khedive in 1867 had been followed six years later by 'an Imperial Rescript making him an independent sovereign with the right to raise loans and grant concessions in Egypt's name without reference to the Porte'.[2] The ability to raise loans gave Ismail free rein to indulge his grand schemes for Egypt by heaping up yet more government debt. He simply did not understand financial matters, and was not the type of personality to ask for advice. Had he not, after all, presided over a trebling of Egypt's exports, a transformation of its infrastructure, and a wholesale modernization of its economy? To finance his limitless ambitions, Egypt's foreign debt soared from $16 million in 1862 to a colossal $443 million in 1875. Unable to meet the interest payments, Ismail decided to sell his 44 per cent holding in the Suez Canal Company to raise some much-needed cash. The British government spotted an opportunity to take a strategic stake in a crucial communication link with India, and moved quickly, paying Ismail the sum of £4 million, raised with the assistance of the Rothschilds. The deal was presented to Parliament as a fait accompli. As a contemporary observer noted: 'The purchase of four million pounds' worth of Suez Canal shares by the British Government was not merely an evidence of Ismail Pasha's dwindling resources; it gave England a foothold in addition to the stake in the country that Disraeli, with his schemes of empire, had recognized as soon as the project of the canal had been put into execution.'[3]

Faced with an ever-growing burden of debt, Ismail soon found that even the funds raised from selling the shares were not enough. Under pressure from British and French bond-holders, and their governments, he was forced to accept foreign control over Egypt's finances. In 1876, an Armenian prime minister, a British finance minister, and a French minister of public works arrived in Cairo to take up their posts. They were joined by a young British civil servant whose job was controller of the collection of debt; his name was Evelyn Baring. Little did he know – little did Egypt know – that he would come to dominate its affairs, economic and political, for the best part of three decades.

So began Anglo-French dominance of Egypt's government, the so-called 'Dual Control'. No matter that Egypt had, in the eyes of some, 'advanced as much in seventy years as many other countries have done in five hundred':[4] it had come at a staggering cost. From now on, the Commission of the Public Debt, and the two executive controllers-general, an Englishman for revenue and a Frenchman for expenditure, oversaw ever greater swathes of the Egyptian economy. Ismail was humiliated, but 'it was not repentance that he suffered, but a sense of injustice'.[5] To start turning the public finances around, taxes were increased across the board, and a concession was even sold to a British firm to use ancient tombs for the storage of fertilizer.[6] In the efforts to rescue modern Egypt, ancient Egypt took second place. In a bitter irony, a new official newspaper appeared for the first time in 1876, named *Al-Ahram* (The Pyramids) after Egypt's greatest monuments. In reality, foreigners called the shots, not the descendants of the pharaohs.

Despite the best efforts of Dual Control, by 1877, the year of Amelia Edwards's *A Thousand Miles Up the Nile*, Egypt was on its knees. The British controller-general proposed halving the rate of interest on the public debt, but Baring, now Commissioner of the Public Debt, was outraged. His plan was to force Ismail to accept an international commission of inquiry into Egypt's revenues and expenditure, and he browbeat all opposition. As Baring had predicted, the commission's report was devastating, pointing the finger squarely at Ismail for corruption and abuse of power.[7] He was forced to cede all his personal and family estates, roughly a fifth of all the cultivated land in Egypt, to the state. From now on, he would be supported by a modest civil list. He tried to put a brave face on it, declaring: 'My country is no longer in Africa; we are now part of Europe. It is therefore natural for us to abandon our former ways and to adopt a new system adapted to our social conditions.'[8] The worst, however, was still to come. A low Nile flood that year led to crop failure the following season, which coincided with an outbreak of cotton blight, devastating Egypt's main export crop. The economy plunged further into crisis, as thousands died from starvation and disease in Upper Egypt. Impoverished peasants parted with everything – household possessions, even the clothes off their backs – to pay their taxes. Ismail tried everything to curry favour with his Western backers, even offering the British Museum the colossus of Ramesses II at Memphis (if they could pay for its removal). But to no avail. It was as if the gods themselves had deserted Egypt.

After the disastrously low inundation in 1877, the Nile flood of 1878 was one of the highest of the nineteenth century. Where the low flood had brought famine, the high Nile wreaked great damage, in particular to the Egyptian Museum at Bulaq, which was sited close to the riverbank. Water flooded its halls, and undermined its foundations. It seemed to sum up the parlous state of the country at large. Eventually, the museum was reinforced, restored and reopened, but by that time, Ismail was no longer khedive. His end, when it came, was relatively swift. In early 1879, he tried to reassert his authority over Dual Control, dismissing his prime minister and informing European diplomats that he planned to form a ministry composed entirely of Egyptians. The response was a general strike throughout Egypt by European officials, whose numbers had swelled under Dual Control. (In 1878, there were over a hundred thousand foreign residents in Egypt, many of them employed in government jobs.) Neither the British nor the French government had much appetite for direct intervention, but when the German and Austrian governments added their pressure over the treatment of foreign bond-holders, the two powers swung into action. They pressured the Ottoman sultan, still nominally Egypt's suzerain, to order Ismail to abdicate in favour of his eldest son, Tewfiq.[9] The note delivered to Ismail in one of his many Cairo palaces was brief and to the point: 'The French and English Governments are agreed to advise Your Highness officially to abdicate and to leave Egypt.'[10] He duly collected the crown jewels and £3 million in cash, and sailed from Alexandria aboard the royal yacht, bound for Naples and later Istanbul. He never returned to Egypt. The British blamed him for bankrupting Egypt, while Egyptian nationalists never forgave him for throwing away the country's independence. A contemporary commentator summed up his predicament most perceptively: 'It was Ismail Pasha's misfortune that he lived too late. The age of tyrants and despots was passing, even in the East, and Egypt was too near to Europe not to have come, to some extent, under its modernising influence.'[11]

The new khedive, Tewfiq, was reluctant to submit to the full political control of Britain and France, so it was agreed that the two controllers-general should have only advisory powers and a consultative role in cabinet; however, the khedive would not be able to dismiss them without their governments' consent. It was a fig-leaf that enabled Tewfiq to salvage some semblance of independence. Baring took up the role of British controller-general; Egypt's debts were finally settled, and taxes on the peasantry reduced. Following the Liberals' victory in the 1880 British general election, the new Viceroy of India, the Marquess of Ripon, appointed Baring to be his financial secretary (Baring had served earlier in his career as private secretary to a previous Viceroy), and he left Egypt in June that year, after barely six months in the country. While he was away, administering the finances of a subcontinent, things came to a head in Egypt.

From the outset, Tewfiq had struggled to assert his legitimacy with Egyptian nationalists; his submission to foreign influence had led to an alliance between the constitutionalists (who demanded constitutional change) and Egyptian officers in the army (who had emerged as champions of Egyptian self-determination). When the khedive promulgated a draft law reserving the higher ranks of the military for the Turkish and

Circassian elite, junior officers of Egyptian nationality, led by one of their number named Arabi, revolted. A botched attempt to place the ringleaders on trial, and their subsequent escape from prison, turned the army into the focus of Egyptian nationalism (a position it has cultivated and maintained to this day) and Arabi into a popular hero. The rebels' demands were readily understood and widely shared by the population at large: a restoration of the Egyptian army to the strength it had enjoyed before the Convention of London, regulation of water rights, restrictions on usury, and the abolition of the hated corvée. Not for the first time in their imperial history, nor for the last, the British gravely underestimated both the scale of people's grievances and the severity of the nationalist threat.

Trapped between his foreign masters and a rebellious army, Tewfiq planned a counter-attack, but the colonels anticipated his move and marched on Cairo's Abdin Palace to confront the khedive. He gave in to some of their demands but refused to accept any permanent changes to the constitution. The British wanted, above all, to preserve the status quo of Dual Control, wary of Bismark's ambitions for a greater Germany; characteristically, the Sultan in Constantinople vacillated, playing for time. A new French government in November 1881 lent its wholehearted support to Tewfiq, while the Egyptian army strengthened its popularity in the provinces. By the spring of 1882, the impasse could no longer endure. Tewfiq invited the Dual Powers to help him snuff out the rebellion, once and for all. It was a disastrous decision.

When news spread of an Anglo-French task force headed for Alexandria, it provoked a great outpouring of patriotic sentiment throughout Egypt. On 11 June 1882, a riot in Alexandria caused the death of at least fifty European residents, including a petty officer in the Royal Navy, and the British consul was badly wounded. While panicking expatriates were evacuated in their thousands, Arabi's forces stepped in to restore order. The French, Austrian and German governments urged Tewfiq to back Arabi, but the British – still reeling from recent nationalist murders in Dublin's Phoenix Park – would not countenance appeasement. As tensions rose in Alexandria, the European powers grew increasingly suspicious of each other's motives and intentions. On Arabi's orders, batteries were built along the harbourside of Alexandria to deter any British assault. The admiral in charge of the taskforce issued an ultimatum demanding their dismantling. It was ignored. The next morning, 11 July, British warships began the bombardment of the city. Egyptian troops left as the city was reduced to rubble. The British, French and Italian consulates were gutted; the Grand Square was almost completely ruined. After two days of heavy shelling, British troops came ashore on 13 July, and Arabi declared war against the foreign invaders of his country. The House of Commons overwhelmingly backed British military intervention, but neither the French nor the Italians would join the assault. The Ottoman sultan procrastinated as usual. Arabi believed that, with the population on his side, he was sure of victory. He was wrong.

A British expeditionary force landed at Alexandria on 16 August, soon to be joined by another from India, sealing the Suez Canal at both ends. As the net tightened, Arabi's forces began to desert their leader. The decisive battle, fought at Tel el Kebir on 13 September, lasted barely forty minutes. At the end of the fighting, 10,000 Egyptians lay dead, against just fifty-seven British fatalities. Arabi retreated to Cairo where he surrendered. After a trial, he was exiled to Ceylon – the last thing the British needed was another nationalist martyr. In a show of force, British troops paraded before Tewfiq on 30 September, before retiring to barracks in all the major Egyptian cities. All the while, the British government maintained the fiction that its forces were in Egypt to protect the khedive.

Having snuffed out Arabi's rebellion and formally abolished Dual Control, the British were faced with the question of what to do next. Although the main expeditionary force had withdrawn shortly after Tel el Kebir, Egypt was simply too strategically important to be left to its own devices. On the other hand, Britain did not particularly want to add Egypt to its colonial possessions. The solution to the dilemma, typically, was to set up an enquiry. Lord Dufferin's report of 1883 was a classic fudge, rejecting both direct and indirect rule. Instead, the British would continue to govern Egypt, but under a 'veiled protectorate' – designed, above all, to avoid further provoking France. Under the novel arrangement, British representatives would have no formal authority over the Egyptian government, but there was an expectation, nonetheless, that their orders would be obeyed. And who better to implement this rule by stealth than Evelyn Baring. Confident to the point of authoritarianism – his nickname was 'over-Baring' – he had already demonstrated his clear-sightedness and fiscal discipline. He arrived back in Cairo in 1883, officially as British agent and consul-general, but in reality he was now de facto ruler of Egypt.

◁◦▷

While the late 1870s and early 1880s thus saw two khedives in turn lose power, in the world of Egyptian archaeology Mariette still reigned supreme. By 1879, he had been in charge of the Antiquities Service for over two decades, leading and guiding it through often turbulent times and wavering political support. He had seen off the rival Khedivial School of Egyptology, launched large-scale excavations at more sites than any previous archaeologist, built up and preserved the collections of Egypt's national museum through his personal drive and determination. One of Tewfiq's first acts as khedive had been to go on a royal progress through Upper Egypt, during which he visited all the major temples that Mariette's workmen had liberated from the sand of centuries. It felt like a royal seal of approval for the Frenchman's continuing mission.

Despite his apparent position of strength, however, Mariette soon found his influence was strictly limited when great power politics got in the way. As soon as Ismail, with his pro-European tastes, had been driven into exile, the United States government had lost no time in lobbying Tewfiq for an ancient Egyptian monument of its own. Paris had acquired an obelisk in the 1830s, and so, more recently, had London. Surely now that America had emerged from civil war and begun to assert itself as the most powerful nation on earth, it was time to erect one of these dramatic monuments in the economic engine room of the United States, the city of New York. The *New York Herald* wrote, tongue-in-cheek: 'It would be absurd for the people of any great city to hope to be happy without an Egyptian obelisk. Rome has had them this great while and so has Constantinople. Paris has one. London has one. If New York was without one, all those great cities might point the finger of scorn at us and intimate that we could never rise to any real moral grandeur until we had our obelisk.'[12]

Journalists may have regarded the project with a degree of cynicism, but civic and national leaders were fulsome in their support. Symbols mattered, and no symbol was more powerful than an Egyptian obelisk.

The monument chosen to satisfy America's international pretensions was the second of Cleopatra's Needles, the companion obelisk to the one recently transported to London. Mariette protested publicly against the export of such an import- ant antiquity – it went against everything he had been trying to achieve in establishing the Bulaq Museum – but he was overruled. Diplomatic relations trumped Egyptology.[13] What he did manage to achieve, however, was a promise that this gift would be the last of its kind. On 20 October 1879 the Egyptian Council of Ministers resolved that 'hereafter no Egyptian monument shall be given to any Power or to any city whatever not forming part of the Egyptian territory'. The following summer, the ship carrying Cleopatra's Needle set out from Alexandria on its long voyage westwards. On 20 July 1880, it reached its destination and moored off 23rd Street, New York City.

Meanwhile, worn down by the continuing struggle to protect and preserve Egypt's heritage, Mariette's health took a turn for the worse. Concern once again started to spread in French government circles about the future leadership of the Antiquities Service and Egyptian Museum. Mariette had seen off the German threat in the dangerous days following France's defeat in the Franco-Prussian War; but Heinrich Brugsch was still highly regarded, and his brother Emile was already employed in the Egyptian Museum. There had been an earlier proposal to establish a French archaeological school in Cairo, on a par with the schools in Athens and Rome, but Mariette had opposed it, wanting no competition to his own fiefdom. Now, in late 1880, as it became clear that Mariette's health would not recover, the plan was revived. By having a French heir apparent on the ground in Cairo, running a French institute, the government in Paris believed it would be able to thwart any attempt to install either of the Brugsch brothers at the Antiquities Service when the inevitable moment arrived. The president of the Council of Ministers in France, Jules Ferry, duly decreed the foundation of the Ecole Française du Caire (later the Institut Français d'Archéologie Orientale du Caire) on 28 December 1880. The man chosen as its first director was someone whom not even Mariette could oppose.

Gaston Maspero (1846–1916) was a member of the French academic elite. In stark contrast to Mariette, he had enjoyed the finest education money could buy: schooling at the Lycée Louis-le-Grand, a Jesuit boarding school, and university at the Ecole Normale Supérieure, the training ground (then as now) of the French ruling class. On a visit to the Egyptian galleries of the Louvre at the age of fourteen, Maspero was transfixed: he later recalled, 'it seemed to me that ancient Egypt was revealing itself in front of me and calling me'.[14] At university, Maspero excelled in his studies, learning Sanskrit as well as hieroglyphics. When Mariette visited Paris in 1867, during Maspero's final year at the Ecole Normale, friends mentioned the young student and his proficiency in ancient Egyptian philology to the undisputed head of Egyptian archaeology. Mariette asked Maspero to demonstrate his translation skills on an unseen text. Maspero accomplished the task without difficulty, and Mariette was duly impressed: 'This young man promises to be an Egyptologist of the first order . . . he must continue,'[15] he is said to have remarked. With a recommendation like that, Maspero could not fail to prosper. However, there seemed to be no immediate opening for a full-time Egyptologist. Mariette tried to bring the young scholar to Egypt, but de Rougé managed to secure for Maspero a chair in Egyptology at the new Ecole des Hautes-Etudes. Maspero was just twenty-three.

In the Franco-Prussian War of 1870–1, Maspero took up arms in defence of his adopted country (he had been born the illegitimate son of a Neapolitan refugee) and was granted French citizenship in recognition of his service. It barely deflected him from his studies. In January 1873, he presented the first doctoral thesis on Egyptology in France, and six months later he succeeded de Rougé as professor of Egyptian philology and archaeology at the prestigious Collège de France. By the end of the 1870s, he had emerged as the leading French Egyptologist of his generation: the perfect candidate to direct the new French school in Cairo.

Maspero arrived in the Egyptian capital in the final weeks of 1880. One of his first tasks was to inform a failing Mariette that inscriptions had been discovered inside two Old Kingdom pyramids. The so-called Pyramid Texts constituted the earliest body of religious literature anywhere in the world. Mariette was elated, declaring: 'So there are, despite everything, inscribed pyramids, which I would never have believed!'[16] But a few days later, on 18 January 1881, Mariette was dead. Telegrams of condolence arrived from all over Europe, reflecting the esteem in which he had been held. Empress Eugénie, in exile in England since her husband's deposition, wrote a long letter to Mariette's sister. The founder director of the Antiquities Service was given the signal honour of a state funeral, and was buried in a stone sarcophagus in the gardens of the Bulaq Museum (later transferred to Giza, and thence to the current Egyptian Museum in Tahrir Square).

It was a great irony that, just four days after Mariette's death, the second Cleopatra's Needle was erected in New York's Central Park, within view of the Metropolitan Museum of Art, an institution that would come to rival Mariette's foundation. The main speech at the event was given by the Met's first president, Henry G. Stebbins, who used the opportunity to encourage wealthy New Yorkers to support their museum and make it among the best in the world.[17] (It was a call to which they would enthusiastically respond.) Never one to be outdone, the US Secretary of State, William M. Evarts, added his own public pronouncements, noting that the great powers of the ancient world had removed obelisks from Egypt, and wondering, optimistically, if France, Britain, and now the United States would achieve similar greatness.[18]

Before Mariette was cold in his stony tomb, the French authorities moved to ensure a seamless succession. Maspero took up the reins of both Museum and Antiquities Service, and took stock of his new domain. The museum had suffered major damage in the high flood of 1878, and although it had been restored and reopened, it was clearly no longer adequate to house Egypt's growing national collection of antiquities. Maspero commissioned an extension, which would tide it over until new premises, larger and safer from the waters of the Nile, could be procured. As for the Antiquities Service, it was in relatively good shape, albeit denuded of funding (neither Ismail nor Tewfiq was particularly interested in archaeology).

After a brief summer vacation in France to collect his possessions and prepare for permanent relocation, Maspero was back in Egypt in September 1881 and launched a major new programme of excavations. Emile Brugsch was despatched to Thebes to supervise the retrieval of a cache of royal mummies that had just been uncovered, while Maspero took charge of work at the pyramid sites of Zawiyet el-Aryan, Dahshur and Meidum. If he had harboured visions of directing operations from the deck of his official steamer, he was quickly disabused. In October he suffered a three-week bout of dysentery, followed by a fall down a tomb shaft, an attack of rheumatism, and a minor stroke. In December, he wrote to a friend:

> Many people imagine that archaeology is an armchair science. I would like to see them dangling from a rope, with a 30-metre shaft beneath their feet and an inscription to copy at the bottom of the shaft; or on their belly in a narrow passage dug through the masonry of a pyramid, aware that one false move dislodging a stone could cause 100 tonnes of stone to fall on your back . . . I have just spent four whole days inside the pyramid of

Pepi II at Saqqara . . . In a couple of places, the masonry is so badly damaged that we never knew if, having entered, we would be able to get out.[19]

But he was well aware of his responsibilities, both to science and to French interests. In a letter to Joseph Ernest Renan, the orientalist whose idea it had been to establish the Ecole Française in Cairo, he wrote:

> I only accepted the role . . . to prevent the succession to Mariette from passing into Brugsch's hands. I hope to keep it only long enough to pass it on to another Frenchman. The Egyptian government, which knows how much store France sets by retaining this office, would love to give it to a native or a German, if I were unlucky enough to give it the slightest excuse to take it back.[20]

The Germans were surprisingly magnanimous in defeat. On 19 May 1882, no less a figure than Lepsius wrote to Maspero: 'Your leadership will mark a new era in the history of modern research in Egypt, Mariette notwithstanding.'[21]

Two months later the British invaded Egypt, and Maspero faced an unprecedented diplomatic and curatorial crisis. There were those in Britain who viewed the bombardment of Alexandria and the accompanying civil unrest with alarm, from the perspective of Egypt's antiquities. Amelia Edwards, keenly interested in ancient Egypt since her voyage up the Nile and an increasingly vocal advocate for the preservation of pharaonic remains, alerted the Foreign Office to the vulnerability of the Bulaq Museum, and requested that it be given armed protection if necessary.[22] Her diplomacy – or perhaps her doggedness – won the day and, from the British army's first entry into Cairo, an officer was despatched to check on the museum, and troops visited regularly to ensure its security. Once the dust had settled on Tel el Kebir and its aftermath, Maspero had to learn to deal with Egypt's new de facto ruler, Evelyn Baring, who was no particular fan of archaeology. Perhaps to assuage native sentiment, the British authorities allowed an Egyptian pupil of Heinrich Brugsch's, Ahmed Kamal, to establish a school of Egyptology for Egyptians. It was a pioneering move, but it lasted only three years and had only one graduating class.[23] In a further nod to nationalists, an Egyptian government decree stipulated that the museum (and any future museum), all its contents (current and future), all monuments and all antiquities belonged to the Egyptian state and were inalienable. It was a bold statement of intent, but without adequate resources to police it, failed to put a stop to the trade in antiquities.

Baring was more concerned to maintain the delicate diplomatic balance between the European powers, which had come under great strain as a result of the British occupation. He went out of his way to support Maspero's position as director of the Museum and the Antiquities Service: let France control Egyptian culture, Britain would concern itself with more important matters, notably the economy. To keep the different European interests happy – or at least engaged – Baring set up a Consultative Archaeological Committee (Egyptian membership was notably lacking), and moved the Antiquities Service under the Ministry of Public Works, to provide a measure of stability. No longer would the director have to go cap in hand to the khedive; he would be able to rely on an agreed budget.

The problem was, the budget was woefully inadequate: there were simply too many other demands on the Egyptian treasury. Moreover, Baring's abolition of the corvée – which, together with the *kurbash* (whip), was one of the most hated aspects of Ottoman rule willingly maintained by Egypt's 'independent' khedives – removed from the director of the Antiquities Service a ready source of manpower. Constrained by scarce financial and human resources, Maspero found his ability to undertake large-scale operations severely restricted. No amount of restructuring or reorganization could alter that basic fact. All the while, Egypt's ancient monuments continued to face neglect, damage and destruction. There was nothing for it: Maspero would have to end his own service's monopoly on excavation, a monopoly that Mariette had fought so hard to implement and defend. The era of the gentleman amateur and the state-sponsored expedition was over. Who, then, might have the wherewithal to take up the slack?

⋘◦⋙

Since her trip up the Nile, Amelia Edwards had set her mind to the study, publication and preservation of Egypt's ancient monuments. In 1879, on her own initiative, she had written to Mariette with the suggestion of raising a fund by subscription to finance a new excavation for scientific ends. She had received no reply. (Perhaps Mariette was too ill to give it serious consideration, or perhaps he was wary of any attempt – especially by the British – to water down his exclusive right to excavate.) To make matters worse, Birch – keeper of oriental antiquities at the British Museum and, after the death of Wilkinson, Britain's leading Egyptologist – made no attempt to hide his opposition. He dismissed the plan as 'sentimental', betraying both contempt and fear of amateur outsiders muscling in on the academic establishment.[24]

Never one to be easily dissuaded, Edwards bided her time and began to rally support for her cause. She signed up Lane's nephew, Reginald Poole, keeper of coins and medals at the British Museum (and clearly no friend of Birch's); the Reverend Archibald Sayce, professor of Assyriology at Oxford, and a

great networker; and Erasmus Wilson, the surgeon and benefactor who had funded the transport of Cleopatra's Needle to
London. They made a powerful and persuasive triumvirate.[25]
Once Mariette was off the scene, in January 1881, Edwards
wrote straight away to his successor, Maspero, with whom she
had already started a friendly correspondence – he had advised
her on hieroglyphic inscriptions during her research for *A
Thousand Miles Up the Nile*. The new director seemed more
amenable, but the political situation in Egypt was tense and
Dual Control was causing a strain in Anglo-French relations.
Maspero advised her to wait a little longer. One of Poole's
acquaintances was a Swiss scholar by the name of Edouard
Naville, who had studied under Lepsius, assisted the French
in the Franco-Prussian War, and had already acquired a reputation across Europe as an up-and-coming Egyptologist. In
early 1882, Poole asked Naville to use his influence and sound
out Maspero once again. The answer this time was favourable:
Maspero had no objection to Edwards's proposal, and would
do what he could to support it. Moreover, he suggested that
the target for any new excavation should be the Nile Delta,
not only because it was relatively unstudied, but also because
a site with possible Old Testament connections would surely
appeal to both Christian and Jewish donors.[26]

On 27 March 1882, in Poole's office at the British Museum,
a meeting took place at which, by formal resolution, the Delta
Exploration Fund came into being. (At Poole's suggestion, it
quickly changed its name to the Egypt Exploration Fund (EEF),
to give it greater scope.) Edwards and Poole were elected joint
honorary secretaries, while Wilson – who had promised a
sizeable donation – was appointed treasurer. Sayce agreed to
be one of the fund's 'agents' in Egypt. A jubilant Edwards sent
a formal announcement to the press (making full use of her
journalistic contacts), stating that the aim of the fund was to

explore the Nile Delta where 'the documents of a lost period of Biblical history must lie concealed'.[27] It was a masterstroke. She began fundraising in earnest, contacting wealthy friends and acquaintances, and the fund started looking for an archaeologist to lead its first expedition.

In typical fashion, Edwards already had someone in mind. In fact, she had already written to him. Heinrich Schliemann, the man who had recently located the ruins of ancient Troy, was just about the most famous archaeologist in the world. Someone of his calibre would give the new fund the launch it needed. He had agreed to Edwards's request, but when the proposal was put to Maspero, he was aghast. Arabi's revolt had seriously destabilized the political balance in Egypt, and had put the Anglo-French relationship under great strain. The last thing Maspero needed was an arrogant and abrasive German wading into the picture. In his view, Schliemann was 'tactless and quarrelsome, sought only publicity for himself and would alienate the authorities';[28] there could be no question of him excavating on behalf of the EEF. Far better to identify a young, more pliable Englishman who would be prepared to work under Maspero's instruction and who, once he had proved himself, might eventually take over as dig director in his own right. The committee's thoughts naturally turned to Naville: he wasn't English, but he fitted the bill in every other respect. That summer, he agreed to be the fund's first archaeologist. Planning for the EEF's first mission started in earnest.

The British invasion of Egypt, in July 1882, temporarily put everything on hold. But, once the dust had settled, British occupation actually made it easier for the EEF's mission to go ahead, and Maspero desperately needed help with his colossal task of excavation. In January 1883, Naville presented his credentials to Maspero in Cairo and set out for the remote Delta site of Tell el-Maskhuta (by coincidence, close to the battlefield of

Tel el Kebir), for the first British-sponsored excavation in Egypt since Vyse and Perring's explosive work at Giza forty years earlier. At the end of the season, that spring, two statues that Naville had found, and which seemed to confirm his identification of Tell el-Maskhuta as the biblical city of Pithom, were graciously presented by khedive Tewfiq to Erasmus Wilson (thus circumventing the new law on the export of antiquities) and by Wilson to the British Museum. Naville gave a public lecture in London, at which it was announced that the EEF's next dig would be at San el-Hagar, the biblical Zoan (a location, mentioned in the Old Testament, where Moses is said to have performed miracles before Pharaoh), where Mariette had uncovered a series of impressive monuments. Public interest was aroused, and new donations flooded in, including a thousand pounds from Wilson and subscriptions from across the Atlantic, where the Reverend William Copley Winslow had started a campaign called, with typical American gusto, 'Spades for Zoan'. All looked set fair for the forthcoming winter season. But, as the day approached, Naville announced to the EEF that he was too preoccupied with other projects and would be unable to continue as the fund's excavation director. His withdrawal left a gaping hole in the fund's plans. They approached Maspero, whose laconic response was: 'Send me a young Englishman and I will train him.'[29]

The death of Mariette, the British occupation, and the foundation of the Egypt Exploration Fund: from the early 1880s, there was a new dispensation for archaeology in Egypt. One man would step forward to make it his own.

◁◯▷

The great Egyptologists of the nineteenth century – or, at least, the great British Egyptologists – tended to come from unexpected quarters. Thomas Young, physician and physicist, came to Egyptian hieroglyphics via forays in comparative linguistics. John Gardner Wilkinson, traveller and artist, fell into Egyptology for want of anything better to do. The third, and greatest, British Egyptologist during the discipline's golden age – and the man credited as 'the father of Egyptian archaeology' – was drawn to the subject through a fascination with ancient measurements and the esoteric work of an unorthodox astronomer.

William Matthew Flinders Petrie (1853–1942) was a sickly child, too weak to attend school. Indeed, he never received any formal education (with the exception of a university extension course on algebra and trigonometry, at the age of twenty-four).[30] Yet, by the end of his long and illustrious career, he had been appointed to the first chair in Egyptology in Britain, elected a fellow of both the Royal Society and the British Academy, a member of the Royal Irish Academy and the American Philosophical Society, received honorary doctorates from Oxford, Cambridge and Edinburgh, and been knighted for services to scholarship. By his own admission, he was entirely self-taught, and his childhood interests focussed on objects. His mother had a collection of fossils and minerals, which he studied avidly, and he 'ransacked the marine store ships of Woolwich for coins, thus beginning archaeology when still accompanied by my nurse, at eight'.[31] At the age of fourteen, young Flinders began joining his father, an engineer and surveyor, on trips to measure and record the ancient earthworks near their home in Kent. It quickly turned into something of an obsession. In 1872, he and his father carried out the first proper survey of Stonehenge. Trips followed to sites across England, conducted with an economy that would remain his hallmark for the rest of his life: 'Travelling always third class, and spending on average 1/- or 1/6 for his lodging . . . he reckoned to spend five shillings and sixpence on food every week.'[32]

The result of all this activity, both in the field and in the

British Museum, was Petrie's first book, *Inductive Metrology, or the Recovery of Ancient Measurements from the Monuments* (1877). Meanwhile, his introduction to the pyramids of ancient Egypt had been through the writings of Charles Piazzi Smyth, Astronomer Royal for Scotland and professor of astronomy at the University of Edinburgh. Petrie's father, William, had once courted Smyth's sister, so when Smyth published his bestselling book *Our Inheritance in the Great Pyramid* (1866) and its successor volume *Life and Work at the Great Pyramid* (1867) – themselves inspired by an earlier speculative work, John Taylor's *The Great Pyramid: Why Was It Built? And Who Built It?* (1859) – the Petries, father and son, took more than a passing interest. The more they read, the more they were intrigued by Smyth's theory of the 'pyramid inch', the supposed basic unit that underpinned the dimensions and construction of the pyramids of Giza, and by his convincing blend of mathematics and fundamental Christianity. Flinders Petrie soon decided that, in order to confirm the veracity of Smyth's theories, a reliable set of measurements was required. The Great Pyramid of Giza would have to be surveyed, and he was the man to do it.

With no experience of Egypt, no Arabic and very little money, Petrie set sail from Liverpool at the end of November 1880, bound for Alexandria. Before leaving, he went to see Birch at the British Museum to seek his advice. Like Petrie, Birch had never actually been to Egypt, but he suggested that the young man might like to copy inscriptions whenever he had the opportunity, and bring back some specimens of pottery – a class of material that was abundant on all archaeological sites, but which had never before been collected. The systematic excavation and study of small finds – pottery, flints, stone vessels – would subsequently be one of Petrie's distinctive contributions to Egyptian archaeology.

Finding his way to Giza, Petrie installed himself in a disused tomb. Despite the rats, mice and fleas, and the almost impossibly meagre rations, he relished the spartan freedom of it all. He wrote to a friend in February 1881: 'Life here is really comfortable, without many of the encumbrances of regular hours: bells, collars and cuffs, blacking, tablecloths or many others of the unnecessaries of Civilization.'[33] Indeed, he made asceticism his guiding principle, even – especially – if it meant thumbing his nose at Victorian respectability: 'It was often most convenient to strip entirely for work, owing to the heat and absence of any current of air, in the interior. For outside work in hot weather, vest and pants were suitable, and if pink they kept the tourist at bay, as the creature seemed to him too queer for inspection.'[34]

Petrie's self-sufficiency and self-discipline were the defining characteristics of his personality from the very start of his life in archaeology. He was focussed, sometimes to the point of coldness, and sentiment seems to have played little, if any, part in his thoughts. His autobiography, written towards the end of a long and eventful career, is surprisingly dull, a straightforward record of actions and achievements, entirely devoid of emotion. In his own words, it had 'nothing otherwise to do with the inner life'; indeed, he was firmly of the view that: 'The affairs of a private person are seldom pertinent to the interests of others, yet the rise of a great branch of knowledge in the archaeological discovery of man's development should be worth some record.'[35] This focus, while it did not necessarily make for easy personal relationships, was greatly to the benefit of Egyptian archaeology.

That first season at Giza, Petrie worked entirely independently, without any permit, but received some assistance from a local man named Ali Gabri, who had started as a basket boy on Vyse's excavations. Despite Petrie's lack of formal Egyptological training, he could not fail to be appalled at the destruction of monuments going on around him. Never one to moderate his views, he did not hesitate to point the finger of blame: 'The savage indifference of the Arabs . . . is only surpassed by a most barbaric sort of regard for the monuments by those in power . . . It is sickening to see the rate at which everything is being destroyed, and the little regard paid to its preservation.'[36]

He returned home to England in June, having completed his survey of the pyramids (which, incidentally, proved Smyth entirely wrong); but he had found his calling. In October, Petrie was back in Egypt for a second season. That winter, he travelled up the Nile with Sayce and a few others, stopping at Luxor to survey the royal tombs in the Valley of the Kings.

It was while Petrie was back at Giza, in the early spring of 1882, that news reached him of the foundation of the Delta Exploration Fund, and of Naville's forthcoming excavation. Petrie desperately wanted to continue his own explorations in Egypt, but had no funding. He decided to take a chance and write direct to Amelia Edwards, setting out his philosophy of archaeology: 'I believe the true line lies as much in the careful noting and comparison of small details, as in more wholesale and off-hand clearances.'[37] It was music to Edwards's ears. When Naville relinquished his duties the following year, and despite opposition from some of the fund's committee, Edwards, backed by Wilson, decided to give the unknown Petrie a chance. His book, *The Pyramids and Temples of Giza*, was published to enthusiastic reviews (including one from Edwards herself) in September 1883; two months later, Petrie started digging for the EEF in the Wadi Tumilat, and then at San el-Hagar. Visiting Tell el-Maskhuta, the site of Naville's excavations the previous year, Petrie found a number of small objects, overlooked or discarded, among the spoil heaps. This merely confirmed him in his approach: 'My duty was that of a salvage man, to get all I could quickly gathered in.'[38]

San el-Hagar might have been promoted by the EEF as the biblical Zoan, but the reality was altogether less prepossessing: 'The miserable Arab huts of San first meet the eye . . . with on one side a muddy stream into which they throw their dead buffalo, and from which they drink, and on the other a swamp full of rotting graves and filth.'[39] Nonetheless Petrie sent regular reports back to England, which Edwards used as the basis of short articles in *The Times*, designed both to keep the fund's subscribers up to date with developments and to encourage new donors. By the middle of June, 'after many dust storms, heat over 100°, and violent rain',[40] Petrie closed down the dig and travelled to Cairo. Edwards wrote to him with genuine enthusiasm and gratitude: 'I wish to tell you again with what deep interest I follow you in these records of your daily life and arduous work . . . I take a hearty pleasure and pride in the task of making your manner of work known to the public, and I feel that you are setting a splendid example of scientific excavation to all Europe', before signing off, 'there is but one W.F.P. and . . . I am delighted to be his prophet'.[41]

Petrie's next season for the EEF, at Naukratis, a trading settlement founded in the Nile Delta by ancient Greek merchants, included the first stratified section ever made on an Egyptian excavation. Petrie was truly setting new standards for Egyptian archaeology. He also broke the mould by speedily publishing his finds at the end of each season and by mounting an annual exhibition of small finds (some of them smuggled through customs, apparently with Maspero's blessing).[42] Despite such successes, however, tensions soon started to develop between Petrie and his colleagues back in England. He fell out spectacularly with the British Museum when it thoughtlessly described the finds it had received from his excavation as 'worthless'. He wrote to Edwards: 'The false statements of that letter, and the gross ignorance it shewed of genuine and scientific archaeology, bar me from having anything to do with that quarter again.'[43] (The estrangement did, indeed, last the rest of his life.) He also fell out with the EEF Committee. He found them bumbling and amateurish, while they questioned his use of funds. Unused and unsuited to criticism or control, he decided to resign. Edwards pleaded with him, but he was implacable. On 16 October 1886, she read out his letter of resignation to the committee, before sending a personal note to Petrie, which read: 'Goodbye, good luck, and God bless you. Ever your faithful friend, A. B. Edwards.'[44]

The Egypt Exploration Fund and Petrie went their separate ways, but the bond between Edwards and her protégé endured. She secured for him the patronage of two wealthy businessmen and philanthropists, Jesse Haworth and Henry Kennard, enabling him to continue excavating in Egypt on his own account. As a result, over the next four decades, he dug at more sites even than Mariette, made more major discoveries than any other archaeologist, before or since, amassed a vast collection of antiquities, and published a thousand books, articles and reviews.

As for Edwards, she may have lost her star excavator, but her enthusiasm for Egyptology and her dedication to the EEF remained undimmed. That year alone, she wrote over four thousand letters to recruit new members and solicit donations. In the winter of 1889–90, despite having just recovered from a serious illness, she embarked on an extensive lecture tour of the United States, again to raise funds for the EEF. Altogether she gave 120 lectures at universities, colleges and learned societies all down the east coast, from Boston to Baltimore. It was a triumphal progress, and the zenith of her Egyptological career. She was particularly impressed by the women's colleges she visited – Vassar, Wellesley and Smith

– and regretted that women's education in England lagged so far behind. Freed from the social conventions of Victorian London, she gave free rein to some of her more radical views. One lecture, for example, was entitled 'The Social and Political Position of Women in Ancient Egypt' – the contemporary resonance and relevance were not lost on her audience, prompting the poet Henry W. Austin to laud her as a pioneer of women's emancipation:

> *Yes, by such lives laborious*
> *Is quicker shapen the plan*
> *Of the day, when woman glorious*
> *Shall arise: arise victorious –*
> *No longer the slave laborious,*
> *Or the tempting toy of man!*[45]

The tour was a huge success, but left Edwards exhausted. She never fully recovered her health and died on 15 April 1892, just three months after her lifelong companion Mrs Braysher. But Amelia Edwards was not finished quite yet. In her will, she endowed the first chair of Egyptology in Britain, at University College London – a radical institution, and the first in England to award degrees to women on a par with men – and drew up the terms so as to ensure that Petrie would be appointed. She also left the college her books and antiquities. Almost single-handedly, by her actions in life and her generosity in death, Edwards established Egyptian archaeology as a serious discipline in Britain. She was a remarkable and pioneering woman in a male-dominated age.

⊲◉▷

For Maspero, the foundation of the Egypt Exploration Fund brought another player into the field of Egyptian archaeology, but it did not, on its own, solve his problems. He was still desperately short of funds for the Museum and Antiquities Service, yet was expected to carry out major projects like the clearance of Luxor Temple. This involved compensating the owners of the houses that had been built up, over the centuries, against, inside and even on top of the monument (including the 'French House' lived in by Lucie Duff Gordon). He negotiated with Thomas Cook to introduce a visitor's tax (later changed to entry tickets), but it was insufficient. Maspero had no option but to petition the British colonial authorities for additional funding. Sir Colin Scott-Moncrieff, undersecretary of state at the Ministry of Public Works, responded by means of an open letter to *The Times*. He praised Maspero's leadership of the Antiquities Service – 'Here is a department where there is no need of Joint Control, for there is only one M. Maspero'[46] – but rejected the request for funds. Scott-Moncrieff asserted, patronizingly: 'We prefer in England to subscribe to the causes of this sort on a voluntary basis, rather than to see our government do it for us,' and went on to encourage personal donations. It was a quintessential civil servant's reply. The result of his appeal was a paltry £90 from English donors, while French subscriptions totalled 21,789 francs. The clearance of Luxor Temple eventually began the following year.

Maspero also had to scrimp and save the necessary funds to improve the Egyptian Museum. This even meant selling some small, duplicate objects from the collection, including *shabti*s, amulets and even mummies. Petrie, with his particular fondness for small finds, was furious. But, by such means, Maspero managed to look after the collection and add Graeco-Roman objects to round out the museum's historical breadth. (After he left office, his successor promptly sent most of the post-pharaonic holdings to Alexandria.)

Although British rule tried to accommodate French

interests, at least in the cultural sphere, it could nonetheless prove frustrating. Whilst maintaining cordial relations with Baring in public, Maspero's private correspondence revealed his true feelings. He criticized the British (and the point was directed particularly at Baring) for importing their 'brutal manners' from India, and for trying to impose 'bizarre rules of English bureaucracy' on a land accustomed to sixty years of French-style administration.[47] Like others, Maspero was unsettled by disturbances in Egypt and the Sudan, a delayed reaction against the British invasion, which only seemed to provoke an even harsher crackdown. A French friend of Maspero's wishfully saw in the unrest a more apocalyptic vision, prophesying 'the English nation is lost and its future is utterly compromised'.[48] A well-meaning Amelia Edwards tried to reassure Maspero that the British authorities would not interfere with his jurisdiction over the Antiquities Service and Museum. But British commercial interests, as well as political ones, were starting to dominate the country, to Maspero's annoyance. In the spring of 1885, he wrote to a friend: 'You might naively have persuaded yourself in Europe that the Khedive and, over him, the English consul-general were the masters of Egypt. You would be singularly mistaken: the real kings of Egypt at the moment are [Thomas] Cook and its two representatives Rostowich and Pagnon. It is Cook who last year transported the army to Dongola, it is Cook this year who is making the railway.'[49]

Another reason, perhaps, for Maspero's unease was the sense, in the early 1880s, that the heroic age of Egyptology was passing. Mariette had died in 1881, followed by Lepsius in 1884 and Birch in 1885. The last links with the age of Champollion and Wilkinson were gone. In their place, a new generation found itself entrusted with the heavy burden of archaeology and scholarship, preservation and stewardship. Alongside Maspero were Petrie (who began his work in Egypt in 1880), Adolf Erman (who started teaching at the University of Berlin in 1881), and Ernest Budge (who succeeded Birch at the British Museum). They would have to redefine Egyptology and take it forward into a new century.

By early 1886, calm had been restored in Egypt and Sudan, excavators working for the Antiquities Service discovered the intact tomb of Sennedjem at Deir el-Medina, and Maspero's confidence began to return. The clearance of the Sphinx, which Mariette had begun, started again in earnest, supported by public donations and contributions from Egyptologists and philanthropists. Maspero had a small railway built to take away vast quantities of sand and 'restore the plateau to how it was in pharaonic times'.[50]

Not all the benefactors were pleased at the results. On being shown 'his' Sphinx, Baron de Rothschild grimaced and agreed a further donation of 20,000 francs to the Museum on the express condition that no further work would be done at the Sphinx. Maspero, though, was unrepentant, writing to his wife: 'The sphinx is such a beautiful work of art. The whole of the front part of the body has now been cleared, the paws freed, and the stela in front of the chest has been revealed. Brugsch has taken a photograph of it which I will send you next week, inshallah . . . When the clearance is finished, I believe I will not be reproached for having wasted my time and my money, or rather France's money.'[51] He was also making good progress with the work at Luxor Temple: 'The clearance of Luxor Temple, having slowed for three weeks, has taken off again. The order has arrived to requisition the sixteen houses situated to the west of the temple, and to give their owners the land to which they are entitled. The house of Mustapha Aga is among them!'[52] And, six weeks later: 'At Luxor, the governor has succeeded in evacuating thirteen houses out of sixteen: the cadi and Mustapha Aga are still resisting, but will come around eventually.'[53]

The other great event of 1886 was the first unwrapping of a royal mummy at the Egyptian Museum, an event of such great historical significance that the khedive attended in person. At nine o'clock on the dot, on the morning of 1 June, the first mummy was released from its 3,000-year-old bandages. It was something of a disappointment. So too was the mummy of Ramesses III. The pharaoh's face was covered with such a thick layer of blackened resin that it was impossible to make out the features.[54] Shortly after eleven, Tewfiq left the museum, and the Egyptologists continued their work undisturbed.

After such a series of achievements, Maspero surprised many when he signalled his wish to step down by the end of the year as director of the Antiquities Service and Museum. He no doubt felt that he had done his bit, and wanted to leave while he would still be missed. With Baring's full support, he was succeeded by another Frenchman, Eugène Grébaut, director of the French archaeological mission to Cairo. Predictably, the Germans were outraged. Heinrich Brugsch had been deprived of the top job when Mariette had died, and now his brother Emile, Maspero's loyal and long-serving deputy, had been similarly passed over. An anonymous letter to *The Times* asserted that Emile Brugsch had 'devoted his entire life to the service of the museum, for a miserly salary. He has unparalleled qualifications for this role, and his likely dismissal would be a grievous loss to Egyptology.'[55] From Germany itself came an even more furious reaction. August Eisenlohr, the recently retired professor of Egyptology at Heidelberg, wrote a withering letter to Maspero, asking: 'Are you such a French nationalist as to have passed over one of us, Brugsch, or Naville, or me?'[56] But Maspero shrugged it all off: it was just another manifestation of the long-running rivalry between France, Britain and Germany in the scramble for Egypt. He returned to his professorships and classes at the Collège de France, and in October 1886 had the satisfaction of being elected an honorary vice-president of the EEF, in recognition of his long-standing support for the fund; this was followed, in December, by an honorary fellowship of the Queen's College, Oxford, and the following summer by an honorary doctorate from Oxford University. Some in Britain, evidently, appreciated his contribution to Egyptology.

Petrie and Maspero may have had their disagreements, for example over the sale of small finds from the Egyptian Museum, but generally the two men got along well. They could not, however, have been more different: Maspero was a product of France's finest academic institutions, well connected, smartly dressed, and worked from his office at the Museum or his official steamer. Petrie was self-taught, a loner by instinct, shabby or déshabillé almost as a point of principle, lived in tents and tombs, and ate out of cans. But the two men shared the same annual rhythm of work, devoting themselves to Egyptian archaeology during the winter months and returning to Europe each summer. Each in his own way was utterly devoted to the cause of Egyptology, and they enjoyed an entente, if not exactly a close friendship.

Maspero's successor, Eugène Grébaut, was a different kettle of fish entirely. Where Maspero had reserved the site of Saqqara for the Antiquities Service, believing (with reason) that there was still much more to discover, Grébaut added the whole of Thebes. Petrie's request to excavate there was refused, and he had to look for an alternative site. On a trip up the Nile in the winter of 1886–7 with a recent Oxford graduate, Francis Llewellyn Griffith, Petrie made a mental note of the most promising sites for future excavation. Amarna, Abydos, Coptos: Petrie's sharp eyes noticed details that others had missed, and he believed 'there is still something to do in a place which every Egyptologist has visited'.[57] The journey was not without incident, and characterized by the privations that became something of a hallmark of a Petrie dig. At Hu, they returned to camp after a long day, had some dinner, then brewed coffee on their stove. Not until Griffith had taken a good sip was it discovered that the camp boy had filled the kettle with paraffin instead of water. At el-Hosh near Edfu, they battled a strong northerly wind while copying inscriptions on the cliffs, and put folded blankets over their heads to protect them from the cold. By the time they reached Aswan, their provisions were nearly exhausted and they subsisted on hard, stale bread, dipped in the Nile to soften it.[58] Unsurprisingly, Griffith went down with a heavy cold and rheumatism. Petrie, characteristically, seems to have thrived on the experience.

Despite Petrie's rupture with the EEF, Amelia Edwards had been busy on his behalf, doing her best to secure him a permanent salaried post at the Egyptian Museum. But both museum and potential candidate realized that it would not work. Petrie admitted: 'I hate officialism and all pertaining to it . . . all I want is liberty to work where, when and how I like, means to work with, and no interference of anyone else in my business nor in the distribution of my finds: that is my ideal.'[59] In place of a job, Edwards did line up new private patrons to fund Petrie's future excavations. As a gesture of thanks, and rather against his principles, Petrie bought a mummy from a dealer in Luxor that Edwards had requested for a friend of hers. It cost just £20. In Edwards's words, mummies in those days were 'as plentiful as strawberries'.[60]

For the 1887–8 excavation season, Petrie chose Hawara, a somewhat unpromising site in the Fayum. Grébaut was only too happy to grant a permit, since, with the exception of a heavily ruined brick pyramid and the bare traces of its adjoining temple – famed in classical times as the Labyrinth, but long since reduced to a confusing jumble of muddy lines in the sand – it seemed to offer little opportunity for major discoveries.

Petrie camped nearby in a small, single tent. As he wrote to Edwards, 'in this I have to live, to sleep, to wash and to receive visitors'[61] – though, one suspects, not much of the third and rather little of the last. By March, the daytime temperature had risen to 106 degrees in the shade, and shade was virtually non-existent. Even the Egyptian workers suffered heatstroke. (This would have concerned Petrie, for, unlike many of his fellow excavators, he was not unsympathetic to his Egyptian workers. He wrote: 'They are not angels by any means, but they are not all bad according to their lights and way of life, and they do deserve honest treatment.'[62]) Petrie took refuge in the tunnel being dug into the pyramid, but it was 'too narrow now to do anything in but sit still, and it swarms with fleas from the workmen so that I have to sit with a big pot of insect powder open at hand to rub in continually'.[63] On another occasion, while clearing a tomb, Petrie had to contend with 'working in the dark for much of the time, stripped naked, and in filthy brackish water . . . you collide with floating coffins or some skulls that go bobbing around'.[64]

The reward for all his suffering and forbearance was one of the most spectacular discoveries ever made in Egypt: a series of painted portrait heads, dating from the Ptolemaic and Roman periods, as fresh as the day they were finished and lively with character and detail. When some of them went on display in his annual summer exhibition, they caused a sensation, and Londoners flocked to see them. In order to accommodate the large number of visitors, the exhibition was held, not at the Royal Institution or University College, but in the Egyptian Hall in Piccadilly, in the very room where Belzoni had staged his exhibition sixty-seven years before.

In August 1888, shortly after the exhibition of portraits had closed, Petrie and a small group of artists and intellectuals met in London to discuss the establishment of a new society, the

Committee (later Society) for the Preservation of the Monuments of Ancient Egypt. Its focus was to be different from that of the EEF: preservation rather than excavation. Petrie was not alone in his despair at the rapid destruction of Egyptian monuments, and the committee laid at least some of the blame at the feet of the British colonial authorities. Not only did Baring's administration have little apparent regard for antiquities, the economic boom ushered in by British rule had also boosted both tourism and industry, with dire consequences for archaeological sites: 'tombs had become quarries, paintings and reliefs were being hacked out, for souvenirs for sale, and whole blocks removed from the walls'.[65] The committee set itself the task of raising funds to pay for guardians and inspectors at archaeological sites, and for flood protection works. It also demanded that metal doors be fixed to the Theban tombs, that the contents of the Egyptian Museum be moved from Bulaq to Giza, where conditions were drier, and that an English inspector-general of monuments be appointed with specific responsibility for site security. During the winter of 1888–9, the committee petitioned the Foreign Office, which agreed to commission a report.

While many of the requests were sensible, and British public opinion was increasingly on the committee's side, Baring was loath to do anything that might upset the French and their hard-won pre-eminence in cultural matters. Eventually he brokered a compromise: doors would be fitted to the Theban tombs, the temple of Karnak would be protected from salt infiltration, and the Antiquities Service would use the revenues from the tourist tax and admissions charges to carry out further conservation work. But the museum would remain for the time being at Bulaq and there would be no British inspector-general in the Antiquities Service. Petrie resigned from the committee in disgust. It was a familiar pattern when things did not go entirely his own way.[66]

In any case, he had other things to occupy him, other battles to fight. For when he returned to Hawara for a second season, in October 1888, he was appalled by what he found. While he had been in England over the summer, Grébaut had given permission to an Egyptian antiquities dealer to dig at the site, to rifle it for saleable treasures. To add insult to injury, a unique and beautiful painted sarcophagus which Petrie had spent hours preserving, before delivering it to the Egyptian Museum for safe keeping, had disappeared. When Petrie asked to see it, he was told it had fallen to pieces: it had been left out on the verandah at Bulaq, exposed to the damp of the river and the unrelenting sun.[67] Under Grébaut's direction, it seemed, neither excavations nor the Museum were safe. His six-year tenure at the Antiquities Service was characterized by nepotism, procrastination, and incompetence. Petrie tried to circumvent Grébaut by appealing directly to Baring, but the British consul-general was wary of upsetting the French and 'the French Consul will go to any length to keep things in French hands'.[68] One of Edwards's last letters to Petrie ended with the words 'Wishing you every success and a glorious victory over the French'.[69]

Within a few months of Edwards's death in 1892, her wish was partly granted when Grébaut was replaced by a more amenable director, Jacques de Morgan. But before Grébaut resigned he saw to it that a raft of antiquities regulations was passed by royal decree. The new laws affirmed the state's ownership of all antiquities, but allowed that a portion of the finds from an excavation could be given to the excavator to defray expenses, although the government reserved the right to buy back any object it wanted for the Museum. Petrie was furious – as much at Baring for permitting the regulations as at Grébaut for devising them – and even threatened to take French or German citizenship to spite the British government and secure more robust diplomatic support.[70] It was never a very serious threat. In the end, on this argument at least, Petrie had to back down, live with the new regulations, and hope for a better relationship with de Morgan.

After completing his spectacularly successful excavations at Hawara, Petrie wrote to a friend that there were five areas in which he considered himself an expert: '(1) The fine art of collecting and securing all the requisite information, of realising the importance of everything found and avoiding oversights . . . (2) The weaving of a history out of scattered evidence . . . (3) All details of material, colour, fabric and mechanical questions of tools (4) Archaeological surveying (5) Weights.'[71] For once, he was being modest. In the space of less than a decade, through his careful observation, meticulous excavation, detailed record-keeping and prompt publication, Petrie had transformed the practice of archaeology from a mixture of dynamite, earth clearance and treasure-hunting into a precise science. He had also changed the role of the archaeologist: where once, digging had been a part-time diversion for gentleman scholars, it was now a full-time profession for experts. Egyptian archaeology under Petrie, like the British presence in Egypt, had become a permanent occupation.

EIGHT

Scholars and scoundrels

Ernest Alfred Thompson Wallis Budge, first keeper of Egyptian antiquities
at the British Museum and a great popularizer of pharaonic civilization.

In the last two decades a change has occurred: the charms of the sensational, which captivated the dilettantes, has for the most disappeared.[1]

ADOLF ERMAN, 1900

The French stranglehold on Egypt's two leading cultural institutions – the Antiquities Service and the Egyptian Museum – not only persisted under British occupation, it thrived. Just as Heinrich Brugsch had been passed over in 1881 on the death of Mariette, so his brother Emile was cast aside in 1886, on the resignation of Maspero, in favour of a less qualified French candidate, Grébaut. And in due course, with the backing of the British authorities, the hapless Grébaut was succeeded by another Frenchman, Jacques de Morgan. This pattern of British support for French control would persist long into the twentieth century. But while German scholars were shut out from positions of authority in Egypt, they did not turn their backs on the subject of Egyptology. Quite the opposite.

The extraordinary achievements of Lepsius in the 1840s and '50s – the expedition to Egypt and Sudan, the publication of the *Denkmäler*, the reorganization of the Berlin Museum – had laid firm foundations for Egyptology in Germany, and the country's academic community took the discipline to their hearts. By the 1870s, it could boast five chairs at German universities, more than any other European country. Victory in the Franco-Prussian War and the subsequent unification of Germany under Bismarck gave the country a growing sense of its own destiny. Scholarship on the great civilizations of the ancient world was an important part of Germany's self-image and served to project her own imperial aspirations. As a result, while the new generation of French and British Egyptologists – led by Maspero and Petrie – were busy in the field, their counterparts in Germany, ensconced in their university libraries and studies, were making major advances in the understanding of pharaonic civilization.

The greatest name in German Egyptology in the generation after Lepsius was Adolf Erman (1854–1937). He was just a year younger than Petrie, but as different in temperament as could be imagined. The Erman family were descended from Swiss Protestant émigrés but had become thoroughly integrated in German academic circles. Adolf's father was a professor of physics at Berlin, and after an initial year of study at Leipzig, Adolf returned to his home city to study under Lepsius. The great man recognized the young scholar's potential, and secured for him assistant positions in Berlin's museum and library. At the age of just thirty, following the death of his mentor, Erman stepped into Lepsius's shoes to become both professor of Egyptology and director of the Egyptian Museum in Berlin. He would remain based in the German capital for the rest of his career, travelling to Egypt only occasionally, but arguably doing more to advance understanding of the country's ancient civilization than any other Egyptologist of his generation, save Petrie.

For German as well as British scholars in the mid-nineteenth century, Wilkinson's *Manners and Customs* remained a fundamental primer. For all its colour and detail, it was not especially erudite, but it was all there was. As a young man, Erman studied the work, believing that it answered many of the questions about pharaonic culture and that the task of subsequent scholars was merely to fill in the gaps. But, as he later wrote, 'as I got to know this famous book more intimately, I could no longer deceive myself that the "ancient Egyptians" as he portrayed them had ever existed'.[2] Half a century had elapsed since Wilkinson's travels in Egypt; scholarship had moved on signifi-cantly, aided by new discoveries. *Manners and Customs* was not just patchy, it was completely out of date. Erman decided therefore to write a new book that would replace it, moreover one that would treat the ancient Egyptians objectively, without any assumption of special wisdom. In his groundbreaking *Ägypten und ägyptisches Leben in Altertum* (1885), Erman aimed to cut through the mysticism that still surrounded the achieve-ments of the pharaohs, arguing instead that the ancient Egyptians were 'normal representations of their level of cultural development'.[3] For the first time in the history of scholarship, his book did not rely on the biblical or classical traditions, instead prioritizing ancient Egyptian sources and allowing pharaonic culture to be studied on its own terms, through its own voice.

At the same time, Erman's compatriot, the historian Eduard Meyer (1855–1930), cemented this radical approach with a five-volume *Geschichte des Alterthums* (1884–1902). The result was not just a fundamental re-evaluation of ancient Egypt, but also a tacit acknowledgement that the dream of earlier gener-ations of scholars – a dream deliberately promoted by the recently established EEF – of finding in Egypt confirmation of the Bible narrative, would never be realized. As more and more Egyptian texts were translated, it turned out that they had little, if anything, to contribute to biblical history; most were in fact rather dull and pedestrian. Moreover, the new evidence being revealed by the archaeologist's trowel often pointed in different directions or could not be related to the written word. It was Erman's genius to recognize that the only way to cut through this mass of contradictions and frustrations was to prioritize indigenous, ancient Egyptian material and treat it as a single body of evidence.[4]

Erman applied the same approach in his role as director of Berlin's Egyptian Museum.[5] He had first worked at the museum as a student, and the wages he had received had given him a measure of financial independence. He never forgot the favour, and when he took over as director in 1884, following Lepsius's death, he was determined to ensure that the Egyptian collection, so assiduously built up by his predecessor, would continue to rank as one of the greatest in the world – even if that meant some radical changes. Erman was not a natural revolutionary, but he presided over a fundamental reordering of the collection, which had remained in aspic for forty years. He changed both the way in which the artefacts were displayed – providing individual descriptive labels, while allowing each object to speak for itself and the whole collection to demonstrate the development of pharaonic culture – and expanded the holdings through judicious acquisitions. On his first visit to Egypt in the autumn of 1885, just months after taking over at the museum, Erman collected antiquities, focussing especially on manuscripts (reflecting his passion for philology). His keen eye for objects of major historical importance also led him, the following year, to acquire the Amarna Letters. These were a group of clay tablets from an Egyptian diplomatic archive dating to the reign of the pharaoh Akhenaten that had been dug up illicitly from the abandoned city of Amarna. Museums in Vienna and Paris had turned them down, believing them to be forgeries. Erman recognized both their authenticity and their historical value. Surpassing even this acquisition, the greatest object to enter the Berlin Museum under Erman's directorship was the famous 'Green Head'. Bought from a private collector in England, this extraordinarily lifelike carved stone head of an Egyptian official dated from the early Ptolemaic period and showed a blend of traditional Egyptian and Hellenistic traits. In his autobiography, Erman described it as 'the greatest masterwork of our collection'.[6] It remains so to this day. All in all, the collection expanded under Erman's direction from 8,500 to an incredible 21,000 objects. In time, he came to be recognized and celebrated as the refounder of the Berlin Egyptian Museum, every bit as influential in its development as his mentor Lepsius.

However, at heart, Erman was neither an archaeologist nor an art historian. By training, instinct and preference, he was a philologist: his first love, and his abiding passion, was the ancient Egyptian language. And it was in this field, above all, that he made a seminal contribution. While Champollion made ancient Egyptian readable, Erman made it truly understandable. His very first monograph, *Pluralbildung des Aegyptischen* (1878), confirmed his credentials as a linguist and grammarian of rare ability and insight. He was the first scholar to distinguish between the three periods of ancient Egyptian – Old, Middle and Late Egyptian – and his second published work was a grammatical study of the late phase of the language. He was also a fine scholar of Coptic, and the first to recognize the connections between ancient Egyptian and early Semitic languages. His major studies of the Egyptian language were concentrated in the last two decades of the nineteenth century, while Petrie was busy revolutionizing Egyptian archaeology. Like Petrie, Erman effectively founded a new discipline – in Erman's case, Egyptian grammar – and put it on a proper scientific footing.

Erman's greatest single achievement, and the one for which he is best remembered today, was also his most monumental. In the year of his birth, 1854, the brothers Grimm – best known for their fairy tales – had begun an ambitious project to codify and collate the German language. Their *Deutsches Wörterbuch* marked a step change from the work of earlier lexicographers. The possibilities of this new systematic approach, combined with a love of the Egyptian language, planted in Erman's mind the idea for his magnum opus. The project began to crystallize in 1894, when Erman asked his friend and pupil, the American philologist James Henry Breasted (1865–1935), to copy ancient Egyptian inscriptions while on his honeymoon trip up the Nile. Three years later, Erman wrote formally to the Royal Academy in Berlin to propose the compilation of an ancient Egyptian dictionary. The project was finally given the go-ahead in 1899. It was a mammoth undertaking, involving over eighty international collaborators from ten countries. Erman was editor-in-chief, and he gathered around him a team of able young assistants, all of them former, current or future pupils: Breasted, Georg Steindorff, Ludwig Borchardt (1863–1938), Heinrich Schäfer, Kurt Sethe, Hermann Junker, and Alan Gardiner. Even with such a stellar group of scholars, the initial manuscript of the *Wörterbuch der ägyptischen Sprache* took nearly three years to complete and ran to almost two thousand pages. It was a worthy successor to Lepsius's *Denkmäler* by the great man's star pupil. The only problem was finding the funds to pay for its publication. Fortunately, Breasted was able to secure the patronage of the wealthiest man in the world, John D. Rockefeller, and persuaded him to finance the *Wörterbuch*.[7] The first five volumes eventually appeared between 1926 and 1931, some time after Erman had retired, to be followed by eight further volumes of appendices and indices in the years up to 1963.

Erman never lived to see the full realization of his dream, and, owing to his Jewish ancestry, the last three years of his life were spent under the shadow of proscription by the Nazis.

But he had done enough to establish his reputation as the founder of a new school of Egyptology (as practised by his many pupils), and Germany's most important Egyptologist since Lepsius. One of his protégés, and his co-editor on the *Wörterbuch* project, Hermann Grapow (1885–1967), made an even bolder claim, saying of Erman that 'after Champollion and Lepsius, he founded Egyptology anew for the third time'.[8] Certainly, in his break with the classical and biblical prejudices of earlier scholars, his emphasis on indigenous sources, his transformational scholarship on the Egyptian language, and – unusually for a scholar of such distinction – his willingness to write books for a popular, non-specialist readership, his career took Egyptology in new directions and pointed the way to the future.[9]

◁◦▷

Erman and his pupils epitomized the 'German school' of Egyptology, which favoured building up a larger picture from carefully collected, detailed data. The rival 'French school', as practised by Champollion's successors, took the opposite approach, seeking to establish a general pattern first, to provide an interpretative context for specific observations. Needless to say, Petrie attacked both: Mariette and Maspero for their large-scale, careless excavations; the Germans for 'armchair' Egyptology.[10] Erman was more accommodating: while he rightly saw himself as pre-eminent in the field of Egyptian philology, he was willing to concede British leadership in Egyptian archaeology, especially as developed and championed by Petrie.[11]

Not everybody digging in Egypt in the 1880s and '90s, however, was as meticulous or principled as Petrie. There were still scoundrels as well as scholars operating in the Nile Valley. One of the most controversial characters was Ernest Alfred

Thompson Wallis Budge (1857–1934). A close contemporary of Erman's, he could not have been more different in temperament or approach. Budge is regarded today as one of the giants of late nineteenth-century Egyptology, but his interests and methods had more in common with the treasure-hunters of the beginning of the century than with the careful scholarship of Petrie and Erman.

Budge's very origins are shrouded in mystery. His birth certificate names his father as a 'Mr Vyvyan', without further details.[12] The name looks to have been hastily added, and it has been suggested that it was a decoy, masking the true identity of Budge's father to protect the reputation of a public figure. The personal interest taken in Budge's education and upbringing by the Liberal statesman and future prime minister William Ewart Gladstone is certainly unexpected, given the boy's modest, provincial origins. In any case, Budge took his mother's surname, moved from Cornwall to London, and became interested in Egyptian civilization at an early age, often visiting the British Museum. It was while Budge was still at school that a friend of his headmaster introduced him to Birch, the keeper of oriental antiquities at the museum and guardian of the flame of British Egyptology during the fallow years of the mid-nineteenth century (after Wilkinson and his circle had moved on to other interests and before Petrie began his excavations). Birch encouraged Budge to pursue his studies, and provided space in his own office for the young scholar. As Budge later recalled:

> When reading or copying in his room I learned to know personally nearly all the great Oriental archaeologists of the day, and nearly all the little band of scholars . . . who had successfully deciphered the Egyptian hieroglyphs and the cuneiform inscriptions . . . I saw Gardner Wilkinson

on various occasions when he came to discuss with Birch the preparation of a second edition of his popular work on the 'Manners and Customs of the Ancient Egyptians' . . . He watched the progress of decipherment with sympathy and interest, but he had no special linguistic talent, and never professed to be an Egyptologist . . . He had neither the gifts nor the enthusiasm which make a great collector . . . On more than one occasion he advised me to get to Egypt as soon as I could, saying that no man who had not seen that country could ever hope to understand its history.[13]

Already we see the combination of self-confidence and arrogance that were to characterize Budge's entire career.

With the support of establishment figures like Gladstone and Birch, Budge secured a place at Cambridge in 1878, initially as a 'non-collegiate student' before transferring within a year to Christ's College where he was elected a scholar. He seems to have applied himself diligently – his own description of his time at Cambridge is that it was 'filled with hard work'[14] – and he graduated in Semitic languages in 1882. His two mentors then agreed to create for him a new post, of assistant keeper in Birch's department; Gladstone (then both prime minister and Chancellor of the Exchequer) used his political influence to have 'the necessary provision made in the British Museum Estimates for the year',[15] and Budge used the intervening months to further his studies in Arabic, Ethiopic and Talmudic literature. In April 1883, at the start of the new financial year, Budge duly took up his post at the British Museum, the institution that would remain his home for the next four decades.

His immediate task was perhaps not quite as glamorous as he had expected. The transfer between 1880 and 1883 of the museum's extensive natural history collection to South

Kensington – where it would form the core of the new Natural History Museum – provided an opportunity to reorganize the remaining holdings, and Budge spent several months packing and unpacking cases of antiquities as the historical collections spread out to fill the additional gallery space. Birch had welcomed the young man into his department, but in reality had little need for an additional orientalist. He therefore decided to train Budge in Egyptology, and soon spotted an opportunity for him to prove his usefulness.

In the summer of 1886, the *sirdar* of the Egyptian army, Sir Francis Grenfell, was visiting England and looking for an Egyptologist to excavate the nobles' tombs at Aswan. Birch recommended Budge, granted him four months' leave of absence from the museum, and gave him the task of establishing contact with 'native dealers from whom a regular supply of antiquities might be obtained for the British Museum'.[16] The excavations at Aswan would provide the perfect cover for collecting. Once the real purpose behind Budge's forthcoming trip became known in museum circles, the Fitzwilliam Museum in Cambridge gave him a sum of £100 for purchases, while HM Treasury sanctioned a grant of £150.

Budge first set foot on Egyptian soil towards the end of 1886, and the country made an instant impression: 'When I saw the variety of lights which accompanied the sunrise, it seemed to me that I had entered a new world, and that I had never seen the sun rise before.'[17] But romantic thoughts of cloudless climes and starry skies soon gave way to the practical business of the mission, and Budge discovered that he had a natural flair for acquiring antiquities. At Zagazig railway station, en route from Port Said to Cairo: 'Dealers in anticas from the site of the ancient city of Bubastis climbed up into the carriages from both sides of the line, and the half hour's halt was agreeably spent in buying good Delta scarabs for two or three piastres apiece, and quite good figures of the cat-headed goddess Bast for a piastre a piece.'[18] He soon 'made the acquaintance and somehow gained the good will of two natives' who, in the years to come, would supply him with 'many valuable objects for the Museum'.[19] Birch had evidently chosen well.

The thirty-one-year-old Budge seems to have had other things on his mind when he first visited Giza, comparing the two larger pyramids to 'a pair of twin breasts against the red light of the western sun'.[20] This same red-blooded confidence and disregard for diplomatic niceties soon brought him into conflict with the British agent and consul-general, Evelyn Baring. At their very first meeting, Baring, perennially wary of upsetting the French, told Budge that any excavations carried out in Egypt by a British government employee were likely to 'complicate political relationships' and that the occupation of Egypt by the British 'ought not to be made an excuse for filching antiquities from the country, whether to England or anywhere else'.[21] The two men were not destined to get on. According to Budge, Baring 'spoke with some irritation of the annoyance which he had suffered from several British archaeologists and amateur dealers who were in Cairo at that moment, and having quite made up his mind that I was of the same kidney, he politely but firmly got me out of his room'.[22]

Baring's colleague (and eventual successor), the controller of taxes Eldon Gorst, was of the same view. Their stance not only irritated Budge, it mystified him, and he decided to press on with his mission regardless: 'As I knew quite well that the agents for the great Continental Museums regularly despatched to them collections of antiquities, I determined to follow their example, if I could find out the way they managed their affairs, and send home collections to the British Museum.'[23]

In December 1886, Budge carried out excavations at Aswan – the ostensible purpose of his expedition – noting that 'the labour involved was enormous, for the rubbish and broken stones mixed with sand had to be cleared by small sledges'. Nonetheless, the results were worth the effort. As Budge described in a letter to *The Times* the following month: 'The whole of the side of the hill is filled with tombs, tier upon tier, and the above rough description of three of them, taken at random, will show what a large and important necropolis awaits excavation.'[24] His sponsor, Grenfell, was delighted, and, taking a leaf out of Amelia Edwards's book, took the opportunity to appeal for further funds:

> We have already collected various sums for the prosecution of the work of clearing out the tombs, and would now, with your permission, through the medium of *The Times*, appeal for help to all archaeologists and others interested in the antiquities of Egypt . . . As during the four years of the British occupation of Egypt but little has been done by our countrymen towards the advancement of the cause of Egyptian archaeology, it would be most unfortunate, now that an opportunity offers, if this important work should fall through for the want of a little pecuniary assistance. I may add that I am able to assist, to some extent, by contributing military labour from the Egyptian regiments at present quartered at Assouan. Subscriptions may be sent to Messrs. Morton, Rose, and Co., Bartholomew-lane, E.C., for Assouan Excavation Fund.[25]

The prosecution of further excavations at Aswan looked set to be stymied by financial constraints, but Budge's mission to acquire artefacts for his museum sponsors back in England was going swimmingly. Having visited the museum at Bulaq and seen the state in which the collections were being kept – 'It seemed as if no one . . . knew or cared about the preservation of the antiquities'[26] – he convinced himself that it was his duty as a scholar to remove antiquities to a place of safety where they could be properly conserved and studied. The Egyptian Museum knew what Budge was up to, and sent a representative to watch his comings and goings; but this merely drove the native antiquities dealers into Budge's arms, since 'the natives treated the Government's claim to all antiquities in Egypt with contempt'.[27]

Budge's efforts to acquire objects for the British Museum became increasingly daring, and increasingly brazen. At Philae, a company of the Royal Engineers discovered some pieces of carved stone while carrying out temple clearance; Budge saw that they were sent to London. He wanted to transport the colossus of Ramesses II at Mit Rahina to England, but met with implacable opposition from the French and blamed the British authorities for caving in: 'Sir E. Baring, for some reason or other, wished to placate the French Colony in Egypt . . . Thus the British lost the statue.'[28] In truth, it would have proved impossible to lift and transport so immense a statue thousands of miles by river and sea. It remains in its original position to this day, prostrate on the ground, too large even to be re-erected.

As Budge neared the end of his four-month mission, and prepared to take his acquisitions out of the country, Baring intervened once again, pressing for the return of any antiquities bought from dealers. Budge tersely reminded him 'that I was not a member of his staff, and that I intended to carry out the instructions of the Trustees, and to do my utmost to increase the collections of the British Museum'.[29] No wonder Baring is said to have declared: 'I wish there were no more antiquities in this country; they are more trouble than anything else.'[30] In Budge, 'over-Baring' had certainly met his match. Next, the Antiquities Service attempted to block the export of Budge's cases from Alexandria, but he colluded with officials and British military officers at the docks to smuggle the objects through customs and onto a waiting ship. Budge and his hoard arrived safely back in London to the delight of his employers at the British Museum. He had done exactly as he had been asked, and had surpassed expectations.

The appointment of Grébaut as director of the Egyptian Museum and the Antiquities Service in 1886 merely strengthened the native dealers' hand. Budge was scathing of the new director at Bulaq, calling him 'by nature, and disposition, and training . . . unsuited for the post into which he was thrust', and averring (with no sense of irony) that 'all those who had at heart the progress of Egyptology, and the welfare of the National Collection in Egypt, regretted the appointment'.[31] The more Grébaut tried to assert the Egyptian government's owernship of antiquities, the more he found himself outwitted by the dealers.

In 1887–8, rumours of a major discovery in Upper Egypt began circulating in archaeological circles throughout Europe. Continental museums dispatched representatives to Cairo, 'each doing his best, as was right, to secure the lion's share'.[32] The discovery in question was that of the Amarna Letters – which Erman would successfully acquire for Berlin's Egyptian Museum – and the fact that the Antiquities Service knew of it at all came about by accident rather than design. A smuggler was taking one of the largest tablets to Cairo, and:

hid it between his inner garments, and covered himself with his great cloak. As he stepped up into the railway coach this tablet slipped from his clothes and fell on the bed of the railway, and broke in pieces. Many natives in the train and on the platform witnessed the accident and talked freely about it, and thus the news of the discovery of the tablets reached the ears of the Director of Antiquities.[33]

Budge revelled in the cat-and-mouse game between the dealers and the authorities, making it perfectly clear on which side he stood. Grébaut in turn, and with good reason, distrusted Budge, and ordered the police to watch him, report his movements, and take the names of any dealers he met. Budge was even threatened with arrest and prosecution; but he pressed on, undeterred and utterly confident of his own rightness.

During one collecting trip to Thebes, he acquired from local dealers a remarkable series of funerary papyri – no doubt illicitly excavated from a nearby tomb – and smuggled them back to his storeroom in Luxor. Grébaut followed in hot pursuit, but the captain of his steamer deliberately ran the boat aground on a sandbank near Naqada, just a few hours' sailing north of Luxor, so that he could attend his daughter's wedding. The boat remained there for two days. Frustrated, Grébaut sent police to arrest Budge and the dealers, but Budge managed to buy off the police. When Grébaut's steamer eventually arrived in Luxor, one of the dealers went straight to the boat and bought antiquities from Grébaut's own servant, 'who handed them down to him from one end of the steamer while his employer was dining at the other!'[34] By now, Antiquities Service guards had been stationed around Budge's storeroom to stop him removing any of his ill-gotten gains. But Budge had learned a lesson or two from his dealer friends. First, he arranged for the guards to be sent a hearty meal. Then, under cover of darkness, he had an underground tunnel dug from the storeroom to the adjoining garden of the Luxor Hotel. While he and the hotel manager watched anxiously, and while the guards were busy eating: 'man after man went into the *sardâb* [basement] of the house, and brought out, piece by piece and box by box, everything which was of the slightest value commercially . . . In this way we saved the Papyrus of Ani, and all the rest of my acquisitions from the officials of the Service of Antiquities, and all Luxor rejoiced.'[35]

Budge used all sorts of ruses to smuggle the antiquities out of Egypt, for example hiding sheets of papyrus between photographic plates. Once again, he was assisted by sympathetic British officers and corrupt customs officials. He remained totally unrepentant, defending his actions by claiming he had done only: 'what every collector for a European Museum did in Egypt . . . dispensed with [the authorities'] permission to take out of the country the smaller and more precious objects which were greatly needed to increase existing groups or to fill up gaps in the collections in the British Museum'.[36] Moreover, he asserted, because of the parlous state of security at the Bulaq Museum: 'The objects would have been smuggled out of Egypt all the same; the only difference would have been that instead of being in the British Museum they would be in some museum or private collection on the Continent or in America.'[37] 'No tomb in Egypt,' he averred, 'however skilfully and cunningly constructed, has protected the mummy or mummies in it against the ancient tomb-robber, and from wreckage and mutilation at his hands. But it is impossible for any mummy to be wrecked or mutilated in the British Museum.'[38]

Altogether, Budge was sent to Egypt to acquire antiquities on thirteen more occasions between 1891 and 1913. By the 1890s, forgeries were becoming increasingly common, but Budge's good relations with all the main dealers allowed him to purchase the best genuine artefacts – much to the chagrin of his European rivals. As he himself put it: 'It only took a couple of winters to teach the dealers that the Trustees of the British Museum always paid fair prices.'[39] He also recognized the importance of local knowledge. Throughout the Nile Valley, as soon as the archaeologists downed tools at the end of a digging season, 'the natives set to work to finish the excavations on their own account'.[40] Moreover, 'the native seekers after antiquities always have known, and always will know, more about the places where antiquities are to be found than European archaeologists, however greatly they be skilled in Egyptology'.[41]

When, in 1892, de Morgan replaced Grébaut as director of the Antiquities Service and Egyptian Museum, Budge immediately recognized a kindred spirit. He found de Morgan 'courteous, sympathetic and broad-minded',[42] principally, one imagines, because the new director had a much more liberal attitude to the export of antiquities, 'provided that they immediately found safe and secure deposit in great national museums like the Louvre and the British Museum . . . He wanted all the great museums in Europe to acquire all they possibly could, while the British occupied Egypt.'[43] To take full advantage of such a benign new regime, Budge's employers sent him to Egypt in early October 1892, 'to arrange with the dealers for a regular supply of Egyptian and Coptic antiquities, and to acquire Greek and Coptic papyri and manuscripts of all kinds'.[44] When he arrived, he discovered that collecting had turned into a free-for-all. Picking up on the signals sent by de Morgan, foreign agents were smuggling antiquities out of Egypt in their diplomatic baggage. Budge sprang into action, and his reputation preceded him. Each time he visited Thebes, he found 'another group of happy natives' awaiting him with antiquities to sell.[45] By such means, he acquired for the British Museum an intact prehistoric grave – 'The body was exhibited at once in the First Egyptian Room, and for the first time the British public saw a neolithic Egyptian'[46] – and, directly from dealers at Giza and Saqqara, a series of false doors, statues and stelae, to create at the

British Museum 'the finest collection of monuments of the Early Empire outside Egypt'.[47]

Even by the standards of his own time, Budge's reputation was decidedly mixed. Some contemporaries denounced him in the press as 'a somewhat unscrupulous collector of antiquities for his Museum', and hoped they might 'arouse scientific public opinion in England against him and his methods';[48] but Budge continued, undaunted. In his autobiography, written after thirty-five years of collecting, his justification was as robust and outspoken as it had been at the beginning of his career: 'from first to last . . . the principal robbers of tombs and wreckers of mummies have been the Egyptians themselves. The outcry against the archaeologist is foolish, and the accusations made against him are absurd.'[49]

⟨o⟩

It was in the context of operations like Budge's that, in 1889, Petrie's young assistant, Francis Llewellyn Griffith, had railed against the mores of contemporary archaeology. He lamented:

If a small portion of the sums of money that, *in the name of scientific research*, have been spent in Egypt on treasure-hunting for antiquities, on uncovering monuments and exporting them to destruction, on *unwatched* excavations from which the limestone sculptures have gone straight to the kiln or the village stone-mason – if a small portion of this had been utilized in securing systematically throughout the country accurate and exhaustive copies of the inscriptions above ground and in danger, the most important part of all the evidence of her past that Egypt has handed down to our day would have been gathered intact, instead of being mutilated beyond recovery.[50]

Such sentiments resonated with Amelia Edwards, for one. The following October, she wrote a letter to *The Times* announcing the establishment of an Archaeological Survey of Egypt under Griffith's direction and editorship, and setting out its goals: 'to map, plan, photograph and copy all the most important sites, sculptures, and paintings and inscriptions yet extant, so as to preserve at least a faithful record of those fast-perishing monuments'.[51] It was to be one of the last significant initiatives of her life.

Edwards's final gift to Egyptology, as we have seen, was to endow a chair at UCL. There is no doubt that Edwards chose University College, rather than one of the two ancient universities, because of its commitment to equality between men and women. Edwards wanted women like her to have the opportunity to study Egyptology at university, and her wish was fulfilled from the outset: of the eight students who enrolled for Petrie's first course of lectures, seven were women. Petrie was determined to use Edwards's legacy to build up a nationally important centre of teaching and research. To add to Edwards's own library, he used his academic contacts to persuade the French government to donate volumes of their archaeological series, and the German Kaiser to donate a complete set of Lepsius's *Denkmäler*; within two years, the library comprised 600 volumes. In his inaugural lecture, Petrie launched the Egyptian Research Account to train students in the field as excavators, backed by private donations; it ran for over fifty years and launched the careers of many successful archaeologists. Petrie ensured that the courses given by his assistant, Margaret Murray, would 'prepare his excavators to be archaeologists and not just diggers'.[52]

UCL had agreed with Petrie that he would lecture in the first and third terms, leaving the winter months free for his annual season of excavation in Egypt. The location he chose for his first dig as Edwards Professor of Egyptology in the winter of 1893–4 was, on the face of it, rather unprepossessing. At Kuft (ancient Coptos, modern Qift), north of Luxor, a public road ran through the centre of the archaeological site, providing looters with easy access to the ruins. Petrie found the town awash with thieves and dealers. The locals were not much better. He described them as 'the most troublesome people that I have ever worked with'.[53] Nonetheless, he was determined to train some in the science of archaeology, to complement his growing band of students back in London. It was an inspired decision, as he later explained:

> Among this rather untoward people we found however, as in every place, a small percentage of excellent men; some half-dozen were of the very best type of native, faithful, friendly, and laborious, and from among these workmen we have drawn about forty to sixty for our work . . . They have formed the backbone of my upper Egyptian staff, and I hope that I may keep these good friends so long as I work anywhere within reach of them.[54]

Within a couple of seasons, Petrie's small band of Kuftis grew into something of a local industry, and by the end of the nineteenth century villagers from Kuft enjoyed a virtual monopoly of skilled archaeological labour on Egyptian excavations.[55] In time, Petrie's original Kuftis passed on their skills, father to son, down the generations. Some of their descendants are still employed as professional diggers working in Egypt today, and 'Kufti' has become shorthand among archaeologists for a skilled site foreman.

While working at Kuft, Petrie 'eyed the hills on the opposite side of the Nile, and heard of things being found there'.[56] So, after finishing at Kuft, he moved his team across the river and started work at the two adjacent sites of Nagada and Ballas. Petrie concentrated on Nagada, with its extensive cemeteries, while his young assistant, James Quibell, sister in tow, worked at Ballas. 'Miss Quibell did most of the drawing of the objects found; she seems to have enjoyed excavating and took very kindly to life in Egypt.'[57] Yet despite her important contribution, Miss Quibell's name never appeared on the title page of any of Petrie's publications, and she is absent from most histories of Egyptology. (Later, during the First World War, she kept a school for children of English residents in Cairo.)

The graves Petrie excavated at Nagada were unlike anything else he had ever encountered in Egypt. The pottery was in strange styles – red with black tops or cream with red-painted decoration – and there were previously unknown classes of object: cosmetic palettes, used for grinding mineral pigments, and flint knives. Petrie held to the 'diffusionist' theory that civilization must have reached Egypt from more advanced lands to the East – *ex oriente lux* – and interpreted the strange burials accordingly. He identified the people buried at Nagada as members of a 'New Race', and stuck resolutely to the theory, even when faced with evidence and arguments to the contrary. (Quibell is said to have had his doubts about the 'New Race' theory from the outset, although he would not have been so unwise as to utter them in Petrie's presence.) Petrie's strength was also his weakness. In the words of his biographer: 'Once he had seized upon a hypothesis it was sometimes difficult for him to envisage that he could be wrong . . . throughout his life he clung to theories of his own . . . till overwhelming evidence forced him to admit his mistakes.'[58] Only in the light of subsequent excavations by Quibell elsewhere in Upper Egypt were the 'New Race' burials correctly identified as those of prehistoric, indigenous Egyptians.

A more lasting achievement from Petrie's excavations at

Nagada was his development of 'sequence dating', a technique now known as seriation, whereby the gradual changes in style over time within a particular class of object, for example pottery or stone vessels, can be used to place a series of archaeological contexts in their relative chronological order. Petrie also established a system for tomb-digging that set the standard for future archaeologists. Altogether he dug over two hundred graves in a single season at Nagada, making scale drawings of each tomb and its contents. He wanted, above all, to distance himself from the old style of excavation, as practised by Mariette, who 'only visited his excavation once in a few weeks and left everything to native reises [overseers], just ordering a particular area to be cleared out'.[59]

While Petrie set new standards of scientific precision and process in his archaeological work, life on one of his digs became synonymous with asceticism to the point of privation. He was fond of the Stoic philosophers, and always took a volume of Epictetus with him when he travelled to Egypt. On his earliest excavations for the EEF in the Nile Delta: 'He dosed himself daily with quinine and strychnine to ward off the marsh fevers, and found that under his strenuous regime he kept surprisingly well.'[60] In February 1895, James Breasted visited Petrie during a honeymoon trip up the Nile. Breasted was looking forward to meeting the archaeologist who had already established an international reputation, but was aghast and genuinely perplexed by Petrie's modus vivendi: 'It was never quite clear to those who endured his deliberately primitive regime why service to archaeology should necessarily entail . . . rags, dirt, malnutrition, chronic dyspepsia and almost total absence of the most rudimentary creature comforts.'[61]

What Breasted had discerned was that Petrie's austerity was not simply a matter of economy, but of choice. Nonetheless, Breasted had to admit, Petrie achieved 'maximum results for minimum expenditure'.[62] His excavations at Kuft, on which he employed seventy men for eleven weeks, cost just £300.

A few years later, the founder of the National Trust, Canon Rawnsley, visited Petrie's excavations at Meidum, and so enjoyed the experience – one suspects it must have been a brief visit – that he sent his son, Noel, as a volunteer to work with Petrie during a subsequent winter season. As finishing schools go, it was certainly memorable:

> First came an ice-cold bath . . . Visions of ham and eggs are lost in the reality of other food . . . We sit on empty boxes to discuss our meals. The dining room is floored with sand. It is an oblong room and down its centre is a rough trestle table. The boards are somewhat warped and stained, and on them range the bowls of food or opened tins, covered with dishes or saucers to exclude the dust. Along each side-wall is a single plank for shelf, where lie the records of the former excavations, a few odd finds, the public ink and pens and rolls of copied hieroglyphs.[63]

The diet consisted of tea, ship's biscuits, and cold tinned tongue. Half-empty tins were left to be served up again the following day. In the heat of Egypt, food poisoning was the regular result. It was even said that tins of food left over from one season were buried, to be dug up again at the start of the next. Each tin would be tested by throwing it against a stone wall. If it survived without exploding, its contents were deemed fit for consumption.[64] As for sanitation, Petrie told one of his students 'the desert is wide and there are many sheltered hollows'.[65] (The result, according to Budge, was that Petrie was 'dirty, verminous and . . . as odiferous as a polecat'.[66]) The young Rawnsley summed the whole experience up thus: 'An excavator's camp in the valley of the Nile is a thing apart . . . a rough sketch in mud bricks and sand, a little settlement of sunburnt men toiling in a thirsty land, alone with nature, in one of her solemnest moods.'[67] His time spent with Petrie had, at the very least, disabused him of romantic notions of the Orient. His lasting impression was that 'the valley of the Nile is not a paradise, for there are dust and flies and smells and other disagreeable things'.[68]

Later visitors to Petrie's excavation camp included T. E. Lawrence, who came for six weeks to learn the rudiments of archaeology from its acknowledged master. He, too, had a memorable experience: 'A Petrie dig is a thing with a flavour of its own: tinned kidneys mingle with mummy-corpses and amulets in the soup: my bed is all gritty with prehistoric alabaster jars of unique types – and my feet at night keep the bread-box from rats.' Lawrence also got the measure of Petrie as a person, and in his brief description we see through the mask of the great archaeologist to the stubborn, single-minded and rather selfish individual that lay beneath. Lawrence described Petrie, with a remarkable degree of indulgence, as 'a man of ideas and systems, from the right way to dig a temple to the only way to clean one's teeth. Also he only is right in all things . . . Further he is easy-tempered, full of humour, and fickle to a degree that makes him delightfully quaint, and a constant source of joy and amusement in his camp.' But, once again, the end of the visit was an occasion for profound relief. Lawrence concluded: 'Am awfully glad I went to him. But what a life!'[69]

That Petrie ever found space in his life for another person is a wonder. That he married is nothing short of miraculous. During the exhibition of his season's finds, at UCL in the summer of 1896, he noticed a young woman making drawings of some of the objects. He found himself attracted to her, and struck up a conversation. Her name was Hilda Urlin, and she had been asked to sketch some of Petrie's finds by a family friend, the Pre-Raphaelite painter Henry Holiday. But Hilda herself preferred more practical pursuits. As a child she had been a tomboy, given to sailing boats, spinning tops, and other activities generally deemed unsuitable for a girl.[70] Petrie seems to have spotted an ideal soul mate, and within a year had declared his love. Hilda initially rejected his advances, but eventually began to reciprocate his feelings. They married in late November 1897, and spent their honeymoon . . . in Egypt. Fortunately for Petrie, his wife 'took to life in an archaeological camp like a duck to water'.[71] She lacked any domestic skills, but her inability to cook was hardly of concern in a camp that ran on tinned food. Her strength, stamina and stoicism were what mattered. On one of their early excavations together, Petrie recalled, 'a man came in the dark and shot at close range at the first person who came out of our mess-hut, which was my wife. Happily she escaped.'[72] On another occasion, Hilda herself wrote 'at the head of my bed are 4 great cartonnage heads of mummy cases with staring faces, at the side are collections of alabasters and many bones hard by; at the foot of the bed are 80 skulls'.[73] She took it all in her stride.

⊲⚬⊳

Neither Petrie nor Budge had found Maspero's successor at the Museum and Antiquities Service, Eugène Grébaut, easy to deal with. His primary concern, to defend French archaeological pre-eminence at all costs, blinded him to other pressing problems. Thefts from archaeological sites, and the illicit trade in antiquities – exploited, if not encouraged by Budge – flourished under Grébaut's stewardship. Just about the only positive development in his six-year tenure was the opening of a new Egyptian Museum at Giza; the collection had finally been relocated from its riverside quarters at Bulaq following the disastrous floods of 1878. Khedive Tewfiq offered an old harem palace built by his father, Ismail, and inaugurated it as Egypt's new national musem on 12 January 1890. But this positive development could not mask Grébaut's wider failings. In private, even the French consul conceded that he was a disaster and would have to be replaced.[74] Grébaut clearly sensed that moves were being made against him; determined to resist demands to hire a German, or – worse still – a Briton, he promoted Ahmed Kamal to the post of assistant curator. Kamal thus became the first Egyptian to be employed in a substantive position in the Egyptian Museum. His appointment was followed shortly afterwards by that of Ahmed Najib as chief inspector of antiquities: the first Egyptian to occupy a senior role in the Antiquities Service. Through his fierce opposition to other European nationalities, Grébaut thus unwittingly became an early champion of Egyptian advancement.

Grébaut's wider ineptitude, however, could not be ignored. Matters came to a head in 1892. In January that year, Tewfiq died unexpectedly at the age of thirty-nine, and was succeeded by his seventeen-year-old son Abbas. (The boy spoke Turkish, German, French and English, but no Arabic: it was little wonder that late nineteenth-century Cairo witnessed the first stirrings of pan-Arab nationalism, as Egyptians began to debate their future under Ottoman rule.) According to Egyptian law, the age of majority was eighteen, and Abbas was still at school in Vienna. More awkward still for Evelyn Baring (newly ennobled as Lord Cromer), Abbas had imbibed Hapsburg ideas and was no friend of the British. Within just one month of his accession, Abbas had appointed an Anglophobe Swiss as his private secretary, and believed he would have French support in any showdown against Cromer. Tewfiq had been relatively easily to manipulate, but Abbas showed every sign of wanting to be his own man. Cromer himself admitted: 'I really wish he was not quite so civilized.'[75]

During the interregnum, while the British authorities were preoccupied with the royal succession, Grébaut took his chance to reassert his position and, in a fit of pique, refused all new concessions to excavate, even to the EEF. It was a step too far. Later that year, by which time Abbas had turned eighteen and returned to Egypt to assume the throne as Abbas II (r.1892– 1914), the French authorities forced Grébaut from office. They replaced him with an unlikely choice, the mining engineer and geologist, Jacques de Morgan. Where Grébaut had been petty, de Morgan was affable. His more conciliatory approach certainly found favour with the likes of Petrie and Budge. Inevitably, some French accused de Morgan of being too friendly towards the British. But it was his lack of expertise in Egyptology rather than any want of national pride that eventually sank his directorship. For example, determined to reinforce the flood defences at Kom Ombo, to protect the Ptolemaic temple from slipping into the river, he turned – as any good engineer would – to the nearest source of stone, a handy pile of sixty blocks, which he proceeded to have pulverized into chippings to strengthen the Nile bank. The blocks subsequently turned out to have formed the ancient floor of the temple. In saving it from flooding, de Morgan had irreparably damaged its very fabric. His cavalier attitude to antiquities also led him to propose selling duplicates in the Egyptian Museum directly to foreign museums, enraging the antiquities dealers. For the head of Egypt's cultural heritage directorate to alienate archaeologists and antique dealers alike was no mean feat. After just five years in post, de Morgan, too, had to go.

Like Grébaut before him, his one moment of triumph concerned the future of the Egyptian Museum. The Giza harem palace was only ever going to be an interim solution, and early in his tenure de Morgan had appointed an international jury to choose the design for a new, permanent museum, to be located in the centre of Cairo. A Frenchman, a Briton and an Italian received designs from all over the world. The five entries they shortlisted were all French; the winner was a relatively unknown architect, Marcel Dourgnon, whose vision was for an imposing edifice in a neoclassical European idiom. On 1 April 1897, Khedive Abbas II laid the cornerstone at the northern end of a grand new square that had been laid out by Ismail as part of his redevelopment of the capital.

By that autumn, however, de Morgan had left office, to be replaced by someone with an unimpeachable background in Egyptology. (Had the authorities proposed another amateur, pressure to appoint the assistant curator at the Egyptian Museum, the German Emile Brugsch, could have proved impossible to resist.) Victor Loret had been a pupil of Maspero's at the Ecole des Hautes Etudes, and had undertaken fieldwork at Thebes. His primary interest was in archaeology, and he relaunched systematic excavations in the Valley of the Kings for the first time since Belzoni's day, discovering the tombs of Thutmose III and Amenhotep II (the latter hiding a cache of royal mummies) within a month of each other, and fourteen private tombs. He also refounded the Ecole du Caire as the Institut Français d'Archéologie Orientale and reinstated the *catalogue général* of the Egyptian Museum, to document all objects entering the collection. Unfortuately, like so many academics, Loret was totally unsuited to a senior administrative role. Clandestine excavations and the illicit trade in antiquities prospered under his incompetent regime. As one British observer put it: 'Egypt was the happy hunting-ground of archaeologists of all nations . . . excavators were inclined to put a free interpretation on the concessions granted to them by the Egyptian Government, and in spite of the embargo set on their exportation, valuable antiquities continued, from time to time, to slip out of the country.'[76]

Faced with such shameless looting, Loret steered through a new decree on the protection of Egypt's cultural heritage, but it was too little, too late. His main talent, besides excavation, seems to have been making enemies. Eventually, all nationalities, including the French, were clamouring for him to go.[77]

The question was, who could be found to replace him? Since Maspero's departure in 1886, there had been three directors of the Antiquities Service and Museum in the space of thirteen years. Each had proved more inept than the last. The French were desperate to maintain their control, so hard won and so diligently maintained. Back in 1890, they had received assurances from the Egyptian foreign minister that, in return for a loan, 'Egypt would not name Britons to the Antiquities Service.'[78] Now, nine years later, the French consul-general had to remind his political masters in Paris of the importance of 'retaining here the Egyptological terrain, the rightful place to which we are entitled by the French origin of this science, the work of Mariette, and the sacrifices France has always made for knowledge of ancient Egypt'.[79] But after the high-handed Grébaut, the incompetent de Morgan, and the disastrous Loret, there were few plausible French candidates left. In fact, there was only one.

Scholars began to plead with Maspero to return. Petrie wrote to him in April 1898: 'I sincerely hope to find you (back) at the Museum next season. The current situation is completely impossible: if French influence has to be represented there by men such as Grébaut and Loret, it would be better for it to disappear to avoid an even greater scandal. Your return would be the only solution acceptable to all parties and all interests.'[80]

But Maspero was loath to involve himself in what he saw as a campaign to unseat his former pupil, Loret. The situation continued to deteriorate, and six months later, a Frenchman begged Maspero: 'I am absolutely certain, after what I have seen and heard, that this important position will be given to an Englishman or a German, given the level of discontent this year . . . Your undisputed and indisputable reputation alone can save for France this legitimate inheritance.'[81]

Meanwhile, Cromer was preoccupied with a matter altogether more important than the future of the Antiquities Service. The Mahdist rebellion in Sudan had been festering for years, but an Anglo-Egyptian army commanded by General Kitchener had been achieving some recent successes. Their efforts at reconquest, facilitated by the newly completed railway from Cairo to Aswan, culminated in the Battle of Omdurman on 2 September 1898, which saw the Khalifa defeated and the death of General Gordon avenged. But no sooner had the British celebrated victory than they were met with another challenge to their control of north-east Africa. While the British and the Mahdist forces had been fighting, a French force had spotted an opportunity to gain a foothold on the Upper Nile, and had marched all the way from the Congo to raise the French flag at Fashoda, less than 500 miles from Khartoum. Kitchener was hastily dispatched, and Britain and France remained on the brink until the French capitulated and withdrew.[82]

While recapturing Sudan and averting a European war were uppermost in Cromer's mind, he could not altogether neglect the future leadership of Egypt's cultural institutions, even though he found archaeological rivalries intensely irritating. His chosen method of intervention was a textbook example of his modus operandi under the 'veiled protectorate'. He approached that doyen of orientalists, Archibald Sayce, who since 1890 had taken to spending each winter on the Nile on his *dahabiya*, *Istar* (complete with an onboard library of 2,000 books and a crew of nineteen). Sayce knew everyone in

Egyptology, and agreed to sound out Maspero's willingness to contemplate a second term. Maspero had refused three previous attempts to bring him back, but this time the very future of the Antiquities Service, and of French pre-eminence, hung on his decision. He agreed to return, but on much more generous terms than before: a salary of £1,500 per annum plus expenses. Cromer did not demur. By September 1899, Maspero was on his way back to Egypt.

As if to signal the dire state into which Egypt's patrimony had fallen during his thirteen-year absence, on the morning of 3 October, just a few days after his arrival in the country, eleven columns in the great Hypostyle Hall at Karnak came crashing down. The roar could be heard in Luxor two miles away. Maspero found himself having to pick up the pieces, quite literally, of his predecessors' incompetence and neglect. The disaster at Karnak confirmed his priorities for his second term of office: from now on, the Antiquities Service would focus on conservation and publication of Egypt's ancient monuments; excavations would be left to foreign missions. As long as they had the money and the requisite skills, overseas expeditions would be welcome in the Nile Valley.

As the world entered the dying days of the nineteenth century, the way was thus opened for new interests to join the scramble for Egypt.

NINE

Egypt and America

Theodore Davis (third from left) outside a tomb in the Valley of the Kings,
accompanied by his two archaeologists Arthur Weigall (second from left)
and Edward Ayrton (right), and Mrs Weigall.

All good things come to those who dig long and deep enough.[1]

THEODORE DAVIS, 1902

Europeans had imbibed the mystique and majesty of ancient Egypt from classical times. The very visible presence, in Rome and Constantinople, of obelisks from the distant Nile Valley set a precedent and an expectation: that any future European empire, actual or self-imagined, would proclaim its credentials by erecting a grand pharaonic monument at the heart of its capital city. Furthermore, from the beginning of the Enlightenment, Europe saw itself as the inheritor of classical civilization; and had not the ancient Greeks themselves inherited much from the ancient Egyptians? So it was that Napoleon Bonaparte went to Egypt wishing to be seen as a new Alexander, while the erection of Cleopatra's Needle on the banks of the Thames signalled the dominance of Victorian London as a new Rome. Imperial France and imperial Britain alike clothed themselves in pharaonic garb, the better to assert their own hegemonic aspirations. Prussia, at first somewhat presumptuously, then, as imperial Germany, more self-confidently, sought to challenge France and Britain in Egypt in order to challenge them in Europe. For most of the nineteenth century, the history of Western enagagement with Egypt was written by these three latter-day empires, with occasional bit parts for the odd Italian or Swiss.

Americans, by contrast, came to Egypt later, and more self-consciously. The influence of ancient Egypt – or, rather, an eighteenth-century European conception of ancient Egypt – on Masonic ritual and symbolism had an important impact on the self-image of the newly independent United States. The country's Great Seal, adopted in 1782, included an Egyptian pyramid radiating light, while a memorial erected to Christopher Columbus in Baltimore ten years later took the form of an obelisk. However, these early public expressions were not accompanied by a great rush of visitors to the Nile Valley. It was simply too far away. When early citizens of the United States travelled abroad, it was usually to Europe. Only a few plucky adventurers made it as far as the Eastern Mediterranean. The first American to visit Egypt was probably John Ledyard, a friend of Thomas Jefferson's, who travelled to Alexandria and Cairo in 1789, dying there before he could return home: hardly a great advertisement to his fellow countrymen and women. The American Academy of Arts and Sciences, founded in 1780, elected both Napoleon and Denon as honorary members, in recognition of their having opened up Egypt to Western scholarship; but it would not be until 1820 that a second American, George Bethune English, reached the banks of the Nile.[2] The lawyer and diplomat Luther Bradish visited Egypt the following year, as part of a wider tour of Europe and the Middle East. In the mid-1820s, a merchant from Smyrna presented an Egyptian mummy and its accompanying coffin to the people of Boston, early examples of the Egyptian artefacts that began to enter American collections sporadically during the formative years of the United States.

During the second and third quarters of the nineteenth century, while Europeans, from Champollion and Wilkinson to Lepsius and Mariette, were opening up and exploring the civilization of the pharaohs, Americans were busy forging their new republic, fighting and emerging from a civil war that would define the parameters of American civilization. Tales from far-off lands were a sideshow compared to the more important business of nation- and fortune-building. In 1832, one Mendes Israel Cohen, a Jewish-American collector from Virginia, boasted that he was the first person to fly the American flag on the Nile,[3] while five years later John Lloyd Stephens was the first American to publish a popular account of his travels, *Incidents of Travel in Egypt, Arabia Petræ and the Holy Land* (1837).[4] In 1839, the *North American Review* presciently described Egypt as 'a quarter of the world, where comparatively few [Americans] have travelled, but where we anticipate they will soon penetrate, with all their characteristic ardor and enterprise'.[5] The person who really put Egypt on the map for Americans in the mid-nineteenth century was the US consul in Cairo, George Gliddon. As well as being a powerful (and outstpoken) advocate for the preservation of Egypt's monuments, he was also a great popularizer of the subject in his home country. His series of lectures on ancient Egypt, first delivered in 1842 and illustrated with antiquities collected by Cohen, was so successful that it toured the United States for two years. The accompanying book, *Ancient Egypt* (1843), sold 24,000 copies. Largely as a result of Gliddon's efforts, American academia accepted the study of ancient Egypt as a subject in its own right in the 1850s: a decade after Prussia, two decades after France, but – it must be said – four decades before Britain.[6]

Other than Gliddon, the first American to live in Egypt for any length of time – and out of personal rather than diplomatic interest – was an adventurer and dealer from Connecticut, Edwin Smith. He settled in Egypt in 1858 and lived for eighteen years in Luxor, where he became friends with Lucie Duff Gordon. Smith made a living as a moneylender and antiquities dealer. Among the objects he acquired were two important medical papyri, and much of his collection went on to form the core of the Brooklyn Museum. However, he is also said to have used his knowledge of ancient Egyptian writing to help unscrupulous dealers produce fake antiquities for sale.[7] While far from being an exemplar of academic integrity, Smith was nonetheless the first American to call himself an Egyptologist (even if his model was more Belzoni than Birch).

American interest in Egypt waned in the 1860s, as domestic struggles convulsed the United States. But after the end of the Civil War, as if the lid had been taken off a pressure cooker, Americans flocked to Egypt, just as Europeans had done after Waterloo. In 1870 alone, 300 American visitors registered at the US consulate-general in Cairo. Veterans of the Civil War even enlisted in the Egyptian army to boost its strength under Ismail, who was disillusioned with Britain and France and keen to throw off the Ottoman yoke. When General Gordon went to the Sudan in 1874 in an attempt to put down the Mahdist rebellion, Ismail sent two American officers to accompany him as a check against Britain's expansionary intentions. Both experiments proved a failure. Within four years, all but one of the American veterans had resigned or been discharged, while one of the officers resigned his position as chief of staff and left Egypt in 1883, following the British invasion and occupation. (He went on to supervise the building of the base for the Statue of Liberty.[8])

The upsurge in American tourism to Egypt was accompanied by a post-bellum drive to found and expand universities and civic museums as pillars of national learning.[9] It was in this context that the Metropolitan Museum of Art in New York acquired its first Egyptian objects in 1874, soon to be joined in Central Park by the second Cleopatra's Needle (which, as we have seen, was erected in 1881). When former president and Civil War hero Ulysses S. Grant visited Egypt on a round-the-world trip in 1878, he apparently showed 'no interest in the ruins, believing Cairo to be more interesting because of the cafes, which remind him of Paris, than the Pyramids, which he regards as entirely useless'.[10] But he was atypical. Many of his fellow citizens who beat a path to Egypt in the latter part of the nineteenth century had a deep interest in the country's ancient civilization; a few of them would become the founders of American Egyptology. They would bring new insights and breathe fresh life into a subject that had, since its origins, been the preserve of Europeans and the prisoner of European prejudice.

The first great figure in American Egyptology came to the subject, like the founder of British Egyptology, John Gardner Wilkinson, somewhat by accident. Charles Edwin Wilbour (1833–96), was born in Little Compton, Rhode Island, attended his local university, Brown, for two years, but left before graduating owing to ill health, and made his way to New York to seek his fortune, working initially as a journalist at the *Tribune* newspaper. There he was able to hone his natural gifts as a linguist – he translated Victor Hugo's *Les Misérables* into English – and make influential friends in the close-knit, not to say corrupt, world of 1860s New York. Through his political and business connections, Wilbour's financial affairs flourished; by the time he had reached his mid-thirties, he had made enough money to indulge his literary interests, so he decided to sail for Europe, which would become his home for the rest of his life.

It is not known when, or from where, Wilbour developed an interest in ancient Egypt, but while in Paris in the 1870s he took lessons with Maspero at the Collège de France, and he also studied with Eisenlohr in Heidelberg. Wilbour first visited Egypt in 1880, and was immediately entranced. Thereafter, he took annual trips up the Nile from 1886 on his own luxurious *dahabiya*, the *Seven Hathors*. Wilbour's fellow Nile traveller, Sayce, called him 'the best Egyptologist living'. In fact, Wilbour was an observer rather than a practitioner, on the sidelines of Egyptology but never at its centre. He published only one, very brief, article, 'Canalizing the Cataract',[11] otherwise amusing himself by copying inscriptions, correcting the work of others (he gained particular satisfaction by pointing out errors in the works of Champollion and Lepsius), and collecting antiquities. While exploring the First Cataract region, Wilbour struck lucky not once but twice: on the island of Sehel, he discovered the so-called Famine Stela, while from a local dealer on the island of Elephantine he bought nine rolls of papyrus which turned out to document the life of Egypt's earliest Jewish community. Indeed, it was as a collector with a keen eye for exceptional artefacts that Wilbour made his name and established his reputation. Acquiring antiquities became his abiding passion and his principal motivation. On a visit to Cairo, he wrote: 'I made no effort to go to the Khédive's reception last night; why should I seek his acquaintance? He has no papyrus.'[12]

Had Wilbour chosen to publish, he could have become an Egyptologist of distinction. He was intimately acquainted with every site of archaeological importance, had a wide circle of scholarly friends, and was also an acute observer of contemporary Egyptian society. (On hearing muttered complaints from the fellahin against the British occupation, he noted that: 'The glee with which all the people, even those in office, recount the victories of the Mahdi . . . indicates which side their sympathies are on even against their own soldiers.'[13]) As it was, his fame rested largely on his munificence, and came posthumously: the Wilbour Library of Egyptology at the Brooklyn Museum, the Wilbour professorship of Egyptology at Brown University, and the great Wilbour Papyrus, bought as a permanent memorial to a great papyrological collector.

Although Wilbour never practised as a professional Egyptologist – he had neither the desire nor the need – his activities laid the foundations for the birth of the discipline in the United States. He must, therefore, have felt a certain satisfaction to live long enough to see the very first academic position in Egyptology established at an American university. The year was 1895, the young scholar appointed as a teaching assistant at the University of Chicago a man by the name of James Henry Breasted. Breasted, like Wilbour, had started out life in a very different career, training as a pharmacist and serving as a counter clerk in local drug stores near his home in Illinois. Breasted's family was deeply religious, and he was influenced by his aunt to enrol at the nearest seminary, the Congregational Institute in Chicago, to study the Bible. It was to help with these studies that Breasted started learning Hebrew and Greek, but he quickly realized he had an innate talent for languages. Where Wilbour had been merely gifted, Breasted was a genius. (He eventually taught himself Greek, Latin, Aramaic, Syriac, Babylonian and Assyrian, Arabic, Egyptian, French, German, 'and a moderate facility in Italian'.[14]) His tutor at the seminary urged him to consider an academic career in the newly emerging subjects of Near Eastern Studies or Egyptology, where his linguistic skills could be put to good use.

Breasted himself had begun to have doubts about his suitability for theological ministry, so decided to take the plunge, leave the seminary, and enrol at Yale. There, his great fortune was to study under William Rainey Harper, probably the leading intellectual of his generation. Harper had been a child prodigy, graduating from college at fourteen and completing his doctoral studies at Yale at the age of twenty. He recognized a fellow genius when he saw one. He also saw an opportunity to advance the subject of Egyptology in the United States. For, within a few months of Breasted entering Yale, Harper had been approached by the millionaire philanthropist John D. Rockefeller to help establish a new university in Chicago. Harper's role was to recruit the very best faculty from across America. In Breasted, he saw the perfect candidate. In the summer of 1891, when Breasted had finished his studies, Harper promised him a new chair in Egyptology at Chicago if he would first bring himself up to date with the latest scholarship. That meant a trip to Germany, since under Erman the University of Berlin had become 'the teaching and research centre of the world for oriental languages, and especially for Egyptology'.[15] Breasted was enthusiastic. The only problem was money: with no family resources behind him, the prospect of trans-Atlantic travel was out of reach. Harper was not going to let a lack of funds derail a brilliant academic career, and agreed to provide support for his star pupil. On 30 July 1891, Harper, his family and a small group of his most able students sailed for Germany. For Breasted, it was the start of a remarkable life in Egyptology.

On arrival in Berlin, Breasted enrolled at the university and began taking classes with Erman, 'the greatest Egyptologist of Germany, and perhaps of the world, in his day – and certainly one of the kindliest, most benign spirits of his generation'.[16] Breasted's progress was nothing short of meteoric. He learned to speak and write German with native fluency. At the end of his first year of study, he joined Erman and Sethe on a summer holiday in the mountains south-west of Berlin, which he described as 'a fortnight in Elysium'.[17] At the end of his third year, he was ready to defend his doctoral thesis, in front of a panel which included Sethe and Borchardt.[18] He passed with flying colours. At the feet of Lepsius's pupils, he had thoroughly imbibed the German approach to scholarship and, with it, a distrust of the 'French model'. His outspoken criticism of French Egyptologists – 'Their methods are inclined to be slipshod . . . The most obvious details escape them, and they hide their distaste for the drudgery of solid research behind a facade of facile, sometimes brilliant, but too often inaccurate generalization'[19] – would later make him many enemies in France. Nonetheless, Breasted's three years in Berlin gave him a firm grounding in Egyptology and 'subjected him to an intellectual discipline which became the keynote of his scientific career';[20] they also made his name in academic and archaeological circles. Suddenly everyone with an eye on the future of the subject wanted a piece of this brilliant young American scholar.

Petrie had already written to Breasted, inviting him to spend a week on his excavations that coming season at Kuft and Nagada. But seven days eating cold food out of a tin was not exactly what Breasted had in mind for his first visit to Egypt – especially as it was also going to be his honeymoon. For, shortly after gaining his doctorate at Berlin, he had married Frances Hart, and a trip up the Nile was to be their first holiday together. It was not quite, perhaps, what a young married woman might have chosen. Breasted still had little money, so the couple took the train from Cairo to Asyut, to save the cost of hiring a boat for the whole journey. Fortunately, Frances 'minded neither dust nor flies nor filth'.[21] What she found harder to bear was her new husband's preoccupation with Egyptian antiquities and inscriptions, at the expense of their time together. She later recalled 'a scholarly honeymoon' where 'work took precedence over play'.[22] Erman had also been in touch with Breasted, asking him to copy inscriptions for the *Wörter-buch*, and the young American set about his task with relentless enthusiasm and an unwavering focus. But his scholarly pursuits masked a deeper void: he was already, at the age of twenty-nine, becoming 'a lonely man of few intimate friendships, who looked upon his personal life as a failure'.[23]

It was while on his honeymoon that Breasted came up with the idea of copying, not merely a representative selection of hieroglyphic inscriptions, but every Egyptian inscription of historical interest. This self-appointed task would preoccupy him for the next decade. Another commission he gladly accepted was to acquire objects for a new Egyptian museum at the University of Chicago. He was assisted by Sayce, 'a unique British institution in the Near East . . . known, trusted and honoured everywhere, by Europeans and orientals alike', and, moreover, a man who 'knew every inch of the Nile for a thousand miles southward from Cairo'.[24] So glowing was Breasted's reputation that archaeologists like Petrie even gave him antiquities they had excavated. The result, to Breasted's satisfaction and Harper's delight, was 'the nucleus of a modest though representative collection'.[25] By way of acknowledgement for Petrie's assistance and support, Breasted took the time to visit his excavations at Nagada. He found the archaeologist 'thoroughly unkempt, clad in ragged, dirty shirt and trousers, worn-out sandals and no socks . . . not merely careless but deliberately slovenly and dirty'.[26] The experience proved salutary, convincing Breasted that his calling lay in epigraphy and history, not field archaeology. He wrote to his father: 'I want to read to my fellow men the oldest chapter in the story of human progress. I would rather do this than gain countless wealth.'[27]

At the same time, it was clear that archaeology in Egypt could not be left to its own devices, nor to continue in the same vein. As Amelia Edwards had discovered on her trip up the Nile in the 1870s, and Petrie had witnessed for himself a decade later, digging in Egypt was a corrupt business: 'the least promising sites were assigned to European excavators, while the richest sites were given to native antiquity dealers who were permitted to carry on haphazard digging solely for commercial purposes'.[28] Breasted was outraged by the appalling condition of many of the sites he visited, and made his feelings clear in a letter home: 'I am so filled with indignation against the French and their empty, blatant boasting, "*la gloire de la France*", that I can hardly contain myself. I could have wept my eyes out in Amarna. Scarcely less indignant must one feel against the English who are here only for the commerce and the politics of it, and who might reform matters if they would. A combination of French rascality, of English philistine indifference & of German lack of money is gradually allowing Egypt to be pillaged and plundered from end to end. In another generation there will be nothing to be had or saved.'[29]

If neither France nor Britain – nor, for that matter, Germany – could be trusted to excavate, preserve and record Egypt's pharaonic heritage, America would have to step in.

Breasted's first visit to Egypt had given him 'the equipment for a great work'.[30] On his way back to the United States in the spring of 1895, he stopped off in Paris (to see Maspero), in London (where he met Budge, and noted numerous errors in the labelling of the British Museum's Egyptian collection), and in Oxford (no doubt at Sayce's suggestion), before arriving in Chicago in April to take up his new teaching post. All thoughts of copying inscriptions or rescuing sites from slipshod archaeology were quickly banished as he faced up to the daunting challenge of establishing a new academic discipline. He wrote: 'In America, Egyptology really did not exist at all – and here was I, proposing single-handedly to introduce it into a Middle Western community.'[31] Moreover, 'Egyptology was then commonly regarded by the public and the Press as something bizarre, an oddity at a county fair.'[32] To make matters worse, Breasted had not received the chair that he had been promised, but only a lowly assistant post. He had to supplement his meagre salary of $800 per year by giving public lectures at gentlemen's and ladies' clubs. Not even the wholehearted support of Harper, who had been appointed as the university's first president, could smooth Breasted's path. The truth was that: 'Amid the hurly-burly and travail of a great university's birth, Egyptology was a super-numerary item of antiquarian bric-à-brac to be laid aside until the rest of the house was in order.'[33] While Breasted set to work creating a new department, his grand ideas had to take a back seat – gone for the time being, but certainly not forgotten.

In 1899, Breasted received an invitation from the Royal Academy in Berlin to copy all the Egyptian inscriptions in European collections for the unfolding *Wörterbuch* project. He jumped at the chance, offering to do the work without payment, on an expenses basis only. His family – by now grown to include a young son – was rather less enthusiastic. Breasted, his wife and child spent the next few years shuttling back and forth between America and Europe, always travelling third-class, skimping on meals, and living 'as scholar gipsies in an unending succession of dreary, grubby little hotels and pensions'.[34] But Breasted could not have been happier. The material he collected provided the basis, not only for the *Wörterbuch*, but also for his own magnum opus. By the time he had finished the manuscript of his *Ancient Records of Egypt*, seven years later, it ran to over ten thousand pages. Even with the backing of John D. Rockefeller, the University of Chicago baulked at the cost of publication. (It was finally issued, in five volumes, in 1906–7.) Breasted's only regret, was that he had not been able to copy '*all* the extant inscriptions along the entire Nile valley'.[35] But, come to think of it, that was an idea worth pursuing.

Breasted's impecunious wanderings around Europe, following his low-budget honeymoon up the Nile, had brought home to him a simple truth of academic scholarship (which is as true today as it was a century ago): research needs money. It had been all very well for the pioneering Egyptologists of independent means, men like Denon and Wilkinson, or for those employed on state-sponsored expeditions, like Champollion and Lepsius; Breasted had neither private funds nor government backing. Instead, he would need to follow the example of Petrie and obtain his own philanthropic support. In the spring of 1903, Breasted secured an interview with John D. Rockefeller's business agent. The result was a gift of $50,000 to the University of Chicago for archaeological fieldwork in the Near East – the 'Oriental Exploration Fund'. Breasted decided that its first mission should be an epigraphic survey of Nubia, hitherto a neglected part of the Nile Valley where there had been little in the way of systematic recording. On Christmas Day 1905, a few months after finally being appointed to a chair in Egyptology – the first in America – Breasted set out on his new expedition. The party arrived at Wadi Halfa on 7 January 1906 and started work the very next day. Breasted's innovative new technique (later dubbed the 'Chicago method') was to collate and correct inscriptions from photographs. This occasionally required feats of acrobatics, such as shimmying up the mast of a *dahabiya* to photograph a stela high up on a cliff face.[36] The aims of the expedition were ambitious, its methods novel, and the scale monumental: 'Sometimes we employed between fifty and a hundred men to excavate temple courts buried in rubbish and drifted sand; or to reassemble like jigsaw puzzles the reliefs on fallen walls; or to relocate and record by modern methods the inscribed monuments mentioned by earlier visitors like Lepsius.'[37]

Like Lepsius and other nineteenth-century visitors to Nubia, Breasted had to face his fair share of trials and tribulations. Nights on the boat were 'a carnival of riotous rats . . . They danced and galloped across the roof in a constant tattoo, they dropped through a window onto my bed so that I would be awakened by one sitting on my face!'[38] Temperatures soared to 135 degrees Fahrenheit in the shade, and, on one occasion: 'It was so hot in the middle of the day that a standing camera scorched the hands. In the camera's spirit level, the liquid expanded until the bubble finally disappeared.'[39] At other times, however, the expedition had to face bitingly cold winds, sandstorms, and swarms of gnats. The meagre provisions were worthy of a Petrie dig, and Breasted hunted wildfowl 'to relieve our monotonous diet of tinned foods'.[40] While excavating the pyramids of Meroë, in far-flung Upper Nubia, he encountered a 'grasshopper in the soup to-night . . . I crunched on him for some time, supposing he was a piece of dried herb. But finding him invulnerable, I pulled him out, still intact, but very dead!'[41] The party nearly capsized at the Fourth Cataract, and while attempting to shoot the rapids of the Third were wrecked on the rocks; fortunately, British surveyors were working nearby and helped repair Breasted's boat.[42]

Despite such adventures and near-disasters, the survey was successfully completed over two seasons. It covered 1,200 miles, and produced more than 1,200 records – photographs, transcriptions and notes. They were never fully published, but are still of inestimable value, especially as many of the monuments recorded have subsequently been damaged or destroyed. Breasted never again travelled south of Wadi Halfa, but his contribution to Nubian archaeology had been, and remains, immense.

Breasted's final service to Egyptology was also his most enduring. A few months after the end of the First World War, he renewed his courtship of the Rockefeller Foundation, putting to them a proposal he had first dreamt up some years earlier – for an Oriental Institute at the University of Chicago. He put it in suitably epochal terms, claiming that the imminent collapse of the Ottoman Empire made 'the study of these lands . . . the birthright and the sacred legacy of all civilized peoples'.[43] Rockefeller was moved by the argument, and agreed to fund an institute for an initial five-year period at $10,000 per year. (He subsequently doubled the figure.) Breasted arrived in Egypt in November 1919 to direct the institute's first mission: an aerial photographic survey of the Memphite necropolis using an RAF plane lent by General Allenby.[44] This visit only confirmed 'the dire need of epigraphic work to save from destruction . . . fast-perishing written records'. Of immediate concern were the storage facilities in the basement of the (new) Egyptian Museum, where 'beautifully painted wooden coffins . . . were submerged in water whenever there was an inundation above the normal level'.[45] Breasted decided that one of the priorities of the Oriental Institute should be to copy and publish all the surviving Coffin Texts in the Egyptian Museum and in museums across Europe. It was but the first of a series of landmark projects to record pharaonic civilization for posterity.

Breasted had dreamed of recopying and republishing every inscription throughout Egypt using the Chicago method, and in 1924 he launched the Epigraphic Survey under the auspices of the Oriental Institute. That same year, thanks to further Rockefeller largesse, a house was built to serve as the Egyptian base of the institute and its survey, on the west bank of Thebes. Chicago House, as it became known, transferred to new premises on the east bank in 1931, and remains to this day a centre of scholarship and hospitality, a welcome oasis for archaeologists of all nationalities in the heart of modern Luxor.

Institute, Survey and House: together they make an invaluable contribution to the discipline of Egyptology in the twenty-first century; none would have been established without Breasted's energy, enthusiasm and persuasion. He also had the good fortune to be the right man in the right place at the right time. Late nineteenth-century and early twentieth-century America was a land of unprecedented wealth creation, and much of that wealth was directed into education, research and culture.

Breasted ensured that Egyptology got its fair share. As his son and biographer put it: 'archaeology is likely to have to wait for some time not only for another such champion as James Henry Breasted, but for a recurrence of the coincidence by which his unique blend of scholarship, executive ability and vision attained its fullest development at the most favourable moment yet to have occurred in his country's economic history.'[46]

⊲◦⊳

When Maspero returned to Egypt in 1899, he was welcomed by archaeologists from all nationalities as the saviour of the Antiquities Service and Egyptian Museum. His three predecessors, in their different ways, had 'seemed to think that good administration meant annoying as many people as possible . . . They succeeded magnificently.'[47] Not only did Maspero have to patch up relations with his fellow Egyptologists, he also faced two particularly pressing challenges. First, there was the repair of the Hypostyle Hall at Karnak, following the disastrous collapse of eleven columns on 3 October 1899. Maspero oversaw the rapid installation of wooden bracing, to prop up the remaining columns and buy some much-needed time to plan a full-scale restoration project. Second, there was the impending move of the national collection of antiquities from its temporary home in Giza to a purpose-built museum in the centre of Cairo. The move had been envisaged back in 1893, and work had started on the new museum the following year, during Grébaut's tenure. There had been the inevitable delays in construction – which the French architect and consul, equally inevitably, blamed on the British[48] – but finally the building was handed over to the Antiquities Service in September 1901. That left the really tricky business of moving thousands of fragile antiquities some nine miles from Giza to Ismail Square. Maspero's inspired solution was to build a narrow-gauge

Decauville railway, to provide a smoother, less bumpy and more direct route from old museum to new. The journey, going at a slow speed to protect the objects, took about two hours. Within twelve months, all the antiquities had been transferred, and the official opening of the Egyptian Museum took place on 15 November 1902. (Petrie was typically outspoken, disapproving not only of the location – he thought it should have been built in the drier climate of Luxor – but also of the design, which he called (not without reason) 'the worst building I ever saw made for such a purpose. Half of it is too dark to be used at all, and much of it is scorched with sun through enormous skylights . . . Nearly half the site is wasted in spaces left to display the abominable architecture.'[49])

Indeed, the building boasted a grand, neoclassical facade, which gave pride of place to the heroes of Egyptology since the Napoleonic expedition a century before: men such as Denon and Champollion, Wilkinson and Birch, Burckhardt and Lepsius. Altogether, the inscriptions honoured six Frenchmen, five Britons, four Germans, three Italians, a Dutchman, a Dane and a Swede.[50] It was a triumphant and unselfconscious monument to the Western rediscovery of Egypt. The only Egyptian immortalized on the building was the reigning khedive, Abbas II – a puppet ruler, propped up by the British – and his inscription was in Latin. Europe's implicit claim to the civilization of ancient Egypt was reinforced when Mariette's sarcophagus was unveiled in its new location, the front garden of the museum – he would lie there for eternity, as the presiding genius and guardian spirit of the institution he had founded.

Just three weeks later, the two European powers who had controlled Egypt and its heritage for over a century, Britain and France, signed the entente cordiale. It was a brilliant diplomatic compromise, recognizing the pre-eminence of British political interests in Egypt while confirming that 'the general direction of Antiquities in Egypt shall continue to be, as in the past, entrusted to a French scholar'.[51] The Franco-British accords effectively ended all the manoeuvring and jostling for position of the previous twenty years.

Maspero's direction of the new Egyptian Museum brought a measure of efficiency and professionalism to what had, for too long, been a somewhat haphazard enterprise. To reduce the risk of theft, he ordered the museum guards to wear Western uniform instead of traditional Egyptian *galabeya*s with their inside pockets. He oversaw the publication of the *catalogue général*, and transformed the museum into a proper scientific institution with its own library and archives. In 1899, there had been just twenty-four staff at the museum; by the time Maspero left office for the second time, in 1914, this number had risen to thirty-nine. In tandem with increasing the staff, he also added significantly to the collection. Most prominent of the new acquisitions was a colossal dyad of Amenhotep III and Queen Tiye, found in pieces at Thebes, and reconstructed in the central hall of the museum. Despite such additions, Maspero confidently believed his new museum would have enough space for forty or fifty years' worth of finds.

In archaeological work, too, Maspero's return signalled an end to what had become a fragmented, laissez-faire, free-for-all. For over a decade, the Antiquities Service had been denuded of resources, its staff demoralized. Maspero sought to diversify its income, through entry tickets, sales from the museum, and sales of Antiquities Service publications – notably a new periodical, the *Annales du Service des Antiquités d'Egypte*, which he founded in 1900. He also managed to negotiate – from a grateful and relieved British administration – a trebling of the Service's budget. With this additional funding, he was able to increase staffing: from just two chief inspectors to five, and from 191 site custodians to 298, by the end of his tenure.

Given the recent disaster at Karnak, the Antiquities Service's first priority was consolidation and conservation. Maspero launched a series of projects to restore and preserve some of Egypt's greatest monuments. At Karnak itself, his colleague Georges Legrain continued the systematic investigations begun under de Morgan. This led to the discovery in November 1903 of a vast cache of stone and bronze statues buried underneath the court of the temple's seventh pylon. The contents were remarkable – within a year, the pit had yielded 472 stone statues and 8,000 bronzes – and it took five years to excavate them all. The final tally was nearly 17,000 objects, perhaps the most important single find in Egypt since Mariette's discovery of the Serapeum. Other excavations near Karnak's Sacred Lake uncovered a giant stone scarab while, across the Nile, a systematic clearance began of the Tombs of the Nobles; this necessitated the forced removal of the local residents, many of whose families had lived among and above the sepulchres for generations. Elsewhere in western Thebes, the Antiquities Service undertook the consolidation of the string of mortuary temples, from Medinet Habu in the south to Qurna in the north.

In the latter decades of the nineteenth century, Egypt's rapid modernization had taken its toll on the monuments, but so too had a massive increase in tourism. By the early 1900s, an electric tram had been installed running from the centre of Cairo at Ezbekiya Gardens to the foot of the pyramids, swelling the number of visitors to the Giza plateau. Further south, the torches and candles used to illuminate Theban tombs for tourists were damaging the precious wall paintings, so Maspero pioneered the installation of electric light into the Valley of the Kings. But as fast as the Service could carry out such work, further challenges came to the fore. In December 1902, the first Aswan Dam was completed and Maspero had to find funds to save the temples of Lower Nubia, which were now partially submerged each year for months on end. There was particular anguish over the fate of Philae, 'jewel of the Nile'. The result was the establishment of an international team of archaeologists, who worked under the auspices of the Service to study and record the Nubian monuments and their inscriptions. After many months' work at the grandest of all the Nubian temples, Abu Simbel, the team's Italian conservator, Alexandre Barsanti, wrote, a tad optimistically: 'there only remains the sand, about 30,000 cubic metres. I think it will require at least another two months, and then everything will be finished.'[52]

The scale of work facing the Service required Maspero to look for innovative solutions. For example, to bring electric light to Abu Simbel, he struck a deal with Cook & Co. whereby the temple generator would be connected to visiting cruise ships. But the truth was that the Service's resources, though better than they had been for years, were still inadequate for the massive task of conservation, taking place on so many fronts simultaneously, let alone sufficient to support additional excavations.

Maspero's solution, from the beginning of his second term of office, was to dispense with the Service's monopoly and license private excavations. At the same time, he tightened control of illicit digs, and appointed two new inspectors, one for Middle Egypt and one for Upper Egypt (James Quibell and Howard Carter, respectively). He was in no doubt about the serious threat facing archaeological sites from economic development, especially the expansion of irrigation and cultivation. Indeed, he believed that within twenty-five years, those sites not already explored and recorded faced being lost forever. In awarding concessions to dig, his preference was for reputable institutions: universities, museums, and organizations like the EEF. But he also recognized individual talent, and one of his first acts was to award Petrie the concession to excavate at the plum site of Abydos. There, among the ruins of antiquity, Petrie formed his credo: that it was the duty of humanity to preserve all the evidence of its past, 'not merely objects of artistic beauty, but samples of the relics of every age, pottery, flint artefacts, skulls and skeletons, objects of everyday life from every age of past history'.[53]

◁◫▷

Despite Petrie's undoubted prowess and reputation as a great field archaeologist, as the nineteenth century concluded and a new century dawned, there was a feeling in Egypt that the days of the old colonial dispensation were numbered. Queen Victoria's death on 22 January 1901, just three weeks into the new century, 'cast an undisguised gloom over the whole British community . . . an event in which everyone dimly perceived the makings of a national calamity, though few guessed that it constituted a definite turning point in English history'.[54]

The entente cordiale three years later brought a century of Anglo-French rivalry in Egypt largely to an end, but the British administration refused to acknowledge that the era of colonial empires was also drawing to a close. The savage punishment of villagers involved in the infamous Denshawai incident of 1906 – in which a British army officer died in an altercation with angry locals, and the colonial authorities meted out collective retribution, including hanging one of the ringleaders in front of his own house – only served to stoke the fires of Egyptian nationalism. By 1907, 'an elderliness was apparent in the British regime';[55] Sayce decided to sell his *dahabiya* and return to England for good, commenting that 'life on the Nile had ceased to be the ideal existence it once was';[56] and even Cromer, who had been Egypt's de facto ruler for a quarter of a century, decided it was time to retire. Thereafter, 'it was as though the soul had gone out of the body of the British administration'.[57] Though Cromer's successors, Sir Eldon Gorst and Lord Kitchener, managed to diffuse some of the Egyptian antipathy towards the British, they were in reality only marking time.

The change at Government House was also felt in archaeological circles. Cromer had shown little interest in Egypt's ancient past, being more concerned about the country's economic future. His extensive, two-volume work, *Modern Egypt*, written immediately after his retirement, reveals much about his view of the country and its inhabitants – its subheadings include: 'Main tenets of Islam – Its failure as a social system', 'Degradation of women', 'Immutability of the law – slavery – Intolerance', 'Coarseness of literature and conversation', and 'Obstacles to England's mission', as well as 'Unsuitability of the French system to form the Egyptian character', and 'Summary of the classes friendly and hostile to England' – but not a single section dealt with antiquities or archaeology. By contrast, just a year after his departure, a new university was established in Cairo to bring education – including knowledge of the past – to the Egyptian middle class. A year after that, the British and French governments were persuaded to renounce their claims to the large monuments 'given' to them by Muhammad Ali. When, in 1909, the American consul-general offered to pay for the removal of the remaining Luxor obelisk and transport it to central Cairo, objections from Egyptologists and the Egyptian cabinet alike scuppered the plan. Instead, provincial authorities in Egypt were encouraged to establish small regional museums.[58]

In the last two years of Cromer's rule and the years immediately succeeding his departure, major American excavations in Egypt really took off. American museums had initially built their collections by subscribing to EEF digs, receiving a share of the finds in exchange for a financial contribution,[59] but the advent of wealthy philanthropists gave American institutions the wherewithal to sponsor their own missions. Within a short time, in addition to Breasted's work for the University of Chicago, expeditions had been launched by the Metropolitan Museum of Art, the Brooklyn Museum, the University of Pennsylvania's Museum of Archaeology and Anthropology, and Harvard University in conjunction with the Museum of Fine Arts, Boston.

The last of these was directed from the outset by a man who would come to rival even the great Petrie as the leading field archaeologist working in Egypt in the early twentieth century. George Andrew Reisner (1867–1942) was born in Indianapolis, the son of a shoe-store owner. Academically gifted, he studied law at Harvard, intending to become a lawyer, but was fascinated by Semitic languages, the study of which was then emerging. On a research trip to Germany to study Assyriology, he met Erman and was drawn instead to Egyptology. Erman employed him for a year as a temporary assistant in the Berlin Museum, after which Reisner returned to Harvard as instructor in Semitics. The turning point in his career was a chance meeting with Phoebe Hearst, wife of a wealthy mine-owner and US senator (and mother of the newspaper proprietor and collector, William Randolph Hearst, the inspiration for *Citizen Kane*). On a trip up the Nile in 1899, Mrs Hearst fell in love with Egypt and decided she would like to sponsor excavations. With her financial backing, Reisner embarked on a series of digs, culminating in the joint Harvard-Boston expedition to Giza in 1903. His investigations at the pyramids – which he would direct for some forty years – were 'some of the finest work ever done in Egypt'.[60] They resulted in two of the most important archaeological discoveries ever made: the perfectly preserved statues of King Menkaura from his pyramid temple, which rank among the foremost examples of ancient Egyptian art; and the intact burial equipment of Queen Hetepheres, including her silver bracelets and her carrying chair inlaid with ebony and gold.

In 1907, immediately after Cromer's departure, the Egyptian government appointed Reisner director of the Nubian Archaeological Survey. A systematic survey of Nubian monuments was Maspero's response to the construction of the Aswan Dam, and the resulting threat posed to Nubian monuments by regular submersion in flood waters. During two seasons of survey and excavation between the First and Fourth Nile Cataracts, Reisner discovered the pyramid tombs of five Nubian pharaohs, and the funerary monuments of a further sixty-eight rulers of the Upper Nile. He later spent a dozen years excavating Nubian fortresses and royal capitals, transforming understanding of Nubian history and shedding historical light on the fabled Kingdom of Kush.

During the course of this work, Reisner effectively laid down the principles of modern archaeological surveying, building significantly on Petrie's work of the previous generation.[61] Reisner consciously eschewed the practices of the Antiquities Service – with its focus on large-scale clearances and the acquisition of museum-quality artefacts – and instead emphasized the importance of careful stratigraphy and complete documentation. He kept a detailed diary, a comprehensive register of finds, and photographs of every object and every stage of a dig. Recognizing that archaeology is a destructive process, Reisner's aim was to 'enable future scholars to reconstruct in every detail the conditions found by the excavator'.[62] His excavation reports were, in consequence, 'dense and exhaustive';[63] they took an age to prepare, and were of monumental proportions themselves. Nonetheless, they have stood the test of time, and may still be consulted with great utility a century later.

Appointed curator of the Egyptian collection at the Museum of Fine Arts in 1910 and professor of Egyptology at Harvard in 1914 (only the second chair in Egyptology in the United States, after Breasted's at Chicago), Reisner actually spent most of his career in Egypt. Like Petrie, he relied on a skilled work-force of Kuftis, with whom he formed a strong bond;[64] moreover, he came to identify closely with the ordinary fellahin, which coloured his view, both of the British colonial administration, and of his fellow Americans.

One suspects that, of all his compatriots working in Egypt during the first decade of the twentieth century, Reisner would have had least time for Theodore Davis (1838–1915). They shared a legal background, but there the similarity ended. Davis grew up in poverty and was largely self-educated. The back-streets of Detroit were a world away from the cloistered quads of Harvard, but were all the education Davis received, or needed. Avoiding the draft, he prospered as a lawyer during the American Civil War. At the end of the war, he moved to New York City, attracted by its culture of unbridled capitalism and cut-throat competition. His law firm, Davis and Edsall, made money quickly, but not all of it cleanly. Like Charles Wilbour, Davis made the acquaintance of William M. Tweed, 'arguably the most corrupt politician in American history'.[65] Like Wilbour, Davis used his connections for profit, and within five years of arriving in New York had amassed a considerable fortune. Besides his legal work, he had interests in canals, railroads, forestry, and iron and silver mines; but it was digging of a different sort – in the sands of Egypt, for golden treasure – that began to pique his interest.

Davis first visited Egypt in 1887, at Wilbour's recommen-dation, as an extension to an annual winter trip to Europe. Davis and his companion Emma Andrews – a cultured, intel-ligent and wealthy widow – reached no further than Cairo, but it made a lasting impression on both of them. Two years later, they rented a *dahabiya* and travelled upstream as far as Thebes. Towards the end of the trip, on 2 February 1890, Davis first set foot in the Valley of Kings. He was struck by the timeless atmosphere (he wrote to a friend: 'All countries seem youthful in comparison with Egypt'[66]), intrigued by the tomb entrances half-hidden in the hillsides, and appalled by the condition of the open tombs. An idea began to form in his mind. When, after a bout of pneumonia, he was advised by his doctor to spend every winter in a warm, dry climate, there was no hesitation. A trip up the Nile became Davis's annual habit for the rest of his life.

By the winter of 1894, he had begun to discuss building his own boat. Finished in January 1897, the *Beduin* was one of the most luxurious *dahabiyas* on the Nile, furnished with all the opulence of Davis's mansion in Newport, Rhode Island. It had a grand piano in the salon, a crystal chandelier in the dining room, bathrooms with hot and cold running water; it was crewed by a score of experienced Nubian sailors who wore white turbans and brown cardigans with the ship's name in red stitching.[67] Live poultry carried on board supplied fresh eggs and meat, so that Davis and Emma could entertain archaeologists up and down the Nile, picking up the latest gossip and learning about the latest discoveries.

On one of his early visits to Egypt, Davis became acquainted with Sayce – who was always on the look-out for wealthy patrons to sponsor new excavations. It was not long before Davis had been introduced to a host of young, impecunious archaeologists, including Percy Newberry and Howard Carter (1874–1939). Carter became a frequent visitor to the *Beduin*, and in January 1901, Newberry brought on board a bronze bowl he had recently excavated from the tomb of the New Kingdom vizier Rekhmira. Davis was entranced. With funds aplenty and the time to indulge his passions, he decided to sponsor his own excavation. His chosen archaeologist was the young Carter, his chosen location, the Valley of the Kings. They were inspired choices.

In January 1903, Carter rewarded his patron with a major discovery: the tomb of pharaoh Thutmose IV. It was the first king's burial unearthed in Egypt in the twentieth century, and yielded a hoard of objects from the golden age of Egypt's eighteenth dynasty: chariots, fine furniture and stone vessels. The Egyptian Museum catalogued a total of 612 artefacts from the tomb, eighty-four of which were given by Maspero to Davis as compensation for his expenditure. Davis in turn presented the bulk of these to the Museum of Fine Arts in Boston, while he kept the remainder for his personal collection. Only one object was left in the tomb: a mummy, perhaps belonging to one of Thutmose IV's sons, which had been found by Carter propped up against the wall of one of the side chambers, its abdomen slashed open. (There it remained, remarkably, for more than a century until, in 2005, the tomb was reopened to the public.[68])

Carter's remarkable instinct soon bore further fruit. A tomb created for Hatshepsut, the female pharaoh, turned out to be the longest and deepest in the Valley of the Kings. Clearing it was 'long, patient, tiresome and dangerous work . . . The serious danger of caving ceilings throughout the entire length of the corridors and chambers was a daily anxiety.'[69] Moreover, the whole tomb, from entrance to burial chamber, was filled with stone chippings, rubbish and bat droppings. The hot, dirty and dangerous work was carried out, not by Davis, but by an army of poorly paid Egyptian workmen, whom Davis barely acknowledged in his publication, other than to reassure readers that: 'Happily the work was so well watched and conducted that no accidents occurred, though many of the men and boys were temporarily overcome by the heat and bad air.'[70] Their reward was barely enough money to keep their families off the bread-line: his was a beautifully carved stone sarcophagus, one of two found inside the tomb, which he promptly took back to Boston, making it the only Egyptian royal sarcophagus in the New World.

The partnership between Davis and Carter, patron and archaeologist, was proving wildly successful, and looked set to continue. But the entente cordiale of 1904 prompted a shake-up in the Antiquities Service; Maspero switched his two chief inspectors, sending Carter to Lower Egypt and replacing him with Petrie's former assistant, James Quibell. Davis was deter-mined to continue sponsoring excavations in the Valley of the Kings, and agreed to hire Quibell as his archaeologist; but before Quibell could begin work, he was summoned back north by Maspero to supervise the Antiquities Service's work at Saqqara. A new chief inspector of antiquities for Upper Egypt was appointed, in the person of Arthur Weigall, but Davis lost patience with the merry-go-round of personnel. He started to make his own decisions about where to dig, despite his total lack of archaeological experience. It could have spelt disaster for his entire mission. Instead, by amazing good fortune, it led to his greatest discovery.

In February 1905, while Davis was aboard the *Beduin*, moored at Thebes alongside *dahabiyas* belonging to Sayce and Maspero, his workmen found another concealed entrance in the side of the valley, in a previously unexplored area between two Ramesside royal tombs. Davis claimed the credit for finding it:

> The site was most unpromising . . . As an original prop-osition I would not have explored it, and certainly no Egyptologist, exploring with another person's money, would have thought of risking the time and expense. But

I knew every yard of the lateral valley, except the space described, and I decided that good exploration justified its investigation, and that it would be a satisfaction to know the entire valley, even if it yielded nothing.[71]

Forcing a way through the blocking stones and the piles of loose chippings, the workmen came face to face with a sumptuous burial of the eighteenth dynasty: not a royal tomb per se, but the magnificent sepulchre created by King Amenhotep III for his parents-in-law. Their names were Yuya and Tjuyu; their funerary goods, a king's ransom. Although the sarcophagus had been prised open and the mummy wrappings torn off by ancient tomb robbers, most of the grave goods had been left in place. They comprised the most spectacular treasure found in Egypt up to that point. Davis noted laconically, 'we could see nothing except the glitter of gold'.[72] Weigall, quickly alerted to the discovery, was more effusive: 'We stood, really dumbfounded, and stared around at the relics of the life of over three thousand years ago, all of which were as new almost as when they graced the palace.'[73] By coincidence, that very day Maspero received a telegram from Cromer to say that Queen Victoria's son, the Duke of Connaught, was visiting Egypt as inspector-general of the army and would be in Luxor the following afternoon. Maspero saw an opportunity to win favour with the British authorities by presenting the duke with a new discovery to coincide with his visit. So, the tomb of Yuya and Tjuyu was quickly resealed, to be officially opened the next day in the royal presence.[74]

Just as remarkable as the gilded coffins, fine furniture and chariots were the intact mummies of Yuya and Tjuyu themselves. Perfectly preserved, they seemed to speak across the centuries. (Their remarkable preservation could have led to disaster. Peering at the face of Yuya, Davis brought his candle so close to the bitumen-encrusted mummy that he nearly set it alight and, with it, the entire contents of the tomb.) A visiting American artist, Joseph Lindon Smith, said that Yuya's features reminded him of Abraham Lincoln. The *New York Times* went into raptures, calling the tomb 'the greatest find in the whole history of Egyptian research', and noting with undisguised pride that its discoverer was 'an American, a New Yorker'.[75]

Davis became something of an international celebrity – lauded as a professor, archaeologist and Egyptologist, even though he was none of those things – and the discovery gave Egyptian archaeology a popular following in America for the first time. This in turn generated funding for further excavations by all the great museums, from Boston and New York to Philadelphia and Chicago. Tourists visited Luxor in record numbers the following year, to gawp at the new discovery; but for the archaeologists a long and painstaking process of cata- loguing the contents lay ahead. The sheer quantity of material in Yuya and Tjuyu's burial forced a change in archaeological practice: there was no question of emptying the tomb quickly; only systematic clearance would do justice to such a remarkable find. As Weigall later recounted, with some feeling: 'The hot days when one sweated over the heavy packing-cases, and the bitterly cold nights when one lay at the mouth of the tomb under the stars, dragged on for many a week; and when at last the long train of boxes was carried down to the Nile en route for the Cairo Museum, it was with a sigh of relief that I returned to my regular work.'[76]

Finally, in 1909, after four years' work, the archaeologists were preparing to pack up the last remaining object, a beautiful gilded chair that had been presented to Tjuyu by her grand- daughter, Princess Sitamun. But, just as one royal visit had interrupted the opening of the tomb, so another would define its closure. That winter, the widowed Empress Eugénie was visiting Thebes, retracing her Nile trip of forty years earlier. She decided to call in at the tomb (by now famous throughout the world), crossed the floor, and – to the horror of those watching – promptly tried Sitamun's chair for size. She was the first person to sit in it for over thirty-five centuries: a suitably royal behind in an ancient royal seat.[77] To the relief of everyone present, both the three-and-a-half-thousand-year-old chair and the eighty-three-year-old empress survived the encounter unscathed.

Bar a few keepsakes, Davis declined a share of the finds. He explained:

Though under the letter of my permission to explore in the 'Valley of the Kings', I was not entitled to any portion of the 'find', Monsieur Maspero, with a generosity common to him, offered me a share. I confess that it was a most attractive offer, but, on consideration, I could not bring myself to break up the collection which I felt ought to be exhibited intact in the Cairo Museum, where it could be seen and studied by probably the greatest number of appreciative visitors.[78]

Today the collection occupies a significant section of the first-floor galleries of the Egyptian Museum.

After the tomb of Yuya and Tjuyu, Davis continued to strike it lucky in the Valley of the Kings. In December 1905, he and his new archaeologist, Edward Ayrton, found a solitary blue faience vase, bearing the name of a little-known pharaoh, Yuya and Tjuyu's great-grandson, Tutankhamun. For those who knew how to interpret it, it was a vital clue. But for Davis, eager for more spectacular discoveries, it was of little consequence. More rewarding was the tomb of Siptah (a king of the twentieth dynasty), and a series of animal burials. These were followed, in January 1907, by a tomb containing fragments of gold foil, that Davis identified as the burial of Queen Tiye. The story of Tiye, a commoner who became the most powerful woman in ancient Egypt, appealed to American sensibilities; Player's issued a cigarette card adorned with her presumed likeness, and describing her – implausibly – as 'blue-eyed, and of very fair complexion'.[79]

All in all, Davis was blessed with remarkable luck during his decade of digging in the Valley of the Kings. Almost every season he was rewarded with yet another spectacular find. As a result of his success, the Nile Valley and its ancient treasures became firmly implanted in the American public consciousness. A book published in Philadelphia in 1907 spoke of Egypt as 'The land of the Mysterious River, the magic country of one's longing dreams of Pharaoh and pyramid and sphinx, of desert and of camel . . . perplexing tokens from when the world was young.'[80] Yet for all their romantic notions of Egypt and their republican principles, Americans were every bit as colonial in their attitudes as their European contemporaries. On one of her first visits to Upper Egypt in 1890, Emma Andrews had written: 'However friendly we may be as individuals, we cannot understand each other.'[81] When recently retired US president, and champion of the working man, Theodore Roosevelt visited Egypt in 1910, he gave a speech at the University of Cairo predicting 'it will be years, perhaps generations, before Egypt is able to govern itself'.[82] Hundreds of Egyptian nationalists gathered outside Shepheard's Hotel to denounce the speech, resulting in the first anti-American demonstration ever seen in the Arab world.

Davis's winter season of 1907–8 began with the modest discovery of a cache of embalming materials, left over from a royal burial, but struck gold, literally, a few weeks later with a burial full of precious jewellery. Dubbed the 'Gold Tomb', its contents included seventy-eight ear pendants, earrings, amulets, bracelets, a head circlet, a silver sandal, rings of gold, silver and electrum, a necklace of 151 filigree gold beads, and a pair of silver gloves The discovery surpassed even the tomb of Yuya and Tjuyu for sheer spectacle, and sparked an international craze for Egyptian-style jewellery. The Duke and Duchess of Devonshire, then on a trip up the Nile,[83] made a point of coming alongside the *Beduin* to see the treasure of the Gold Tomb for themselves. In distant Waterloo, Iowa, the *Daily Courier* of 4 August 1909 wrote: 'the present craze for jewelry fashioned after old Egyptian pieces is likely to receive a fillip from the discoveries of the American explorer, Theodore Davis'.[84] Davis himself had written to a friend: 'It would seem that I have more success than any other explorer, but I brave the danger of conceit by saying I find because I exhaust every spot in the valley regardless of time, expense and promise.'[85]

True to his word, just a month after finding the Gold Tomb, Davis (or, rather, his employee Ayrton) uncovered the tomb of the general-turned-pharaoh Horemheb, with its immaculately preserved decoration. The press went into a frenzy. A lengthy, syndicated profile of Davis was carried by the American newspapers. Davis explained to readers that: 'These tombs are cut in solid rock, on hillsides, and the sands of ages have drifted firmly over them'; then, with more than a touch of false modesty, declared that: 'The only way to find a tomb is to dig for it.'[86]

The tomb of Horemheb, however, was to be Davis's last major discovery in the Valley of the Kings. In December 1908, his latest archaeologist, Harold Jones, uncovered a poorly preserved tomb, numbered, according to the system invented by Wilkinson, KV58. Davis believed it to be the tomb of the missing pharaoh, Tutankhamun, and published it as such. (Everyone agreed, with the exception of Davis's first archaeologist, Howard Carter.) Davis's final discovery, in January 1910, was an entirely empty tomb. Harold Jones died the following year, while working in the Valley of the Kings. It seemed as if the royal burial ground was biting back, having given up all its secrets. In Davis's 1912 book, *The Tombs of Harmhabi and Touatânkhamanou* (his rather tortured renderings of Horemheb and Tutankhamun), he reluctantly concluded that 'the Valley of the Tombs is now exhausted'. The final page was devoted to a colour plate of the blue faience vase bearing Tutankhamun's name, which Davis and Ayrton had found under a rock seven years earlier.

Davis had funded excavations for the thrill of the chase, and to give him something to occupy his time during his winter sojourns in Egypt. But, as a friend observed: 'His interest in archaeology was that of a hobbyist; therefore, at the first test, it was quick to go.'[87] Once he had determined that there were no more discoveries to be made in the Valley of the Kings, he briefly turned his attention to the mortuary temple of Ramesses III at Medinet Habu, a few miles to the south, leaving his workmen to finish up in the valley. They put down their picks and shovels in February 1914. Returning to Cairo that spring, Davis informed Maspero that his years of digging in Egypt had come to an end. In June, Maspero granted the concession for the Valley of the Kings to Lord Carnarvon. It was Maspero's last act as director of the Antiquities Service, for he resigned the following month and returned to France, as Europe went to war. Davis sold his beloved *Beduin* to Newberry and left Egypt, never to return. Without the excitement of excavations to keep him going, his health began to fail and he died in Florida on 23 February 1915. The same day, Turkish troops crossed the Sinai to attack the Suez Canal.

During his years in Egypt, Davis had amassed an impressive collection of antiquities, which he called 'the child of my mind'.[88] On his death, he bequeathed it to the Metropolitan Museum of Art. Although no archaeologist, he demonstrated the efficacy of the long-term, systematic study of a single site. Though no scholar, he published his results promptly, supported Howard Carter during his years as an impecunious artist, and also partially funded Breasted's work. Altogether, Davis discovered eighteen tombs in the Valley of the Kings and cleared another four. He was, for a few years in the mid-1900s, the most famous Egyptologist in the world. Yet today, few people recognize the name of Theodore Davis. A discovery seven years after his death, and just six feet from where his workmen stopped digging, would erase his achievements from popular memory.

TEN

Imperial ambitions

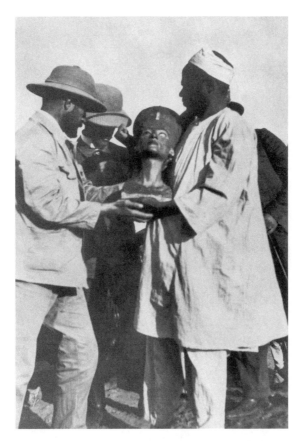

Ludwig Borchardt inspecting the bust of Nefertiti shortly after its discovery
in the ruins of Amarna.

A constant struggle to maintain a balance between the various interests, keeping the English happy while not upsetting the French or the Egyptians.[1]

GASTON MASPERO, 1910

In the six decades following Lepsius's expedition, whilst Egyptology thrived in Germany and scholars such as Erman added immeasurably to the development of the discipline, only a very few Germans were active in Egypt itself. Other than the Brugsch brothers, Heinrich and Emile, the history of Egyptian archaeology in the second half of the nineteenth century is almost devoid of notable German figures. Partly, this was down to the very success of Lepsius's endeavours: the collection of antiquities he brought back from Egypt, and the extraordinary accomplishment of the *Denkmäler*, could not easily be replicated, still less surpassed; by contrast, a focus on developing outstanding museum collections and establishing Egyptology at the major universities gave Germany the opportunity to assert cultural and academic leadership over its European rivals. Moreover, North Africa in general and Egypt in particular had little importance in German foreign policy, which was predominantly focussed on geopolitics closer to home. Partly, though, the lack of German archaeological activity in Egypt in the decades after Lepsius was a simple matter of political influence. Mariette's establishment and subsequent leadership of the Antiquities Service and Egyptian Museum ensured that, from the late 1850s onwards, the key posts in Egyptian archaeology were reserved for Frenchmen, and guaranteed French excavators the support of their government, always keen to preserve cultural hegemony in North Africa. The British occupation of Egypt from 1882 onwards likewise meant that British excavators could count on some measure of official assistance, even if Cromer regarded archaeology as a diplomatic irritant.

Not everyone in Germany, however, was willing to accept this state of affairs. In November 1881, nine months before the British invasion, the professor of Egyptology at Heidelberg, Eisenlohr, had petitioned the German emperor, Wilhelm I (r.1871–88), to set up an Institute for Egyptian Archaeology in Cairo to support field research and publication, and provide assistance to German scholars active in the Nile Valley. The government in Berlin turned to the Royal Academy for an expert opinion: its conclusion was that there were too few German scholars active in Egypt, or likely to be so, to warrant the expense of creating a dedicated institute. But, by the mid-1890s, the situation had changed. In a letter to Maspero of 18 April 1893, Heinrich Brugsch bemoaned the fact that 'German Egyptology, since the death of Lepsius, has lost its importance in the eyes of the public and even of scholars'.[2] The new generation of German Egyptologists – pupils of Erman like Schäfer and Steindorff – were quick to add their voices, and began to question the status quo. When, in 1895, Erman mooted the idea of the *Wörterbuch* in his inaugural address to the academy, the idea of German scholars becoming active throughout Egypt, gathering material for the dictionary and even excavating new sites, no longer seemed out of the question.

Another consideration was the recent upsurge in collecting by the agents of European museums (led by Budge for the British Museum). The Berlin Museum, propelled by Lepsius's expedition to the first rank, had started to lose its lustre. Indeed, there had been no major additions to the collection since the early 1840s. The German government's immediate response, in 1898, was to establish the Deutsche Orient-Gesellschaft to conduct research in the field of 'oriental antiquity'. After a lengthy period when the conservative Christian views of the German establishment, combined with the dominance of the Catholic Church, had effectively suppressed the study of non-Christian cultures (ancient Egypt, with its biblical resonances, was spared), a relaxing of censorship and a lessening of clerical influence under Wilhelm II (r. 1888–1918) gave the green light to orientalists.[3] However, the Orient-Gesellschaft was no mere learned society. It also had the explicit task of acquiring oriental antiquities, works of art, and other cultural artefacts for the Royal Museums of Berlin and other public collections across Germany. From the very outset, it was thus conceived as an instrument of German cultural imperialism.[4]

All these changes combined to give German Egyptology in the late 1890s a renewed confidence and ambition. The zeitgeist was captured in a speech to the Prussian parliament in March 1898 by the founder of the Progressive Party, Rudolf Virchow. In front of the assembled representatives, he lamented the state of Egyptian archaeology in the Vaterland, and made a powerful declaration of intent:

> Germany, which for a while – especially under Lepsius – made so significant a contribution to this field, has gradually been left entirely behind . . . If one wants to study ancient Egypt, one cannot do so in Berlin but has to go elsewhere. Our wish, therefore, is that Germany might establish itself more actively in these new developments; and we are confident that we have the men to undertake such work on a completely equal footing to the foreigners.[5]

357

The premise won broad support, but Germany still had to tread carefully in the face of Anglo-French control over Egypt's affairs. Rather than establish a German institute in Cairo in direct competition with the Institut Français, the government decided instead to appoint a scientific attaché to the German consulate-general in the Egyptian capital. It was a permanent establishment, albeit not in bricks and mortar. The aim was that the attaché would be able to visit excavations and archaeological sites, but would be seen as relatively independent of political control. On 9 October 1899, the Berlin Academy named its choice. There was really only one candidate.

Ludwig Borchardt was an architect by training, but had also studied Egyptology in Berlin under Erman. Combining his two interests, he had carried out research on the construction of the pyramids, proving Lepsius's theories correct. Furthermore, he had the great advantage of already being on the ground in Egypt. The academy had sent him there in 1895 to investigate the effects of periodic submergence on the temples of Philae, and he had subsequently been hired by the Antiquities Service to develop the plans for the *catalogue général*. In the summer of 1899, the Berlin Academy's Commission on the Publication of the Dictionary of the Egyptian Language – the body overseeing the *Wörterbuch* project – pre-empted the German government's decision by giving Borchardt instructions to report on all archaeological developments in Egypt – in effect, to be Germany's eyes and ears on the ground – and to assist German scholars and German museums with the acquisition of Egyptian antiquities.

Borchardt's appointment coincided with a renewed interest in the Middle East in the context of Germany's foreign policy. Since the mid-1880s, the country had set about competing with the other European powers by actively acquiring colonies in Africa (South West Africa and Tanganyika), the Pacific

(Samoa and the Caroline Islands) and even China (the trading colony of Kiaochow, on the shore of the Yellow Sea). Wilhelm II sought to extend German influence further, targeting in particular the Ottoman lands, as a counterweight to British, French and Russian interests and to position Germany for the expected demise of the Ottoman Empire.[6] In 1898–9, the kaiser gave the clearest signal yet of Germany's interests and intentions by touring the Middle East as the guest of the Ottoman sultan. Wilhelm II's *Orientreise*, which included visits to Constantinople, Haifa, Jerusalem and Bethlehem, Jaffa, Beirut and Damascus, underscored the importance of Borchardt's role as scientific attaché and paved the way for its future expansion.

Directly following Borchardt's appointment, German orientalists began to make the most of their new-found political support. The professor of Egyptology at Leipzig, Ebers, had died the year before, leaving an important collection of books, which had been purchased by a fellow professor, Friedrich Wilhelm von Bissing. No sooner had Borchardt taken up his role at the German consulate-general than von Bissing (who had dug with Borchardt a decade earlier), sent the entire library to his friend in Cairo. Borchardt found room for it in his own house, but this was no personal acquisition. Bit by bit, the foundations were being laid for a full-scale German institute.

The alignment of German foreign policy and scholarly interests had another significant impact: for the first time since the 1840s, German archaeological missions in the Middle East could call upon state funds.[7] Before Borchardt's appointment as scientific attaché, he had taken part in excavations at Abu Ghurab, west of Cairo. In 1901, he persuaded Maspero to award him the concession in his own right. The beginning of the twentieth century was thus marked by the first official German excavation in the Nile Valley since the days of Lepsius.

Lepsius's star pupil, the torch-bearer for his achievements, and Germany's pre-eminent living Egyptologist, Erman, was politically astute enough to sense a golden opportunity. In a speech to the Ministry of Culture in Berlin, he noted how German scholars had lacked confidence in the 1860s, but approved of the recent change in their fortunes, linking it to German scientific rigour. This blatant appeal to German national sentiment was merely a warm-up act for Erman's coup de grâce: the publication of a memorandum entitled '*Bericht über die Lage der deutschen Ägyptologie in Kairo*'. His hope was that the German government might build upon Borchardt's recent appointment, go a step further, and give its backing to ending the Anglo-French dominance of excavations in Egypt.[8] His call did not go unheeded. In 1902, a personal donation from the Kaiser enabled the construction of a 'German House' on the west bank at Thebes, a permanent base for future arch-aeological missions; it opened in 1904.

Erman's success spurred him on to press for his ultimate goal. In July 1907, he asked the German Ministry of Religious, Educational and Medical Affairs to propose a motion to estab-lish Borchardt, his assistant staff, the Ebers Library, scientific equipment and the German House as the constituent elements of a new institution, to be called the 'Wissenschaftliche Station für Ägyptische Altertumskunde' ('Scientific Station for Egyptian Archaeology') and to confirm Borchardt as its director with professorial standing. In other words, Erman was asking the German government to formally recognize something that already existed.[9]

Aware, no doubt, that the proposal would prove controver-sial, Erman had been busy building his coalition of support. He had persuaded his fellow members of the academy that it would not be possible to complete the *Wörterbuch* without a permanent base for German scholars in Cairo. But the diplo-matic sensitivies could not be brushed aside so lightly. Erman had proposed the designation 'station' as relatively unthreatening, but the German consul-general in Cairo wanted nothing less than a 'German Egyptological Institute'. The foreign ministry in Berlin was wary of appearing to compete directly with French interests. Eventually, all parties rallied round a suggestion from Borchardt himself, and on 5 September 1907 he was confirmed as inaugural director of the Kaiserlich-Deutsches Institut für Ägyptische Altertumskunde, 'the Imperial German Institute for Egyptian Archaeology'.

With a permanent base, a prestigious position, and government support, Borchardt sought to make his own mark by establishing a new branch of Egyptology. His plan was to draw on his experience and focus on the architectural history of pharaonic civilization. But Erman, who considered himself the leading voice of German Egyptology, and who had backed the creation of the institute to advance German national interest, not Borchardt's private ambitions, was less enthusiastic. No doubt the politics of setting up the institute had left a sour taste, and he opposed the idea of Borchardt undertaking large-scale excavations on his own account.[10] But while Erman's views held sway at the Berlin Academy, Borchardt, too, was an accomplished political operator. He bypassed the academy, went straight to the Orient-Gesellschaft, and persuaded their members to finance a dig at Amarna, the city founded by the heretic pharaoh Akhenaten in the fourteenth century BC, where Petrie had excavated in the early 1890s with notable results. The Antiquities Service, overstretched and consequently open to requests from well-funded, high-status foreign teams, acquiesced and awarded Borchardt the Amarna concession.

By 1911, German colonization was proceeding apace, and African and oriental artefacts were being shipped in their hundreds to the Royal Museums in Berlin.[11] Germany was also increasing its cultural, political and economic influence throughout the Ottoman Empire, including Egypt. Both developments culminated, at the end of 1912, in one of the greatest discoveries ever made in the Nile Valley: a find which not only marked a new high point of Egyptian archaeology, but also confirmed Germany's emergence as a full-blown imperial power. On 6 December 1912, digging through the dunes in the residential quarter of Amarna, Borchardt's workers came across the house and workshop of a sculptor named Thutmose. He had evidently abandoned his premises in a hurry, for on the shelves in his workshop – long since collapsed onto the floor and buried under sand and rubble – he had left behind a large number of plaster casts, trial pieces, and sculptor's models. There were rough plaster busts of royalty and wealthy private clients, and unfinished stone heads destined for statues of the royal princesses. But the greatest find of all was a sculptor's model: a beautifully painted and immaculately preserved limestone bust of Nefertiti, Akhenaten's queen. It was without doubt one of the finest objects ever found in Egypt, an icon of female beauty as fresh as the day it had been made, thirty-five centuries before.

Borchardt had been granted the Amarna concession on the basis that any finds would be divided between the Egyptian Museum and the excavator – or, rather, his private sponsors in Berlin. Now, he contrived to have both the bust of Nefertiti and a painted limestone altarpiece awarded to Berlin. (The Egyptian authorities later alleged dishonesty, but it could just as well have been down to official laxness: the division of finds often took place on the spot, and the local inspectors at Amarna may not have realized the historic importance or cultural significance of a couple of dusty old limestone pieces with little apparent intrinsic value.) The bust of Nefertiti was sent to Berlin where it was displayed, triumphantly, in the villa of the financier James Simon, the principal supporter of Borchardt's excavations. Simon in due course gave it to the Royal Museum on permanent loan, where it formed the centrepiece of the newly expanded Egyptian collection. (The bust was gifted to the Prussian state in 1920.) A quarter of a century earlier, Erman had outbid the British Museum to acquire the Amarna tablets. Now, Berlin had acquired the great prize of Nefertiti's bust. The site at Amarna was transformed in German public consciousness from a remote, archaeological backwater to a source of national pride.[12]

Pride, however, comes before a fall and for Borchardt, Erman and the whole of the German Egyptological establishment, nemesis followed hubris with startling rapidity. Intent on European domination, the German government had started to build up its armed forces; archaeology in far-off Egypt suddenly seemed a very low priority for state resources. When Borchardt's funds ran out in 1913, the excavations at Amarna came to an abrupt halt. Erman's grip on the Berlin Museum also began to falter, and in 1914 he was forced to relinquish his directorship in favour of his pupil Heinrich Schäfer. His consolation prize, wrung as a concession from the state authorities, was the creation of the 'Egyptological Seminar' which gave Erman, along with other staff and students of Berlin University, continued access to the museum and its Egyptian collections. But in August that year, the European geopolitics that the German government had been so intent on shaping to its own advantage exploded, plunging the entire continent into a long and bloody war – a conflict from which German Egyptology would emerge weakened, with German archaeologists frozen out of Egypt for a generation.

⟨◦⟩

The imperial rivalry that culminated, with such devastating consequences, on the Western front and the fields of Flanders, had also been felt in the Nile Valley, in the years leading up to the outbreak of the First World War. Archaeologists from Britain, France, Germany, Austria, Italy and America had all – consciously or unconsciously, actively or unwittingly – been pursuing national agendas.[13] Anglo-French competition in Egypt dated back to the time of Napoleon. Germany saw its entry onto the Egyptological scene in similarly imperialist terms. The relatively tardy unification of Italy, together with the distraction of its colonial priorities elsewhere in Africa (Libya and Abyssinia), meant that Italian archaeologists were latecomers to the Nile Valley. The leading Italian Egyptologist of the early twentieth century, Ernesto Schiaparelli, who had studied under Maspero in Paris, first visited Egypt in 1903 and began his excavations in Thebes shortly afterwards. He was rewarded with two spectacular discoveries: the incomparably beautiful tomb of Nefertari in the Valley of the Queens, uncovered in 1904, and the intact tomb of Kha at Deir el-Medina two years later. The former may have hit the headlines, but it was the latter, with its extraordinary collection of grave goods, that was the real archaeological prize. Alongside furniture, intricate basketry and bolts of fine linen, Kha's tomb contained loaves of bread, joints of meat, and bowls of fruit. According to Arthur Weigall, then inspector of antiquities for Upper Egypt: 'Everything looked new and undecayed.'[14] Just as remarkable was Schiaparelli's agreement with the Antiquities Service which allowed him to take the entire tomb contents back to Turin.[15] It was Maspero at his most generous; within a few years, the ceding of whole collections would be ended for good.

Not far away from Deir el-Medina, in another part of western Thebes, Anglo-German archaeological rivalry was reaching fever pitch. The underlying cause was not so much conflicting imperial interests (although those no doubt added spice) as different approaches to scholarship.[16] British Egyptology had a long and distinguished tradition of attracting the gentleman amateur: men like Young and Wilkinson carried out their research to indulge a personal interest, not to advance scientific understanding – although they accomplished both. Even Budge followed a rather dilettantish path, publishing a raft of popularizing books – which earned him a great deal of money – rather than scholarly tomes. By contrast, Lepsius and Erman had taken a purist approach: scholarship for its own sake, unsullied by any thought of trying to win popular acclaim. The heirs of Wilkinson regarded the Germans as dry, stuffy and unimaginative; Erman's pupils thought the British insufficiently academic. The difference was epitomized by two rival missions working side by side during the season of 1904–5 at the mortuary temple of Hatshepsut at Deir el-Bahri. The German dig was led by Sethe, while Naville directed the British excavations for the EEF. Despite close proximity in the field, the two men were not on speaking terms, and Sethe refused to be in the same room as Naville.[17] The feud was awkward in the close-knit community of European excavators; but, as Petrie's biographer would later explain, 'archaeology is not a science but a vendetta'.[18]

It was Maspero's unenviable task, as director of the Antiquities Service, to mediate between such bitter rivalries. He described his job as 'a constant struggle to maintain a balance between the various interests, keeping the English happy while not upsetting the French or the Egyptians'.[19] On the whole, he succeeded remarkably well, managing to keep all parties happy – even when the Americans entered the fray. His approach was, above all, pragmatic. Recognizing the impossibility of putting a complete stop to the antiquities trade, he regulated it rather than trying to ban it outright, drawing up a list of authorized dealers, location by location. While happy to outsource the expensive business of excavation to foreign missions, Maspero nonetheless took pains to visit sites the length and breadth of the Nile Valley. He would spend about three months a year away from Cairo, aboard his official steamer, inspecting excavations, checking on the progress of Antiquities Service projects, meeting and entertaining his fellow Egyptologists. Friends called him 'pharaoh' – it was a double-edged compliment.

The reward for Maspero's tireless diplomacy came in 1909 with a trio of significant events. First, there was the visit by Empress Eugénie, her first to Egypt since she had opened the Suez Canal four decades earlier. On her way from central Cairo to the pyramids she passed along the avenue which she had ceremonially planted on her earlier visit; it now comprised mature trees. (On arrival at Giza, she found that the royal hunting lodge where she had stayed in sumptuous luxury back in 1869 had since been converted into the Mena House Hotel to accommodate an ever-increasing number of tourists.) Second, there was the International Congress of Archaeology, which Maspero succeeded in bringing to Cairo. Concerned at the steady rise of the English language at the expense of French among the Egyptian population, he planned the congress as a triumphant display of '*francophonie militante*' – assertive francophony. Of the 906 delegates who attended, the largest group by far (160) was from France, and the French language was given prominence in the congress proceedings. Last, but by no means least, in 1909 Maspero was made a Knight Commander of the Order of St Michael and St George – an honour reserved for eminent diplomats – by Edward VII, in recognition of his services to Egyptian archaeology but also, one suspects, to the entente cordiale.

Bolstered by such plaudits, and confident of his own position, Maspero decided to take the radical step of authorizing excavations privately financed by wealthy *Egyptians*. For the first time in over a century of excavation, citizens of the Nile Valley were allowed to sponsor digs in their own land. Not surprisingly, the decision met with howls of disapproval from Western interests, but Maspero stuck to his guns, appointing his Egyptian colleague, Ahmed Kamal, to direct such excavations. It was as if he saw the future coming, and was determined that his Service would be prepared.

That future, however, was being determined by the forces of imperial rivalry and colonial conflict. In 1911, Italy went to war with the Ottoman Empire over the fate of Tripolitania. Italy's invasion of Egypt's North African neighbour scuppered Schiaparelli's plans for an Italian archaeological institute in Cairo, and set back Italian scientific activity in the Nile Valley for nearly half a century. A wider Balkan conflict erupted in 1912, sowing the seeds that would lead, two years later, to the assassination in Sarajevo of Archduke Franz Ferdinand and the declaration of a Europe-wide war. Sensing, perhaps, that the old order and his own time in Cairo were coming to an end, Maspero's final objective was to pass a new antiquities law.

Following Cromer's retirement in 1907, control of British interests in Egypt had passed to a new consul-general, Sir Eldon Gorst. He was better disposed towards ordinary Egyptians than his precedessor, and introduced reforms designed to improve the lot of the native population. (In 1908 he authorized the creation of the first university for Egyptians.) But British public sentiment was in no mood for such concessions, and Gorst was harshly judged. When he died of cancer in July 1911, the government replaced him with Lord Kitchener, veteran of the Sudan campaign and a confirmed imperialist, a man who could be counted on to take a more robust approach with Egyptian nationalists. To Maspero's surprise and great good fortune, Kitchener turned out – unlike his two predecessors – to be keenly interested in Egyptian antiquities. Maspero lost no time in pleading his case: 'I saw Kitchener on Saturday morning . . . He wants to pass an antiquities law that applies to natives – my 1902 project, which was at first accepted by Lord Cromer but then refused by him at Brugsch's instigation.'[20]

The law was eventually passed, with Kitchener's support, in 1912. But the British consul-general had not finished with the subject of antiquities. Indeed, he harboured visions of grandeur. Once again, Maspero recorded the discussion in his diary: 'Cairo, 27 October 1913: I saw Kitchener and he kept me an hour and a half, during which we spoke about just two subjects, his project to bring to Cairo the two colossi of Mit Rahina, and provincial museums . . . It is an idée fixe: he wants the two [colossi] to be set up in front of the main station.'[21]

A colossus of Ramesses II was eventually erected in front of Cairo's main railway station, giving its name to what would become one of the busiest locations in the capital: Ramses Square.

During the first half of 1914, the world of Egyptology was preoccupied with largely parochial concerns: Erman's forced retirement from the Berlin Museum, and the question of who would succeed him; rivalry between French and German interests over appointments to the Egyptian Museum, following Emile Brugsch's departure; the discovery at Lahun by Petrie's pupil Guy Brunton of the jewellery of a twelfth-dynasty princess; and the impending publication, by the EEF, of the inaugural edition of the first English-language periodical in Egyptology, the *Journal of Egyptian Archaeology* (*JEA*). (True to form, when Petrie learned of the EEF's plans, which did not include a position for him as editor, he launched his own journal, *Ancient Egypt*, in direct competition. Its first issue came out a month before the first *JEA*.) The most momentous event of all, however, for Egyptologists was the retirement, in July 1914, of Maspero. At the age of sixty-eight, having accomplished so much, he had decided it was time to hand over the reins of the Museum and Antiquities Service to a younger man. Erman voiced the concerns of the entire discipline when he expressed the hope that Maspero's successors would demonstrate the same generosity of spirit. (It was not to be.) On 24 July 1914, on returning to Paris, Maspero was elected permanent secretary of the Académie des Inscriptions et Belles-Lettres – the position held, a century before, by Champollion's friend and mentor, Bon-Joseph Dacier. One week later Maspero's sons were mobilized. On 3 August, war was declared.

Cut off from his beloved Egypt and weighed down with the concerns of wartime, Maspero's health began to fade. On 30 June 1916, during a session of the *académie*, he was about to rise to speak when a pain forced him to remain seated. It was his heart. He died later that day, mourned by archaeologists of all nationalities, and was laid to rest in the cemetery of Montparnasse. No one, with the possible exception of Mariette, had done more to advance the cause of Egypt's ancient heritage.

<hr>

In the years leading up to the outbreak of the First World War, the speed of change in Egypt had accelerated, and the country had undergone profound transformation, both economically and socially. The population nearly doubled from 6.8 million at the time of the British invasion to over 12 million a generation later. (By contrast, Egypt's population under Ottoman rule had more than halved, from 7 million in Roman times to just 2.5 million at the time of Napoleon's expedition.[22]) In tandem with this rapid increase in people, crime also rose steadily. Cromer blamed it on foreigners (from which he excluded British expatriates), asserting that 'all that was least creditable to European civilization was attracted to Egypt, on whose carcase swarms of needy adventurers preyed at will'.[23] It seems never to have occurred to him that the root cause might have been the desperation of Egypt's hard-pressed citizens, for whom the country's rapid industrialization had brought nothing but misery. Under British rule, literacy rates continued to be dire – just 8.5 per cent for men and 0.3 per cent for women by 1910 – and Cromer actively discouraged tertiary education, fearing that the growth of an Egyptian intellectual class might undermine British rule. The French, for their part, could never understand Britain's lack of interest in Egypt's cultural and intellectual development, regarding it as symptomatic of a general philistinism.[24]

Certainly, the British authorities, and Cromer in particular, were always more interested in economic matters, in restoring and maintaining financial stability and productive capacity. By the end of the nineteenth century, Egypt had one of the most extensive railway networks in the world per head of population. The railway was the largest employer in the country, and the number of passengers using the service increased from less than 5 million in 1890 to almost 30 million in 1906. Alongside the railways, the road and telegraph networks were expanded; ports were developed to handle burgeoning volumes of trade; police stations were built throughout the country to maintain order. But the greatest changes by far were felt in the sphere of agriculture. British rule saw changes in patterns of land ownership, an expansion of irrigation, and a commensurate – and unprecedented – increase in agricultural production.[25] Most of this increase was down to a single crop, cotton. Egypt's most important cash crop from the time of Muhammad Ali onwards, cotton came to dominate the economy under British rule: it accounted for 92 per cent of Egyptian exports by value on the eve of the First World War.[26] It has been said that 'no other place in the world in the nineteenth century was transformed on a greater scale to serve the production of a single industry'.[27] The down-side of the expansion of cotton production was that, by 1913, Egypt – famed as the breadbasket of the Roman Empire – had become dependent on imported grain to feed its population. It fell to Kitchener to take drastic action in preparation for wartime, sharply reducing the acreage devoted to cotton to make way for wheat, and establishing Egypt's first Ministry of Agriculture to monitor food production.

Aside from agriculture, however, the British administration took a decidedly laissez-faire approach to other sectors of the economy. It was the French who dominated the sugar industry and controlled the Suez Canal. They also ran most of the best schools in the country. All Cairo's main hotels (Shepheard's, the Gezira Palace and the Savoy) were under European management, and the area around Shepheard's was a European enclave. Expatriate life in Cairo, as in other cities of the British Empire, revolved around clubs. The Gezira Sporting Club had been founded immediately after the British invasion of 1882, on land 'gifted' by the khedive. Modelled on the Hurlingham Club in London, it was frequented by British administrators, Cairo's other foreign residents, and a few members of the Egyptian ruling class. Even more exclusive was the Turf Club, which was reserved exclusively for the British. In the early 1920s, Lord Edward Cecil, at that time the only Englishman permitted to attend the Egyptian Council of Ministers, visited the Turf Club two or three times a day between business meetings. While the men lunched and dined at their club, their wives maintained their own social calendar. Lady Cromer took different groups of British ladies for a fortnightly audience with the khedive. According to one expatriate Englishwoman: 'For many years the Khedive's ball was the culminating event in the winter festivities in Cairo, and was as brilliant a function as oriental splendour and cosmopolitan fashion in combination could compass.'[28]

Throughout the period of colonial rule, the British simply never understood the Egyptians. They lived separate lives, in different worlds. Cromer, though he effectively ran Egypt for a quarter of a century, never learned Arabic. Many Europeans – figures like Lucie Duff Gordon were exceptional – thought the Egyptians indolent and in need of moral reform. Cromer detested Islam, regarding it as 'a complete failure', and liked to describe colonial administration as a process of 'continual tutoring'.[29] He believed the Egyptians incapable of self-government. His deputy from 1894 to 1902, Rennell Rodd, was even more contemptuous, writing that: 'the Oriental mind did not appeal to him, and that in so far as he understood it he regarded it as an obstacle to be overcome rather than a factor to be studied with sympathetic attention'.[30] There were plenty of British expatriates who swallowed their own propaganda, genuinely believing that: 'The poor fellaheen, who had suffered deception for more centuries than they could count, realized that they had at last found justice and hugged it to themselves as a precious discovery.'[31]

Such sentiments were totally at odds with the true character of British rule. Martial law, military raids, widespread imprisonment, a network of informants, and the systematic use of torture were Cromer's instruments of government.[32] His secret intelligence service was extensive and highly effective: 'He was kept informed of everything that went on, and often staggered people by his knowledge of their most intimate affairs.'[33] Against this background, nationalism started to emerge at the end of the nineteenth century, in Cairo's cafes and newspapers, as prolonged exposure to Europeans and European ideas started to transform Egyptian politics.

The British had never intended to colonize Egypt. Successive governments steadfastly resisted annexing it to the British Empire, ruling instead through the 'veiled protectorate'. This made it even harder for Egyptian patriots to challenge the status quo, since it had no legal standing or structure. Cromer was a strong advocate of the veiled protectorate, fearing that formal annexation might provoke a war with France. Those particular concerns were largely put to rest after the signing of the entente cordiale in 1904, but there were indigenous threats to British rule. One was the unpredictable nature of the Egyptian succession. Muhammad Ali had successfully played one European power off against another. Said had been decidedly pro-French, Abbas I more even-handed. Ismail had fought to assert his own authority, while Tewfiq had been a pawn of the British. The accession of Abbas II in 1892 threatened to be a disruption, as his schooling in Vienna had taught him, if not outright Anglophobia, then certainly 'Hapsburg notions of sovereign power and prerogative' and an 'intolerance of British control'.[34] Cromer had had to assert his authority with the young khedive, who subsequently retreated into a life of indolence and self-aggrandizement.

By 1910, Egyptian nationalists were on the rise but in despair. Their own prime minister, Boutros Ghali,[35] had been accused of siding with the British during the Denshawai incident in 1906, and was shot by an assassin while leaving the foreign ministry. In the ensuing international outcry, Theodore Roosevelt declared that the British should 'govern or get out' of Egypt.[36] In the House of Commons, the leader of the opposition, Arthur Balfour, justified continuing British control on the back of advances in Egyptology, arguing: 'We know the civilization of Egypt better than we know the civilization of any other country, we know it further back; we know it more intimately.'[37] Egyptians saw it rather differently, making their own connections between their country's glorious, ancient past and its current, parlous situation. The journalist Ahmad Lufti al-Sayyid wrote that: 'Our nation today does not exist independently from the nation of our past. The nation is a single unbroken, unbreakable whole'; he looked upon pharaonic civilization as an inspiration to action 'so that this miserable present might pass, and so that our Egypt might be returned to its ancient past'.[38] Kitchener, by contrast, dreamed of creating 'a new viceroyalty of Egypt and Sudan, with himself as the first viceroy'.[39] Events in Europe in the summer of 1914 would shatter his dreams, and bring those of men like al-Sayyid a step closer.

When the Turks joined the Central Powers on 5 November 1914, Britain found itself at war with the Ottoman Empire, of which Egypt was still technically a part. The British response was to declare a formal protectorate the following month. Abbas II, who was in Constantinople and whom Kitchener had called 'that wicked little khedive',[40] was prevented from returning to Egypt and deposed. The British replaced him with his eldest uncle, Hussein Kamel (r.1914–17). He was 'elevated' to the style of sultan, but it was clear to everyone where true power lay. The British representative, Sir Milne Cheetham (Kitchener had been recalled to London at the outbreak of hostilities, to serve as Secretary of State for War), now styled high commissioner, reintroduced martial law, suspended the legislative assembly, banned political parties and closed down outspoken newspapers.

Egypt was turned into a fortified army camp for Indian and Australian regiments en route to the Western front. Troops flooded Cairo: the main British garrison was in the district of Abbassia, while the barracks at Kasr el-Nil occupied a prime site in the city centre; the Australians were based at Mena Camp, near the pyramids. Alexandria became the base of operations for the naval war in the Eastern Mediterranean, including the Gallipoli campaign. A British soldier temporarily stationed at Mustapha Camp, outside Alexandria, commented: 'The eastern half of Alexandria is not really Oriental at all. It differs only in matters of detail from the modern quarters of other seaports across the Mediterranean. The streets are labelled with French names, while on the pavement one seems to meet far more English and French and Italians and Greeks than Egyptians.'[41] It was a measure of just how Europeanized Egypt had become after a century of foreign involvement.

At the height of the war, while the Prince of Wales was practising his golf at Giza – according to legend he drove a ball from the summit of the pyramid of Khafra onto a green at the Mena House Hotel[42] – his loyal troops were 'encamped on the bare sands of Sinai, on the unknown Libyan coast, in remote oases far out in the western desert, or in little mosquito-ridden towns on the Nile'.[43] British officers, meanwhile, frequented the Gezira Sporting Club. In addition to hosting tens of thousands of troops awaiting manoeuvres, Egypt was also used as a base where injured servicemen were sent to convalesce: 'At Heliopolis the Army has taken over one of the largest and most gorgeous hotels in the world, and many other buildings in Cairo – Government offices, barracks, private houses – have all been pressed into the service, especially for hospital purposes.'[44] So full was the capital of British officers, civil servants, engineers, and temporarily jobless archaeologists that, on the island of Gezira, some of the roads resembled 'Wimbledon or Beckenham or some other prosperous London suburb'.[45]

The British and the Egyptians, as was their wont, generally kept separate company, meeting only in the local cinemas. Serving in Egypt certainly opened the eyes of British soldiers, for whom Egypt had previously been a fabled land, 'vaguely associated with camels, plagues, bullrushes, Potiphar's wife, Moses, and crocodiles'. As a member of the Egypt Expeditionary Force wrote: 'We who are serving in Egypt and Palestine know that we are fortunate to have had such a chance of seeing these ancient lands, a chance that would never have come to most of us in the ordinary course of our tranquil lives.'[46]

But the war also opened the eyes of the Egyptians, for whom the prospect of the British fighting fellow Muslims (the Turks) merely stoked their desire for independence.

⊲o⊳

The First World War marked not just an interruption in the work of archaeologists in Egypt, but also the end of an era in Egyptology. Maspero retired in 1914 and died two years later. Cromer – no particular friend of archaeologists, but a major figure in their story, nonetheless – died in 1917. Both Maspero and Erman lost sons in the conflict, while the German House at Thebes was deliberately destroyed by British troops in 1915. Maspero's successor at the Antiquities Service and Museum, Pierre Lacau, was unable to take up his post until September 1915, leaving the institutions rudderless for over a year. From 1916 to 1917, he had to return to France, and delegated temporary responsibility for affairs in Egypt to the secretary-general of the Institut d'Egypte, Georges Daressy. Not that there was much to be done in the realm of Egyptian archaeology. Foreign missions were halted for the duration of the war. Breasted, profoundly distressed both by the war itself and by the anti-German sentiment it provoked, tried to lose himself in his work. In London, he stayed with H. G. Wells, and was invited to Highclere by Lord Carnarvon – a man he described as 'devoted to Egypt'.[47] Breasted's wartime scholarship resulted in a high-school textbook, *Ancient Times* (1916), which proved so popular that the royalties finally put its author on a secure financial footing.[48] Petrie also found himself stuck in London, where he spent his time at University College London, 'doing regular lectures and working up material'.[49] (His politics were the polar opposite of Breasted's, and he was a member of the Anti-Socialist Society and President of the British Constitution Association.)

Once the armistice had been declared and four long years of war had finally come to an end, archaeologists began to make preparations to return to Egypt. Predictably, Petrie was on the first civilian ship back. He later recounted: 'Although it was difficult to secure passages even a year after the Armistice, we managed to return to Egypt, leaving November 19, 1919.'[50] By the following year, he was busy digging again, this time in the cemeteries of Middle Egypt.

The most significant impact of the war on Egyptian archaeology was the banning of German missions. The German Institute was stripped of its concessions, and the plum site of Amarna was given to the EEF (which changed its name, in 1919, to the Egypt Exploration Society) as archaeological war reparations. Erman, who had done so much to promote German interests in Egypt, was incensed, describing it as '*Raub*' ('robbery'). Gardiner's testy reply laid bare the feelings aroused by the war. He wrote to Erman:

Do you really imagine that the French Director of the Service of Antiquities, who has seen one sixth of his country overrun and devastated by the German armies would willingly countenance the resumption of German excavations in Egypt, so long as he could possibly prevent it? And do you think it likely that the British who stood shoulder to shoulder with the French in defending Egypt against Turkish and German invaders, would be disposed in this matter to adopt the German point of view in preference to the French? . . . what you describe as Raub would necessarily be regarded by the average Frenchman or Englishman as an obvious compensatory act of *justice*.[51]

German Egyptologists had hoped that their scholarship would not be influenced by geopolitical events, so the loss of the Amarna concession was a bitter blow.[52] But the ever-undiplomatic Gardiner pointed out that 'it is the consideration that the Egyptians themselves would certainly interpret concessions made to Germany at the present moment as a sign of weakness on the part of the *Entente*'.[53] For several decades after the war, Anglo-German relations within Egyptology resumed their former antagonism.

An aspect of Egyptian archaeology that had not changed was the perennial lack of funding for British digs. In a long and impassioned letter to *The Times* in March 1919, Sir Arthur Evans, the discoverer of Minoan civilization, president of the Society of Antiquaries, and one of the most decorated archaeologists of his generation, pleaded the case for a properly funded British Institute of Archaeology in Egypt, with a library and a budget for research and publications, to match the government-backed French, American and (temporarily suspended) German institutions. He began by describing the competition faced by British excavators in the Nile Valley:

> Forty years have now passed since the French Government founded the Institut Français d'Archéologie du Caire . . . In 1906 Germany established the Imperial Archaeological Institute in Cairo and its work has been greatly assisted by the wealthy society known as the Orientgesellschaft, itself largely under official auspices. With the United States, on the other hand, the functions of a Centralized National Institution have been more than filled by several parallel organizations, lavishly equipped and practically permanent in their nature.[54]

He then asked, plaintively: 'Beside all this, what is the position of Britain – the protecting Power, the moral trustee of Egypt's inheritance?' Echoing the sentiments of Amelia Edwards three decades earlier, Evans lamented the fact that: 'As a whole the moneyed classes in this country – unlike their aristocratic predecessors of a century and a half ago – show little of that enthusiasm for the advancement of knowledge which ensures such a liberal response to appeals on the other side of the Atlantic.'

His proposition was simple and bold, and was deliberately designed to stir British imperial pride: 'a uniquely qualified committee, formed under the auspices of the British Academy . . . has presented a memorial to the Lords of the Treasury, strongly urging the creation of an Imperial British Institute of Archaeology in Cairo, to be subsidized by an annual grant from the Treasury at least sufficient to make our position as protecting Power not appreciably inferior in this respect to [that] of other countries'. His concluding sentence was a call to action, and an appeal to the national conscience: 'Our good name among civilized peoples will largely depend on the manner in which our Government fulfils its grave responsibilities as trustee not only of Egypt's present, but of its past.'[55]

Needless to say, Evans's appeal fell on deaf ears. British excavations in Egypt continued to be funded privately and run on a shoestring. In this aspect, at least, Egyptological history was destined to repeat itself – again and again. Twelve years later, Petrie concluded his memoir with the same hope, undaunted by fifty years of fruitless pleading: 'The whole machinery of research has never been so well developed, and the only hindrance is insufficiency of means, for in the absence of any government help, the progress of researches depends entirely on the public.'[56]

As for Borchardt, though he continued in office as director of the Imperial German Institute for Egyptian Archaeology (renamed, after the war, the Egyptian section of the German

Archaeological Institute), his research in the Nile Valley was, perforce, restricted to the collections of the Egyptian Museum. He published an extensive study of the museum's royal and private statuary, to complement the publication of his greatest archaeological discovery, the bust of Nefertiti. More than the Rosetta Stone or the Dendera zodiac, the Luxor obelisk or Cleopatra's Needles, more even than the pieces smuggled out by Budge, the bust of Nefertiti came to represent for Egyptian nationalists the exploitation and appropriation of their history by foreigners – a perennial insult that had gone on for more than a century. Outrage over the bust's removal to Berlin – keenly felt in 1912, and rekindled after the war – stoked the fires of nationalism and forced the colonial authorities to face the inevitable reckoning.

Sultan Hussein Kamel had died during the war, in October 1917, and was succeeded by his entirely ill-prepared and ill-suited younger brother, Ahmed Fuad (r.1917–36). The new sultan spoke little Arabic, and appeared to his people just as much a stooge of the British as his predecessor. 'Secret societies flourished in the revolutionary atmosphere and Cairo was a hotbed of plots and conspiracies.'[57] Egyptians were actively questioning their colonial status, and just two days after the armistice, the prime minister, Zaghloul Pasha, requested permission to lead a delegation to London to negotiate independence.[58] The British authorities, however, thought they could deny nationalist demands. Their North African protectorate was simply too strategically important, lying across the route to India and giving access to Britain's newly won colonial possessions in East Africa. As the Ottoman Empire collapsed and began to be dismantled, Egypt also gave Britain an advantage over France – whose North African interests were far to the west, in Algeria and Tunisia.[59]

The British authorities' response to the calls for independence

was therefore to arrest the nationalist leaders. That was incen-
diary enough, but an attempt to deport them was a provocation
too far. Full-scale riots spread from Cairo to the countryside.
Insurgents, bolstered by Bedouin from the deserts, cut telegraph
wires, tore up railway tracks and besieged British garrisons –
every symbol of colonial domination was a legitimate target.
The British responded with force, meting out harsh sentences
to the rioters – but, at the same time, opened negotiations on
Egypt's future. The new high commissioner, Lord Allenby,
'made up his mind that the only way to pacify the Egyptians
was to give them all – or nearly all – they wanted'.[60]

The last gasp of the British imperial presence in Egypt is
recorded in Lord Edward Cecil's memoir, subtitled 'pictures
of the lighter side of Egyptian life' and published two years
after the end of the war. In its diffident tone, it perfectly captures
the attitudes and interests of the British ruling class in the
dying days of the protectorate. The first section, subtitled 'My
Daily Life', is divided into the following chapters: 'Getting up
and breakfasting; Office Part I; Office Part II; Council; Office
Part III, and lunch; Golf; Committee; Office, Club, and Dinner;
Evening Party; Supper Part I; Supper Part II; My Dream'. The
second section, 'Going on Leave', charts the journey from Cairo
to Calais via Port Said and Marseilles. Cecil said of himself,
'like all sane men, I dislike work', and of his Cairo club, 'it is
the only place where one can get decent food at a price less
than that paid at a Monte Carlo restaurant'. He was unself-
consciously condescending towards the Egyptians – referring
to 'the undeveloped state of their intelligence, and to the tradition of bad government' – but also perceptive enough to realize
that Egyptian politics were 'a web of personal intrigue and
counter-intrigue' and that 'he who follows not custom in the
East is a fool'. His account is full of the social whirl of Cairo's
glittering balls, and of the thoughts of home that always loomed

large among the expatriate community: 'If you see two Anglo-Egyptians in deep conversation, you will find that five times out of ten they are discussing steamship lines, their virtues and iniquities.'[61]

But the sands of time were fast running out on British rule in Egypt. Just a year after Cecil's memoir, the Egyptians' longing for self-rule would be brought to a head – not by a nationalist politician or a popular uprising, but by the greatest archaeological discovery ever made in the Nile Valley.

ELEVEN

Wonderful things

Howard Carter (first from left) meeting his patron Lord Carnarvon and Lady Evelyn Herbert on their arrival at Luxor railway station in November 1922, accompanied by the provincial governor.

Our sensations and astonishment are difficult to describe as the better light revealed to us the marvellous collection of treasures.[1]

HOWARD CARTER, 1922

The name of Tutankhamun barely features in the annals of nineteenth-century Egyptology. None of the classical authors, on whose accounts of Egyptian history most European scholars relied, made mention of him at all. Nor did he feature in the king list compiled from ancient sources by the third-century BC Egyptian priest Manetho and preserved in later fragmentary copies. Only after Champollion's decipherment of hieroglyphics in 1822 made it possible to read ancient Egyptian inscriptions directly for the first time did antiquarian visitors to Egypt begin to notice occasional, brief texts that mentioned a little-known pharaoh bearing the throne name Nebkheperura and the birth name Tutankhamun. In the later 1820s, during Wilkinson's twelve-year sojourn in the Nile Valley, he travelled into the Eastern Desert between the river and the Red Sea; at the remote site of Bir Abbad, east of Edfu, his eagle eyes noted a stone block bearing the names of Tutankhamun. In 1828, Wilkinson made another discovery that mentioned the same pharaoh: a tomb cut into the hillside of western Thebes that had been created for a high official named Huy – a viceroy of Kush, the king's personal representative in Egyptian-controlled Nubia – during the reign of Tutankhamun.

While Wilkinson was exploring the deserts and hills of Upper Egypt, his friend Lord Prudhoe (later the fourth Duke of Northumberland) was venturing even further afield, to Upper Nubia. At the ancient religious capital of Gebel Barkal, near the Fourth Nile Cataract, Prudhoe collected two magnificent statues of recumbent lions, each carved from a single block of red granite. Reused and reinscribed by a Nubian ruler, Amanislo, in the third century BC, the beasts had originally been carved by the pharaoh Amenhotep III a thousand years earlier. One of them bore a dedicatory inscription of Tutankhamun, recounting how he had renewed the monument in honour of its original patron, his grandfather Amenhotep III. In 1835, Prudhoe presented both lions to the British Museum, where they had the distinction of becoming the first two objects to be registered in its nascent collection of Egyptian antiquities. (They bear the registration numbers EA1 and EA2.) Thus far, Tutankhamun was no more than a minor footnote in the unfolding history of ancient Egypt.

Further evidence for the existence and achievements of this king had to wait until Mariette's excavations of the Serapeum in the 1850s. The third of the great bull burials uncovered in the underground vaults had, it transpired, been carried out during the reign of Tutankhamun; a few objects from the burial found their way to the Louvre, part of the steady stream of artefacts dug from the sands of Saqqara with which Mariette repaid his Parisian employer. Another four decades later, one of the more notable discoveries made by the hapless Emile Amélineau during his disastrous excavations at Abydos was a box of gilded wood, bearing Tutankhamun's royal cartouche. But it was Petrie's dig in the winter of 1891–2 at the site of Amarna that made the real breakthrough, shining new light on the history of Akhenaten's reign and its immediate aftermath, at the end of the eighteenth dynasty. Numerous inscribed objects from the ruined city, including the Amarna Letters that Erman had purchased for the Berlin Museum, mentioned Nebkheperura Tutankhamun by name, and made it clear that he was Akhenaten's son and successor. Moreover, the evidence suggested that the royal court had remained at Amarna under Tutankhamun, at least during the early years of his reign. Suddenly his absence from the king-lists made sense: Akhenaten's royal revolution had been so radical, such a break with centuries of pharaonic tradition, that, after his death and the restoration of orthodoxy, he and all his associates had been expunged from history as if they had never existed. What the ancient Egyptians had tried so hard to suppress was, only now, being rediscovered, thanks to the meticulous efforts of Egyptologists.

With the dawn of the twentieth century, the name of Tutankhamun started to crop up, if not everywhere, then certainly more frequently. Suddenly, this little-known pharaoh began to emerge from a hundred generations of obscurity to take his place among the kings of Egypt's golden age. In 1905, investigations in the temple of Karnak, north of Luxor, uncovered a great stone slab, covered with hieroglyphic inscriptions. At some point in its long history, the stela had been earmarked for reuse; it still bore a series of deep incisions down its front, where workmen had tried to cut it into pieces. But enough survived of the text to enable scholars to translate it. It turned out to be a dedicatory inscription celebrating the restoration of Karnak, and the other temples of Egypt, following their abandonment under Akhenaten. The king responsible for this glorious renaissance was none other than Tutankhamun. For those who knew how to interpret it, the 'Restoration Stela' gave a clear indication that Tutankhamun had broken with the teachings of his father, and the city of Amarna, and had restored Thebes as both the religious capital of Egypt and a centre of royal activity.

A further, chance discovery, that same archaeological season, confirmed the fact: while digging in the Valley of the Kings for the Davis mission, Ayrton found, concealed under a rock, a small faience cup bearing the name Nebkheperura. Two years later, Davis and Ayrton discovered a hole in the ground above the entrance to the tomb of Seti I. 'Pit 54', as they termed it, contained a cache of materials left over from the embalming of a royal mummy – not just any royal mummy but, according to the hieroglyphic inscriptions on some of the objects, the mummy of Tutankhamun. This seemed unequivocal evidence that, not only had Tutankhamun been active in Thebes, he had also been buried in its royal necropolis, the Valley of the Kings. Now the hunt was on for his tomb. In January 1909, Davis discovered what he had been looking for: a small, undecorated chamber (numbered KV58), abandoned in antiquity and filled with mud, but crucially containing a stone *shabti*, fittings from a horse's harness, and several fragments of gold foil bearing the names of Tutankhamun and his wife Ankhesenamun. Davis proudly announced his discovery in the resulting publication:

> The finding of the blue cup with the cartouche of Touatânkhamanou, and not far from it the quite undec- orated tomb containing the gold leaf inscribed with the names of Touatânkhamanou and Ankhousnamanou . . . and the pit containing the jars with the name of Touatânkhamanou, lead me to conclude that Touatânkhamanou was originally buried in the tomb described above, and that it was afterwards robbed, leaving the few things that I have mentioned.[2]

For Davis, this was not merely a triumph but the culmin- ation of his nine years of work in the Valley of the Kings. 'I began my work of exploration in 1903,' he recounted, 'and between that date and 1909, I found seven important inscribed tombs . . . also nine uninscribed tombs, one of them containing the beautiful gold jewellery of Setuî and Taouasrît, one with pieces of gold leaf with the names of Touatânkhamanou and Aîya, and a small alabaster figure.'[3]

In the published account of what was to be Davis's last major discovery, a chapter on the life and reign of Tutankhamun was contributed by no less a scholar than Maspero, the grand old man of Egyptology. He began it by confessing: 'Very little is known about the origin of this king . . . The length of his reign is unknown.'[4] In the few succeeding pages, the much-admired director of the Antiquities Service and Egyptian Museum listed the major monuments attributable to Tutankhamun's reign – the lions from Gebel Barkal, the tomb of Huy, the Restoration Stela, and the objects found by Ayrton and Davis – before summarizing: 'Such are the few facts we know about Touatânkhamanou's life and reign.'[5] As for Davis, he famously concluded 'the Valley of the Tombs is now exhausted'. In February 1914, at the end of Davis's final season in Egypt, his workmen stopped digging into the floor of the valley, fearing that further work would undermine the adjacent path.[6] In any case, Davis could not imagine for a moment that the ancient Egyptians would have cut a royal tomb into the valley floor where it would be vulnerable to flooding. With the discovery of KV58, he was sure that the Valley of the Kings really had given up the last of its secrets.

<del>—◁o▷—</del>

The man who would prove Davis spectacularly wrong – and, in the process, cause him to be all but forgotten – was his former employee, a man who happened to be working nearby in the hills of western Thebes. Howard Carter had worked for Davis a decade earlier, and had taken part in the excavation of the tomb of Hatshepsut. By 1914, Carter was one of the most experienced archaeologists of his age. But his journey to prominence had been anything but smooth. Born in Brompton, London,[7] into a comfortable middle-class family, he spent much of his childhood in Norfolk. Like Champollion and Petrie before him, Carter suffered from ill-health as a child, and was consequently educated at home. As with his great Egyptological predecessors, the freedom to follow his own interests and explore his passions was, in retrospect, a key factor in his later success. Carter's father was an accomplished painter, specializing in animals, and passed on his skill to his son. Howard soon became a talented watercolourist, also preferring natural history subjects, and he found plenty of inspiration for his work in the countryside around the Carter family home in Swaffham. Rural Norfolk also had another advantage: the county boasted a number of aristocratic families who might, directly or through their connections, offer preferment to a budding young artist. The patrons who took an interest in the young Howard Carter were Lord and Lady Amherst of nearby Didlington Hall. By chance, Lord Amherst was not only a man of considerable means, he was also a keen amateur antiquarian who used his wealth to sponsor excavations and collect antiquities. Through a series of judicious purchases, and his own trips to Egypt, he amassed one of the finest private collections of ancient Egyptian artefacts in England, which he proudly displayed at Didlington. Carter must have seen some of the objects on his visits: his first encounter with the civilization of the pharaohs, the study of which was to consume the rest of his life.

In 1891, at the age of seventeen, Carter was given his first break. At Lady Amherst's recommendation, he was taken on by Newberry (who, alongside his archaeological duties, acted as an agent for Lord Amherst, buying choice Egyptian antiquities when they came on the market) as an assistant member of staff of the Archaeological Survey of Egypt. Newberry was a botanist by training; his knowledge of plant remains had proved useful to Petrie on his digs in the late 1880s. With this experience, and through connections at the EEF, Newberry was subsequently given his own expedition, the Archaeological Survey mission to Beni Hasan. At this site in Middle Egypt, there was a series of fine, decorated tombs cut into the cliffs overlooking the Nile. The job of recording their beautifully preserved, complex and detailed reliefs required not just epigraphic skill but also the eye of a trained artist. In Howard Carter, the Amhersts believed they had found the ideal candidate. In late 1891, therefore, Carter travelled for the first time to Egypt, and worked for several weeks at Beni Hasan under Newberry's supervision. Carter's talents as a copyist and painter quickly confirmed his patrons' judgement, and he was soon switched to another of Lord Amherst's funded excavations, Petrie's dig at the nearby site of Amarna. In the space of a few weeks, Carter began to build his knowledge of the late eighteenth dynasty, to familiarize himself with the names of its shadowy rulers: Akhenaten, Nefertiti, and Tutankhamun.

Petrie, for his part, was distinctly underwhelmed by the new addition to his team: 'Mr Carter is a good-natured lad whose interest is entirely in painting and natural history: he only takes on this digging as being on the spot . . . and it is of no use to me to work him up as an excavator.'[8]

But Carter had been bitten by the Egyptian bug, and was only too delighted to be retained by the Archaeological Survey to work on their other missions. He resumed his work at Beni Hasan and nearby el-Bersha the following season (1892–3) before moving to Deir el-Bahri – the mortuary temple of Hatshepsut in western Thebes – as official expedition draughtsman, working under Naville. During the next six years, while copying all the scenes and inscriptions in the temple, Carter gained a deep – perhaps unparalleled – knowledge of the surrounding area. Wandering the hills, valleys and embayments, he developed an unerring eye for potential archaeological sites, and came to know every inch of the Theban necropolis: Deir el-Bahri, Sheikh Abd el-Qurna, the Valley of the Kings.

After half a dozen seasons at Deir el-Bahri, Carter gained his second lucky break in 1899. Maspero's much-heralded return as director of the Antiquities Service ushered in a major reorganization of senior posts. Carter, with his proven abilities as a copyist, his training under Newberry, Petrie and Naville, and his deep understanding of Thebes, had all the necessary credentials, and he was duly appointed chief inspector of antiquities for Upper Egypt, a newly created post and one of the most important roles in Egyptian archaeology. He did not disappoint. Maspero's initial impressions were perceptive: 'very active, a very good young man, a little obstinate'.[9] Taking up his position in January 1900, Carter set to work at once with his customary energy and dedication. The administration of the Upper Egyptian inspectorate was reformed, and electric light installed at the major tourist sites. The results of this particular project were transformative. Davis's companion, Emma Andrews, recorded in her diary a visit to the tomb of Amenhotep II shortly after the power had been switched on:

> We entered Amenhotep's tomb – now lighted with electricity, showing arrangement and decoration delightfully . . . Carter has arranged the whole thing most artistically. A shrouded electric light is at the head of the sarcophagus, throwing the fine face into splendid relief – and when all the other lights were extinguished, the effect was solemn and impressive. Carter has done

wonderful work . . . No more stumbling about amongst
yawning pits and rough staircases, with flickering candles
dripping wax all over one.[10]

Nor was Carter merely concerned with restoration and
display. He plunged himself into a series of hands-on excavations, uncovering and recording royal tombs for the
Antiquities Service and for various private sponsors. In 1900,
working for two local Egyptians, Chinouda Macarios and
Boutros Andraos, Carter revealed a previously unknown tomb
(KV42) dating to the early eighteenth dynasty. The next year
he discovered another empty tomb and a series of small finds.
It was when he started working for Davis, in the winter of
1902, that Carter's archaeological instincts really proved their
worth, culminating in the discovery of the richly appointed
tomb of Thutmose IV (KV43) in 1903 and the clearance of
the tomb of Hatshepsut (KV20) the following season. In the
latter, Carter showed not only his deep commitment to archaeology, but also his willingness to risk life and limb in the
furtherance of Egyptological enquiry. Davis was hugely
impressed, if a little incredulous, recounting in the subsequent
publication:

The long, patient, tiresome, and dangerous work executed
by Mr Carter, the difficulties which he overcame, and
the physical discomforts which he suffered, are not fairly
described in his modest official report . . . the air had
become so bad, and the heat so great, that the candles
carried by the workmen melted, and would not give
enough light to enable them to continue their work . . .
Braving all these dangers and discomforts, Mr. Carter
made two or three descents every week, and professed to
enjoy it.[11]

Such dedication did not go unnoticed, and in 1904 Carter was promoted to chief inspector of antiquities for Lower Egypt. (The north of the Nile Valley, with the iconic monuments of Giza, Alexandria and the Memphite necropolis, was considered more prestigious than Thebes and the south.) It was a vote of confidence by Maspero, but a calamitous move for Carter. The ever-observant Emma Andrews had summed up Carter as 'always so pleasant – in spite of his dominant personality'.[12] That character trait, which other less generous commentators dubbed an irascible temper, soon got Carter into trouble. In January 1905, only a few months into his new job, Carter was at Saqqara, inspecting the Serapeum. Though a popular tourist destination, it had not yet benefited from the installation of electric light. A group of French tourists, coming to see for themselves the greatest discovery of their compatriot Mariette, objected to paying an entrance fee; then, on finding there were no candles to illuminate the subterranean galleries, demanded their money back. Carter refused, an argument ensued, and punches were thrown. Realizing that he had overstepped the mark, he sent a telegram at once to Lord Cromer, explaining the situation and pinning the blame squarely on the tourists:

> My Lord I am exceedingly sorry to inform you that a bad affray has occurred today here Mariette House Saqqara 5 p.m. with 15 French Tourists who were here in a drunken state The cause of the affray was started by their rough handling both my inspector + gaffirs As both sides have been cut and knocked about I feel it my duty to inform ~~you~~ Lordship immediately + will report the matter to you personally tomorrow morning. Carter Service of Antiquities.[13]

Ever anxious to avoid a diplomatic incident, especially with the French, Cromer summoned Carter and demanded an explanation. To smooth ruffled feathers and prevent any escalation, Cromer asked Carter to apologize. Carter, certain that he had acted within his rights, refused. The only way open to him was to resign, not just as chief inspector, but from the Antiquities Service entirely. He later admitted: 'I have a hot temper, and that amount of tenacity of purpose which unfriendly observers sometimes call obstinacy, and which nowadays . . . it pleases my enemies to term . . . *un mauvaise caractère*. Well, that I can't help.'[14]

In November 1905, Carter returned to his old stamping ground of Thebes and, for the next two years, eked out an existence as a guide and jobbing watercolourist. His former patron, Davis, gave him work recording the objects from the newly discovered tomb of Yuya and Tjuyu. At other times, Carter supported himself by selling his paintings to well-heeled tourists. For example, in the winter of 1907–8, the ailing eighth Duke of Devonshire was travelling up the Nile with a small party that included his personal physician (and amateur Egyptologist), Ferdinand Platt. On a visit to Thebes, Platt met the impecunious Carter, and described the encounter in a letter home:

> Carter has done some very beautiful work. What he does is to copy some of the best Egyptian figures or scenes very accurately as to the matter of outline and general colour. He leaves out all the cracks and damage and restores what is left. But the great charm is that he shades the colours to make it look real; for instance the golden vulture head dress of a queen he has shaded in such a way that without altering the drawing in the least it looks like real gold . . . After lunch I went with Carter to the

Tombs of the Queens and saw the tomb of Queen
Nefert-Ari, the wife of Rameses II . . . She was a beautiful woman and Carter's painting brings this out in a
wonderful way . . . If I had the money spare I would buy
this particular picture without a moment's hesitation. As
you can imagine Carter's loss of his appointment is a
serious thing for him, and he was and is I believe very
hard up. I told the Duke about him and he has asked
me to go over to Medinet Habu with him to see Carter's
sketches as he wants to help him by buying some. I am
very glad to have been the means of doing this.[15]

In the end, however, it was not the Duke of Devonshire
who turned Carter's fortunes around, but another English aristocrat wintering in Egypt that season: a man who was attracted
to Luxor, not just for its restorative climate, but for its antiquities and its promise of undiscovered treasures.

◁◻▷

George Edward Stanhope Molyneux Herbert, son and heir of
the fourth Earl of Carnarvon, was born in 1866 at Highclere
Castle, the family's magnificent country seat on the Hampshire–
Berkshire border, remodelled in high Gothic Revival taste by
Charles Barry in the 1840s while the architect (who had travelled up the Nile in 1818) was also engaged in rebuilding the
Houses of Parliament. Herbert's mother died when he was just
nine years old, leaving him the valuable estates she had inherited from her forebears, the earls of Chesterfield. This made
Herbert – known initially by his courtesy title of Lord
Porchester – independently wealthy. At Eton and Cambridge,
the young 'Porchy' paid little attention to his studies, focussing
instead on his primary interest – sport – and a growing fascination for archaeology.[16] When he succeeded to the earldom, on

the death of his father in 1890, he enjoyed free rein to indulge his passions. He travelled the world, visiting North and South America, Asia and Europe; he even attempted (but did not complete) a circumnavigation of the globe by sea.

By the time he reached his late twenties, he had spent much of his considerable inheritance and racked up huge debts. Fortunately, as for many British aristocrats of the time living well beyond their means, salvation appeared in the form of a wealthy bride. Almina Wombwell was the illegitimate daughter of the millionaire banker Alfred de Rothschild. As part of her marriage settlement in 1892, her father paid off all Carnarvon's debts and settled the vast sum of £300,000 on the couple. Carnarvon picked up where he had left off, indulging his love of sport by building up a major stud at Highclere, and betting on his own horses. His obsession with speed also led him into the nascent world of fast cars. It was to prove a turning point in his career. A motoring accident in Germany[17] left him injured and prone to persistent bouts of painful rheumatism, exacerbated by the cold wet winters of England. Seeking respite from his discomfort and a new hobby to occupy his time, Carnarvon had no hesitation in following his doctor's advice and joining the steady stream of well-heeled patients who repaired for the winter months to warmer, drier climates. In January 1903, in San Francisco's Bohemian Club, Carnarvon met a former US senator by the name of Jeremiah Lynch who had recently been to Egypt and had published a book of his travels.[18] Inspired, no doubt, by Lynch's account, Carnarvon decided to make Egypt his winter home. So it was that, towards the end of the year, Carnarvon set off to spend the first of many seasons in Luxor, in the Winter Palace Hotel on the banks of the Nile.

The earl was not a man to stand still: he needed a project to occupy his energies. During his stay in Luxor in 1905, he was present for Davis's discovery of the tomb of Yuya and

Tjuyu, with its remarkable contents and 'the glitter of gold'. The excitement of archaeology struck a chord with Carnarvon, and before long he followed Cromer's advice and decided to take up Egyptology himself. (He later claimed that, 'It had always been my wish and intention even as far back as 1889 to start excavating.'[19]) Carnarvon duly applied to Maspero for a concession; the director of the Antiquities Service was only too happy to oblige, welcoming privately funded excavations as a way of supplementing the Service's stretched resources. Carnarvon's permit was for an area of the Theban necropolis known as Sheikh Abd el-Qurna. It was situated on the west bank of the Nile, but easily accessible from the Winter Palace (Carnarvon's hotel of choice). Carnarvon may have been attracted by the romance of archaeology, but he was not well suited to its daily rigours. Indeed, he is said to have described excavation in Egypt as 'an occupation for the damned'.[20] The heat, dust and flies were a persistent irritation, and he took to sitting in a large, screened cage to watch his workmen dig. On occasions, he was joined by his wife, 'dressed for a garden party rather than the desert, with charming patent-leather, high-heeled shoes and a good deal of jewellery flashing in the sunlight'.[21] Even for the inhabitants of Luxor used to Western tourists in their three-piece suits and voluminous dresses, the fifth Earl and Countess of Carnarvon must have presented a queer spectacle.

After six weeks' work on his first excavation, Carnarvon had little to show for his efforts except an empty chamber and a rather unprepossessing mummified cat. But archaeology seemed to offer the prospect of adventure, and he was keen to take on a more promising site. Rivalry no doubt played a big part in his calculations. In February 1907, as his own disappointing excavations were drawing to a close, Carnarvon and his wife were entertained on board the *Beduin* by Theodore

Davis and Emma Andrews. The contrast between Carnarvon's paltry results and Davis's continued success – he had just discovered a tomb in the Valley of the Kings which he believed to be that of the fabled Queen Tiye – could not have been starker. For an English aristocrat, to be outdone by a nouveau riche American businessman was especially galling, and the atmosphere between Carnarvon and Davis was strained. Carnarvon later declared: 'I should not speak to the man again.'[22]

Carnarvon's problem was not his own lack of archaeological prowess – Davis possessed little more – but his lack of an experienced excavator to direct the work. Davis had always employed trained archaeologists: Newberry, then Carter, then Weigall. So, when Carnarvon wrote to Maspero later in 1907 requesting a new concession, the advice came back loud and clear: hire a good director – not just any director, but one of the most experienced. Maspero had a specific suggestion: Howard Carter. Before resigning from the Antiquities Service, Carter had proved his strengths as an archaeologist. Despite his hot-headedness, there was no doubting his abilities. And so, following Maspero's advice, Carnarvon approached Carter. The deal was struck and the partnership was forged – a partnership that would last the rest of Carnarvon's life and result in the greatest archaeological discovery of all time.

Almost immediately, Carter's training and expert eye began to bear fruit, and Carnarvon's fortunes as an archaeological patron were transformed. With Carter in charge, Carnarvon's second digging season was marked by a series of notable finds, including a writing tablet bearing an account of the battles against the Hyksos at the beginning of the New Kingdom. (The 'Carnarvon tablet' remains, to this day, our most important single source for this crucial turning point in ancient Egyptian history.) Further discoveries followed in subsequent winters, including several private tombs, another temple built by Hatshepsut, a series of Ptolemaic vaulted tombs, and an extensive necropolis. Together these finds justified the publication of a lavish, heavily illustrated volume to mark the first five seasons of the Carnarvon–Carter partnership, *Five Years' Explorations at Thebes* (1912). In the preface, the patron paid fulsome tribute to his archaeologist: 'Mr Howard Carter has been in charge of all operations, and whatever successes have resulted from our labours are due to his unremitting watchfulness and care in systematically recording, drawing, and photographing everything as it came to light.'[23] Within a decade, this 'unremitting watchfulness and care' would prove vital, and would be tested to the limit.

Although Carnarvon and Carter were focussed principally on Thebes, their curiosity and thirst for new discoveries led them to explore other, more remote sites as well. Thus, in 1912, while continuing to dig at Thebes, they decided to carry out some exploratory work at the isolated Delta village of Sakha, site of the ancient Graeco-Roman city of Xoïs, which had lain abandoned and largely unvisited for centuries. Unfortunately, conditions for excavation were less than propitious, and they had to abandon their efforts after just two weeks, 'on account of the number of cobras and *cerastes* [horned vipers] that infested the whole area'.[24] The following season, having tried and failed to win the concession for the pyramid field of Dahshur, Carnarvon and Carter turned their attention to another promising spot in the Delta, Tell el-Balamun. Once again, however, their hopes were dashed and they finished the season with little to show for their efforts except some silver jewellery.

Whatever the accounts of classical authors might have suggested, it seemed that the sites of the Ptolemaic and Roman age in the north of Egypt held little promise for archaeologists, and were hardly worth the investment of time and resources. There really was only one site where the efforts of excavation were more or less guaranteed to be rewarded, and that was Thebes. In Carnarvon's own description: 'No ancient site has yielded a greater harvest of antiquities than this famous stretch of rocky land.'[25] Moreover, everyone knew that the plum concession in the whole Theban necropolis – and hence in the whole of Egypt – was the Valley of the Kings. For now, however, the concession was firmly held by Davis. His string of spectacular discoveries made it highly unlikely that he would relinquish his rights any time soon.

All that changed within the space of a few months in the spring and early summer of 1914. In February, Davis's workmen downed tools, their patron convinced that the valley had nothing more to reveal. A few weeks later, Davis formally relinquished the concession, handing it back to the Antiquities Service. Meanwhile, Carter had not been idle in promoting his credentials. During the early weeks of 1914, the appearance of illicit antiquities in the markets of Luxor suggested that locals had been plundering a newly discovered tomb in the hills of western Thebes. Using his unparalleled knowledge of the area, Carter tracked down the tomb in question – it turned out to have been created for Amenhotep I and his mother Ahmose-Nefertari – and carried out his own, exemplary clearance. His swift action and expert archaeological skills won plaudits. Back in Cairo, Maspero was preparing to retire for good and return to Paris. Eager, no doubt, to ensure that Egypt's most prized archaeological site remained in good hands, Maspero showed his magnanimity and good judgement. In June 1914, in his very last act as director of antiquities, he awarded the concession for the Valley of the Kings to Carnarvon. Carter's indiscretion at Saqqara had been forgiven, if not forgotten. After years of waiting and manoeuvring, the ultimate prize had fallen into Carnarvon's hands.

Not that he was able to enjoy it in person: the outbreak of

the First World War kept him in England. All attempts to get back to Egypt were thwarted. Carter, by contrast, had remained behind in the country, to offer his services and knowledge as a diplomatic courier. Conveniently, this also allowed him the time and space to undertake limited excavations. On 8 February 1915, he formally started work under the new concession, excavating the tomb of Amenhotep III in the western branch of the Valley of the Kings. Once again, his meticulous approach yielded valuable results, rescuing a number of overlooked finds from the debris of earlier digs. The following year he cleared an unused tomb in the cliffs above the valley; prepared for Hatshepsut while she was still queen, it yielded nothing except an abandoned sarcophagus. But, all the while, Carter was honing his already intimate knowledge of the valley, identifying the most likely spots where an undiscovered tomb might yet lie concealed. As a boy, he had been inspired by reading Belzoni's memoirs, and had dreamed of finding a lost tomb in the Valley of the Kings. Carter later admitted: 'Ever since my first visit to Egypt in 1890 it had been my ambition to dig in The Valley, and when . . . I began to excavate for Lord Carnarvon in 1907, it was our joint hope that eventually we might be able to get a concession there.'[26]

In 1916, Breasted, the giant of American Egyptology, published his landmark book *Ancient Times: A History of the Early World*. It placed particular emphasis on the history of pharaonic Egypt, although one pharaoh passed without a single mention: Tutankhamun. The obscure king of the late eighteenth dynasty simply did not merit inclusion. But Carter remained convinced that the pharaoh's final resting place might yet reveal itself.

Davis had found three vital clues – the faience cup, the mud-filled chamber with fragments of gold leaf, and the embalming cache – all of which bore the name of Tutankhamun, and all of which pointed to his tomb being located somewhere in the Valley of the Kings. In KV58, Davis thought he had found the missing tomb; but Carter, with his superior Egyptological training, thought otherwise. As he later explained: 'With all this evidence before us we were thoroughly convinced in our own mind that the tomb of Tut.ankh.Amen was still to find, and that it ought to be situated not far from the centre of The Valley.'[27]

Earlier archaeologists had sought to find new tombs by sinking pits through the accumulated rubble and rubbish on the valley floor. By 1917, however, Carter knew that only way to locate the tomb of Tutankhamun – if it still existed – was to clear the remaining section of valley all the way down to the bedrock.[28] And so, motivated by a single goal, in the autumn of that year he set to work.

Over the next five years, with an army of workers and a grim determination, Carter oversaw the systematic clearance of the remaining, unexcavated section of the valley. Altogether, his team moved some 150,000–200,000 tons of rubble and loose chippings, carried away by means of a Decauville railway, specially installed for the purpose. Five years of strenuous and expensive work yielded little: a few finds, and no tombs. Carnarvon started to lose faith and interest. Even his fortune was not inexhaustible, and in the fruitless search for the undiscovered tomb of a largely unknown pharaoh it seemed he was merely throwing good money after bad. By the summer of 1922, he had decided to call it a day and concentrate on his horse racing. But Carter, spurred on by a conviction as solid as the bedrock of Thebes, felt in his bones that he was on the right track. That summer, he decided to take the highly unusual step of travelling to Highclere in person, to plead his case with Carnarvon and beg the earl's support for one more season. Reluctantly, Carnarvon agreed.

⊲○⊳

After the excitements of the Davis years, and the retirement and death of Maspero, Egyptology in the immediate aftermath of the First World War was in the doldrums. Among the millions of young men killed during the conflict were a number of promising archaeologists, while leading figures on both sides had lost sons. The British army had deliberately flattened the German House at Thebes in an act of retribution, and, even after the armistice, German expeditions found themselves banned from working in the Nile Valley. By 1921, even Gardiner had overcome his hostility towards Germany and was missing its contribution to Egyptology. Nearly three years after the end of the war, he wrote to Erman: 'What a fatality it is, how disastrous for the science, that Germans cannot be working in Egypt still.'[29] (It would be another eight years before the German Archaeological Institute reopened and German excavations resumed in Egypt.)

By contrast, some American missions had returned to the Nile Valley after the war. Foremost among them was an expedition funded by the Metropolitan Museum of Art in New York and directed by Herbert Winlock. Winlock had studied at Harvard and began excavating in Egypt for the Met in 1906; but when war was declared he was evacuated back to New York and enlisted in the US forces, serving as a major. Only when hostilities ceased was he able to return to civilian life and to his work as an archaeologist, and he resumed digging at Deir el-Bahri in the winter of 1919, continuing the work begun by Naville a generation earlier. No less an authority than Petrie praised Winlock's field technique, while Weigall went further, describing the young American as the most brilliant archaeologist of his generation.[30] Winlock's skill as an excavator was rewarded with a succession of important finds: the tomb of Meketra with its extensive collection of wooden tomb models, in that first post-war season of 1919–20, followed two years later by a remarkable archive of letters penned by an Egyptian farmer named Heqanakht in *c.*2000 BC. As Winlock's friend, John Wilson, put it, the letters 'bring us face to face with the ancient Egyptian, not in the frozen dignity of his tombs and temples, but in the homely busyness of his kitchen and his fields'.[31]

But such notable American discoveries did nothing to lift the gloom that had settled over British archaeology in Egypt. The cause was as much political as cultural. Although hundreds of thousands of men from the British Empire had fought – and died – for king and country, there was a strong sense that the old imperial rivalries had led the world to disaster. While the Académie des Inscriptions et Belles-Lettres in Paris prepared to mark the centenary of Champollion's decipherment with official meetings and receptions, Britain's imperial power was ebbing away. The future of its colonies and protectorates, Egypt included, looked uncertain – and so too did the future of the expatriates and archaeologists who had treated Egypt as their playground for the best part of forty years.

This post-imperial malaise was vividly captured in the writings of Arthur Weigall, who had more reason than most to look back on the pre-war years with a sense of deep nostalgia. Weigall had joined the Egyptian Research Account as a student of Petrie's in 1901, and had been lauded by his mentor as 'the most capable student we have ever had'.[32] Within three years Weigall's meteoric rise – assisted by his close friendship with Cromer – had taken him from research student to inspector-general of antiquities for Upper Egypt (in succession to Carter). Moreover, Weigall's connections extended beyond the upper echelons of the British establishment across the Atlantic: he counted Theodore Roosevelt among his friends. With his network of influential acquaintances, Weigall's views were keenly sought and his writings had influence on British policy towards Egypt. But the Nile Valley did not treat him kindly: in 1914, after a decade in post as inspector-general, he suffered a nervous breakdown and returned to England, turning his back on archaeology. In its place, he 'occupied his spare time by painting designs for stage scenery',[33] in the London theatre, and by writing novels, song lyrics and reactionary articles for the *Daily Mail*.

Weigall's most extensive surviving work, written in 1922 (and published the following year), is a book entitled, with headline-grabbing intent, *The Glory of the Pharaohs*. But the title is misleading: Weigall's account was, in fact, a critical discourse on the discipline of archaeology, as practised in Egypt in the first two decades of the twentieth century. It is revealing, both of the turning point at which Egyptology now found itself, and of the contradictions and challenges that faced Britain as the colonial power in a country that clamoured for independence. Weigall had learned his trade from Petrie, and he continued to espouse the notion that, by 'roughing it', the body could be 'toughened'. He boldly asserted that: 'the study of archaeology in the open helps to train up young men in the path of health in which they should go. Work in the Egyptian desert, for example, is one of the most healthy and inspiring pursuits that could be imagined.'[34]

Nonetheless, he reserved special scorn for Petrie's brand of asceticism: 'It is not roughing it to eat canned food out of the can when a plate might be used: it is either hypocrisy or slovenliness.'[35] With only a little more self-restraint, he observed:

> If the experiences of a digger in Professor Petrie's camp are to be regarded as typical, they will probably serve to damp the ardour of eager young gentlemen in search of ancient Egyptian treasure. One lives in a bare little hut constructed of mud, and roofed with cornstalks or

corrugated iron . . . For seven days in the week one's work continues, and it is only to the real enthusiast that work is not monotonous and tiresome.[36]

Weigall was at his most passionate and iconoclastic when writing about the tension between Western archaeology and native Egyptian sentiment. He advocated keeping Egyptian monuments in Egypt, and was much more outspoken than most contemporary commentators, declaring:

> the craze for recklessly dragging away monuments from Egypt to be exhibited in western museums for the satisfaction of the untravelled man is the most pernicious bit of folly to be found in the whole broad realm of Egyptological misbehaviour . . . No curator should endeavour to procure for his museum any antiquity which could be safely exhibited on its original site and in its original position.[37]

He also argued fiercely against the trade in illicit antiquities, which he accused museums of fuelling: 'It is felt . . . that the objects exhibited in European museums have been rescued from Egypt and recovered from a distant land. This is not so. They have been snatched from Egypt and lost to the country of their origin.'[38]

Budge, one suspects, would not have been amused.

In his views on the limitations of archaeology, Weigall was both ahead of his time and unfashionable: 'The archaeologist, so eager to add to his knowledge by new discoveries, should remember that there is already quite enough material on hand to keep him busy for the rest of his life.'[39] Why, he asked, 'add to the burden of Egypt by increasing the number of monuments which have to be protected?' In his opinion: 'The longer an excavation is postponed the better chance there wll be of recording the discoveries adequately.'[40] The Committee of the Egypt Exploration Society must have squirmed to read one of their own protégés advocating such views.

Weigall's writings were deeply influenced by the trauma of the First World War. He found in ancient Egypt an escape from the horrors of the early twentieth century, and it was when describing the attractions of distant antiquity that he became most lyrical:

> To the Past we must go as a relief from To-day's harshness; for the Past is spread out before us as a children's garden, where jolly laughter and sudden, quick-ended tears are to be experienced; where the waters are alive with mermen and the woods are filled with brownies; where nymphs and fairies dwell among the flowers, and enchanted castles crown the hilltops; where heroes die for fame, and the victors marry kings' daughters. There in that garden we may forget the mature cruelty and the sins of the present time; for if there be wickedness in the Past, we may usually name it the thoughtless mischief of childhood . . . One contemplates with positive relief the tortures and massacres of the distant ages, for they are child's play as compared with the reasoned brutality of these wicked olden days in which we now live.[41]

He was, at the same time, mindful of the modern Egyptians' growing sense of their own nationhood – aspirations to which those who knew the country well could not be insensible: 'In Egypt, where scientific excavations are conducted entirely by Europeans and Americans, one has to consider . . . one's duty to the Egyptians, who care not one jot for their history, but who, nevertheless, as the living descendants of the Pharaohs should be the nominal stewards of their ancient possessions.'[42]

This combination of condescension towards other peoples and grudging acceptance of their right to self-determination characterized colonial attitudes towards Egypt in the years after the First World War. Ever since the Napoleonic invasion, Egypt's traditional leadership structures had been steadily eroded under the pressure of Western influence. A succession of rulers, from Muhammad Ali to Fuad, had sought protection or investment from Western powers in return for ceding sovereignty. The British invasion of 1882 had met with only minor resistance, but the apparent Egyptian passivity towards foreign occupation had lulled the British into a false sense of security. Only a few in the British establishment recognized the inherent injustices of occupation, and could see the writing on the wall.

The colonial authorities had first attempted to contain Egyptian nationalism before the war, through Gorst's more liberal approach; but this had been deemed a failure and had been replaced by Kitchener's more traditional, paternalistic attitude. This did not work either. The nationalist uprising of 1919 caught the British authorities by surprise. So did the passive resistance led by Zaghlul in 1921, modelled on Gandhi's civil disobedience in India. That same year, the British opened an airport at Heliopolis; the Royal Air Force began flying mail routes from Cairo to Baghdad, while Imperial Airways launched a Cairo to Karachi service. But even modern communications could not save the Empire.

The colonial authorities calculated that significant concessions to the Egyptian nationalists might yet prevent an all-out revolution and preserve a degree of British influence. London's proposal was for the protectorate to be replaced by an Anglo-Egyptian treaty, granting Egypt independence as a constitutional monarchy. Britain would retain the right to maintain an army in Egypt, a financial adviser, and a permanent official in the ministry of justice, and to protect the rights of foreigners resident in Egypt. It was, in other words, self-determination in name only. With great fanfare, Egyptian 'independence' was declared on 28 February 1922. Two weeks later, Sultan Fuad assumed the title King Fuad I.

Archaeology was not immune to these political developments. The director of the Antiquities Service, Lacau, immediately announced that henceforth all finds would be claimed for Egypt, with only duplicates given to the excavators at the Service's discretion.[43] The measures were not universally popular. Petrie, predictably, railed against the new strictures, seeing in them the latest skirmish in the Anglo-French rivalry that had characterized Egyptology since the days of Young and Champollion:

> The issue of new and arbitrary conditions by Lacau was a repetition of what former French Directors of Antiquities had tried to do, by ignoring their subordination to the Ministry in Egypt, and trying to establish an autocracy . . . This attempt had been checked before . . . by the strength of British management. Now that Britain was leaving much more to Egyptian direction, there was not the same check, and French autocracy was left uncontrolled.[44]

The new regulations meant that, without the prospect of new acquisitions, foreign museums would no longer be interested in supporting digs in Egypt. For Petrie, this was intolerable. In a fit of pique he decided to stay in England for the winter season of 1922–3 to tackle a backlog of publications and muster opposition to Lacau's decision. He called a joint meeting of the Egypt Exploration Society, the Metropolitan

Museum of Art and the British School of Archaeology in Egypt, resulting in a formal protest being sent to the Council of Ministers in Cairo, the British High Commissioner in Egypt, Lord Allenby, and Lacau himself. In response, the introduction of the new law was suspended for two years.[45] Even so, Petrie decided to confine himself in future to 'excavations in which there was little likelihood of finding anything of value'.[46]

Not that the prospect of discovering further treasure beneath the sands of Egypt was thought particularly likely. As Weigall noted that same season: 'There is painful disillusionment awaiting the man who comes to dig in Egypt in the hope of finding the golden cities of the Pharaohs or the bejewelled bodies of their dead.'[47]

◁〇▷

Digging in the Valley of the Kings seemed to many a particularly thankless task. As far back as 1869, Mariette had written: 'There is every reason to believe that the excavations . . . however persevering, will not yield results commensurate with the difficulties caused by the remoteness of the location and the want of a water supply.'[48] Over half a century later, Weigall summed up the task thus: 'There is much drudgery to be faced, and for a large part of the season's work it is the excavator's business to turn over endless masses of rock chippings, and to dig huge holes which have no interest . . . At other times a tomb-chamber is reached and is found to be absolutely empty.'[49]

In the autumn of 1922, after five seasons of systematic but fruitless work, Carnarvon's reluctance to persevere was understandable. One final season, and he would call it a day.

Carter arrived in Luxor on 28 October and excavations resumed on 1 November. Just three days into the dig, the workmen uncovered a step cut into the valley floor. Twenty-four hours later, a flight of twelve descending steps had been exposed, leading to a blocked doorway covered in plaster and impressed with the seals of the ancient royal necropolis. Carter could scarcely believe his eyes: 'The design was certainly of the Eighteenth Dynasty. Could it be the tomb of a noble buried here by royal consent? Was it a royal cache, a hiding place to which a mummy and its equipment had been removed for safety? Or was it actually the tomb of the king for whom I had spent so many years in search?'[50]

On 6 November, Carter ordered the staircase to be refilled with rubble and he sent the now-famous telegram to his patron in England: 'At last have made wonderful discovery in Valley; a magnificent tomb with seals intact; re-covered same for your arrival; congratulations.' Carnarvon cabled back the reply: 'Possibly come soon,' followed, a little later, by, 'Propose arrive Alexandria 20th'.[51] That gave Carter and his excavation team 'a fortnight's grace', and they devoted it 'to making preparations of various kinds, so that when the time of the re-opening came, we should be able, with the least possible delay, to handle any situation that might arise'.[52]

Carnarvon, accompanied by his daughter Lady Evelyn Herbert, arrived at Luxor by train on 23 November, to be greeted by Carter and the provincial governor. The next day, patron and archaeologist watched together as the staircase was cleared to its full depth, revealing the whole of the plastered doorway. Now there could be no doubt what they had found: 'On the lower part the seal impressions were much clearer, and we were able without difficulty to make out on several of them the name of Tut.ankh.Amen.'[53] In due course, the blocked doorway was dismantled, only to reveal a sloping tunnel, filled from floor to ceiling with limestone chippings. As workmen struggled in the dusty confined space to clear the tunnel, a second doorway was encountered, likewise covered with sealings naming Tutankhamun. To Carter and Carnarvon's horror, this inner doorway, like the first, showed signs of earlier forced entry. Robbers had clearly entered the tomb in antiquity. The question was, had they left anything behind?

By four o'clock in the afternoon on 26 November, the corridor had been fully cleared. Carter, watched by Carnarvon, Lady Evelyn, an English engineer Arthur 'Pecky' Callender, and the Egyptian overseers, prised some of the stones out of the top of the second doorway. Carter's journal entry for that 'day of days'[54] relates what happened next:

Candles were procured – the all-important tell-tale for foul gases when opening an ancient subterranean chamber – I widened the breach and by means of the candle looked in, while Ld. C., Lady E, and Callender with the Reises waited in anxious expectation. It was sometime before one could see, the hot air escaping caused the candle to flicker, but as soon as one's eyes became accustomed to the glimmer of light the interior of the chamber gradually loomed before one, with its strange and wonderful medley of extraordinary and beautiful objects heaped upon one another. There was naturally short suspense for those present who could not see, when Lord Carnarvon said to me 'Can you see anything' I replied to him Yes, it is wonderful.[55]

In Carter's published account of the discovery, which appeared the following year (written with the 'literary help' of the novelist Percy White, professor of English Literature at the Egyptian University), the episode had acquired a touch more drama and panache:

At first I could see nothing, the hot air escaping from the chamber causing the candle flame to flicker, but presently, as my eyes grew accustomed to the light, details of the room within emerged slowly from the mist, strange animals, statues, and gold – everywhere the glint of gold. For the moment – an eternity it must have seemed to the others, standing by – I was struck dumb with amazement, and when Lord Carnarvon, unable to stand the suspense any longer, inquired anxiously, 'Can you see anything?' it was all I could do to get out the words, 'Yes, wonderful things.'[56]

Carnarvon, with more typical British understatement, described it as 'a most extraordinary sight'.[57]

Breaking through the doorway, Carter entered the chamber beyond. Even for a man who prided himself on his meticulous, detached professionalism, the experience conjured up powerful emotions:

Three thousand, four thousand years maybe, have passed and gone since human feet last trod the floor on which you stand, and yet, as you note the signs of recent life around you – the half-filled bowl of mortar for the door, the blackened lamp, the finger-mark upon the freshly painted surface, the farewell garland dropped upon the threshold – you feel it might have been but yesterday. The very air you breathe, unchanged throughout the centuries, you share with those who laid the mummy to its rest.[58]

Carter summed up that day as 'the most wonderful I have ever lived through, and certainly one whose like I can never hope to see again'.[59] As the first person to enter the tomb of Tutankhamun in modern times, he experienced 'the exhilaration of discovery, the fever of suspense . . . the strained expectancy

– why not confess it? – of the treasure-seeker'.[60] Soon, however, other thoughts came to the fore, as the magnitude of the discovery – and of the work that lay ahead – began to dawn. In Carter's words, 'our brains began to reel at the thought of the task in front of us'.[61] Neither archaeologist nor patron had been prepared for 'the greatest find ever made',[62] and they were 'wholly unprepared to deal with the multitude of objects'[63] – 5,398 in total. As Carnarvon put it: 'There is enough stuff to fill the whole Egyptian section upstairs of the B. M. [British Museum].'[64] 'Carter,' he confidently predicted, 'has weeks of work ahead of him.'[65]

Fortunately, Egyptologists around the world were quick to offer assistance. Breasted, who had visited the tomb shortly after its discovery, helped in the clearance and worked on the seal impressions. Albert Lythgoe, curator of the Egyptian department at the Metropolitan Museum of Art in New York, cabled Carter as soon as he heard about the discovery, to offer any assistance needed. Carter gratefully accepted, and was soon joined in the Valley of the Kings by the museum's photographer, Harry Burton, and two architects, Walter Hauser and Lindsley Foote Hall, who drew all the objects in situ. (Hauser and Hall subsequently left, finding Carter difficult to work with.) Gardiner arrived within weeks, to start work on the inscriptions. Eventually, the excavation team comprised an unprecedented, multidisciplinary team of experts: alongside Carter, Callender, Breasted, Burton, Hauser, Hall and Gardiner, there were Arthur Mace (Lythgoe's associate curator at the Met), Alfred Lucas (director of the chemical department of the Egyptian government), Newberry (now honorary reader in Egyptian art at Liverpool University), Douglas Derry (anatomist at the Cairo Anatomy School), L. A. Boodle (botanist from Kew Gardens), G. F. Hulme (Geological Survey of Egypt), James Ogden (jeweller), and Battiscombe Gunn (epigrapher and philologist).

It would take them seven weeks to clear the antechamber, and a total of seven seasons to record, conserve and clear the entire tomb.

Following the official opening of the tomb on 29 November 1922 and the official inspection by Lacau the following day, Carnarvon and Lady Evelyn left for Cairo and made their way back to England. Carter, too, repaired to Cairo for ten days while bespoke steel gates were made for the tomb. The discovery had made headlines around the world, and as a result the site was plagued with visitors. As Breasted remarked, the discovery:

> broke upon a world sated with post-First World War conferences, with nothing proved and nothing achieved, after a summer journalistically so dull that an English farmer's report of a gooseberry the size of a crab-apple achieved the main news page of the London metropolitan dailies. It was hardly surprising therefore that the Tutenkhamun discovery should have received a volume of world-wide publicity exceeding anything in the entire history of science.[66]

Back home in London, Carnarvon was invited to a private audience at Buckingham Palace where he recounted the adventure to King George V and Queen Mary. Unused and ill-suited to worldwide media attention, Carter expressed the forlorn hope that: 'Whatever our discoveries next season may be, we may be allowed to deal with them in a proper and dignified manner.'[67] It was not to be. Instead: 'The seasonal volume of mail at the Luxor post office was doubled and trebled . . . The two leading hotels of Luxor set up tents in their gardens' to accommodate the hordes of visitors.[68]

The discovery of Tutankhamun's tomb had a profound impact on the Egyptians themselves. Coming just eight months after

Egypt's declaration of independence, it was inevitable that the find and its aftermath should become entangled with nationalist politics. To Egyptians, the richness and sophistication of the boy-king's treasures offered 'vindicating proof of past glory and inspiration at a critical moment in their struggle for independence'.[69] Interest in Egypt's pharaonic past, which had hitherto been the preserve of Western archaeologists and a few native scholars, was suddenly propelled into the mainstream of Egyptian cultural and political thought.[70] The teaching of pharaonic history was introduced in government schools, a state university was founded, programmes were introduced to train Egyptian Egyptologists, and the Antiquities Service and Museum – for so long bastions of Western influence – were steadily Egyptianized.[71]

Above all, the unearthing of a tomb so extraordinarily rich in objects marked a turning point in the history of Egyptian archaeology, when the old system of dividing finds between the archaeologist and the state came to an end. Carnarvon's 1914 permit to excavate in the Valley of the Kings had specified an even distribution of finds, except in the event of an unrobbed tomb being found. The Egyptian authorities now invoked that exception, and sought to retain the entire contents of the tomb as part of Egypt's patrimony. Carter, Breasted and their ilk were aghast, believing that only trained (Western) Egyptologists could properly appreciate and care for Egyptian antiquities. Moreover, they regarded the moves by Fuad's government and Lacau's Antiquities Service as 'either nationalist political posturing or crass opportunism in anticipation of future tourist revenues'.[72] But the world – and Egypt with it – had moved on since the days of Champollion and Lepsius. Mariette's vision – for a national museum that would curate and safeguard pharaonic artefacts on behalf of the Egyptian people – had come to pass. In an era of renewed Egyptian national pride, in a newly independent country with a spring in its step, figures like Petrie and Budge looked like relics of the past. When the first object was removed from Tutankhamun's tomb on 27 December 1922, it was taken not to Highclere Castle or the British Museum, but to the Egyptian Museum in the heart of Cairo.

Exactly a century after the decipherment of hieroglyphics first opened a window on remote antiquity and allowed the ancient Egyptians to speak again, the discovery of Tutankhamun's tomb, coming hot on the heels of Egyptian independence, prompted the country's modern inhabitants to rethink their relationship with their own past and chart a new course for the future. It would be a future which the Egyptians themselves, rather than Westerners, would determine.

The future of the past

Carter with King Fuad I and Egyptian officials in the Valley of the Kings.

It is the business of the archaeologist to wake the dreaming dead: not to send the living to sleep.[1]

ARTHUR WEIGALL, 1923

The worldwide publicity that attended the discovery of Tutankhamun's tomb in November 1922 reached fever pitch the following year with the official opening of the burial chamber. As the *New York Times* reported:

> There is only one topic of conversation . . . One cannot escape the name of Tut-Ankh-Amen anywhere. It is shouted in the streets, whispered in the hotels, while the local shops advertise Tut-Ankh-Amen art, Tut-Ankh-Amen hats, Tut-Ankh-Amen curios, Tut-Ankh-Amen photographs, and tomorrow probably genuine Tut-Ankh-Amen antiquities. Every hotel in Luxor today had something a la Tut-Ankh-Amen . . . There is a Tut-Ankh-Amen dance tonight at which the piece is to be a Tut-Ankh-Amen rag.[2]

The 'Egyptomania' that the discovery sparked in Europe and America was accompanied by a national awakening in Egypt itself. The boy-pharaoh from ancient Egypt's golden age became an icon of the country's new independence.[3] Egyptian nationalist politicians paid well-publicized visits to the tomb, discovering that the magic of ancient Egypt could be as powerful a weapon for contesting Western influence in the twentieth century as it had been for bolstering it in the nineteenth.[4]

The team brought together by Carter to study, record and conserve the thousands of objects from Tutankhamun's tomb marked a new departure in Egyptian archaeology. The expedition was the first to have its own chemist (Alfred Lucas), and the sheer number of different specialisms required to do the tomb and its contents justice signalled the end of the heroic age of gentleman amateurs. Also gone were the days when a single scholar – a Young or Wilkinson, Champollion or Mariette – could hope to encompass the whole discipline of Egyptology. The sheer number of discoveries during the nineteenth and early twentieth centuries had outstripped the ability of any one individual to keep pace with and master such a raft of new knowledge.

The orgy of treasure-seeking in the immediate aftermath of the Napoleonic expedition had resulted in countless thousands of objects entering European collections, to be admired as curios and objets d'art; but the proper interpretation and understanding of Egyptian antiquities – as insights into pharaonic civilization – only really began with Champollion's decipherment of hieroglyphics in 1822. His achievement allowed ancient Egyptian culture to emerge out of the fog of Classical myth and esoteric legend into the spotlight of serious scientific enquiry, to be studied and appreciated as a sophisticated culture in its own right and on its own terms. At the same time, Wilkinson's careful observations on the ground in Egypt brought new breakthroughs in understanding. He recognized the pyramids of Giza for what they really were – the tombs of fourth-dynasty kings – while his accurate drawings of the scenes in the Tombs of the Nobles at Thebes rounded out the picture of pharaonic culture by illuminating the daily life of the ancient

Egyptians. As Wilkinson was the first to observe, their manners and customs were as rich and varied as those of any other people, ancient or modern. Hunting and fishing, music and dance, arts and crafts, banquets and festivals: all were recorded in intimate detail on tomb walls, but it took a man of Wilkinson's curiosity and diligence to bring them back to life.

Building on these foundations, scholars in the middle of the nineteenth century were able to bring a sharper focus to the study of ancient Egypt, elucidating the different periods of its long history and charting the development of its extraordinary art and architecture. Thanks to the efforts of Lepsius and his expedition, Egyptian civilization gained some texture and nuance: instead of being seen as a single, amorphous entity, it came to be understood as a succession of distinct epochs of cultural creativity (which were named the Old, Middle and New Kingdoms), each with its own recognizable artistic style. In the 1850s, Mariette's excavations unexpectedly revealed the degree to which ancient Egypt had maintained close relations with, and been influenced by, its neighbours. The burial of King Kamose at Thebes, with its objects of Levantine inspiration; the reliefs depicting an ancient voyage to Punt (modern coastal Sudan), discovered in the Theban temple of Hatshepsut; and the lion-headed sphinxes, found at Tanis in the Nile Delta, with their strange Asiatic features: this succession of notable finds demonstrated that the pharaohs had not only traded with other cultures, but had also absorbed influences from abroad. Ancient Egypt had not, after all, been the pristine 'civilization apart' that earlier scholars had assumed (or wished).

With the establishment of the Antiquities Service in the late 1850s, new discoveries came thick and fast.[5] The Pyramid Age was revealed in all its glory by a series of beautiful objects unearthed from cemeteries at Saqqara, Giza and Meidum: a life-sized wooden statue of a high official, nicknamed by the workmen who found it Sheikh el-Beled ('village elder'); the majestic diorite statue of King Khafra, uncovered in situ in his pyramid temple; delicately carved wooden relief panels from the tomb of Hesira, a dentist at the court of a third-dynasty king; the exquisite statues of husband and wife, Rahotep and Nofret, found in their tomb chapel, undisturbed for over three thousand years; and the beautifully observed painting of geese from a nearby tomb. Antiquities Service excavations also revealed the world's oldest body of religious writings, the Pyramid Texts, enabling scholars to appreciate the antiquity and complexity of ancient Egyptian beliefs; and a cache of royal mummies, allowing faces to be put to some of the great names of antiquity.

From the 1880s onwards, Petrie's focus on small finds – the objects thrown away or disregarded by earlier archaeologists – and on meticulous, systematic excavation led to some of the most elusive and fragile remains being discovered, recorded and studied. His unerring eye and enquiring mind revealed for the first time the long prehistory of ancient Egyptian civilization, by finding a series of unassuming shallow graves, cut in the low desert north of Thebes and dating back to the early fourth millennium BC; rescued the precious mummy portraits from Hawara, which testified to the artistic and cultural sophistication of a hybrid Graeco-Egyptian culture at the end of ancient Egypt's immense time span; and unearthed delicate paintings in the royal palaces at Amarna, illuminating life in the royal court under the heretic pharaoh Akhenaten during Egypt's 'golden age' (*c.*1350 BC). Petrie also had the luck – or judgement – to find the only known instance of the word 'Israel' in Egyptian hieroglyphics, on a reused slab of stone. But, by the late 1880s, the study of ancient Egypt was no longer seen as a branch of biblical history, but as a fully formed discipline with its own questions to answer.

As knowledge grew, so further discoveries in the late nine-teenth and early twentieth centuries were able to add yet more colour and detail. The Amarna Letters, discounted as forgeries by many, but recognized and acquired by Erman for Berlin, turned out to be an invaluable diplomatic archive, charting relations between Egypt and her neighbours at a time of great intrigue and power politics. A cache of delicate royal jewellery, found by de Morgan at Dahshur, illustrated Egyptian crafts-manship at its zenith. A ceremonial stone palette, dug from the mud by Quibell, turned out to have been commissioned by Egypt's very first king, Narmer (*c.*3000 BC), to celebrate his rule over a united realm. And the tomb of Kha, excavated by Schiaparelli at Thebes, yielded the greatest array of objects belonging to a private individual ever found in one place – basketry, furniture, clothing, food: the perfectly preserved possessions of a man who lived over twenty centuries ago.

By the time Davis, then Carter and Carnarvon, began to dig in the Valley of the Kings, ancient Egypt was no longer just an amalgam of garbled classical accounts, no more a myth-ical realm of esoteric knowledge, but a complex and vibrant civilization, every bit as innovative and sophisticated as Greece or Rome – the crucible of great feats of artistic and architectural achievement, but inhabited by real people.

<∘>

While assisting Carter in the Valley of the Kings, Gardiner, the foremost philologist of his generation, published his land-mark *Egyptian Grammar*. It was, and remains, the seminal text on the ancient Egyptian language. It is not, however, easy reading. Would that Gardiner, or myriad Egyptologists in the century since, had heeded the comments of Weigall, also writing in 1923: 'It is the business of the archaeologist to wake the dreaming dead: not to send the living to sleep.'[6] But it would be Gardiner's heirs rather than Weigall's, specialists rather than generalists, who would chart the future of the discipline. In embracing scientific rigour, Egyptology would lose its panache.

The sense that Carter's discovery marked the end of an era was only strengthened by the sudden and tragic death of his long-term patron and friend, Lord Carnarvon. Returning to Luxor in early 1923, after a whirlwind of interviews and audiences in England, Carnarvon was bitten on the cheek by a mosquito, allegedly while crossing the Theban plain to or from the Valley of the Kings. He subsequently nicked the top of the bite while shaving, and it became infected. Blood poisoning set in, and on 14 March he was transferred to Cairo, where he developed pneumonia. Concerned friends and colleagues hoped for the best while fearing the worst. On 20 March, Gardiner wrote to his wife: 'Our great sorrow during the last few days has been Carnarvon's serious illness. He . . . is not yet out of danger. It is difficult to think that only last Friday he and I dined and spent the evening together. It would be terrible if – but I just won't think of it.'[7]

Just over two weeks later, Carnarvon was dead. His body was brought back to Highclere and buried on Beacon Hill – the site of an ancient earthwork – overlooking the estate. His death gave rise to speculation about the 'pharaoh's curse', a myth that has proved hard to dislodge in the century since.[8] Carnarvon's sister, Lady Burghclere, recognized at once that: 'A story that opens like Aladdin's Cave and ends like a Greek myth of Nemesis cannot fail to capture the imagination of all men and women.'[9] Carter persuaded Carnarvon's widow to take over her late husband's concession, so that the clearance of the tomb could continue, uninterrupted. She agreed, but the old deference by the Egyptian authorities towards aristocratic English patrons had gone forever.

In 1923, even as Petrie was being knighted by King George V 'for services to Egypt' (not 'Egyptology'), the Egyptian government was re-establishing the Cairo School of Egyptology, which had lasted only three years during its first incarnation. That had been back in the 1880s, as Petrie was beginning his career in archaeology. In a bitter irony, the announcement coincided with the death of Ahmed Kamal, the first Egyptian to undertake scholarly work in Egyptology. He did not live to see his ultimate wish – for Egyptians to administer their own Antiquities Service (in which he had served faithfully for thirty-five years) – but he had done more than most to hasten the day.

Egypt's new constitution was promulgated on 19 April 1923, and the following year, after parliamentary elections resulted in a government dominated by nationalists, the Antiquities Service promptly cancelled Carter's permit to work in the Valley of the Kings. The symbolism was clear for all to see. Eventually, after much wailing and gnashing of teeth, the concession was restored in 1925, but on the Egyptian government's terms. *The Times* lost its monopoly (negotiated by Carnarvon) on news coverage of the excavation, while the Carnarvon estate had to formally renounce any claim to a share of objects from the tomb.

The one area where Westerners continued to exercise significant influence was at the Egyptian Museum. The building had been designed by a Frenchman, bore the names of exclusively Western Egyptologists, and was still the preserve of a largely European curatorial staff. But under their leadership, the building, as opposed to the antiquities inside it, had not been particularly well looked after. Only twenty years old, the roof had already started to leak and the basement flooded regularly when the Nile rose. Moreover, nobody back in 1902 had envisaged that the museum would one day have to accommodate so vast a collection of objects as had recently been unearthed in Tutankhamun's tomb. By the 1920s, the museum was overcrowded and in a bad state of disrepair. The Egyptian government had other, more pressing priorities for public investment, but Western Egyptologists were aghast, and decided to take matters into their own hands. In 1925, Breasted persuaded his benefactor, John D. Rockefeller, to promise funding for a brand new museum – a grand, riverside building in ancient Egyptian revival style. There was one condition: that Western scholars would be guaranteed control of the museum and its associated research institute for a period of thirty-three years. The Egyptian government refused.[10]

The days of Western interests infringing on Egyptian sovereignty in the name of archaeology were gone forever. Breasted, like Carter, had shown himself hopelessly out of touch with Egyptian national sentiment.[11] In a rare show of Egyptological discord, Reisner bitterly opposed the Rockefeller scheme. In the end, Rockefeller directed his philanthropy towards the building of the Palestine Archaeological Museum in Jerusalem, and gave additional funds to the Oriental Institute, allowing for the construction of Chicago House.

Plans for a new, Western-controlled Egyptian museum may have been thwarted, but the existing museum continued to be run by European – specifically French – directors, right up to the overthrow of the Egyptian monarchy. Etienne Drioton – the last in an unbroken line stretching back to Mariette in the 1850s – was forced from office after the revolution of July 1952. In a further gesture of anti-imperialism, the British army barracks at Qasr el-Nil, right next to the museum, were razed to the ground (to be replaced by the Nile Hilton, the first of Cairo's modern hotels). The Suez debacle, four years later, merely confirmed and cemented the permanent loss of British and French influence in Egypt. For better or worse, the fate of the

Antiquities Service and Egyptian Museum, and with them the direction of archaeology in Egypt, would henceforth be controlled by the people of the Nile Valley, not by foreigners from distant shores.

Acknowledgements

I would like to record my thanks to my agent, Peter Robinson, and my editor at Picador, George Morley; to the unfailingly helpful staff of the Cambridge University Library; to the many scholars and antiquarians, from the seventeenth century to the present day, upon whose research I have drawn; to Edward Hanna at the University of Lincoln and Richard Cornes at the Royal Netherlands Meteorological Institute for helping me track down the 1822 meteorological records from the Paris Observatoire; and, as always, to Michael Bailey for his unstinting support.

Notes

Introduction

1. Belzoni (1821): 80.
2. Quoted by Ambrose Lansing in Cone, ed. (1976): 5, and in Adams (2013): 51.
3. Colla (2007): 21.

PROLOGUE: Travellers in an antique land

1. Norden (1757): 77.
2. Felix Fabri, *Evagatorium in Terræ Sanctæ, Arabiæ et Egypti peregrinationem*, quoted in Thompson (1992): 17.
3. Anon. (1589).
4. Reid (2002): 27.
5. Sicard (1982): 23.
6. Quoted in Tyldesley (2005): 43.
7. Pococke (1743): 13.
8. Pococke (1743): 46.
9. Pococke (1743): iii.
10. They included 'Martin Folkes, Esq. President of the Royal Society', and 'The Right Hon'ble Thomas, Earl of Pomfret, Knight of the Most Hon'ble Order of the Bath'.
11. Norden (1757), I: 39.
12. Norden (1757): 65.
13. Norden (1757): 77, 79.
14. Norden (1757): 67, 69.
15. Norden (1757): pl. CVI.
16. Norden (1757): 44.
17. Norden (1757): 129.
18. Norden (1757): 121.

19. Thompson (1992): 21.

20. Norden (1757), I: dedication.

21. Thompson (1992): 21.

22. Rauch (2006): 325.

23. Colla (2007): 21.

24. For which see Volney (1787).

25. Rauch (2006): 325–6.

26. *Edinburgh Review*, I (January 1803): 330.

27. Reid (2002): 31.

28. Quoted in Gillispie and Dewachter (1987): 3.

29. Jeffreys (2003): 2–3.

30. Gillispie and Dewachter (1987): 3. It is no coincidence that on the Egyptian campaign, Napoleon carried with him the very book that had accompanied Alexander, Homer's *Iliad*, together with Xenophon's *Anabasis* and Plutarch's *Parallel Lives*. He also carried a copy of Volney's *Les Ruines*. See Reid (2002): 139–41; Rodenbeck (2004): 130.

31. Gillispie and Dewachter (1987): 5.

32. Ceram (1978): 77.

33. Tyldesley (2005): 48.

34. Denon (2003): 20.

35. Elshakry (2015): 191

36. Gillispie and Dewachter (1987): 19.

37. Lehner and Hawass (2017): 91.

38. Lehner and Hawass (2017): 91.

39. Quoted in Dixon (2003): 87.

40. Tyldesley (2005): 49.

41. Quoted in Sattin (1988): 25.

42. Reid (2002): 32.

43. Reported to have been quoted by Burckhardt: see Sattin (1988): 59.

44. Quoted in Mayes (1959): 114.

45. Burton (1880).

46. Jeffreys (2003): 4.

47. Quoted in Sattin (1988): 59.

48. Belzoni (1821): 1.

49. Belzoni (1821): 1.

50. 'Ozymandias' is a Greek corruption of the ancient Egyptian 'Usermaatra', the throne name of Pharaoh Ramesses II, for whom the temple had been built. Today, the entire edifice is known as the Ramesseum.

51. In the Napoleonic *Description de l'Egypte*, the second volume of plates of Egyptian antiquities, published in 1812, includes a map of western Thebes (plate 19) entitled 'Thèbes. Memnonium'. It marks the entire edifice as *'Tombeau d'Osymandyas, désigné par les voyageurs sous la dénomination de Palais de Memnon'*. The map marks the location of two colossal heads, plus a pedestal and a fallen colossus, labelled *'Restes de la statue d'Osymandyas'*. One of the colossal heads is illustrated on plate 32.

52. Long (1832), I: 253.

53. Belzoni (1821): 21.

54. Quoted in Belzoni (1821): 26.

55. Quoted in Belzoni (1821): 22, 24.

56. In the introduction to his own account, Belzoni rather pointedly noted: 'I am not an Englishman, but I prefer that my readers should receive from myself, as well as I am able to describe them, an account of my proceedings . . . rather than run the risk of having my meaning misrepresented by others' (Belzoni, 1821: v). By 'others' he no doubt meant Salt.

57. Belzoni (1821): 46.

58. Reid (2002): 40.

59. Belzoni (1821): vii.

60. While Belzoni was uncovering a world beneath the sands, his wife Sarah, 'took the opportunity, while in Egypt, to observe the manners of the women in that country'; the result, published in an appendix to her husband's compendious memoir (Belzoni, 1821: 441), was a 'short account of the women of Egypt, Nubia, and Syria' – perhaps the first such study by a Westerner.

61. *Quarterly Review*, XVIII (1817–18): 368.

62. *Quarterly Review*, XIX (April 1818): 204.

63. Hogg (1933), I: 76.

64. Among the likely sources of inspiration for Shelley's poem are Pococke's *Description* and Denon's *Travels in Upper and Lower Egypt*. In particular, Denon's description of the site of Oxyrhynchus in Middle Egypt as 'a boundless barrenness, which oppresses the

mind by immensity of distance, and whose appearance, where level, is only a dreary waste' employs imagery uncannily similar to Shelley's language; see Waith (1995).

65. Manley and Rée (2009).

66. Manley (2001): 189.

67. Usick and Manley (2007): 3.

68. Usick and Manley (2007): 1.

69. Usick and Manley (2007): 1. The account of Caviglia's work at Giza, written by Salt, only came to light in 2002 during a reorganization at the British Museum.

70. After the translation in Ray (2007): 170.

71. *Courier de l'Egypte*, 37 (*le 29 fructidor*, an VII), quoted in Thompson (1992): 22.

72. Tyldesley (2005): 52.

73. Henniker (1823): 139.

74. Saulnier (1822): 76.

75. On his visit in 1820, Henniker was 'lost in admiration, even though the concomitant filth hill is nearly on a level with the top of the portal' (Henniker 1823: 119).

76. Saulnier (1822): 77–8.

77. Saulnier (1822): 77–8.

78. Little is known about Lelorrain, other than his expedition to remove the Dendera zodiac.

79. Saulnier (1822): 84.

80. Saulnier (1822): 84.

81. Champollion (1986): 154–5.

ONE: Description and decipherment

1. Young to William Hamilton, 29 September 1822, quoted in Robinson (2006): 209.

2. Anon. (1822).

3. Robinson (2012): 142.

4. Nowinski (1970): 33.

5. Nowinski (1970): 66.

6. Ceram (1978): 80.

7. Ceram (1978): 79.

8. Reid (2002): 3.

9. Quoted in Robinson (2006): 144.

10. Thomas Young, quoted in Robinson (2006): 144.

11. Quoted in Wilson (1964): 11.

12. Pococke (1743): 230.

13. Quoted in Ceram (1978): 87.

14. Quoted in Ray (2007): 24.

15. Tyldesley (2005): 56.

16. Quoted in Robinson (2006): 15.

17. Quoted in Robinson (2006): 1.

18. Young (1823): ix.

19. Young (1823): 2.

20. Young (1823): 2.

21. Quoted in Robinson (2006): 158.

22. Quoted in Robinson (2006): 211.

23. Reproduced in Young (1823): 29–30.

24. Belzoni (1821): 162.

25. Jacques-Joseph subsequently altered his surname to 'Champollion-Figeac' to distinguish himself from his (more famous) younger brother.

26. Quoted in Robinson (2012): 49.

27. Salt to Mr Lee, quoted in Halls (1834): 186.

28. G. H. Noeden, 'Über das sogenannte Memnons-Bild im Brittischen Museum in London', quoted in Long (1832), 1: 251.

29. Young to William Hamilton, 29 September 1822, quoted in Robinson (2006): 209.

30. Young (1823): 43.

31. Young (1823): ix.

32. Young (1823): xiii–xiv.

33. Young to Hudson Gurney, 18 December 1820, quoted in Robinson (2006): 5–6.

34. Young (1823): 9.

35. Young (1823): 39, 46.

36. Young (1823): 53–4.

37. Quoted in Robinson (2006): 219.

38. Hudson Gurney, quoted in Robinson (2006): 211.

39. Champollion-Figeac (1887): 58.
40. Champollion (1824): 327.
41. Champollion (1824): 7.
42. Gurney, quoted in Robinson (2006): 234.
43. Quoted in Robinson (2006): 230.
44. Young to Gurney, undated, quoted in Robinson (2006): 230.
45. Champollion to Champollion-Figeac, 25 March 1829 – Champollion (1986): 249–50.
46. http://www.westminster-abbey.org/our-history/people/thomas-young, accessed 3 May 2018.
47. Ray (2007): 6.

TWO: In the footsteps of Napoleon

1. Champollion to Champollion-Figeac, July 1829 (*Lettres de Champollion le Jeune*, 2: 387), quoted in Robinson (2012): 222–3.
2. Champollion-Figeac 1887, quoted in Robinson (2012): 130.
3. Kitchen (2001): 235.
4. *Lettres de Champollion le Jeune*, 1: 87, quoted in Robinson (2012): 158.
5. Robinson (2012): 163.
6. Quoted in Robinson (2012): 165.
7. Reid (2002): 142.
8. Quoted in Robinson (2012): 170.
9. Mitchell (1988): 36.
10. Drovetti to Champollion, 3 May 1828, quoted in Champollion (1986): 1–2.
11. Champollion to Champollion-Figeac, 29 August 1828 – Champollion (1986): 41.
12. Champollion to Champollion-Figeac 30 July 1828 – Champollion (1986): 15.
13. Champollion (1986): 33–4.
14. Champollion (1986): 33–4.
15. Champollion to Champollion-Figeac, 10 September 1828 – Champollion (1986): 44.
16. Champollion to Champollion-Figeac, 14 January 1830, near Toulon – Champollion (1986): 469.

17. Champollion to Champollion-Figeac – Champollion (1986): 46.

18. Champollion's journal, 20 September 1828 – Champollion (1986): 77–8.

19. Champollion's journal, quoted in Robinson (2012): 199.

20. Champollion (1986): 119–20.

21. Champollion to Champollion-Figeac, 27 September 1828, Cairo – Champollion (1986): 88.

22. Champollion to Champollion-Figeac, quoted in Robinson (2012): 206.

23. Champollion to Champollion-Figeac, 24 November 1828, Thebes – Champollion (1986): 164.

24. Champollion to Champollion-Figeac, 24 November 1828, Thebes – Champollion (1986): 150.

25. Champollion (1986): 153.

26. Henniker (1823): 158–61.

27. Champollion to Champollion-Figeac, 1 January 1829, Wadi Halfa – Champollion (1986): 177.

28. Champollion to Champollion-Figeac, 12 January 1829, Abu Simbel – Champollion (1986): 213.

29. Champollion to Dacier, 1 January 1829, Wadi Halfa – Champollion (1986): 181.

30. Champollion to Champollion-Figeac, 1 January 1829, Wadi Halfa – Champollion (1986): 180.

31. Champollion's diary, 17 January 1829, Lower Nubia – Champollion (1986): 203.

32. Champollion to Champollion-Figeac, 10 February 1829 – Champollion (1986): 217.

33. Denon (2003): 58.

34. Champollion to Champollion-Figeac, 12 March 1829, Thebes – Champollion (1986): 244.

35. Champollion to Champollion-Figeac, 25 March 1829, Valley of the Kings – Champollion (1986): 273.

36. Champollion to Champollion-Figeac, 4 July 1829, Thebes – Champollion (1986): 387.

37. Champollion (2009): 241.

38. Champollion to Champollion-Figeac, 25 March 1829, Valley of the Kings – Champollion (1986): 249.

39. Quoted in Robinson (2012): 183.
40. Owen (1981): 66, 69, 71.
41. Quoted in Elshakry (2015): 187.
42. Quoted in Hassan (2003): 61.
43. Champollion to Champollion-Figeac, 28 November 1829, Alexandria – Champollion (1986): 418.
44. Quoted in Robinson (2012): 225.
45. Paul de Lagarde to Heinrich Rückert, 18 June 1867, quoted in Marchand (2009): 90.
46. Champollion to Rosellini, 29 January 1830, Aix-en-Provence – Champollion (1986): 476.
47. Quoted in Robinson (2012): 235.
48. Quoted in Ray (2007): 59.

THREE: Englishman abroad

1. Wilkinson to Robert Hay, 20 May 1832, quoted in Thompson (1992): 119.
2. Levine (1986) passim.
3. Madden (1841): 25–6.
4. Catherwood first visited Egypt in 1823–4, and returned in 1832 to make a series of drawings of Karnak Temple, which formed the basis of a painted panorama exhibited in his friend Robert Burford's circular viewing room in Leicester Square. Catherwood later travelled to the Americas, and died when the SS *Arctic* sank off Newfoundland.
5. Reid (2002): 43.
6. Henniker (1823): vi, 76, 82, 130, 135, 144.
7. *Eclectic Review*, N.S. XVIII (November 1822): 444.
8. *Eclectic Review* N.S. XXI (April 1824): 306.
9. Sherer (1824): iii.
10. Macmichael (1828): 157.
11. Ahmed (1978): 5.
12. Hall (1915): 78–9.
13. Thompson (1992): 30.
14. Salt to Gell, 16 September 1822, quoted in Hall (1915): 138.
15. Quoted in Thompson (1992): 49.

16. Quoted in Thompson (1992): 51.

17. A talented artist, Burton published a volume of plates, *Excerpta Hieroglyphica* (1825–8), and left an important collection of drawings, plans and antiquities, most of which are now in the British Museum. His younger brother was Decimus Burton, architect of the Athenaeum, among other London landmarks.

18. His collection of drawings, plans, copies and antiquities is also in the British Museum.

19. Bierbrier (ed.) (2012): 68.

20. Gell to Wilkinson, July 1822, quoted in Thompson (1992): 78.

21. Gell to Wilkinson, 1823, quoted in Thompson (1992): 74.

22. Caminos (1997): 24.

23. Thompson (1992): 123.

24. Quoted in Thompson (1992): 124.

25. Quoted in Blake (1982): 92.

26. Thompson (1992): 88.

27. Wilkinson (1835): 127.

28. Wilkinson to Hay, Cairo, 15 April 1832, quoted in Thompson (1992): 126.

29. Gell to Wilkinson, Naples, 10 April 1832, quoted in Thompson (1992): 78.

30. Wilkinson to Gell, 3 October 1832, quoted in Thompson (1992): 126.

31. Wilkinson to Gell, 3 October 1832, quoted in Thompson (1992): 118.

32. *Literary Gazette*, 13 April 1833, quoted in Moshenska (2015): 206.

33. Pettigrew is a remarkable, if marginal, figure in the history of Egyptology. His acquaintances included Dickens, Disraeli, Coleridge, Turner, Landseer and Faraday. The *'conversaziones'* he held in his Savile Row house were attended by the cream of London society, including peers, judges, members of the House of Commons and eminent scientists. As surgeon to the Duke and Duchess of Kent, Pettigrew vaccinated the future Queen Victoria as a baby. In 1841, with the encouragement of Wilkinson and others, he embarked on an *Encyclopaedia Aegyptiaca*, to present the recent achievements in Egyptology. It was due to be published in twenty-four monthly instalments, but failed to attract enough subscriptions so never appeared, beyond a short extract in the

prospectus. In 1852, Pettigrew presided over the mummification of Alexander, tenth Duke of Hamilton, and his interment in an Egyptian sarcophagus in the family mausoleum at Hamilton House, Scotland.

34. Dawson (1934): 170.
35. Rifaud (1830).
36. Wilkinson (1835): xiv.
37. Wilkinson (1835): 559–60.
38. Wilkinson (1835): 560.
39. Wilkinson (1835): 560.
40. Quoted in Ahmed (1978): 1.
41. Halls (1834): 273–4.
42. Quoted in Ahmed (1978): 24.
43. Quoted in Sattin (1988): 69.
44. Quoted in Ahmed (1978): 32.
45. Quoted in Ahmed (1978): 33.
46. Clarke (1814): 95.
47. *Retrospective Review*, III (1821): 96–7.
48. Ahmed (1978): 103.
49. *Quarterly Review*, LIX (July 1837): 165.
50. Ahmed (1978): 121.
51. Poole (1851), 1: 206.
52. Quoted in Ahmed (1978): 44.
53. Mitchell (1988): 41.
54. St John (1834), 1: viii.
55. Reid (2002): 52.
56. Sattin (1988): 49.
57. Wilkinson (1843), 1: 264.
58. Colla (2007): 118.
59. de Verninac Saint-Maur 1835, quoted in translation in Reid (2002): 1.
60. Quoted in Colla (2007): 111.
61. Gliddon (1841): 138.
62. Gliddon (1841): 88–9.
63. Gliddon (1841): 3–4.

64. Gliddon (1841): 146.

65. Colla (2007): 123.

66. He was subsequently promoted to colonel in 1837 and major-general in 1846.

67. Vyse (1840–2), 1: 1.

68. Vyse (1840–2), 1: 199.

69. Vyse (1840–2), 1: 200.

70. Vyse (1840–2), 2: 33.

71. Quoted in Tyldesley (2005): 110.

72. Vyse (1840–2), 2: 34.

73. Vyse (1840–2), 1: 236.

74. Vyse (1840–2), 1: 274.

75. Usick and Manley (2007).

76. *Laws and Regulations of the Egyptian Society*, Alexandria, no date, 1; quoted in Reid (2002): 49.

77. Wilkinson to Ada Lovelace, 18 May 1842, quoted in Thompson (1992): 169.

78. David Roberts (1796–1864) was the first professional artist to travel in Egypt, spending the winter of 1838–9 visiting and sketching the ancient monuments along the Nile, as well as the mosques of Cairo. During his stay, he corresponded with Hay and rented the house that had belonged to Osman Effendi, while Thomas Pettigrew unrolled one of his mummies in Roberts's London studio. On leaving Egypt, Roberts wrote: 'Well, I have no doubt all will end well – then for home with one of the richest folios that ever left the East. It is worth the hazard' (quoted in Sim, 1984: 159). Indeed it was. His earlier training as a set designer gave his work a theatrical flair, while technological advances allowed him to print his images in rich colours. They were, and have remained, the most popular, evocative and influential paintings of Egypt ever made.

79. Thompson (1992).

FOUR: The Prussian project

1. Lepsius to Friedrich Wilhelm IV of Prussia, December 1840, quoted in Freier (1988): 98.

2. Reid (2002): 43.

3. Clark (2006).

4. Baron d'Haussez to Charles X, 25 November 1829, quoted in Lebas (1839): 15.

5. Thompson (1992): 75.

6. Lepsius to Friedrich Wilhelm IV, December 1840, quoted in Freier (1988): 98.

7. Lepsius to Eichhorn, 4 March 1841, quoted in Freier (1988): 101.

8. Lepsius to Eichhorn, 24 May 1842, quoted in Freier (1988): 103.

9. Lepsius (1853): 6, author's preface.

10. Conradus Leemans (1809–93), director of the museum of antiquities in Leiden, and the first Egyptologist to publish a systematic catalogue of the contents of a major European collection.

11. Quoted in Freier (1988): 102.

12. Lepsius (1853): 12.

13. Lepsius to Eichhorn, 1843, quoted in Freier (1988): 110.

14. Lepsius (1853): 6, author's preface.

15. Ebers (1887): 140.

16. Lepsius to Graf Usedom, 23 October 1842, quoted in Freier (1988): 110.

17. His request was clearly taken seriously: just a week after his letter to Usedom, Wagner was recalled from Constantinople and posted to Alexandria as Prussian consul-general, with the approval of both the sultan and the pasha. He arrived in January 1843.

18. Lepsius (1853): 40.

19. Kröger (1991): 19.

20. Wilkinson (1843): 202.

21. Wilkinson (1843): 203.

22. Quoted in Sattin (1988): 86.

23. Lepsius (1853): 47, 49 (Letter from Cairo, 16 October 1842).

24. Lepsius (1853): 57.

25. Wilkinson to an unidentified correspondent, quoted in Thompson (1992): 238 n.33.

26. Lepsius (1853): 13.

27. Lepsius (1853): 51.

28. Lepsius (1853): 54.

29. Lepsius (1853): 69 (Letter from Saqqara, 13 April 1843).

30. Lepsius (1853): 80 (Letter from Cairo, 22 April 1843).

31. Lepsius (1853): 87 (Letter from the Labyrinth, 31 May 1843).

32. Lepsius (1853): 103.

33. Letter from Memphis, quoted in Ebers (1887): 146.

34. Wilkinson (1843): 264.

35. Reid (2002): 46.

36. Lepsius (1853): 17.

37. Lepsius (1853): 17.

38. Lepsius day book 12°, Nr. VII, 172, quoted in Rainer (1988): 59.

39. Lepsius (1853): 133 (Letter from the Blue Nile, Province of Sennar, Lat. 13°, 2 March 1844).

40. Letter from Thebes, 24 November 1844, quoted in Ebers (1887): 159.

41. Lepsius (1853): 20.

42. Lepsius (1853): 271 (Letter from Thebes, 25 February 1845).

43. Quoted in Freier (1988): 105.

44. The tomb chapels of Merib (Giza), Metjen and Manofer (Saqqara).

45. Lepsius (1853): 26.

46. Lepsius (1853): 28.

47. Lepsius (1853): 29.

48. Lepsius (1853): 32.

49. Bonomi and Arundale (1842–3): 1.

50. Ebers (1887): 189.

51. Lepsius (1853): 7.

52. Quoted in Rainer (1988): 40–1, n.27.

53. Auguste Mariette, quoted in Ebers (1887): 168.

54. Ebers (1887): 171.

55. The very first Egyptological photograph was published by Fox Talbot in 1846.

56. Lepsius (1853): 7.

FIVE: French foundations

1. Quoted in Reid (2002): 100.

2. Quoted in Lambert (1997): 43 ('Le canard égyptien est un animal redoutable. Quand il vous mord, il ne vous lâche plus').

3. Quoted in Lambert (1997): 79.

4. Reeves (2000): 40; Reid (2002): 99.

5. Strabo, *Geography*, XVII.1.32 – Strabo (1949): 88–9.

6. Piacentini (2009): 424.

7. Mariette (1857): 5–6, quoted in Tyldesley (2005): 122.

8. There is controversy surrounding the circumstances of the discovery of the *Le scribe accroupi*, one of the masterpieces of the Louvre's collection. While Mariette insisted that he excavated it at Saqqara, Prisse d'Avennes (never the most trustworthy source) claimed that it was bought from Salomon Fernandez for 120 francs.

9. Lambert (1997): 13.

10. Quoted in Lambert (1997): 19.

11. Lambert (1997): 13.

12. Reid (2002): 99.

13. Moser (2015): 250.

14. Reid (2002): 99.

15. Tyldesley (2005): 122.

16. The duke had been inspired by the work of Thomas 'Mummy' Pettigrew (see chapter 3).

17. Kluckert (2006): 245.

18. Lehner and Hawass (2017): 99.

19. Quoted in Lambert (1997): 33.

20. Quoted in Lambert (1997): 33.

21. Reid (2002): 100.

22. Mariette (1857): dedication.

23. Quoted in Lambert (1997): 154.

24. Quoted in Reeves (2000): 49.

25. Quoted in Reid (2002): 100.

26. Piacentini (2009): 429.

27. Quoted in Lambert (1997): 158.

28. The first entry in the museum's *Journal d'Entrée* dates to June 1858, the very month of Mariette's appointment.

29. The story of the Queen of Punt illustrates the sensitive diplomacy required of Mariette's role. Shortly after the discovery of the relief by his workmen, he learned that labourers working for an amateur collector, Lord Dufferin, had hacked out the relief and were

planning to take it back to Britain. Rather than creating a public scandal, Mariette met quietly with Birch (then British vice-consul) at Shepheard's Hotel to agree a diplomatic solution: Dufferin would keep a small part of his 'finds' but the majority of objects, including the scene of the Queen of Punt, would be restored to Mariette for the Egyptian Museum. Honour was served and, most importantly, the incident was kept from the ears of the viceroy.

30. Reid (2002): 100.
31. Piacentini (2009): 425.
32. Mariette to Heinrich Brugsch, 10 April 1859, quoted in Piacentini (2009): 426.
33. Quoted in Lambert (1997): 193.
34. Mariette (1868): 10.
35. Colla (2007): 133.
36. Quoted in Reid (2002): 109.
37. Mariette (1868): 8.
38. Mariette (1868): 8.
39. Mariette (1868): 8.
40. Reid (2002): 135.
41. Quoted in Maspero (1904): cxxxvii.
42. Reid (2002): 105.
43. A. E. M. Ashley, *Life and Correspondence of Palmerston* (London, 1879), 338, quoted in Mansfield (1971): 4.
44. Wilkinson to Thomas Pettigrew, Beirut, 18 May 1844, quoted in Thompson (1992): 195.
45. Quoted in Mansfield (1971): 4.
46. Mansfield (1971): 5.
47. Quoted in Sattin (1988): 62.
48. British trade accounted for two-thirds of the tonnage through the Suez Canal the year after it opened, rising to 79 per cent within a decade; see Wilson (1964): 48.
49. Reid (2002): 113.
50. Quoted in Piacentini (2009): 431.

SIX: A thousand miles up the Nile

1. Edwards (1889): 353.

2. Caroline Norton, quoted in Duff Gordon (1969): 11.

3. Duff Gordon (1969): 42 (27 October 1862).

4. Duff Gordon (1969): 3.

5. Kröger (1991): 19.

6. Duff Gordon (1969): 42 (27 October 1862).

7. Duff Gordon (1969): 44 (11 November 1862).

8. Duff Gordon (1969): 51 (21 November 1862).

9. Duff Gordon (1969): 52 (30 November 1862).

10. Duff Gordon (1969): 56 (1 December 1862).

11. Duff Gordon (1969): 52 (21 November 1862).

12. Duff Gordon (1969): 57 (10 December 1862).

13. Sattin (1988): 95.

14. Quoted in Sattin (1988): 97.

15. Duff Gordon (1969): 60 (11 February 1863).

16. Duff Gordon (1969): 116 (22 January 1864).

17. Duff Gordon (1969): 65 (February 1863).

18. Duff Gordon (1969): 62.

19. Duff Gordon (1969): 65.

20. Duff Gordon (1969): 61.

21. Duff Gordon (1969): 66.

22. Duff Gordon (1969): 63.

23. Duff Gordon (1969): 73, n.1.

24. Joseph Hekekyan to Nassau Senior, quoted in Duff Gordon (1969): 73, n.1.

25. Duff Gordon (1969): 66–7.

26. Duff Gordon (1969): 76, 78 (25 May 1863).

27. Duff Gordon (1969): 113–14 (13 January 1864).

28. Duff Gordon (1969): 113–14.

29. Duff Gordon (1969): 73, n.2.

30. Duff Gordon (1969): 85–6.

31. Duff Gordon (1969): 86 (21 May 1863).

32. Duff Gordon (1969): 185.

33. Duff Gordon (1969): 171 (23 May 1864).

34. Duff Gordon (1969): 224 (13 April 1865).

35. Duff Gordon (1969): 202 (11 January 1865).

36. Duff Gordon (1969): 4.

37. Duff Gordon (1969): 201 (9 January 1865).

38. Duff Gordon (1969): 5.

39. Duff Gordon (1969): 126 (12 February 1864).

40. Duff Gordon (1969): 184 (21 October 1864).

41. Duff Gordon (1969): 167 (17 May 1864).

42. Reid (2002): 114–15.

43. Marchand (2009): 204.

44. Duff Gordon (1969): 243 (December 1865).

45. Duff Gordon (1969): 257 (April 1866).

46. Duff Gordon (1969): 286–7 (21 November 1866).

47. Duff Gordon (1969): 145 (22 March 1864).

48. Duff Gordon (1969): 180 (7 July 1864).

49. Duff Gordon (1969): 180–1.

50. Duff Gordon (1969): 233.

51. Duff Gordon (1969): 207 (13 March 1865).

52. Duff Gordon (1969): 224 (29 April 1865).

53. Duff Gordon (1969): 213 (30 March 1865).

54. Duff Gordon (1969): 282 (19 October 1866).

55. Duff Gordon (1969): 317 (19 April 1867).

56. Duff Gordon (1969): 329 (28 July 1867).

57. Mitchell (1988): 63.

58. Duff Gordon (1969): 297 (22 January 1867).

59. Duff Gordon (1997): xi.

60. Duff Gordon (1997): 36.

61. Duff Gordon (1969): 348.

62. Duff Gordon (1969): 358 (22 January 1869).

63. Duff Gordon (1969): 360 (25 January 1869).

64. Duff Gordon (1969): 361 (15 June 1869).

65. Duff Gordon (1969): 362.

66. *The Times*, 26 July 1869, quoted in Duff Gordon (1969): 364.

67. Mansfield (1971): 6.

68. Caillard (1935): 20.

69. Caillard (1935): 19.

70. Quoted in Maspero (1904): clxxxii.

71. Reid (2002): 117.

72. Maspero (1904): cxci.

73. Edwards (1889): 415.

74. Quoted in Rees (1998): 18.

75. Edwards (1889): 2.

76. Cook & Son (1887): 4.

77. Cook & Son (1887): 4.

78. Caillard (1935): 58.

79. Reid (2002): 80.

80. Quoted in Rees (1998): 39.

81. Edwards (1889): 90.

82. Edwards (1889): 70.

83. Quoted in Rees (1998): 47.

84. Edwards (1889): 66.

85. Edwards (1889): 207.

86. Edwards (1889): 65.

87. Edwards (1889): 116.

88. Edwards (1889): 480.

89. Edwards (1889): 91.

90. Edwards (1889): 85.

91. Edwards (1889): 454, 455.

92. Caillard (1935): 5.

93. Edwards (1889): ix.

94. Edwards (1889): 1.

95. Edwards (1889): 37.

96. Edwards (1889): 139.

97. Edwards (1889): 487.

98. Edwards (1889): 285.

99. Edwards (1889): 353.

100. Edwards (1889): xvi, preface to the first edition.

101. Wilkinson to Birch, 22 December 1865, quoted in Thompson (1992): 193.

102. Hassan (2003): 64.

SEVEN: A permanent occupation

1. Petrie (1931): 35 (Petrie to Amelia Edwards, summer 1882).
2. Mansfield (1971): 6.
3. Caillard (1935): 16.
4. *The Times*, January 1876, quoted in Mansfield (1971): 7.
5. Caillard (1935): 28.
6. Mansfield (1971): 10.
7. Mansfield (1971): 10.
8. Quoted in Mansfield (1971): 11.
9. Mansfield (1971): 13–14.
10. Quoted in Wilson (1964): 46.
11. Caillard (1935): 28.
12. Quoted in Hassan (2003): 64.
13. Reid (2002): 102.
14. Quoted in David (1999): 22.
15. Quoted in David (1999): 25.
16. Maspero (1904): ccxx.
17. Hassan (2003): 64.
18. Sattin (1988): 174.
19. Maspero to G. d'Eichthal, 23 December 1881, quoted in David (1999): 100.
20. Maspero to Renan, 19 April 1882, quoted in David (1999): 103.
21. Quoted in David (1999): 110.
22. Amelia Edwards to Maspero, 17 December 1882, quoted in David (1999): 129.
23. Elshakry (2015): 189.
24. Melman (1995): 258; see Drower (1982b): 301, for the full text of Birch's haughty reply.
25. By February 1882, Edwards had also signed up as supporters the Archbishop of Canterbury, Cardinal Manning, the chief rabbi, and the eminent archaeologists of Mesopotamia, Sir Henry Layard and Sir Henry Rawlinson; see Drower (1982b).
26. Drower (1985): 58.
27. Quoted in Drower (1985): 65.
28. Quoted in Drower (1985): 66.

29. Quoted in Drower (1982a): 18.

30. Tyldesley (2005): 140.

31. Petrie (1931): 7.

32. Drower (1985): 22.

33. Petrie to Flaxman Spurrell, 11 February 1881, quoted in Drower (1985): 38.

34. Petrie (1931): 21.

35. Petrie (1931): 1.

36. Quoted in Drower (1985): 43.

37. Petrie (1931): 36.

38. Quoted in Drower (1985): 64.

39. Quoted in Rees (1998): 58.

40. Petrie (1931): 50.

41. Quoted in Drower (1985): 80.

42. Reid (2002): 177.

43. Quoted in Drower (1985): 105.

44. Drower (1985): 104.

45. Quoted in Melman (1995): 265; see also Rees (1998): 80.

46. *The Times*, 23 February 1884, quoted in David (1999): 124.

47. Maspero, 17 January 1884, quoted in David (1999): 154.

48. Gabriel Charmes to Maspero, 20 May 1884, quoted in David (1999): 156.

49. Maspero to Henri Marion, 6 April 1885, quoted in David (1999): 155.

50. Maspero to his wife, 2 May 1886, quoted in David (1999): 128.

51. Maspero (2003): 207 (Maspero to his wife, Bulaq, 5 April 1886).

52. Maspero (2003): 173 (Maspero to his wife, Luxor, 2 March 1886).

53. Maspero (2003): 217 (Maspero to his wife, Bulaq, 16 April 1886).

54. David (1999): 139.

55. Quoted in David (1999): 173.

56. Quoted in David (1999): 173.

57. Quoted in Drower (1985): 115.

58. Drower (1985): 109, 114–15.

59. Quoted in Drower (1985): 127.

60. Quoted in Drower (1985): 120.

61. Quoted in Drower (1985): 131.
62. Petrie (1931): 44.
63. Quoted in Drower (1985): 137.
64. Quoted in Drower (1985): 146–7.
65. Drower (1985): 168.
66. Drower (1985): 169–71.
67. Drower (1985): 143.
68. Petrie, quoted in Drower (1985): 179.
69. Edwards to Petrie, December 1891, quoted in Drower (1985): 199.
70. Drower (1985): 196.
71. Petrie (1931): 106.

EIGHT: Scholars and scoundrels

1. Speech to the German Ministry of Culture in Berlin, quoted in Marchand (2009): 203.
2. Quoted in Marchand (2009): 205.
3. Marchand (2009): 205.
4. Wilson (1964): 112; Marchand (2009): 196, 203.
5. Spinelli (2006).
6. Quoted in Spinelli (2006): 207.
7. Seidlmayer (2006): 172.
8. Quoted in Schipper (2006): 1.
9. Marchand (2009): 206.
10. Wilson (1964): 109.
11. Gertzen (2015): 37.
12. A copy of Budge's birth certificate is held in the collections of the Old Library, Christ's College, Cambridge.
13. Budge (1920), 1: 17 and 25 n.2.
14. Budge (1920), 1: 55.
15. Budge (1920), 1: 67. Gladstone also told Budge that 'if it were necessary . . . to visit Paris, or Munich, or Rome, to work in the libraries there, he would be glad to find the necessary funds' (Budge, 1920, 1: 68).
16. Budge (1920), 1: 75.
17. Budge (1920), 1: 77–8.

18. Budge (1920), 1: 79.
19. Budge (1920), 1: 80.
20. Budge (1920), 1: 80.
21. Budge (1920), 1: 81.
22. Budge (1920), 1: 81.
23. Budge (1920), 1: 81
24. Budge (1887).
25. Grenfell (1887).
26. Budge (1920), 1: 83.
27. Budge (1920), 1: 111.
28. Budge (1920), 1: 104.
29. Budge (1920), 1: 117.
30. Quoted in Sayce (1923): 285.
31. Budge (1920), 1: 133.
32. Budge (1920), 1: 133.
33. Budge (1920), 1: 142.
34. Budge (1920), 1: 145.
35. Budge (1920), 1: 144.
36. Budge (1920), 1: 333.
37. Budge (1920), 1: 333, 334.
38. Budge (1920), 2: 395.
39. Budge (1920), 1: 328.
40. Budge (1920), 1: 359.
41. Budge (1920), 1: 329.
42. Budge (1920), 1: 330.
43. Budge (1920), 1: 330.
44. Budge (1920), 1: 326.
45. Budge (1920), 1: 342.
46. Budge (1920), 1: 361.
47. Budge (1920), 1: 338.
48. Budge (1920), 1: 367.
49. Budge (1920), 1: 389.
50. Griffith, *Inscriptions of Siut and Dêr Rîfeh*, 1889, quoted in James (1982): 144.
51. *The Times*, 15 October 1890, quoted in Drower (1985): 171.

52. Sheppard (2015): 118.

53. Petrie (1896): 1.

54. Petrie (1896): 2.

55. Doyon (2015): 148.

56. Petrie (1931): 155.

57. Drower (1985): 214.

58. Drower (1985): 215–16.

59. Petrie (1931): 49.

60. Drower (1985): 83.

61. Breasted (1948): 78.

62. Breasted (1948): 78.

63. Rawnsley (1904): 15.

64. Adams (2013): 98.

65. Quoted in Drower (1985): 269.

66. Budge to Emma Andrews, January 1903, quoted in Adams (2013): 60–1.

67. Rawnsley (1904): 32.

68. Rawnsley (1904): 47.

69. Lawrence to D. G. Hogarth, 20 February 1912, quoted in Drower (1985): 319.

70. Drower (1985): 232.

71. Drower (1985): 243–4.

72. Petrie (1931): 185.

73. Quoted in Drower (1985): 325.

74. Reid (2002): 183.

75. Cromer to Lord Rosebery, quoted in Mansfield (1971): 151.

76. Caillard (1935): 145.

77. Reid (2002): 185.

78. French foreign ministry archives, *Correspondance politique*, vol. 117, fol. 279, MAE to Cairo, 13 May 1890, quoted in Reid (2002): 182.

79. French foreign ministry archives, Cagordan to MAE, 19 March 1898 and 18 May 1899, quoted in Reid (2002): 185.

80. Petrie to Maspero, 11 April 1898, quoted in David (1999): 192.

81. Loret to Maspero, 17 October 1898, quoted in David (1999): 192.

82. Mansfield (1971): 79.

NINE: Egypt and America

1. Davis to Harvard professor David G. Lyon, 1 March 1902, quoted in Adams (2013): 57–8.
2. Kalfatovic (2001): 240.
3. Reid (2002): 75.
4. Kalfatovic (2001): 241.
5. Quoted in Kalfatovic (2001): 248.
6. Wilson (1964): 58.
7. According to Naville, quoted in Bierbrier (ed.) (2012): 515.
8. Wilson (1964): 64.
9. Reid (2002): 198.
10. John Russell Young, quoted in Kalfatovic (2001): 244.
11. *Recueil des Travaux* (1890).
12. Quoted in Wilson (1964): 105.
13. Letter of Charles Wilbour, quoted in Wilson (1964): 104.
14. Breasted (1948): 25.
15. Breasted (1948): 37.
16. Breasted (1948): 45.
17. Breasted (1948): 50.
18. Abt (2011): 35.
19. Breasted (1948): 84.
20. Breasted (1948): 46.
21. Breasted (1948): 71.
22. Breasted (1948): 68.
23. Breasted (1948): 132.
24. Breasted (1948): 70.
25. Breasted (1948): 69.
26. Breasted (1948): 78.
27. Breasted (1948): 79.
28. Breasted (1948): 78.
29. Letter from Cairo, 24 January 1895, quoted in Tyldesley (2005): 214.
30. Quoted in Abt (2011): 51.
31. Breasted (1948): 87.
32. Breasted (1948): 96.

33. Breasted (1948): 93.

34. Breasted (1948): 103; see also Wilson (1964): 140.

35. Breasted (1948): 128.

36. Abt (2011): 136.

37. Breasted (1948): 184.

38. Breasted (1948): 189–91.

39. Wilson (1964): 136.

40. Breasted (1948): 185.

41. Breasted (1948): 173.

42. Wilson (1964): 137.

43. Quoted in Abt (2011): 228.

44. Abt (2011): 233.

45. Breasted (1948): 304.

46. Breasted (1948): 5–6.

47. Maspero to Henri Cordier, 17 January 1900, quoted in David (1999): 204.

48. Reid (2002): 195.

49. Petrie, *Journal*, I, xvii (Abydos 1902–3), entry for 17 November 1902, quoted in Drower (1985): 301.

50. Reid (2002): 3.

51. Quoted in David (1999): 259.

52. Barsanti, 8 March 1910, quoted in David (1999): 214.

53. Petrie, paper to the Royal Society of Arts, quoted in Drower (1985): 337.

54. Caillard (1935): 153.

55. Caillard (1935): 155.

56. Sayce (1923): 338.

57. Caillard (1935): 156.

58. Reid (2002): 204.

59. Wilson (1964): 129.

60. Wilson (1964): 145.

61. Wilson (1964): 145.

62. Wilson (1964): 148.

63. Doyon (2015): 149.

64. Wilson (1964): 149.

65. Adams (2013): 90.
66. Davis to David G. Lyon, 23 June 1902, quoted in Adams (2013): 58.
67. Adams (2013): 5–6.
68. Adams (2013): 67.
69. Davis (1906): xii–xiii.
70. Davis (1906): xiii.
71. Davis (1907): xxv.
72. Davis (1907): xxviii.
73. Quoted in Adams (2013): 13.
74. Adams (2013): 8.
75. Quoted in Adams (2013): 22–3.
76. Weigall (1923): 130.
77. Adams (2013): 105–6.
78. Davis (1907): xxx.
79. Adams (2013): 130.
80. Tyndale (1907): 3.
81. Quoted in Adams (2013): 77.
82. Quoted in Adams (2013): 76.
83. Wilkinson and Platt (2017).
84. Quoted in Adams (2013): 273–4.
85. Davis to Nellie Knagenhjelm, 20 January 1908, quoted in Adams (2013): 201–2.
86. *Evening News*, Ada, Oklahoma, 10 April 1908, quoted in Adams (2013): 212.
87. Joseph Lindon Smith, quoted in Wilson (1964): 123.
88. Adams (2013): 172.

TEN: Imperial ambitions

1. Maspero (2003): xii.
2. Quoted in David (1999): 180.
3. Marchand (2009): 158.
4. Marchand (2009): 352.
5. Quoted in Thissen (2006): 195.
6. Marchand (2009): 158.

7. Marchand (2009): 195.

8. Marchand (2009): 203.

9. Thissen (2006): 198.

10. Thissen (2006): 200.

11. Marchand (2009): 339.

12. Gertzen (2015): 40.

13. Reid (2002): 13.

14. Weigall (1923): 132.

15. Wilson (1964): 127.

16. Gertzen (2015): 38–9.

17. Wilson (1964): 110.

18. Drower (1985): 280.

19. Maspero (2003): xii.

20. Maspero (2003): 516 (diary, Cairo, 29 October 1911).

21. Maspero (2003): 542.

22. Mansfield (1971): 110, 115.

23. Quoted in Mansfield (1971): 133.

24. Mansfield (1971): 148.

25. Owen (1981): 226.

26. Owen (1981): 219.

27. Mitchell (1988): 16.

28. Caillard (1935): 139.

29. Quoted in Mitchell (1988): 175.

30. Rennell Rodd, *Social and Diplomatic Memories 1894–1901*, (London, 1922–5), 16, quoted in Mansfield (1971): 63.

31. Caillard (1935): 149.

32. Mitchell (1988): 97.

33. Caillard (1935): 127.

34. Caillard (1935): 125.

35. Grandfather of the one-time UN Secretary-General, Boutros Boutros Ghali.

36. Mansfield (1971): 188.

37. Quoted in Colla (2007): 101.

38. 'Al-Athar al-qadima': 17, 14, quoted in Colla (2007): 149, 150.

39. Mansfield (1971): 201.

40. Quoted in Adams (2013): 213.
41. Briggs (1918): 17.
42. Sattin (1988): 204.
43. Briggs (1918): 5.
44. Briggs (1918): 28.
45. Briggs (1918): 37.
46. Briggs (1918): 177, 272.
47. Breasted (1948): 232.
48. Wilson (1964): 142.
49. Petrie (1931): 236.
50. Petrie (1931): 240.
51. Gardiner to Erman, 19 August 1920 and 3 September 1920, quoted in Gertzen (2015): 42 and 44, respectively.
52. Gertzen (2015): 46.
53. Quoted in Gertzen (2015): 45.
54. Evans (1919).
55. Evans (1919).
56. Petrie (1931): 269.
57. Caillard (1935): 226.
58. Wilson (1964): 127.
59. Mansfield (1971): 232.
60. Caillard (1935): 225.
61. All quotes from Cecil (1921); specific quotations are from pages 15, 9, 71, 117, 79 and 272, respectively.

ELEVEN: Wonderful things

1. Carter's journal entry for 26 November 1922, reproduced in Collins and McNamara (2014): 29.
2. Davis (1912): 3.
3. Davis (1912): 3.
4. Maspero (1912): 111–12.
5. Maspero (1912): 123.
6. Adams (2013): 302.
7. In his entry for *Who's Who*, Carter claimed to have been born in Swaffham, Norfolk, on 9 May 1873; in fact, he was born in

Brompton, London, exactly one year later. It is not clear whether the mistake was accidental or deliberate.

8. Quoted in Drower (1985): 194.

9. Maspero, letter to Naville, 5 January 1900, quoted in Reeves and Wilkinson (1996): 70.

10. Emma Andrews's diary, 13 January 1903, quoted in Reeves and Wilkinson (1996): 72.

11. Davis (1906): xii–xiii.

12. Emma Andrews's diary, 17 January 1902, quoted in Reeves and Wilkinson (1996): 70.

13. Telegram from Carter to Cromer, 8 January 1905, illustrated in Reeves (1990): 42.

14. Griffith Institute, Carter archive, VI, autobiographical sketch, quoted in Reeves (1990): 42.

15. Letter from Ferdinand Platt to his wife, Luxor, 22 January 1908, quoted in Wilkinson and Platt (2017): 108–9.

16. Fagan (2004): 686.

17. Sources differ as to whether the accident took place in 1901 or 1903.

18. Fagan (2015): 57.

19. Quoted by Carnarvon's sister, Lady Burghclere, in Carter and Mace (1922–3), I: 29.

20. Carnarvon to Weigall, quoted in Adams (2013): 169.

21. Lindon Smith (1956): 79–80.

22. Carnarvon to Weigall, 14 April 1907, quoted in Reeves (1990): 48.

23. Carnarvon and Carter (1912): preface.

24. Letter from Newberry to Gardiner, 25 December 1947, Griffith Institute, Gardiner archive, quoted in Reeves (1990): 46.

25. Carnarvon and Carter (1912): 1.

26. Carter and Mace (1922–3), I: 75.

27. Carter and Mace (1922–3), I: 78.

28. Fagan (2004): 687.

29. Gardiner to Erman, 15 August 1921, quoted in Gertzen (2015): 45.

30. Bierbrier (ed.), (2012): 585.

31. Wilson (1964): 186.

32. Quoted in Drower (1985): 266.

33. Weigall (1923): 11.

34. Weigall (1923): 15.

35. Weigall (1923): 16.

36. Weigall (1923): 126–7.

37. Weigall (1923): 19.

38. Weigall (1923): 23.

39. Weigall (1923): 97.

40. Weigall (1923): 97–8.

41. Weigall (1923): 280.

42. Weigall (1923): 98.

43. Reid (2015): 165.

44. Petrie (1931): 249.

45. Drower (1985): 356.

46. Drower (1985): 356.

47. Weigall (1923): 135.

48. Quoted in Piacentini (2009): 430.

49. Weigall (1923): 130–1.

50. Carter and Mace (1922–3), I: 89–90.

51. Carter and Mace (1922–3), I: 91.

52. Carter and Mace (1922–3), I: 91.

53. Carter and Mace (1922–3), I: 92.

54. Carter and Mace (1922–3), I: 94.

55. Quoted in Collins and McNamara (2014): 28–32.

56. Carter and Mace (1922–3), I: 95–6.

57. Carnarvon (1923)

58. Carter and Mace (1922–3), I: 97.

59. Carter and Mace (1922–3), I: 94.

60. Carter and Mace (1922–3), I: 97.

61. Carter and Mace (1922–3), I: 100.

62. Carnarvon to Gardiner, 28 November 1922, quoted in Collins and McNamara (2014): 32–4.

63. Carter and Mace (1922–3), I: 105.

64. Carnarvon to Gardiner, 28 November 1922, quoted in Collins and McNamara (2014): 32–4.

65. Carnarvon to Gardiner, 28 November 1922, quoted in Collins and McNamara (2014): 34.
66. Breasted (1948): 325.
67. Carter and Mace (1922–3), I: 150.
68. Breasted (1948): 325.
69. Reid (2015): 159.
70. Colla (2007): 177.
71. Reid (2002): 293.
72. Abt (2011): 312.

EPILOGUE: The future of the past

1. Weigall (1923): 27.
2. *New York Times*, 18 February 1923, quoted in Collins and McNamara (2014): 63.
3. Colla (2007): 206.
4. Colla (2007): 273.
5. Reeves (2000) passim.
6. Weigall (1923): 27.
7. Gardiner, *My Early Years*, 68, quoted in Reeves (1990): 62.
8. Tyldesley (2012) passim.
9. Winifred, Lady Burghclere, in Carter and Mace (1922–3), I: 1.
10. Abt (2011): 317–27.
11. Reid (2015): 165.

Bibliography

Abt, Jeffrey, *American Egyptologist: The Life of James Henry Breasted and the Creation of His Oriental Institute*, Chicago and London: University of Chicago Press, 2011

Adams, John M., *The Millionaire and the Mummies: Theodore Davis's Gilded Age in the Valley of the Kings*, New York: St Martin's Press, 2013

Ahmed, Leila, *Edward W. Lane: A Study of His Life and Works and of British Ideas of the Middle East in the Nineteenth Century*, London and New York: Longman, 1978

Anon., *Voyage Made in the Year 1589 from Cairo to Ebrim by Way of the Nile*, 1589

———'*Observations météorologiques faites à l'observatoire royal de Paris dans le mois de Septembre 1822*', in *Journal de physique, de chimie, d'histoire naturelle*, pp. 318–19, http://www/gallica/bnf.fr, accessed 11 March 2018

Baring, Evelyn, Earl of Cromer, *Modern Egypt*, 2 vols, London: Macmillan, 1908

Belzoni, G., *Narrative of the Operations and Recent Discoveries within the Pyramids, Temples, Tombs, and Excavations, in Egypt and Nubia, and of a Journey to the Coast of the Red Sea, in Search of the Ancient Berenice; and another to the Oasis of Jupiter Ammon*, London: John Murray, 1820, second edition, 1821

Bierbrier, Morris L., 'Art and antiquities for government's sake', in David Jeffreys (ed.), *Views of Ancient Egypt since Napoleon Bonaparte: imperialism, colonialism and modern appropriations*, pp. 69–76, London: UCL Press, 2003

———(ed.), *Who Was Who in Egyptology*, fourth revised edition, London: the Egypt Exploration Society, 2012

Birch, Samuel, J. Bonomi, G. R. Gliddon, A. C. Harris and W. H. F. Talbot, *The Talbotype applied to Hieroglyphics*, Reading: Talbot, 1846

Blake, Robert, *Disraeli's Grand Tour: Benjamin Disraeli and the Holy Land 1830–31*, London: Weidenfeld and Nicolson, 1982

Blumenthal, Elke, 'Carl Peter Lepsius und die Ägypten-Expedition des

Bibliography

Sohnes', in Elke Freier and Walter F. Reineke (eds), *Karl Richard Lepsius (1810–84): Akten der Tagung anläßlich seines 100. Todestages, 10–12.7.1984 in Halle*, pp. 133–66, Berlin: Akademie-Verlag, 1988

Blunt, Wilfred S., *The Secret History of the English Occupation of Egypt*, Stroud/Dublin: Nonsuch Publishing, 2007 (first published 1907)

Bonomi, Joseph and Francis Arundale, *Gallery of Antiquities Selected from the British Museum*, London: John Weale, 1842–3

Breasted, Charles, *Pioneer to the Past: The Story of James Henry Breasted, Archaeologist*, London: Herbert Jenkins, 1948

Briggs, Martin S., *Through Egypt in War-Time*, London: T. Fisher Unwin, 1918

Budge, E. A. Wallis, 'Description of the tombs of Mechu, Ben, and Se-Renpu, discovered by Major-General Sir F. Grenfell in 1885', *The Times*, 28 January 1887, p. 13

Budge, Sir E. A. Wallis, *By Nile and Tigris: A narrative of journeys in Egypt and Mesopotamia on behalf of the British Museum between the years 1886 and 1913*, 2 vols, London: John Murray, 1920

Burton, Sir Richard, 'Giovanni Battista Belzoni', *Cornhill Magazine*, 42 (July 1880), pp. 39–40

Caillard, Mabel, *A Lifetime in Egypt 1876–1935*, London: Grant Richards, 1935

Caminos, Ricardo A., 'Peasants', in Sergio Donadoni (ed.), *The Egyptians*, tr. Robert Bianchi, Anna Lisa Crone, Charles Lambert and Thomas Ritter, pp. 1–30, Chicago and London: University of Chicago Press, 1997

Carnarvon, The Earl of, 'The Treasures of Luxor: Lord Carnarvon's Account', *The Times*, 12 January 1923, p. 10

Carnarvon, The Earl of and Howard Carter, *Five Years' Explorations at Thebes*, London, New York, Toronto and Melbourne: Henry Frowde, Oxford University Press, 1912

Carter, Howard and Arthur C. Mace, *The Tomb of Tut.ankh.Amen*, 3 vols, London: Cassell, 1922–3

Cecil, Lord Edward, *The Leisure of an Egyptian Official*, London: Hodder and Stoughton, 1921

Ceram, C. W., *Gods, Graves, and Scholars: The Story of Archaeology*, second edition, London: Book Club Associates, 1978

Champollion, Jean-François, *Précis du système hiéroglyphique des anciens Egyptiens, ou Recherches sur les élémens premiers de cette écriture sacrée, sur leurs diverses combinaisons, et sur les rapports de ce système avec les autres méthodes graphiques égyptiennes*, Paris: Treuttel et Würtz, 1824

466

———(ed. H. Hartleben), *Lettres et journaux écrits pendant le voyage d'Egypte*, Paris: Christian Bourgois, English tr. Martin Rynja (2009), *The Code-Breaker's Secret Diaries: The Perilous Expedition through plague-ridden Egypt to uncover the ancient mysteries of the hieroglyphs*, London: Gibson Square, 1986

Champollion-Figeac, Aimé, *Les Deux Champollion, Leur vie et leurs oeuvres, leur correspondance archéologique relative au Dauphiné et à l'Egypte: Etude complète de biographie et de bibliographie 1778–1867*, Grenoble: Xavier Drevet, 1887

Clark, Christopher, *Iron Kingdom: The Rise and Downfall of Prussia, 1600–1947*, London: Allen Lane, 2006

Clarke, Edward D., *Travels in Various Countries of Europe, Asia, and Africa*, vol. 3, London: Printed for T. Cadell and W. Davies, by R. Watts, 1814

Colla, Elliott, *Conflicted Antiquities: Egyptology, Egyptomania, Egyptian Modernity*, Durham NC and London: Duke University Press, 2007

Collins, Paul and Liam McNamara, *Discovering Tutankhamun*, Oxford: Ashmolean Museum, 2014

Cone, Polly (ed.), *Wonderful Things: The Discovery of Tutankhamun's Tomb*, New York: Metropolitan Museum of Art, 1976

Cook, Thomas & Son, *Programme of Cook's International Tickets to Egypt including The Nile to the Second Cataract, Philae, Luxor, Thebes, Assouan, Aboo Simbel, &c., &c. Also particulars of arrangements for Steamers and Dahabeahs, With maps and plans of steamers. Under the special and exclusive contracts and arrangements of Thos. Cook & Son, sole owners of the only First Class Tourist Steamers specially built for the Nile (Price Sixpence, Post Free)*, London: Thomas Cook & Son, 1887

David, Elisabeth, *Gaston Maspero 1846–1916, Le gentleman égyptologue*, Paris: Pygmalion/Gérard Watelet, 1999

Davis, Theodore M., *The Tomb of Hâtshopsîtû*, London: Constable & Co., 1906

———*The Tomb of Iouiya and Touiyou*, London: Constable & Co., 1907

———*The Tomb of Queen Tîyi*, London: Constable & Co., 1910

———*The Tombs of Harmhabi and Touatânkhamanou*, London: Constable & Co., 1912

Dawson, W. R., 'Pettigrew's Demonstrations upon Mummies: A Chapter in the History of Egyptology', *Journal of Egyptian Archaeology*, 20 (1934), pp. 170–82

Degardin, Jean-Claude, 'Les acquis irremplaçables de l'expedition de

Bibliography

Lepsius', in Elke Freier and Walter F. Reineke (eds), *Karl Richard Lepsius (1810–84), Akten der Tagung anläßlich seines 100. Todestages, 10–12.7.1984, in Halle,* pp. 125–32, Berlin: Akademie-Verlag, 1988

Denon, Dominique Vivant (ed. Bernard Bailly), *Les Monuments de la Haute Egypte,* Chalon-sur-Saône: Comité Vivant Denon, Université pour tous de Bourgogne, 2003

de Verninac Saint-Maur, E., *Voyage du Luxor en Egypte: enterpris par ordre du roi pour transporter, de Thèbes à Paris, l'un des obélisques de Sésostris,* Paris: Arthus Bertrand, 1835

Dixon, David M., 'Some Egyptological sidelights on the Egyptian war of 1882', in David Jeffreys (ed.), *Views of Ancient Egypt since Napoleon Bonaparte: imperialism, colonialism and modern appropriations,* pp. 87–94, London: UCL Press, 2003

Doyon, Wendy, 'On Archaeological Labor in Modern Egypt', in William Carruthers (ed.), *Histories of Egyptology: Interdisciplinary Measures,* pp. 141–56, New York and London: Routledge, 2015

Drower, Margaret S., 'The Early Years', in T. G. H. James (ed.), *Excavating in Egypt: The Egypt Exploration Society 1882–1982,* pp. 9–36, London: British Museum Publications, 1982 (1982a)

———'Gaston Maspero and the birth of the Egypt Exploration Fund (1881–3)', *Journal of Egyptian Archaeology,* 68 (1982), pp. 299–317 (1982b)

———*Flinders Petrie: A Life in Archaeology,* London: Victor Gollancz, 1985

du Camp, Maxime, *Egypte, Nubie, Palestine et Syrie: dessins photographiques recueillis pendant les années 1849, 1850 et 1851 accompagnés d'un texte explicatif,* Paris: Gide & Baudry, 1852

Duff Gordon, Lucie, *Letters from Egypt (1862–69),* London: Routledge & Kegan Paul, 1969

———*Letters from Egypt,* London: Virago, 1997

Ebers, Georg, *Richard Lepsius: A Biography,* tr. Zoe Dana Underhill, New York: William S. Gottsberger, 1887

Edwards, Amelia B., *A Thousand Miles up the Nile,* second edition, London: Routledge, 1889

Elshakry, Marwa, 'Histories of Egyptology in Egypt: Some Thoughts', in William Carruthers (ed.), *Histories of Egyptology, Interdisciplinary Measures,* pp. 185–97, New York and London: Routledge, 2015

Endesfelder, Erika, '*Der Beitrag von Richard Lepsius zur Erforschung der altägyptischen Geschichte*', in Elke Freier and Walter F. Reineke (eds),

Karl Richard Lepsius (1810–84), Akten der Tagung anläßlich seines 100. Todestages, 10–12.7.1984 in Halle, pp. 216–46, Berlin: Akademie-Verlag, 1988

Evans, Arthur, 'England in Egypt, Need for an Institute of Research, State Aid for Archaeology', *The Times*, 4 March 1919, p. 8

Fagan, Brian, 'Herbert, George Edward Stanhope Molyneux, fifth earl of Carnarvon (1866–1923)', in *Oxford Dictionary of National Biography*, vol. 26, pp. 686–7, Oxford: Oxford University Press, 2004

——*Lord and Pharaoh: Carnarvon and the Search for Tutankhamun*, Walnut Creek, California: Left Coast Press, 2015

Freier, Elke, '*Die Expedition von Karl Richard Lepsius in den Jahren 1842– 1845 nach den Akten des Zentralen Staatsarchivs, Dienststelle Merseburg*', in Elke Freier and Walter F. Reineke (eds), *Karl Richard Lepsius (1810–84), Akten der Tagung anläßlich seines 100. Todestages, 10–12.7.1984 in Halle*, pp. 97–115, Berlin: Akademie-Verlag, 1988

Freitag, Michael, '*Expeditionszeichnungen als Zeugnisse der Kunst und der Wissenschaft*', in Elke Freier and Walter F. Reineke (eds), *Karl Richard Lepsius (1810–84), Akten der Tagung anläßlich seines 100. Todestages, 10–12.7.1984 in Halle*, pp. 167–84, Berlin: Akademie-Verlag, 1988

Frith, Francis, *Egypt and Nubia: Descriptive Catalogue of One Hundred Stereoscopic Views of the Pyramids, the Nile, Karnak, Thebes, Aboo-Simbel and All the Most Interesting Objects of Egypt and Nubia*, London: Negretti and Zambra, 1857

Gertzen, Thomas L., 'The Anglo-Saxon Branch of the Berlin School: the Interwar Correspondence of Adolf Erman and Alan Gardiner and the Loss of the German Concession at Amarna', in William Carruthers (ed.), *Histories of Egyptology, Interdisciplinary Measures*, pp. 34–49, New York and London: Routledge, 2015

Gillispie, Charles Coulston and Michel Dewachter (eds), *Monuments of Egypt: The Napoleonic Edition, The Complete Archaeological Plates from la Description de l'Egypte*, Princeton: Princeton Architectural Press, 1987

Gliddon, George, *An Appeal to the Antiquaries of Europe on the Destruction of the Monuments of Egypt*, London: James Madden, 1841

Grenfell, Francis, 'Egyptian Discoveries', *The Times*, 28 January 1887, p. 13

Gurney, Hudson, 'Memoir', in Thomas Young, *Rudiments of an Egyptian Dictionary in the Ancient Enchorial Character; Containing All the Words of Which the Sense Has Been Ascertained*, pp. 5–47, London: J. and A. Arch, 1831

Bibliography

Hall, H. R., 'Letters to Sir William Gell', *Journal of Egyptian Archaeology* 2 (1915), pp. 133–67

Halls, J. J., *The Life and Correspondence of Henry Salt, Esq, F.R.S. &c. His Britannic Majesty's Late Consul-General in Egypt*, 2 vols, London: Richard Bentley, 1834

Hassan, Fekri A., 'Imperialist appropriations of Egyptian obelisks', in David Jeffreys (ed.), *Views of Ancient Egypt since Napoleon Bonaparte: imperialism, colonialism and modern appropriations*, pp. 19–68, London: UCL Press, 2003

Henniker, Sir Frederick, Bt., *Notes During a Visit to Egypt, Nubia, the Oasis, Mount Sinai, and Jerusalem*, London: John Murray, 1823

Hintze, Fritz and Gerhard Rühlmann, 'Karl Richard Lepsius: Begründer der deutschsprachigen Ägyptologie', in Elke Freier and Walter F. Reineke (eds), *Karl Richard Lepsius (1810–84), Akten der Tagung anläßlich seines 100. Todestages, 10–12.7.1984 in Halle*, pp. 17–28, Berlin: Akademie-Verlag, 1988

Hogg, Thomas Jefferson, *The Life of Percy Bysshe Shelley*, 2 vols, London and Toronto: J. M. Dent & Sons, 1933

James, T. G. H., 'The Archaeological Survey', in T. G. H. James (ed.), *Excavating in Egypt, The Egypt Exploration Society 1882–1982*, pp. 141–59, London: British Museum Publications, 1982

Jeffreys, David, 'Introduction – Two Hundred Years of Ancient Egypt: Modern History and Ancient Archaeology', in David Jeffreys (ed.), *Views of Ancient Egypt since Napoleon Bonaparte: imperialism, colonialism and modern appropriations*, pp. 1–18, London: UCL Press, 2003

Kalfatovic, Martin R., 'Nile Notes of a *Howadji*: American Travellers in Egypt, 1837–1903', in Paul and Janet Starkey (eds), *Unfolding the Orient: Travellers in Egypt and the Near East*, pp. 239–59, Reading: Ithaca Press, 2001

Kapoïan, Angèla, 'Egypt in 1615–1616 as seen through the eyes of the Armenian Simeon of Poland', in Paul and Janet Starkey (eds), *Unfolding the Orient: Travellers in Egypt and the Near East*, pp. 111–17, Reading: Ithaca Press, 2001

Kircher, Athanasius, *Oedipus Aegyptiacus*, 4 vols, Rome: Ex typographia Vitalis Mascardi, 1652–4

Kitchen, Kenneth, 'King lists', in Donald B. Redford (ed.), *The Oxford Encyclopedia of Ancient Egypt*, vol. 2, pp. 234–8, New York: Oxford University Press, 2001

Kluckert, Ehrenfried, 'The Landscape Garden', in Rolf Toman (ed.),

Neoclassicism and Romanticism, Architecture, Sculpture, Paintings, Drawings 1750–1848, pp. 230–49, Könemann, 2006

Kröger, Martin, *'Le bâton égyptien' – Der ägyptische Knüppel, Die Rolle der 'ägyptischen Frage' in der deutschen Außenpolitik von 1875/6 bis zur 'Entente Cordiale'*, Frankfurt, Bern, New York and Paris: Peter Lang, 1991

Lambert, Gilles, *Auguste Mariette, L'Egypte ancienne sauvée des sables*, Paris: J.-C. Lattès, 1997

Lebas, Jean-Baptiste Apollinaire, *L'obélisque de Luxor, Histoire de sa translation à Paris*, Paris: Carilian-Goeury et Vr Dalmont, 1839

Leclant, Jean, 'Champollion, Bunsen, Lepsius', in Elke Freier and Walter F. Reineke (eds), *Karl Richard Lepsius (1810–84), Akten der Tagung anläßlich seines 100. Todestages, 10–12.7.1984 in Halle*, pp. 53–9, Berlin: Akademie-Verlag, 1988

Lehner, Mark and Zahi Hawass, *Giza and the Pyramids*, London: Thames and Hudson, 2017

Lepsius, Richard, *Letters from Egypt, Ethiopia, and the Peninsula of Sinai*, tr. L. and J. B. Horner. London: Henry G. Bohn, 1853

———*Denkmäler aus Aegypten und Aethiopien: nach den Zeichnungen der von seiner Majestät dem Koenige von Preussen Friedrich Wilhelm IV nach diesen Ländern gesendeten und in den Jahren 1842–45 ausgeführten wissenschaftlichen Expedition*, 12 vols, Berlin: Nicolaische Buchhandlung, 1849–59

Levine, Philippa, *The Amateur and the Professional: Antiquarians, Historians and Archaeologists in Victorian England, 1838–86*, Cambridge: Cambridge University Press, 1986

Lindon Smith, Joseph (ed. Corinna Lindon Smith), *Tombs, Temples and Ancient Art*, Norman, Oklahoma: University of Oklahoma Press, 1956

Long, George, *The British Museum: Egyptian Antiquities*, 2 vols, London: Charles Knight, 1832

Loprieno, Antonio, 'Adolf Erman und die ägyptische Literatur', in Bernd U. Schipper (ed.), *Ägyptologie als Wissenschaft: Adolf Erman (1854–1937) in seiner Zeit*, pp. 150–68, Berlin and New York: de Gruyter, 2006

Macmichael, William, *The Gold-Headed Crane*, London: John Murray, 1828

Madden, Richard R., *Egypt and Mohammed Ali*, London: Hamilton, Adams & Co., 1841

Manley, Deborah, 'Lord Belmore proceeds up the Nile in 1817–1818', in Paul and Janet Starkey (eds), *Unfolding the Orient: Travellers in Egypt and the Near East*, pp. 179–91, Reading: Ithaca Press, 2001

Manley, Deborah and Peta Rée, 'Encounters on the Nile: tourists, artists, scholars, explorers, a missionary and an obelisk: Cairo to the Second Cataract, October 1818 to August 1819', in Diana Magee, Janine Bourriau and Stephen Quirke (eds), *Sitting Beside Lepsius: Studies in Honour of Jaromir Malek at the Griffith Institute*, pp. 327–42, Leuven: Peeters, 2009

Mansfield, Peter, *The British in Egypt*, London: Weidenfeld and Nicolson, 1971

Marchand, Suzanne L., *German Orientalism in the Age of Empire*, New York/Washington DC: Cambridge University Press/German Historical Institute, 2009

Mariette, Auguste, *Le Sérapéum de Memphis*, Paris: Gide, 1857

————*Notice des principaux monuments exposés dans les galeries provisoires du Musée d'Antiquités Egyptiennes de S.A. le Vice-Roi à Boulaq*, Alexandria: Mourès, Rey & Cie; Paris: A. Franck, 1868, third edition, 1869

Maspero, Gaston, 'Mariette (1821–81): Notice biographique', in Auguste Mariette, *Œuvres diverses*, volume 1, i–ccxxiv, Paris: Ernest Leroux, 1904

————*Egypt: Ancient Sites and Modern Scenes*, London: T. F. Unwin, 1910

————'Note on the life and reign of Touatânkhamanou', in Theodore M. Davis, *The Tombs of Harmhabi and Touatânkhamanou*, pp. 111–23, London: Constable and Co., 1912

————(ed. Elisabeth David) *Lettres d'Egypte, Correspondance avec Louise Maspero*, Paris: Seuil, 2003

Mayes, Stanley, *The Great Belzoni*, London: Putnam, 1959

Melman, Billie, *Women's Orients: English Women and the Middle East, 1718–1918, Sexuality, Religion and Work*, second edition, Basingstoke and London: Macmillan, 1995

Mitchell, Timothy, *Colonising Egypt*, Cambridge: Cambridge University Press, 1988

Moser, Stephanie, 'Legacies of Engagement: The Multiple Manifestations of Ancient Egypt in Public Discourse', in William Carruthers (ed.), *Histories of Egyptology, Interdisciplinary Measures*, pp. 242–52, New York and London: Routledge, 2015

Moshenska, Gabriel, 'Thomas "Mummy" Pettigrew and the Study of Egypt in Early Nineteenth-Century Britain', in William Carruthers (ed.), *Histories of Egyptology, Interdisciplinary Measures*, pp. 201–14, New York and London: Routledge, 2015

Müller, Wolfgang, 'Das historische Museum – die Neugestaltung des Berliner Ägyptischen Museums durch Richard Lepsius', in Elke Freier and Walter F. Reineke (eds), *Karl Richard Lepsius (1810–1884), Akten der Tagung anläßlich seines 100. Todestages, 10–12.7.1984 in Halle*, pp. 276–83, Berlin: Akademie-Verlag, 1988

Nicholson, Paul T., 'Egyptology for the masses: James Henry Breasted and the Underwood brothers', in Diana Magee, Janine Bourriau and Stephen Quirke (eds), *Sitting Beside Lepsius: Studies in Honour of Jaromir Malek at the Griffith Institute*, pp. 381–422, Leuven: Peeters, 2009

Norden, Frederick Lewis, *Travels in Egypt and Nubia*, 2 vols, London: Lockyer Davis and Charles Reymers, 1757

Nowinski, Judith, *Baron Dominique Vivant Denon (1747–1825): Hedonist and Scholar in a Period of Transition*, Rutherford, Madison and Teaneck: Fairleigh Dickinson University Press, 1970

Owen, Roger, *The Middle East in the World Economy 1800–1914*, London and New York: Methuen, 1981

Petrie, W. M. F., *Koptos*, London: Quaritch, 1896

——*The Royal Tombs of the First Dynasty*, part 1, London: Egypt Exploration Fund, 1900

——*Seventy Years in Archaeology*, London: Sampson Low, Marston & Co., 1931

Piacentini, Patrizia, 'Auguste Mariette in the Egyptological archives and library of the University of Milan', in Diana Magee, Janine Bourriau and Stephen Quirke (eds), *Sitting Beside Lepsius: Studies in Honour of Jaromir Malek at the Griffith Institute*, pp. 423–38, Leuven: Peeters, 2009

Pocoke, Richard, *A Description of the East and some other countries*, 2 vols, London: W. Bowyer, 1743–5

Poole, Sophia, *The Englishwoman in Egypt: letters from Cairo written during a residence there in 1842, 3, & 4, with E. W. Lane, Esq author of the 'Modern Egyptians', By his sister*, 2 vols, London: C. Cox, 1851

Rainer, M., 'Richard Lepsius und seine Familie – Bildungsbürgertum und Wissenschaft', in Elke Freier and Walter F. Reineke (eds), *Karl Richard Lepsius (1810–84), Akten der Tagung anläßlich seines 100. Todestages, 10–12.7.1984 in Halle*, pp. 29–52, Berlin: Akademie-Verlag, 1988

Rauch, Alexander, 'Neoclassicism and the Romantic Movement: Painting in Europe between Two Revolutions 1789–1848', in Rolf Toman (ed.), *Neoclassicism and Romanticism, Architecture, Sculpture, Paintings, Drawings 1750–1848*, pp. 318–479, Könemann, 2006

Bibliography

Rawnsley, Canon Hardwicke and Noel Rawnsley, *The Resurrection of Oldest Egypt, Being the Story of Abydos as Told by the Excavations of Dr Petrie, Sketches of Life & Labour in the Excavator's Camp by Noel Rawnsley*, Lalcham: The Beaver Press, 1904

Ray, John, *The Rosetta Stone and the Rebirth of Ancient Egypt*, London: Profile, 2007

Rees, Joan, *Amelia Edwards: Traveller, Novelist and Egyptologist*, London: The Rubicon Press, 1998

Reeves, Nicholas, *The Complete Tutankhamun*, London: Thames and Hudson, 1990

——*Ancient Egypt: The Great Discoveries, A Year-by-Year Chronicle*, London: Thames and Hudson, 2000

Reeves, Nicholas and Richard H. Wilkinson, *The Complete Valley of the Kings*, London: Thames and Hudson, 1996

Reid, Donald M., *Whose Pharaohs? Archaeology, Museums, and Egyptian National Identity from Napoleon to World War I*, Berkeley, Los Angeles and London: University of California Press, 2002

—— 'Remembering and Forgetting Tutankhamun, Imperial and National Rhythms of Archaeology, 1922–72', in William Carruthers (ed.), *Histories of Egyptology, Interdisciplinary Measures*, pp. 157–73, New York and London: Routledge, 2015

Rifaud, Jean-Jacques, *Tableau de l'Egypte, de la Nubie et des lieux circon-voisins: ou itinéraire à l'usage des voyageurs qui visitent ces contrées*, Paris: Treuttel et Würz, 1830

Robinson, Andrew, *The Last Man Who Knew Everything, Thomas Young, The Anonymous Polymath Who Proved Newton Wrong, Explained How We See, Cured the Sick, and Deciphered the Rosetta Stone, Among Other Feats of Genius*, New York: Pi Press, 2006

——*Cracking the Egyptian Code: The Revolutionary Life of Jean-François Champollion*, London: Thames and Hudson, 2012

Rodenbeck, John, 'Travelers from an Antique Land: Shelley's Inspiration for "Ozymandias"', *Alif: Journal of Comparative Poetics* 24 (2004), pp. 121–8

St John, James A., *Egypt and Mohammed Ali, or Travels in the Valley of the Nile*, London: Longman, Rees, Orme, Brown, Green & Longman, 1834

Sattin, Anthony, *Lifting the Veil: British Society in Egypt 1768–1956*, London: J. M. Dent & Sons, 1988

Saulnier, M., fils, *A Journey in Egypt, by M. Lelorrain; and observations on the circular zodiac of Denderah*, in *New Voyages and Travels: consisting of originals and translations*, vol. 3, pp. 75–96, London: Sir Richard Phillips & Co. (English translation of *Notice sur le voyage de M. Lelorrain en Egypte; et observations sur le zodiaque circulaire de Denderah*, Paris: Chez l'Auteur), 1822

Sayce, Archibald H., *Reminiscences*, London: Macmillan, 1923

Schenkel, Wolfgang, 'Bruch und Aufbruch: Adolf Erman und die Geschichte der Ägyptologie', in Bernd U. Schipper (ed.), *Ägyptologie als Wissenschaft: Adolf Erman (1854–1937) in seiner Zeit*, pp. 224–47, Berlin and New York: de Gruyter, 2006

Schipper, Bernd U., 'Adolf Erman (1854–1937), Leben und Werk', in Bernd U. Schipper (ed.), *Ägyptologie als Wissenschaft: Adolf Erman (1854–1937) in seiner Zeit*, pp. 1–26, Berlin and New York: de Gruyter, 2006

Scholz, John Martin Augustus, *Travels in the Countries Between Alexandria and Paraetonium, the Lybian Desert, Siwa, Egypt, Palestine, and Syria, in 1821*, London: Sir Richard Phillips & Co., 1822

Seidlmayer, Stephan Johannes, 'Das Ägyptische Wörterbuch an der Berliner Akademie: Entstehung und Konzept', in Bernd U. Schipper (ed.), *Ägyptologie als Wissenschaft: Adolf Erman (1854–1937) in seiner Zeit*, pp. 169–92, Berlin and New York: de Gruyter, 2006

Sheppard, Kathleen L., 'Margaret Alice Murray and Archaeological Training in the Classroom: Preparing "Petrie's Pups"', in William Carruthers (ed.), *Histories of Egyptology, Interdisciplinary Measures*, pp. 113–28, New York and London: Routledge, 2015

Sherer, Moyle, *Scenes and Impressions in Egypt and in Italy*, London: Printed for Longman, Hurst, Rees, Orme, Brown, and Green, 1824

Sicard, Claude (ed. Serge Sauneron and Maurice Martin), *Œuvres III, Parallèle géographique de l'ancienne Egypte et de l'Egypte moderne*, Cairo: Institut Français d'Archéologie Orientale du Caire, 1982

Sim, Katharine, *David Roberts R.A., 1796–1864: A Biography*, London, Melbourne and New York: Quartet Books, 1984

Spinelli, Birgit, 'Der Erwecker des ägyptischen Sammlung', Adolf Erman und das Berliner Museum', in Bernd U. Schipper (ed.), *Ägyptologie als Wissenschaft: Adolf Erman (1854–1937) in seiner Zeit*, pp. 202–23, Berlin and New York: de Gruyter, 2006

Stevenson, Alice, 'The Object of Study: Egyptology, Archaeology, and Anthropology at Oxford, 1860–1960', in William Carruthers (ed.), *Histories of Egyptology, Interdisciplinary Measures*, pp. 19–33, New York and London: Routledge, 2015

Bibliography

Strabo, *Geography, Book XVII* (tr. Horace Leonard Jones), Cambridge (Massachusetts) and London: Harvard University Press (Loeb Classical Library), 1949

Thissen, Heinz J., 'Adolf Erman und die Gründung des Deutschen Archäologischen Instituts in Kairo', in Bernd U. Schipper (ed.), *Ägyptologie als Wissenschaft: Adolf Erman (1854–1937) in seiner Zeit*, pp. 193–201, Berlin and New York: de Gruyter, 2006

Thompson, Jason, *Sir Gardner Wilkinson and His Circle*, Austin, Texas: University of Texas Press, 1992

——'"Purveyor-General to the hieroglyphics": Sir William Gell and the development of Egyptology', in David Jeffreys (ed.), *Views of Ancient Egypt since Napoleon Bonaparte: imperialism, colonialism and modern appropriations*, pp. 77–85, London: UCL Press, 2003

Tyldesley, Joyce, *Egypt: How a Lost Civilization Was Rediscovered*, Berkeley and Los Angeles: University of California Press, 2005

——*Tutankhamen's Curse*, London: Profile Books, 2012

Tyndale, Walter, *Below the Cataracts*, Philadelphia: J. B. Lippincott, 1907

Usick, Patricia and Deborah Manley, *The Sphinx Revealed: A Forgotten Record of Pioneering Excavations*, London: The British Museum, 2007

Volney, Constantin-François Chasseboeuf, comte de, *Voyage en Syrie et en Égypte, pendant les années 1783, 1784, et 1785*, Paris: Desenne, Volland, 1787

Vyse, Howard, *Operations Carried on at the Pyramids of Gizeh in 1837, With an Account of a Voyage into Upper Egypt, and an Appendix*, 3 vols, London: James Fraser, 1840–2

Waith, Eugene M., 'Ozymandias: Shelley, Horace Smith, and Denon', *Keats-Shelley Journal* 44 (1995), pp. 22–8

Weigall, Arthur, *The Glory of the Pharaohs*, London: Thornton Butterworth, 1923

Wilkinson, John Gardner, *Topography of Thebes and General View of Egypt, Being a Short Account of the Principal Objects Worthy of Notice in the Valley of the Nile, to the Second Cataract and Wadee Semneh, with the Fyoum, Oases, and Eastern Desert, from Sooez to Berenice; with Remarks on the Manners and Customs of the Ancient Egyptians and the Productions of the Country, &c. &c.* London: John Murray, 1835

——*Modern Egypt and Thebes, Being a Description of Egypt, Including the Information Required for Travellers in That Country*, 2 vols, London: John Murray, 1843

——*A Handbook for Egypt, Including descriptions of the course of the Nile* to the Second Cataract, Alexandria, Cairo, The Pyramids, and Thebes, the overland transit to India, the Peninsula of Mount Sinai, the Oases, etc., London: John Murray, 1846

————*The Architecture of Ancient Egypt: in which the columns are arranged in orders, and the temples classified, with remarks on the early progress of Architecture, etc.*, 2 vols, London: private publication, 1850

Wilkinson, Toby and Julian Platt, *Aristocrats and Archaeologists, An Edwardian Journey on the Nile*, Cairo: American University of Cairo Press, 2017

Wilson, John A., *Signs and Wonders Upon Pharaoh, A History of American Egyptology*, Chicago and London: University of Chicago Press, 1964

Young, Thomas, *An Account of Some Recent Discoveries in Hieroglyphical Literature, and Egyptian Antiquities*, London: John Murray, 1823

————*Rudiments of an Egyptian Dictionary in the Ancient Enchorial Character; containing all the words of which the sense has been ascertained*, London: John & Arthur Arch, 1830

Index

Page numbers in **bold** refer to illustrations.

21982319694653